Principles of Physiological Psychology, Volume 1

Wilhelm Max Wundt, Edward Bradford Titchener

Nabu Public Domain Reprints:

You are holding a reproduction of an original work published before 1923 that is in the public domain in the United States of America, and possibly other countries. You may freely copy and distribute this work as no entity (individual or corporate) has a copyright on the body of the work. This book may contain prior copyright references, and library stamps (as most of these works were scanned from library copies). These have been scanned and retained as part of the historical artifact.

This book may have occasional imperfections such as missing or blurred pages, poor pictures, errant marks, etc. that were either part of the original artifact, or were introduced by the scanning process. We believe this work is culturally important, and despite the imperfections, have elected to bring it back into print as part of our continuing commitment to the preservation of printed works worldwide. We appreciate your understanding of the imperfections in the preservation process, and hope you enjoy this valuable book.

VOL. I.

INTRODUCTION

PART I. THE BODILY SUBSTRATE OF THE MENTAL LIFE

PRINCIPLES OF PHYSIOLOGICAL PSYCHOLOGY

BY

WILHELM WUNDT

PROFESSOR OF PHILOSOPHY IN THE UNIVERSITY OF LEIPSIC

Translated from the Fifth German Edition (1902)

BY

EDWARD BRADFORD TITCHENER

SAGE PROFESSOR OF PSYCHOLOGY IN THE CORNELL UNIVERSITY

VOL. I.

WITH 105 FIGURES IN THE TEXT

LONDON
SWAN SONNENSCHEIN & CO. LIM.
NEW YORK: THE MACMILLAN CO.
1904

Phil 3915.46.6

15 Mr. 1917
HARVARD UNIVERSITY,
Philos. Dept. Library.

HARVARD
UNIVERSITY
LIBRARY
46*143

Author's Preface to the First Edition

THE work which I here present to the public is an attempt to mark out a new domain of science. I am well aware that the question may be raised, whether the time is yet ripe for such an undertaking. The new discipline rests upon anatomical and physiological foundations which, in certain respects, are themselves very far from solid; while the experimental treatment of psychological problems must be pronounced, from every point of view, to be still in its first beginnings. At the same time the best means of discovering the blanks that our ignorance has left in the subject matter of a developing science is, as we all know, to take a general survey of its present status. A first attempt, such as this book represents, must show many imperfections; but the more imperfect it is, the more effectively will it call for improvement. Moreover, it is especially true in this field of inquiry that the solution of many problems is intimately bound up with their relation to other groups of facts, facts that often appear remote and disconnected; so that the wider view is necessary, if we are to find the right path.

In many portions of the book I have made use of my own investigations; in the others, I have at least tried to acquire an independent judgment. Thus, the outline of the anatomy of the brain, contained in Part I, is based upon a knowledge of morphological relations which I have obtained by repeated dissection of human and animal brains. For part of the material employed in this work, and for frequent assistance in the difficulties which such a study offers, I am indebted to the former Director of the Heidelberg Anatomical Museum, Professor Fr. Arnold. The finer structure of the brain, as revealed by the microscope, is, of course, a subject for the specialist; all that I have been able to do is to compare the statements of the various authors with one another and with the results of the gross anatomy of the brain. I must leave it to the expert to decide whether the account of the central conduction paths, as drawn from these sources in chapter iv., is, at least in its main features, correct. I am fully conscious that, in detail, it requires to be supplemented and emended on many sides. Still, it receives a certain confirmation from the fact that the functional derangements induced experimentally by the extirpation and transsection of various parts of the brain are, as I seek to show in chapter v., readily explicable in terms of the anatomical plan. Most of the phenomena here described I have had frequent opportunity to observe in my own experiments. In chapter vi. I have brought together the results of my *Untersuchungen zur Mechanik der Nerven und Nervencentren*,[1] so far as these relate to the question—which is one of psychological importance—regarding the nature of the forces operative in the nervous elements.[2]

Parts II and III are concerned with the topics that first drew me, many years ago, to psychological studies. When in 1858 I began to work upon my *Beiträge zur Theorie der Sinneswahrnehmung*,[3] German physiology was dominated, almost exclusively, by nativistic conceptions. My principal purpose in writing that work was to demonstrate the insufficiency of current hypotheses regarding the origin of our spatial ideas of touch and sight, and to discover a physiological basis for a psychological theory. The views there set forth have since found general acceptance among physiologists as well as among psychologists; though in the form which they have usually taken in the physiologies they could, perhaps, hardly hold their own against a rigorous criticism. I hope that, in the present work, I have succeeded in showing the inadequacy of modern physiological empiricism, as well as the relative justification for nativism and the necessity with which both conceptions alike point to a more profound psychological theory. The hypothesis of specific sensory energies, which is really a survival from the older nativism, has, in my opinion, become untenable, despite the convenient explanation it affords of a large body of facts. My critical treatment of this subject will, no doubt, call forth many objections. But if the facts are viewed as a whole, the cogency of the argument will hardly be disputed.

The investigations of Part IV,[4] especially the experiments on the appearance and course in consciousness of the sensory ideas aroused by external impressions, have occupied me for fourteen years, though, it is true, with many interruptions, due to other work and to the necessity of procuring appropriate apparatus. The first results were presented, as early as 1861, to the Natural Science Conference at Speyer. Since that time a number of notable papers on the same subject have been published by other investigators. No one, however, has hitherto turned these results to account for a theory of consciousness and of attention. I have here sought to give this important chapter of physiological psychology at any rate a tentative systematic setting.

Finally, I would ask the reader, when he comes upon polemical passages directed against Herbart, to remember that my criticisms are, at the same time, a proof of the importance which I attach to the psychological works

---

[1] Erlangen, 1871. A second volume followed later: Stuttgart, 1876.—Translator.
[2] Chapters iv. and v. of the previous editions represent chapters v. and vi. of the present edition. What was formerly chapter vi. now becomes chapter iii.
[3] Leipsic and Heidelberg, 1862.—Translator.
[4] Now Part V.

of this philosopher. It is to Herbart, next after Kant, that I am chiefly indebted for the development of my own philosophical principles. So with regard to Darwin; while I have, in one of the concluding chapters, opposed Darwin's theory of expressive movements, I need hardly say that the present work is deeply imbued with those far-reaching conceptions which, by his labours, have become an inalienable possession of natural science.

W. WUNDT.

HEIDELBERG, *March*, 1874.

Author's Preface to the Fifth Edition

WHEN this book first came before the world, nearly eight and twenty years ago, the status of the science for which it hoped to prepare a place was very different from that of the physiological psychology of to-day. At that time only one successful attempt had been made—in Fechner's *Elemente der Psychophysik*—to throw the light of an exact procedure upon philosophical problems that might, in the last resort, be regarded as psychological. Fechner apart, the adventurer of an 'experimental psychology'[1] was still reduced, in most instances, to borrow what he could from other disciplines, especially from the physiology of sense and nervous system. To-day all this is changed; there is pouring in from all sides—from the psychological laboratories proper, from neighbouring disciplines, from every science that comes into contact with psychological problems—an amount of expository material that, even now, is hardly calculable. At that time the investigator who sought to employ accuracy of method in any question of psychology was challenged at every point, by philosophy as by natural science, to prove that his endeavours were legitimate. To-day these doubts are hardly to be feared. But, to offset our advantage, there have appeared within psychology itself strongly divergent tendencies, some of which cover profound differences of principle regarding the problems and aims of the science, and the paths that it should pursue.

From edition to edition of the present work, as I have attempted to adapt each successive revision to its altered circumstances, these changes of the times have been to me a source of ever-increasing difficulty. Hence, when the need arose for this fifth edition, I was strongly inclined to close my account with the book, and to leave it in the form which it had finally taken, unsatisfactory as I now felt that form to be. But, tempting as the idea was for many reasons, there was one paramount objection. The former edition contained many passages which I could not allow to pass as an adequate expression of my present convictions : for I would be the last to refuse, in the onward endeavour of our youthful science, to learn all that I can from new experiences, and in their light to better my theories. I resolved, accordingly, at least to put the book into such a shape that these discrepancies should, so far as possible, be done away with. However, I soon found that this plan could not be carried out; the result would

---

[1] This phrase appears to have been introduced by Wundt; see *Beiträge*, 1862 Vorrede, vi.—Translator.

Author's Preface to Fifth Edition

be, after as before, a book that, in all probability, should satisfy the reader as little as it satisfied myself. And so, almost unawares, the new edition has become practically a new work. My principal purpose in this thorough recasting of the material has been not so much to give a complete survey of the entire literature of the subject, in its manifold branches,—the numerous journals that are now published in the interests of experimental psychology render this an easy task for any one who will undertake it,—as rather to present, in more adequate form and (where it seemed desirable) with greater detail of proof than had appeared in previous editions, those experiences and those interpretations of experience which had come to me in the years of helpful association in research with all the younger investigators who have worked in the psychological laboratory at Leipsic. In its present form, therefore, the book is intended, first and foremost, to serve the purpose not of a compilation, but of an exposition of my own experiences and convictions; though I have, of course, everywhere made grateful use of whatever I could take from the works of others.

Although the text has been curtailed to the utmost, where curtailment was possible,—particularly by the omission of a number of argumentative passages, directed against opinions and theories, current in philosophy or in the older psychology, which may now be regarded as obsolete,—the change of programme has brought with it an increase in the bulk of the work. The two volumes of the previous editions have now become three. Volume ii. will contain the conclusion of the doctrine of mental elements, and the theory of ideas; volume iii., Parts dealing with emotion and voluntary action and with the interconnexion of mental processes, together with a closing chapter of philosophical import.[1] Dr. W. Wirth has undertaken the preparation of an index of names and subjects, to be included in this last volume.[2] I have also to thank Dr. Wirth for assistance in reading the proof-sheets.

W. WUNDT.

LEIPSIC, *February*, 1902.

---

[1] The present volume contains the Introduction and Part I, On the Bodily Substrate of the Mental Life. The remaining Parts are entitled as follows: Part II, Of the Elements of the Mental Life; Part III, Of the Formation of Sensory Ideas; Part IV, Of the Affective Processes and of Voluntary Actions; Part V, Of the Course and the Connexions of Mental Processes; Part VI, Final Considerations.—Translator.

[2] Now (1903) published separately.—Translator.

Translator's Preface

WHEN I went to Leipsic in 1890, I carried with me a completed translation of the third (1887) edition of the *Grundzüge der physiologischen Psychologie*. I spent nearly a year upon its revision, and did not mention it to the author until the late summer of 1891. Professor Wundt took my presumption very kindly; but the fourth edition was already on the horizon, and my manuscript was never offered to a publisher.

I had not, however, given up the idea of a translation. As soon as other engagements allowed—at the end of 1896—I set to work upon the edition of 1893. The work was finished, except for final revision, in 1899. But I found, on going over the first volume for the press, that certain chapters, especially those dealing with embryology and neurology, must be corrected and brought up to date. A year went by, with nothing to show for it but the writing of footnotes and additional paragraphs; and when I was again ready, the fifth edition was in prospect for the immediate future.

I fear that—apart from my rather dearly bought experience, which should have profited me something—the present translation is the worst of the three. I might plead in excuse that one does not undertake the task of translating a large work for the third time and in mature life with the enthusiasm that one brings to it as a young student. I might also plead that the publishers, disappointed in the matter of the fourth edition, and naturally anxious, in any event, to bring out the translation as soon as possible after the appearance of the original, have put some little pressure upon me, though always of the friendliest kind, to get the work done out of hand. On the whole, however, I prefer to rest my case upon the difficulties of the book itself. Wundt's style has often, of late years, been termed diffuse and obscure. I should not care to call it either of these things; but I am sure that it is difficult. It has, perhaps, in a somewhat unusual degree, the typical characteristics of scientific German; the carelessness of verbal repetitions, the long and involved sentences, the lapses into colloquialism, and what not. It has, besides, two special difficulties. The one is intrinsic: Wundt, if I read him aright, has always had the habit of thinking two or three things at once, of carrying on certain secondary trains of thought while he develops his central idea; and the habit has grown upon him. The consequence is that his use of connecting particles, of parentheses, of echo clauses, is now always complex, and at times extraordinarily complex. The reader who opens the *Physiologische Psychologie* at haphazard, and runs through a paragraph or two, will think this statement exaggerated. If he will try not to understand, but to translate, and to translate not a page, but a chapter, its truth will be borne in upon him. I had hoped to use, for the present translation, certain parts of my former manuscript. But a new opening or closing sentence, even a new set of connectives, changes the whole colour of the German, and so demands a new phrasing, oftentimes a new vocabulary, from the translator. I soon found that my previous work was more of a hindrance than a help, and relegated it to the waste-paper basket. The second special difficulty in Wundt's style has also grown with the years; it is his increasing tendency to clothe his ideas in conceptual garb, to write in a sort of shorthand of abstractions. I have never thought him, for this or for the other reason, obscure; the meaning is always there, and can be found for the searching. But there are many and many passages where a half-way literal English rendering would be unintelligible; where one is forced, in translating, to be concrete without losing generality; and in cases like this the translator's lot is not a happy one.

The present volume covers the first 338 pages of the German work, or the Introduction and Part I: On the Bodily Substrate of the Mental Life. The German pagination is printed, for convenience of cross-reference, in the page-headings of the translation. For reasons stated in their place, I have included a section from the fourth edition which the author has omitted. I have also added an index of names and subjects.

E. B. TITCHENER.

CORNELL HEIGHTS, ITHACA, N.Y.

Contents of Vol. I

INTRODUCTION

	PAGE
§ 1. THE PROBLEM OF PHYSIOLOGICAL PSYCHOLOGY	1
§ 2. SURVEY OF THE SUBJECT	11
§ 3. PREPSYCHOLOGICAL CONCEPTS	16

PART I.

THE BODILY SUBSTRATE OF THE MENTAL LIFE

CHAPTER I

THE ORGANIC EVOLUTION OF MENTAL FUNCTION

§ 1. THE CRITERIA OF MIND AND THE RANGE OF THE MENTAL LIFE	27
§ 2. THE DIFFERENTIATION OF MENTAL FUNCTIONS AND OF THEIR PHYSICAL SUBSTRATE	33

CHAPTER II

STRUCTURAL ELEMENTS OF THE NERVOUS SYSTEM

§ 1. MORPHOLOGICAL ELEMENTS	39
a. The Nerve Cells	40
b. The Nerve Fibres	44
c. Peripheral Nerve Terminations	47
d. The Neurone Theory	48
§ 2. CHEMICAL CONSTITUENTS	54

CHAPTER III

PHYSIOLOGICAL MECHANICS OF NERVE SUBSTANCE

§ 1. GENERAL PRINCIPLES AND PROBLEMS OF A MECHANICS OF INNERVATION	57
a. Methods of a Mechanics of Innervation	57
b. The Principle of the Conservation of Work	60
c. Application of the Principle of the Conservation of Work to the Vital Processes and the Nervous System	65
§ 2. THE COURSE OF THE PROCESSES OF STIMULATION IN THE NERVE FIBRE	67
a. Course of the Muscular Contraction following Stimulation of the Motor Nerve	67
b. Excitatory and Inhibitory Processes in Nerve Stimulation	70
c. After-effects of Stimulation: Practice and Fatigue	75
d. Stimulation of Nerve by the Galvanic Current	79

		PAGE
§ 3.	THEORY OF NERVOUS EXCITATION	80
§ 4.	INFLUENCE OF THE CENTRAL PARTS UPON THE PROCESSES OF EXCITATION	85
	a. Course of the Reflex Excitation	85
	b. Enhancement of Reflex Excitability	88
	c. Inhibitions of Reflexes by Interference of Stimuli	91
	d. Chronic Effects of Excitation and Inhibition: Positive and Negative Tonus	93
§ 5.	THEORY OF CENTRAL INNERVATION	94
	a. General Theory of the Molecular Processes in the Nerve Cell	94
	b. Relation of Nervous to Psychical Processes	101

CHAPTER IV
MORPHOLOGICAL DEVELOPMENT OF THE CENTRAL ORGANS

§ 1.	GENERAL SURVEY	104
	a. Object of the Following Exposition	104
	b. The Neural Tube and the Three Main Divisions of the Brain	106
	c. The Brain Ventricles and the Differentiation of the Parts of the Brain	109
§ 2.	THE MYEL IN THE HIGHER VERTEBRATES	114
§ 3.	THE OBLONGATA	118
§ 4.	THE CEREBELLUM	121
§ 5.	THE MESENCEPHALON	123
§ 6.	THE DIENCEPHALON	124
§ 7.	THE PROSENCEPHALON	126
	a. The Brain Cavities and the Surrounding Parts	126
	b. Fornix and Commissural System	132
	c. The Development of the Outward Conformation of the Brain	137

CHAPTER V
COURSE OF THE PATHS OF NERVOUS CONDUCTION

§ 1.	GENERAL CONDITIONS OF CONDUCTION	150
§ 2.	METHODS OF INVESTIGATING THE CONDUCTION PATHS	153
§ 3.	CONDUCTION IN THE NERVES AND IN THE MYEL	155
	a. Origin and Distribution of the Nerves	155
	b. Physiology of the Conduction-Paths of the Myel	159
	c. Anatomical Results	163
§ 4.	PATHS OF CONDUCTION IN OBLONGATA AND CEREBELLUM	167
	a. General characteristics of these Paths	167
	b. Continuations of the Motor and Sensory Paths	168
	c. The Regions of Origin of the Cranial Nerves and the Nidi of Cinerea in the Oblongata	170
	d. Paths of Conduction in Pons and Cerebellum	172
§ 5.	CEREBRAL GANGLIA AND CONDUCTION PATHS OF THE HIGHER SENSORY NERVES	178

		PAGE
	a. The Cerebral Ganglia	178
	b. Conduction Paths of the Nerves of Taste and Smell	179
	c. Conduction Paths of the Acoustic Nerve	182
	d. Conduction Paths of the Optic Nerve	185
§ 6.	PATHS OF MOTOR AND SENSORY CONDUCTION TO THE CEREBRAL CORTEX	190
	a. General Methods for the Demonstration of the Cortical Centres	190
	b. Motor and Sensory Cortical Centres in the Brain of the Dog	193
	c. Motor and Sensory Cortical Areas in the Monkey	198
	d. Motor and Sensory Cortical Centres in Man	204
§ 7.	ASSOCIATION SYSTEMS OF THE CEREBRAL CORTEX	213
§ 8.	STRUCTURE OF THE CEREBRAL CORTEX	218
§ 9.	GENERAL PRINCIPLES OF THE PROCESSES OF CENTRAL CONDUCTION	225
	a. The Principle of Manifold Representation	225
	b. The Principle of the Ascending Complication of Conduction Paths	226
	c. The Principle of the Differentiation of Directions of Conduction	227
	d. The Principle of the Central Colligation of Remote Functional Areas; Theory of Decussations	229

CHAPTER VI
PHYSIOLOGICAL FUNCTION OF THE CENTRAL PARTS

§ 1.	METHODS OF FUNCTIONAL ANALYSIS	241
§ 2.	REFLEX FUNCTIONS	242
	a. Spinal Reflexes	242
	b. Metencephalic and Mesencephalic Reflexes	244
	c. Purposiveness of the Reflexes. Extent of Reflex Phenomena	250
§ 3.	AUTOMATIC EXCITATIONS	253
	a. Automatic Excitations in Myel and Oblongata	253
	b. Automatic Excitations in the Brain Cortex	256
§ 4.	FUNCTIONS OF THE MESENCEPHALON AND DIENCEPHALON	258
	a. Functions of the Mesencephalon and Diencephalon in the Lower Vertebrates	258
	b. Functions of the Mesencephalon and Diencephalon in Man	269
	c. Striatum and Lenticula	270
§ 5.	FUNCTIONS OF THE CEREBELLUM	271
§ 6.	FUNCTIONS OF THE CEREBRAL HEMISPHERES	280
	a. Phenomena of Abrogation after Partial Destruction of the Prosencephalon	280
	b. Phenomena of Abrogation after Total Loss of the Cerebral Hemispheres	283
	c. Results from Comparative Anatomy and Anthropology	285
	The Hypotheses of Localisation and their Opponents; the Old and the New Phrenologies	287

		PAGE
§ 7.	ILLUSTRATIONS OF THE PSYCHOPHYSICAL ANALYSIS OF COMPLEX CEREBRAL FUNCTIONS	29
	a. The Visual Centres	29
	b. The Speech Centres	3
	c. The Apperception Centre	3
§ 8.	GENERAL PRINCIPLES OF THE CENTRAL FUNCTIONS	32
	a. The Principle of Connexion of Elements	32
	b. The Principle of Original Indifference of Functions	32
	c. The Principle of Practice and Adaptation	32
	d. The Principle of Vicarious Function	32
	e. The Principle of Relative Localisation	32
INDEX OF SUBJECTS		33
INDEX OF NAMES		34

INTRODUCTION

§ 1. The Problem of Physiological Psychology

THE title of the present work is in itself a sufficiently clear indication of the contents. In it, the attempt is made to show the connexion between two sciences whose subject-matters are closely interrelated, but which have, for the most part, followed wholly divergent paths. Physiology and psychology cover, between them, the field of vital phenomena; they deal with the facts of life at large, and in particular with the facts of human life. Physiology is concerned with all those phenomena of life that present themselves to us in sense perception as bodily processes, and accordingly form part of that total environment which we name the external world. Psychology, on the other hand, seeks to give account of the interconnexion of processes which are evinced by our own consciousness, or which we infer from such manifestations of the bodily life in other creatures as indicate the presence of a consciousness similar to our own.

This division of vital processes into physical and psychical is useful and even necessary for the solution of scientific problems. We must, however, remember that the life of an organism is really one; complex, it is true, but still unitary. We can, therefore, no more separate the processes of bodily life from conscious processes than we can mark off an outer experience, mediated by sense perceptions, and oppose it, as something wholly separate and apart, to what we call 'inner' experience, the events of our own consciousness. On the contrary: just as one and the same thing, e.g., a tree that I perceive before me, falls as external object within the scope of natural science, and as conscious contents within that of psychology, so there are many phenomena of the physical life that are uniformly connected with conscious processes, while these in turn are always bound up with processes in the living body. It is a matter of every-day experience that we refer certain bodily movements directly to volitions, which we can observe as such only in our consciousness. Conversely, we refer the ideas of external objects that arise in consciousness either to direct affection of the organs of sense, or, in the case of memory images, to physiological excitations within the sensory centres, which we interpret as after-effects of foregone sense impressions.

It follows, then, that physiology and psychology have many points of contact. In general, there can of course be no doubt that their problems are distinct. But psychology is called upon to trace out the relations that obtain between conscious processes and certain phenomena of the physical life; and physiology, on its side, cannot afford to neglect the conscious contents in which certain phenomena of this bodily life manifest themselves to us. Indeed, as regards physiology, the interdependence of the two sciences is plainly in evidence. Practically everything that the physiologists tell us, by way of fact or of hypothesis, concerning the processes in the organs of sense and in the brain, is based upon determinate mental symptoms: so that psychology has long been recognised, explicitly or implicitly, as an indispensable auxiliary of physiological investigation. Psychologists, it is true, have been apt to take a different attitude towards physiology. They have tended to regard as superfluous any reference to the physical organism; they have supposed that nothing more is required for a science of mind than the direct apprehension of conscious processes themselves. It is in token of dissent from any such standpoint that the present work is entitled a "physiological psychology." We take issue, upon this matter, with every treatment of psychology that is based on simple self-observation or on philosophical presuppositions. We shall, wherever the occasion seems to demand, employ physiology in the service of psychology. We are thus, as was indicated above, following the example of physiology itself, which has never been in a position to disregard facts that properly belong to psychology,—although it has often been hampered in its use of them by the defects of the empirical or metaphysical psychology which it has found current.

Physiological psychology is, therefore, first of all *psychology*. It has in view the same principal object upon which all other forms of psychological exposition are directed: *the investigation of conscious processes in the modes of connexion peculiar to them.* It is not a province of physiology; nor does it attempt, as has been mistakenly asserted, to derive or explain the phenomena of the psychical from those of the physical life. We may read this meaning into the phrase 'physiological psychology,' just as we might interpret the title 'microscopical anatomy' to mean a discussion, with illustrations from anatomy, of what has been accomplished by the microscope; but the words should be no more misleading in the one case than they are in the other. As employed in the present work, the adjective 'physiological' implies simply that our psychology will avail itself to the full of the means that modern physiology puts at its disposal for the analysis of conscious processes. It will do this in two ways.

(1) Psychological inquiries have, up to the most recent times, been undertaken solely in the interest of philosophy; physiology was enabled, by

the character of its problems, to advance more quickly towards the application of exact experimental methods. Since, however, the experimental modification of the processes of life, as practised by physiology, oftentimes effects a concomitant change, direct or indirect, in the processes of consciousness,—which, as we have seen, form part of vital processes at large,—it is clear that physiology is, in the very nature of the case, qualified to assist psychology on the side of *method*; thus rendering the same help to psychology that it itself received from physics. In so far as physiological psychology receives assistance from physiology in the elaboration of experimental methods, it may be termed *experimental psychology*. This name suggests, what should not be forgotten, that psychology, in adopting the experimental methods of physiology, does not by any means take them over as they are, and apply them without change to a new material. The methods of experimental psychology have been transformed—in some instances, actually remodelled—by psychology itself, to meet the specific requirements of psychological investigation. Psychology has adapted physiological, as physiology adapted physical methods, to its own ends.

(2) An adequate definition of life, taken in the wider sense, must (as we said just now) cover both the vital processes of the physical organism and the processes of consciousness. Hence, wherever we meet with vital phenomena that present the two aspects, physical and psychical, there naturally arises a question as to the relations in which these aspects stand to each other. So we come face to face with a whole series of special problems, which may be occasionally touched upon by physiology or psychology, but which cannot receive their final solution at the hands of either, just by reason of that division of labour to which both sciences alike stand committed. Experimental psychology is no better able to cope with them than is any other form of psychology, seeing that it differs from its rivals only in method, and not in aim or purpose. Physiological psychology, on the other hand, is competent to investigate the relations that hold between the processes of the physical and those of the mental life. And in so far as it accepts this second problem, we may name it a *psychophysics*.[1] If we free this term from any sort of metaphysical implication

---

[1] The word was coined by Fechner; see his *Elemente der Psychophysik*, 1860, i. 8. In this passage, Fechner defines psychophysics as an "exact science of the functional relations or relations of dependency between body and mind, or, in more general terms, between the bodily and mental, the physical and psychical worlds"; and his main object in the *Elemente* is, accordingly, to establish the *laws* that govern the interaction of mental and bodily phenomena. It is clear that we have implied here the metaphysical assumption of a substantial difference between body and mind; we can hardly conceive, in any other way, of the existence of such a borderland, with facts and laws of its own. Fechner himself, however, rejected this substantial difference, for theoretical reasons; so that in strictness he could hardly have raised objection to such a purely empirical formulation of the problem of psychophysics as is given in the text. Cf. the concluding Chapter of this work.

as to the relation of mind and body, and understand by it nothing more than an investigation of the relations that may be shown empirically to obtain between the psychical and the physical aspects of vital processes, it is clear at once that psychophysics becomes for us not, what it is sometimes taken to be, a science intermediate between physiology and psychology, but rather a science that is auxiliary to both. It must, however, render service more especially to psychology, since the relations existing between determinate conditions of the physical organisation, on the one hand, and the processes of consciousness, on the other, are primarily of interest to the psychologist. In its final purpose, therefore, this psychophysical problem that we have assigned to physiological psychology proves to be itself psychological. In execution, it will be predominantly physiological, since psychophysics is concerned to follow up the anatomical and physiological investigation of the bodily substrates of conscious processes, and to subject its results to critical examination with a view to their bearing upon our psychical life.

There are thus two problems which are suggested by the title " physiological psychology " : the problem of *method*, which involves the application of experiment, and the problem of a psychophysical *supplement*, which involves a knowledge of the bodily substrates of the mental life. For psychology itself, the former is the more essential; the second is of importance mainly for the philosophical question of the unitariness of vital processes at large. As an experimental science, physiological psychology seeks to accomplish a reform in psychological investigation comparable with the revolution brought about in the natural sciences by the introduction of the experimental method. From one point of view, indeed, the change wrought is still more radical : for while in natural science it is possible, under favourable conditions, to make an accurate observation without recourse to experiment, there is no such possibility in psychology. It is only with grave reservations that what is called ' pure self-observation ' can properly be termed observation at all, and under no circumstances can it lay claim to accuracy. On the other hand, it is of the essence of experiment that we can vary the conditions of an occurrence at will and, if we are aiming at exact results, in a quantitatively determinable way. Hence, even in the domain of natural science, the aid of the experimental method becomes indispensable whenever the problem set is the analysis of transient and impermanent phenomena, and not merely the observation of persistent and relatively constant objects. But conscious contents are at the opposite pole from permanent objects ; they are processes, fleeting occurrences, in continual flux and change. In their case, therefore, the experimental method is of cardinal importance ; it and it alone makes a scientific introspection possible. For all accurate observation implies that the object of observation (in this case the psychical process) can be held fast by the attention, and any changes that it undergoes attentively followed. And this fixation by the attention implies, in its turn, that the observed object is independent of the observer. Now it is obvious that the required independence does not obtain in any attempt at a direct self-observation, undertaken without the help of experiment. The endeavour to observe oneself must inevitably introduce changes into the course of mental events, —changes which could not have occurred without it, and whose usual consequence is that the very process which was to have been observed disappears from consciousness. The psychological experiment proceeds very differently. In the first place, it creates external conditions that look towards the production of a determinate mental process at a given moment. In the second place, it makes the observer so far master of the general situation, that the state of consciousness accompanying this process remains approximately unchanged. The great importance of the experimental method, therefore, lies not simply in the fact that, here as in the physical realm, it enables us arbitrarily to vary the conditions of our observations, but also and essentially in the further fact that it makes observation itself possible for us. The results of this observation may then be fruitfully employed in the examination of other mental phenomena, whose nature prevents their own direct experimental modification.

We may add that, fortunately for the science, there are other sources of objective psychological knowledge, which become accessible at the very point where the experimental method fails us. These are certain products of the common mental life, in which we may trace the operation of determinate psychical motives: chief among them are language, myth and custom. In part determined by historical conditions, they are also, in part, dependent upon universal psychological laws; and the phenomena that are referable to these laws form the subject-matter of a special psychological discipline, *ethnic* psychology. The results of ethnic psychology constitute, at the same time, our chief source of information regarding the general psychology of the complex mental processes. In this way, experimental psychology and ethnic psychology form the two principal departments of scientific psychology at large. They are supplemented by *child* and *animal* psychology, which in conjunction with ethnic psychology attempt to resolve the problems of psychogenesis. Workers in both these fields may, of course, avail themselves within certain limits of the advantages of the experimental method. But the results of experiment are here matters of objective observation only, and the experimental method accordingly loses the peculiar significance which it possesses as an instrument of introspection. Finally, child psychology and experimental psychology in the narrower sense may be bracketed together as *individual* psychology, while animal psychology and ethnic psychology form the two halves of a *generic* or *comparative* psychology. These distinctions within psychology are, however, by no means to be put on a level with the analogous divisions of the province of physiology. Child psychology and animal psychology are of relatively slight importance, as compared with the sciences which deal with the corresponding physiological problems of ontogeny and phylogeny. On the other hand, ethnic psychology must always come to the assistance of individual psychology, when the developmental forms of the complex mental processes are in question.

Kant once declared that psychology was incapable of ever raising itself to the rank of an exact natural science.[1] The reasons that he gives for this opinion have often been repeated in later times.[2] In the first place, Kant says, psychology cannot become an exact science because mathematics is inapplicable to the phenomena of the internal sense; the pure internal perception, in which mental phenomena must be constructed,—time,—has but one dimension. In the second place, however, it cannot even become an experimental science, because in it the manifold of internal observation cannot be arbitrarily varied,— still less, another thinking subject be submitted to one's experiments, conformably to the end in view; moreover, the very fact of observation means alteration of the observed object. The first of these objections is erroneous; the second is, at the least, one-sided. It is not true that the course of inner events evinces only one dimension, time. If this were the case, its mathematical representation would, certainly, be impossible; for such representation always requires at least two variables, which can be subsumed under the concept of magnitude. But, as a matter of fact, our sensations and feelings are *intensive* magnitudes, which form temporal series. The course of mental events has, therefore, at any rate two dimensions; and with this fact is given the general possibility of its representation in mathematical form. Otherwise, indeed, Herbart could hardly have lighted upon the idea of applying mathematics to psychology. And his attempt has the indisputable merit of proving once and for all the possibility of an application of mathematical methods in the sphere of mind.[3]

If Herbart, nevertheless, failed to accomplish the task which he set himself, the reason of his failure is very simple; it lay in the overweening confidence with which he regarded the method of pure self-observation and the hypotheses whereby he filled out the gaps that this observation leaves. It is Fechner's service to have found and followed the true way; to have shown us how a 'mathematical psychology' may, within certain limits, be realised in practice. Fechner's method consists in the *experimental* modification of consciousness by sensory stimuli; it leads, under favourable circumstances, to the establishment of certain quantitative relations between the physical and the psychical.[4] At

---

[1] KANT, *Metaphysische Anfangsgründe d. Naturwissenschaft.* In *Sämmtliche Werke*, ed. by ROSENKRANZ, v. 310.

[2] Cf. esp. E. ZELLER, *Abh. d. Berliner Akad.*, 1881, *Phil.-hist. Cl., Abh. iii.*; *Sitzungsber.* of the same, 1882, 295 ff.; and my remarks upon the question, *Philos. Studien*, i. 250, 463 ff.

[3] HERBART, *Psychologie als Wissenschaft neu gegründet auf Erfahrung, Metaphysik u. Mathematik.* In *Ges. Werke*, ed. by HARTENSTEIN, vols. v., vi.

[4] FECHNER, *El. d. Psychophysik*, ii. 9 ff. An interesting light is thrown upon the

the present day, experimental psychology has ceased to regard this formulation of mental measurements as its exclusive or even as its principal problem. Its aim is now more general ; it attempts, by arbitrary modification of consciousness, to arrive at a causal analysis of mental processes. Fechner's determinations are also affected, to some extent, by his conception of psychophysics as a specific science of the 'interactions of mind and body.' But, in saying this, we do not lessen the magnitude of his achievement. He was the first to show how Herbart's idea of an 'exact psychology' might be turned to practical account.

The arguments that Kant adduces in support of his second objection, that the inner experience is inaccessible to experimental investigation, are all derived from purely internal sources, from the subjective flow of processes ; and there, of course, we cannot challenge its validity. Our psychical experiences are, primarily, indeterminate magnitudes ; they are incapable of exact treatment until they have been referred to determinate units of measurement, which in turn may be brought into constant causal relations with other given magnitudes. But we have, in the experimental modification of consciousness by external stimuli, a means to this very end,—to the discovery of the units of measurement and the relations required. Modification from without enables us to subject our mental processes to arbitrarily determined conditions, over which we have complete control, and which we may keep constant or vary as we will. Hence the objection urged against experimental psychology, that it seeks to do away with introspection, which is the *sine quâ non* of any psychology, is based upon a misunderstanding. The only form of introspection which experimental psychology seeks to banish from the science is that professing self-observation which thinks it can arrive directly, without further assistance, at an exact characterisation of mental facts, and which is therefore inevitably exposed to the grossest self-deception. The aim of the experimental procedure is to substitute for this subjective method, whose sole resource is an inaccurate inner perception, a true and reliable introspection, and to this end it brings consciousness under accurately adjustable objective conditions. For the rest, here as elsewhere, we must estimate the value of the method, in the last resort, by its results. It is certain that the subjective method has no success to boast of ; for there is hardly a single question of fact upon which its representatives do not hold radically divergent opinions. Whether and how far the experimental method is in better case, the reader will be able to decide for himself at the conclusion of this work. He must, however, in all justice remember that the application of experiment to mental problems is still only a few decades old.[1]

The omission, in the above list of the various psychological disciplines, of any mention of what is called *rational* psychology is not accidental. The term was introduced into mental science by C. Wolff (1679–1754), to denote a knowledge of the mental life gained, in independence of experience, simply and solely

origination of the idea of 'mental measurement' in Fechner's mind, and also upon the inspiration that he derived from Herbart, by the "Kurze Darstellung eines neuen Princips mathematischer Psychologie" in his *Zendavesta*, 1851, ii. 373 ff. For a detailed treatment of mental measurement, see Ch. ix. below.

[1] On the question of method in general, cf. my *Beiträge zur Theorie der Sinneswahrnehmungen*, 1862, Einleitung : Ueber die Methoden in der Psychologie; *Logik*, 2nd ed., ii. 2, 151 ff. ; the essay on the problems of experimental psychology in my *Essays*, Leipzig, 1885, 127 ff. ; the article *Selbstbeobachtung u. innere Wahrnehmung*, in the *Philos. Studien*, iv. 292 ff. ; and *Völkerpsychologie*, i. 1, 1900, Einleitung.

from metaphysical concepts. The result has proved that any such metaphysical treatment of psychology must, if it is to maintain its existence, be constantly making surreptitious incursions into the realm of experience. Wolff himself found it necessary to work out an empirical psychology, alongside of the rational : though it must be confessed that, in fact, the rational contains about as much experience as the empirical, and the empirical about as much metaphysics as the rational. The whole distinction rests upon a complete misapprehension of the scientific position, not only of psychology, but also of philosophy. Psychology is, in reality, just as much an experiential science as is physics or chemistry. But it can never be the business of philosophy to usurp the place of any special science ; philosophy has its beginnings, in every case, in the established results of the special sciences. Hence the works upon rational psychology stand in approximately the same relation to the actual progress of psychological science as does the nature-philosophy of Schelling or Hegel to the development of modern natural science.[1]

There are certain psychological works, still current at the present time, which bear the word 'empirical' upon their title-pages, but make it a matter of principle to confine themselves to what they term a 'pure' introspection. They are, for the most part, curious mixtures of rational and empirical psychology. Sometimes the rational part is restricted to a few pages of metaphysical discussion of the nature of mind ; sometimes—as in the great majority of books of the kind emanating from the Herbartian School—certain hypotheses of metaphysical origin are put forward as results of self-observation. It has been well said that if a prize were offered for the discovery by this whole introspective school of one single undisputed fact, it would be offered in vain.[2] Nevertheless, the assurance of the Herbartians is incredible. Their compendia appear, one after another ; and the memory of the students who use them is burdened with a mixed medley of purely imaginary processes. On the other side, the supreme advantage of the experimental method lies in the fact that it and it alone renders a reliable introspection possible, and that it therefore increases our ability to deal introspectively with processes not directly accessible to modification from without. This general significance of the experimental method is being more and more widely recognised in current psychological investigation ; and the definition of experimental psychology has been correspondingly extended beyond its original limits. We now understand by 'experimental psychology' not simply those portions of psychology which are directly accessible to experimentation, but the whole of individual psychology. For all such psychology employs the experimental method : directly, where its direct use is possible ; but in all other cases indirectly, by availing itself of the general results which the direct employment of the method has yielded, and of the refinement of psychological observation which this employment induces.

Experimental psychology itself has, it is true, now and again suffered relapse into a metaphysical treatment of its problems. We recognise the symptoms whenever we find 'physiological psychology' defined, from the outset, in such a way as to give it a determinate metaphysical implication. The task now assigned to the science is that of the interpretation of conscious phenomena by

---

[1] Cf. with this the essay *Philosophie u. Wissenschaft*, in my *Essays*, 1 ff. ; and the article *Ueber d. Eintheilung d. Wissenschaften*, in the *Philos. Studien*, v. 1 ff.

[2] F. A. LANGE, *Geschichte des Materialismus*, 2te Aufl., ii. 383 ; *History of Materialism*, iii., 1892, 171.

their reference to physiological conditions. Usually, the infection spreads still farther, and the same view is taken of the problem of psychology at large. As regards sensations, the elements out of which they are compounded, conscious processes (we are told) have their specific character, their peculiar constitution; but it is impossible by psychological means to discover uniformities of connexion among these elements. Hence the only road to a scientific description or explanation of complex mental experiences lies through the knowledge of the physiological connexions obtaining among the physiological processes with which the psychical elements are correlated.[1] On this conception, there is no such thing as psychical, but only physical causation, and every causal explanation of mental occurrence must consequently be couched in physiological terms. It is accordingly termed the theory of 'psychophysical materialism.' The theory as such is by no means a new thing in the history of philosophy. All through the eighteenth century it was struggling for mastery with the rival theory of mechanical materialism, which explained the psychical elements themselves as confused apprehensions of molecular motions. But it presents a novel feature in its endeavour to press physiological psychology into the service of the metaphysical hypothesis and thus apparently to remove this hypothesis from the metaphysical sphere,—so that psychological materialism becomes for its representatives compatible even with a philosophical idealism of the order of Kant or Fichte. Since psychology, from this point of view, forms a supplement to physiology, and therefore takes its place among the natural sciences, it need, as a matter of fact, pay no further regard either to philosophy or to the mental sciences. That the mental life itself is the problem of psychology,—this is mere dogma, handed down to us by past ages.[2] Yet after all, the assertion that there is no such thing as psychical causation, and that all psychical connexions must be referred back to physical, is at the present day nothing else than it has always been, a metaphysical assumption. More than this: it is an assumption which, on its negative side, comes into conflict with a large number of actually demonstrable psychical connexions, and, on the positive, raises a comparatively very limited group of experiences to the rank of an universal principle. It is, we must suppose, a realisation of the inadequacy of the arguments offered in support of these two fundamental propositions that has led certain psychologists, who would otherwise take the same theoretical position, to divide the problem of psychology, and to recognise the interconnexions of mental processes as a legitimate object of inquiry, alongside of the investigation of their dependence upon determinate physiological processes within the brain. In the psychological portion of their works, these writers usually adopt the theory of the 'association of ideas,' elaborated in the English psychology of the eighteenth century.[3] They adopt it for the good and sufficient reason that the doctrine of association, from David Hartley (1705-1757)

---

[1] H. MÜNSTERBERG, *Ueber Aufgaben und Methoden der Psychologie*, in *Schriften der Gesellschaft f. psychol. Forschung*, i. 111 ff. Practically the same position, though with minor changes of expression, is taken by the author in his *Grundzüge der Psychologie*, i., 1900, 382 ff.

[2] MÜNSTERBERG, *Grundzüge der Psychologie*, Vorwort, viii. Cf. the same author's *Psychology and Life*, 1899. This view, of the irrelevancy of psychology to the mental sciences, is further shared by certain modern philosophers: see the criticism of it in my *Einleitung in die Philosophie*, 1901, § 4.

[3] Cf., e.g., T. ZIEHEN, *Leitfaden der physiologischen Psychologie*, 5te Aufl., 1900, 3 ff.; *Introduction to Physiological Psychology*, 1895, 3 ff.

down to Herbert Spencer (1820–1904), has itself for the most part attempted merely a physiological interpretation of the associative processes.

The materialistic point of view in psychology can claim, at best, only the value of an heuristic hypothesis. Its justification must, therefore, be sought first of all in its results. But it is apparent that the diversion of the work of psychology from its proper object, the related manifold of conscious processes, is precisely calculated to make the experimental method comparatively barren, so far as concerns psychology itself. And, as a matter of fact, the books upon physiological psychology that are written from the standpoint of materialism confine themselves almost entirely, when they are not borrowing from the physiology of brain and sense organs, to the beaten track of the traditional doctrine of association. Ideas are treated, after as before, as if they were immutable objects, that come and go, form connexions of sequence with one another, obey in these connexions the well-known laws of habit and practice, and finally, when arranged in certain groups, yield the not very startling result that they can be brought under the same logical categories that have proved generally serviceable for the classification of all sorts of concepts.[1]

Now physiology and psychology, as we said just now, are auxiliary disciplines, and neither can advance without assistance from the other. Physiology, in its analysis of the physiological functions of the sense organs, must use the results of subjective observation of sensations; and psychology, in its turn, needs to know the physiological aspects of sensory function, in order rightly to appreciate the psychological. Such instances might easily be multiplied. Moreover, in view of the gaps in our knowledge, physiological and psychological alike, it is inevitable that the one science will be called upon, time and again, to do duty for the other. Thus, all our current theories of the physical processes of light excitation are inferences from the psychological course and character of visual sensations; and we might very well attempt, conversely, to explain the conditions of practice and habituation, in the mental sphere, from the properties of nervous substance, as shown in the changes of excitability due to the continued effect of previous excitations. But one cannot assert, without wilfully closing one's eyes to the actual state of affairs or taking theories for facts, that the gaps in our knowledge which demand this sort of extraneous filling are to be found only on the one side, the side of psychology. In which of the two sciences our knowledge of processes and of the interconnexion of processes is more or less perfect or imperfect is a question that, we may safely say, hardly admits of an answer. But however this may be, the assertion that the mental life lacks all causal connexion, and that the real and primary object of psychology is therefore not the mental life itself but the physical substrate of that life,—this assertion stands self-condemned. The effects of such teaching upon psychology cannot but be detrimental. In the first place, it conceals the proper object of psychological investigation behind facts and hypotheses that are borrowed from physiology. Secondly and more especially, it recommends the employment of the experimental methods without the least regard to the psychological point of view, so that for psychology as such their results are generally valueless. Hence the gravest danger that besets the path of our science to-day comes not from the speculative and empirical dogmas of the older schools, but

---

[1] On the doctrine of association, see Part v., below. For a general criticism of psychological materialism, cf. the articles *Ueber psychische Causalität* and *Ueber die Definition der Psychologie*, in the *Philos. Studien*, x. 47 ff., xii. 1 ff.

rather from this materialistic pseudo-science. Antipsychological tendencies can hardly find clearer expression than in the statement that the psychological interpretation of the mental life has no relation whatever to the mental life itself, as manifested in history and in society.

Besides this application of the term 'experimental psychology' in the interests of pyschological materialism, we find it used in still another sense, which is widely different from that of our own definition. It has become customary, more especially in France, to employ the name principally, if not exclusively, for experiments upon hypnotism and suggestion. At its best, however, this usage narrows the definition of 'experimental psychology' in a wholly inacceptable way. If we are to give the title of 'psychological experiment' to each and every operation upon consciousness that brings about a change of conscious contents, then, naturally, hypnotisation and the suggestion of ideas must be accounted experiments. The inducing of a morphine narcosis, and any purposed interference with the course of a dream consciousness, would fall under the same category. But if the principal value of the psychological experiment lies in the fact that it makes an exact introspection possible, very few of these modifications of consciousness can be termed true psychological experiments. This does not mean, of course, that experiments with suggestion may not, under favourable circumstances,—in the hands of an experimenter who is guided by correct psychological principles, and who has at his command reliable and introspectively trained observers,—yield results of high importance to psychology : so much, indeed, is proved by Vogt's observations on the analysis of the feelings in the hypnotic state.[1] But in such cases the conditions necessary to the performance of accurate experiments are, it is plain, peculiarly difficult of fulfilment ; and the great majority of what are called 'hypnotic experiments' either possess, accordingly, no scientific value at all, or lead to the observation of interesting but isolated facts, whose place in the psychological system is still uncertain.[2]

§ 2. Survey of the Subject

Physiological psychology is primarily psychology, and therefore has for its subject the manifold of conscious processes, whether as directly experienced by ourselves, or as inferred on the analogy of our own experiences from objective observation. Hence the order in which it takes up particular problems will be determined primarily by psychological considerations ; the phenomena of consciousness fall into distinct groups, according to the points of view from which they are successively regarded. At the same time, any detailed treatment of the relation between the psychical and physical aspects of vital processes presupposes a digression into anatomy and physiology such as would naturally be out of place in a purely psychological exposition. While, then, the following Chapters of this work are arranged in general upon a systematic plan, the author has not always observed the rule that the reader should be adequately prepared, at each stage

---

[1] O. VOGT, *Die directe psychologische Experimentalmethode in hypnotischen Bewusstseinszuständen.* In the *Zeitschr. für Hypnotismus,* v., 1897, 7, 180 ff.
[2] For a general discussion of hypnotism, see Part v., below.

of the discussion, by the contents of preceding Chapters. Its disregard has enabled him to avoid repetition; and he has acted with the less scruple, in view of the general understanding of psychology which the reading of a book like the present implies. Thus a critical review of the results of brain anatomy and brain physiology, with reference to their value for psychology, presupposes much and various psychological knowledge. Nevertheless, it is necessary, for other reasons, that the anatomical and physiological considerations should precede the properly psychological portion of the work. And similar conditions recur, now and again, even in Chapters that are pre-eminently psychological.[1]

Combining in this way the demands of theory and the precepts of practical method, we shall in what follows (1) devote a first Part to the *bodily substrate of the mental life*. A wealth of new knowledge is here placed at our disposal by the anatomy and physiology of the central nervous system, reinforced at various points by pathology and general biology. This mass of material calls imperatively for examination from the psychological side: more especially since it has become customary for the sciences concerned in its acquisition to offer all varieties of psychological interpretation of their facts. Nay, so far have things gone, that we actually find proposals made for a complete reconstruction of psychology itself, upon an anatomical and physiological basis! But, if we are seriously to examine these conjectures and hypotheses, we must, naturally, acquaint ourselves with the present status of the sciences in question. Even here, however, our presentation of the facts will depart in some measure from the beaten path. Our aim is psychological: so that we may restrict ourselves, on the one hand, to matters of general importance, while on the other we must lay special emphasis upon whatever is significant for psychology. Thus it cannot be our task to follow brain anatomy into all the details which it has brought to light concerning the connexions of fibres within the brain,—into all those minute points whose interpretation is still altogether uncertain, and whose truth is often and again called in question. It will only be necessary for us to obtain a general view of the structure of the central organs and of such principal connexions of these with one another and with the peripheral organs as have been made out with sufficient certainty. We may then, in the light of reasonably secure principles of nerve physiology and of our psychological knowledge, proceed to discuss the probable relations of physiological structure and function to the processes of consciousness.

(2) We shall then, in a second Part, begin our work upon the problem

---

[1] In my *Grundriss der Psychologie* (4te Aufl., 1901; *Outlines of Psychology*, 1897), in which I have attempted to give an elementary exposition of psychology so far as possible under the exclusive guidance of psychological principles, I have adhered more strictly to the systematic point of view. Hence the *Grundriss* may be regarded in this connexion both as supplement and as introduction to the present work.

of psychology proper, with the doctrine of the *elements of the mental life*. Psychological analysis leaves us with two such elements, of specifically different character: with *sensations*, which as the ultimate and irreducible elements of ideas we may term the objective elements of the mental life, and with *feelings*, which accompany these objective elements as their subjective complements, and are referred not to external things but to the state of consciousness itself. In this sense, therefore, we call blue, yellow, warm, cold, etc., sensations; pleasantness, unpleasantness, excitement, depression, etc., feelings. It is important that the terms be kept sharply distinct, in these assigned meanings, and not used indiscriminately, as they often are in the language of everyday life, and even in certain psychologies. It is also important that they be reserved strictly for the psychical elements, and not applied at random both to simple and to complex contents,—a confusion that is regrettably current in physiology. Thus in what follows we shall not speak of a manifold of several tones or of a coloured extent as a 'sensation,' but as an 'idea'; and when we come to deal with the formations resulting from a combination of feelings we shall term them expressly 'complex feelings' or (if the special words that language offers us are in place) 'emotions,' 'volitions,' etc. This terminological distinction cannot, of course, tell us of itself anything whatsoever regarding the mode of origin of such complex formations from the psychical elements. It does, however, satisfy the imperative requirement that the results of psychological analysis of complex conscious contents be rendered permanent, when that analysis is completed, by fitting designations. As for these results themselves, it need hardly be said that the mental elements are never given directly as contents of consciousness in the uncompounded state. We may learn here from physiology, which has long recognised the necessity of abstracting, in its investigations of these products of analysis, from the connexions in which they occur. Sensations like red, yellow, warm, cold, etc., are considered by physiologists in this their abstract character, i.e., without regard to the connexions in which, in the concrete case, they invariably present themselves. To employ the single term 'sensation' as well for these ultimate and irreducible elements of our ideas as for the surfaces and objects that we perceive about us is a confusion of thought which works sufficient harm in physiology, and which the psychologist must once and for all put behind him.

But there is another and a still worse terminological obscurity, common both to physiology and to psychology, which has its source in the confusion of conscious processes themselves with the outcome of a later reflection upon their objective conditions. It is all too common to find sensations so named only when they are directly aroused by external sensory stimuli, while the sensations dependent upon any sort of internal condition are termed ideas, and the word idea itself is at the same time restricted to the contents known as memory images. This confusion is psychologically inexcusable. There is absolutely no reason why a sensation—blue, green, yellow, or what not—should be one thing when it is accompanied simply by an excitation in the 'visual centre' of the cortex, and another and quite a different thing when this excitation is itself set up by the operation of some external stimulus. As conscious contents, blue is and remains blue, and the idea of an object is always a thing ideated in the outside world, whether the external stimulus or the thing outside of us be really present or not. It is true that the memory image is, oftentimes, weaker and more transient than the image of direct perception. But this difference is by no means constant; we may sense in dreams, or in the state of hallucination, as intensively as we sense under the operation of actual sensory stimuli.[1] Such distinctions are, therefore, survivals from the older psychology of reflection, in which the various contents of consciousness acquired significance only as the reflective thought of the philosopher read a meaning into them. It was an accepted tenet of this psychology that ideas enjoy an immaterial existence in the mind, while sensation was regarded as something that makes its way into mind from the outside. Now all this may be right or wrong; but, whether right or wrong, it evidently has no bearing whatever upon the conscious process as such.

The attitude of physiological psychology to sensations and feelings, considered as psychical elements, is, naturally, the attitude of psychology at large. At the same time, physiological psychology has to face a number of problems which do not arise for general psychology: problems that originate in the peculiar interest which attaches to the relations sustained by these ultimate elements of the mental life to the physical processes in the nervous system and its appended organs. Physiology tells us, with ever-increasing conviction, that these relations, especially in the case of sensations, are absolutely uniform; and with an improved understanding of bodily expression, of affective symptomatology, we are gradually coming to see that the feelings too have their laws of correlation, no less uniform, if of an entirely different nature. But this growth of knowledge lays all the heavier charge upon psychology to determine the significance of the various psychophysical relations. A pure psychology could afford, if needs must, to pass them by, and might confine itself to a description of the elements and of their direct interrelations. A physiological psychology, on the other hand, is bound to regard this psychophysical aspect of the problems of mind as one of its most important objects of investigation.

(3) The course of our inquiry proceeds naturally from the mental ele-

---

[1] For a more extended discussion of these terminological questions, see Ch. vii. § 1, below.

ments to the complex psychical processes that take shape in consciousness from the connexion of the elements. These mental formations must be treated in order; and our third Part will be occupied with that type of complex process to which all others are referred as concomitant processes: with the *ideas* that arise from the connexion of sensations. Since physiological psychology stands committed to the experimental method, it will here pay most regard to the sense ideas aroused by external stimuli, these being most easily brought under experimental control. We may accordingly designate the contents of this section a study of the *composition of sense ideas*. Our conclusions will, however, apply equally well to ideas that are not aroused by external sensory stimuli; the two classes of ideas agree in all essential characters, and are no more to be separated than are the corresponding sensations.

The task of physiological psychology remains the same in the analysis of ideas that it was in the investigation of sensations: to act as mediator between the neighbouring sciences of physiology and psychology. At the same time, the end in view all through the doctrine of ideas is pre-eminently psychological; the specifically psychophysical problems, that are of such cardinal importance for the theory of sensation, now retire modestly into the background. Physiological psychology still takes account of the physical aspect of the sensory functions involved, but it hardly does more in this regard than it is bound to do in any psychological inquiry in which it avails itself of the experimental means placed at its disposal.

(4) The doctrine of sense ideas is followed by a fourth Part, dealing with the analysis of mental processes that, as complex products of the interconnexion of simple feelings, stand in a relation to the affective elements analogous to that sustained by ideas to the sensations of which they are compounded. It must not, of course, be understood that the two sets of formations can, in reality, be kept altogether separate and distinct. Sensations and feelings are, always and everywhere, complementary constituents of our mental experiences. Hence the conscious contents that are compounded of feelings can never occur except together with ideational contents, and in many cases the affective elements are as powerful to influence sensations and ideas as these are to influence the feelings. This whole group of subjective experiences, in which feelings are the determining factors, may be brought under the title of *Gemüthsbewegungen und Willenshandlungen*. Of these, *Gemüthsbewegungen* is the wider term, since it covers volitional as well as affective processes. Nevertheless, in view of the peculiar importance of the phenomena of will, and of the relation which external voluntary actions bear to other organic movements,—a relation whose psychophysical implications constitute it a special problem of physiological psychology,—we retain the two words side by side in the title of our section, and limit the meaning

of *Gemüthsbewegungen* on the one hand to the *emotions*, and on the other to a class of affective processes that are frequently bound up with or pass into emotions, the *intellectual feelings*.[1]

(5) Having thus investigated sense ideas, emotions and voluntary actions, the complex processes of the mental life, we pass in a fifth Part to the doctrine of *consciousness* and of the *interconnexion of mental processes*. The results of the two preceding sections now form the basis of an analysis of consciousness and of the connexions of conscious contents. For all these conscious connexions contain, as their proximate constituents, ideas and emotions, and consciousness itself is nothing else than a general name for the total sum of processes and their connexions. So far as our analysis of these connexions is experimental, we shall be chiefly concerned with the arbitrary modification of sense ideas and of their course in consciousness. When, on the other hand, we come to consider the interconnexions of emotions and voluntary actions, our principal dependence will be upon the results of analysis of the processes of consciousness at large.

In these five Parts, then, we confine ourselves to a purely empirical examination of the facts. (6) A sixth and final Part will treat of the *origin and principles of mental development*. Here we shall endeavour to set forth, in brief, the general conclusions that may be drawn from these facts for a comprehensive theory of the mental life and of its relation to our physical existence. So far, we have set conscious processes and the processes of the bodily life over against each other, without attempting any exact definition of either. Now at last, when our survey of their interrelations is completed, we shall be able to ascribe a definitive meaning to the terms physical and psychical. And this will help us towards a solution of the well worn problem of ' the interaction of mind and body,' a solution that shall do justice to the present status of our physiological and psychological knowledge, and shall also meet the requirements of a philosophical criticism of knowledge itself. Physiological psychology thus ends with those questions with which the philosophical psychology of an older day was wont to begin,— the questions of the nature of the mind, and of the relation of consciousness to an external world; and with a characterisation of the general attitude which psychology is to take up, when it seeks to trace the laws of the mental life as manifested in history and in society.

§ 3. Prepsychological Concepts [2]

The human mind is so constituted, that it cannot gather experiences

---

[1] *Gemüthsbewegungen*, as first used above, means "complex affective, affective-volitional and volitional processes." There is no exact English equivalent. See BALDWIN's *Dict. of Phil. and Psych.*, ii. 1902, 680. *Willenshandlungen* means, of course, voluntary actions, internal and external.—TRANSLATOR.

[2] In the first four editions of the *Physiologische Psychologie*, the Introduction con-

without at the same time supplying an admixture of its own speculation. The first result of this naïve reflection is the system of concepts which language embodies. Hence, in all departments of human experience, there are certain concepts that science finds ready made, before it proceeds upon its own proper business,—results of that primitive reflection which has left its permanent record in the concept-system of language. 'Heat' and 'light,' e.g., are concepts from the world of external experience, which had their immediate origin in sense-perception. Modern physics subsumes them both under the general concept of motion. But it would not be able to do this, if the physicist had not been willing provisionally to accept the concepts of the common consciousness, and to begin his inquiries with their investigation. 'Mind,' 'intellect,' 'reason,' 'understanding,' etc., are concepts of just the same kind, concepts that existed before the advent of any scientific psychology. The fact that the naïve consciousness always and everywhere points to internal experience as a special source of knowledge, may, therefore, be accepted for the moment as sufficient testimony to the rights of psychology as science. And this acceptance implies the adoption of the concept of 'mind,' to cover the whole field of internal experience. 'Mind,' will accordingly be the subject, to which we attribute all the separate facts of internal observation as predicates. The subject itself is determined wholly and exclusively by its predicates; and the reference of these to a common substrate must be taken as nothing more than an expression of their reciprocal connexion. In saying this, we are declining once and for all to read into the concept of 'mind' a meaning that the naïve linguistic consciousness always attaches to it. Mind, in popular thought, is not simply a subject in the logical sense, but a substance, a real being; and the various 'activities of mind,' as they are termed, are its modes of expression or action. But there is here involved a metaphysical presupposition, which psychology may possibly be led to honour at the conclusion of her work, but which she cannot on any account accept, untested, before she has entered upon it. Moreover, it is not true of this assumption as it was of the discrimination of internal experience at large, that it is necessary for the starting of the investigation. The words coined by language to symbolise certain groups of experiences still bear upon them marks which show that, in their primitive meanings, they stood not merely

---

sists of two sections, entitled respectively *Aufgabe der physiologischen Psychologie*, and *Psychologische Vorbegriffe*. In the present, fifth edition, the second of these sections is replaced by an *Uebersicht des Gegenstandes*. I here reprint the section on *Psychologische Vorbegriffe* as it appeared in 1893. It was, in all probability, omitted mainly for reasons of space. Cf. Preface to the fifth edition. It will, I think, be found useful by English readers in its present form, although a good deal of its criticism is implicit in the constructions of the final chapter of the work. I print it only after much hesitation, and with the express reminder to the reader that the author, for whatever reason, has *not* included it in the current edition of his book.—TRANSLATOR.

for separate modes of existence, for 'substances,' in general, but actually for personal beings. This personification of substances has left its most indelible trace in the concept of genus. Now the word-symbols of conceptual ideas have passed so long from hand to hand in the service of the understanding, that they have gradually lost all such fanciful reference. There are many cases in which we have seen the end, not only of the personification of substances, but even of the substantialising of concepts. But we are not called upon, on that account, to dispense with the use whether of the concepts themselves or of the words that designate them. We speak of virtue, honour, reason; but our thought does not translate any one of these concepts into a substance. They have ceased to be metaphysical substances, and have become logical subjects. In the same way, then, we shall consider mind, for the time being, simply as the logical subject of internal experience. Such a view follows directly from the mode of concept-formation employed by language, except that it is freed of all those accretions of crude metaphysics which invariably attach to concepts in their making by the naïve consciousness.

We must take up a precisely similar attitude to other ready-made concepts that denote special departments or special relations of the internal experience. Thus our language makes a distinction between 'mind' and 'spirit.' The two concepts carry the same meaning, but carry it in different contexts: their correlates in the domain of external experience are 'body' and 'matter.' The name 'matter' is applied to any object of external experience as it presents itself directly to our senses, without reference to an inner existence of its own. 'Body' is matter thought of with reference to such an inner existence. 'Spirit,' in the same way, denotes the internal existence as considered out of all connexion with an external existence; whereas 'mind,' especially where it is explicitly opposed to spirit, presupposes this connexion with a corporeal existence, given in external experience.[1]

While the terms 'mind' and 'spirit' cover the whole field of internal experience, the various 'mental faculties,' as they are called, designate the special provinces of mind as distinguished by a direct introspection. Language brings against us an array of concepts like 'sensibility,' 'feeling,' 'reason,' 'understanding,'—a classification of the processes given in internal perception against which, bound down as we are to the use of these words, we are practically powerless. What we can do, however, and what science is obliged to do, is to reach an exact definition of the concepts, and to arrange them upon a systematic plan. It is probable that the mental faculties stood originally not merely for different parts of the field of internal

---

[1] The German terms for 'body' and 'matter' are *Leib* and *Körper*; for 'mind' and 'spirit,' *Seele* and *Geist*. See BALDWIN'S *Dict. of Phil. and Psych.*, ii. 680.—TRANSLATOR.

experience, but for as many different beings; though the relation of these to the total being, the mind or spirit, was not conceived of in any very definite way. But the hypostatisation of these concepts lies so far back in the remote past, and the mythological interpretation of nature is so alien to our modes of thought, that there is no need here to warn the reader against a too great credulity in the matter of metaphysical substances. Nevertheless, there is one legacy which has come down to modern science from the mythopœic age. All the concepts that we mentioned just now have retained a trace of the mythological concept of *force*; they are not regarded simply as—what they really are—class-designations of certain departments of the inner experience, but are oftentimes taken to be forces, by whose means the various phenomena are produced. Understanding is looked upon as the force that enables us to perceive truth; memory as the force which stores up ideas for future use; and so on. On the other hand, the effects of these different 'forces' manifest themselves so irregularly that they hardly seem to be forces in the proper sense of the word; and so the phrase 'mental faculties' came in to remove all objections. A faculty, as its derivation indicates, is not a force that must operate, necessarily and immutably, but only a force that may operate. The influence of the mythological concept of force is here as plain as it could well be; for the prototype of the operation of force as faculty is, obviously, to be found in human action. The original significance of faculty is that of a being which acts. Here, therefore, in the first formation of psychological concepts, we have the germ of that confusion of classification with explanation which is one of the besetting sins of empirical psychology. The general statement that the mental faculties are class concepts, belonging to descriptive psychology, relieves us of the necessity of discussing them and their significance at the present stage of our inquiry. As a matter of fact, one can quite well conceive of a natural science of the internal experience in which sensibility, memory, reason and understanding should be conspicuous by their absence. For the only things that we are directly cognisant of in internal perception are individual ideas, feelings, impulses, etc.; and the subsumption of these individual facts under certain general concepts contributes absolutely nothing toward their explanation.

At the present day, the uselessness of the faculty-concepts is almost universally conceded. Again, however, there is one point in which they still exercise a widespread influence. Not the general class-concepts, but the individual facts that, in the old order of things, were subsumed under them, are now regarded in many quarters as independent phenomena, existing in isolation. On this view there is, to be sure, no special faculty of ideation or feeling or volition; but the individual idea, the individual affective process, and the individual voluntary act are looked upon as independent processes, connecting with one another and separating from one another as circumstances determine. Now introspection declares that all these professedly independent processes are through and through interconnected and interdependent. It is evident, therefore, that their separation involves just the same translation of the products of abstraction into real things as we have charged to the account of the old doctrine of faculties,—only that in this case the abstractions come a little nearer to the concrete phenomena. An isolated idea, an idea that is separable from the processes of feeling and volition, no more exists than does an isolated mental force of 'understanding.' Necessary as these distinctions are, then, we must still never forget that they are based upon abstractions,—that they do not carry with them any real separation of objects. Objectively, we can regard the individual mental processes only as inseparable elements of interconnected wholes.

The argument of the text may be supplemented here by some further critical remarks upon the two parallel concepts of 'mind' and 'spirit,' and upon the doctrine of mental faculties.

The English language distinguishes spirit from mind as a second substance-concept, with the *differentia* that it is not, as mind is, necessarily bound up, by the mediation of the senses, with a corporeal existence, but either stands in a merely external connexion with body or is entirely free of bodily relations. The concept of spirit is accordingly used in a two-fold meaning. On the one hand, it stands for the substrate of all inner experiences which are supposed to be independent of the activity of the senses; on the other, it denotes a being which has no part or lot at all in corporeal existence. It is, of course, only in the former of these two meanings that the concept of spirit comes into psychology. We can, however, see at once that the first signification must logically pass over into the second. If the connexion of spirit with body is merely external and as it were accidental, there is no reason why spirit should not occur in the form of pure undivided substance.

Philosophical reflection could not leave the relation of mind and spirit in the obscurity which had satisfied the needs of the naïve consciousness. Are mind and spirit different beings? Is mind a part of spirit, or spirit a part of mind? The earliest philosophical speculation shows clearly enough into what perplexity these questions plunged its authors. On the one hand, they are forced by the interconnexion of the inner experience to postulate a single substance as its substrate; on the other, they can see no way to escape a separation of the more abstract spiritual activities from the bodily entanglements of sense-perception. Alongside of the universal dualism of matter and spirit there remains the more restricted antithesis of spirit and mind. And ancient philosophy never succeeded in wholly overcoming this antithesis,—whether, with Plato, it tries to get rid of the substantiality of mind by regarding mind as a mixture of matter and spirit,[1] or whether, with Aristotle, it transfers to spirit the notion that it has abstracted from mind, and so substitutes a coincident

---

[1] *Timaeus*, 35. JOWETT's *Plato*, iii. 453-4.

form of definition for unity of substance.¹ Modern spiritualistic philosophy has, in general, followed the path laid down by PLATO, though it affirms more decidedly than PLATO did the unity of substance in mind and spirit. The result is that all real discrimination of the two concepts disappears from the scientific vocabulary. If a difference is made, it is made in one of two ways. Either spirit is taken as the general concept, within which the individual mind is contained ;² or spirit is confused with the mental faculties, of which we shall speak presently, and retained as a general designation for the 'higher' mental faculties or, specifically, for intelligence or the faculty of knowledge. The second usage is often accompanied, in the later works, by the inclusion of feeling and desire in the common concept of ' disposition ' ; so that the mind as a whole divides into intellect and disposition,³ without any implication of a separation into distinct substances. Sometimes, again, a mere difference of degree is made between the two terms mind and spirit, and spirit ascribed to man, while mind alone is assigned to the animals. Thus the distinction becomes less and less definite, while at the same time the concept of spirit loses its substantial character. So that, if we are to give the word a meaning that shall not anticipate the results of later investigation, we can do no more than say that spirit, like mind, is the subject of the inner experience, but that in it abstraction is made from the relations of this subject to a corporeal being. Mind is the subject of the inner experience as conditioned by its connexion with an external existence ; spirit is the same subject without reference to such connexion. We shall, accordingly, speak of spirit and of spiritual phenomena only when we can afford to neglect those moments of the inner experience which render it dependent upon our sensuous existence, i.e., upon that side of our existence which is accessible to external experience. This definition leaves entirely open the question whether spirit really is independent of sensibility. We can abstract from one or more of the aspects of a phenomenon without denying that these aspects are actually presented.

It has long been an object with philosophers to reduce the various mental faculties distinguished by language—sensation, feeling, reason, understanding, desire, imagination, memory, etc.—to certain more general forms. As early as Plato's *Timaeus* we find an indication of a tripartite division of the mind, in accordance with the later discrimination of the three faculties of knowledge, feeling and desire. Parallel with this threefold division runs another, into the higher and lower faculties. The former, the immortal reason, corresponds to knowledge ; the latter, sensibility or the perishable part of mind, embraces feeling and desire. Feeling or emotion is here looked upon as mediating between reason and appetite, just as the true idea mediates between sensuous appearance and knowledge. But while sensation is expressly referred to the same part of the mind as desire,⁴ the mediating thought ($\delta\iota\acute{a}\nu o\iota a$) and the emotion

---

¹ The Aristotelian definition of mind in general as ' earlier or implicit entelechy (i.e. perfect realisation) of a natural body possessed potentially of life,' holds also of the $\nu o\hat{u}s\ \pi o\iota\eta\tau\iota\kappa\acute{o}s$, the spirit as independent of sensibility. Spirit is, however, the reality of the mind itself, and so can be conceived of as separated from the body ; which is not the case with the other parts of mind. *De anima*, ii. 1 *sub fin*. WALLACE's trans., 65 ; HAMMOND's trans., 44 f.
² So WOLFF, *Psychologia rationalis*, §§ 643 ff.
³ *Geist* and *Gemüth*.—TRANSLATOR.
⁴ *Timaeus*, 77. JOWETT's Plato, iii. 449-50.

appear to stand in similar relation only to the faculty of reason. Hence these attempts at classification give us the impression that Plato worked out his two principles of division independently of each other,—the one based upon observation of a fundamental difference between the phenomena of cognition, feeling and appetition, and the other upon the recognition of stages in the process of knowledge; and that his not altogether successful attempt to reduce the two to one came only as an afterthought. In Aristotle the mind, regarded as the principle of life, divides into nutrition, sensation, and faculty of thought, corresponding to the three most important stages in the succession of vital phenomena. It is true that he occasionally introduces other mental faculties in the course of his discussion; but it is quite clear that he considers these three as the most general. Desire, in particular, is subordinated to sensation.[1]

PLATO obtains his tripartite division by ranking the properties of mind in the order of ethical value; Aristotle obtains his, conformably with his definition of mind, from the three principal classes of living beings. The plant mind is nutritive only; the animal mind is nutritive and sensitive; the human mind is nutritive, sensitive and rational. We can hardly doubt that the classification, with its three separable faculties, was originally suggested by the observation of the three kinds of living things in nature. But, however different the source from which it springs, we have only to omit the distinction of nutrition as a specific mental faculty, and we find it coinciding outright with the Platonic division into sensibility and reason. Hence it cannot itself, any more than the various later attempts at classification, be regarded as a really new system.

The most influential psychological systematist of modern times, WOLFF, employs both of the Platonic divisions, side by side, but makes the faculty of feeling subordinate to that of desire. The consequent dichotomy runs through his whole system. He first of all separates cognition and desire, and then subdivides each of these into a lower and a higher part. The further progress of the classification is shown in the following table.

I. FACULTY OF KNOWLEDGE

1. *Lower Faculty of Knowledge.*—Sense, Imagination, Poetic faculty, Memory (remembering and forgetting).
2. *Higher Faculty of Knowledge.*—Attention and reflection. Understanding.

II. FACULTY OF DESIRE

1. *Lower Faculty of Desire.*—Pleasantness and unpleasantness, Sensuous desire and sensuous aversion. Emotions.
2. *Higher Faculty of Desire.*—Volition (affirmation and negation). Freedom.

This classification has its proximate source in the Leibnizian distinction of ideation and appetition as the fundamental forces of the monads. It shows a great advance upon previous systems in not confining the faculty of feeling and desire to emotion and sensuous desire, but giving it the same range as the faculty of knowledge, so that the old difference in ethical value disappears. On the other hand, it is obvious that the special faculties grouped under the four main rubrics are not distinguished upon any systematic principle; their arrangement is purely empirical. The classification underwent many changes at the hands of WOLFF's disciples. We frequently find knowledge and feeling taken as the

---

[1] *De anima*, ii. 2, 3. WALLACE's trans., 65–77; HAMMOND's trans., 48–56.

two principal faculties, or feeling added as intermediary to knowledge and desire. This last scheme is that adopted by KANT. WOLFF's thought, even in the empirical psychology, is guided by his endeavour to reduce all the various faculties to a single fundamental force, the faculty of ideation ; and his rational psychology is largely devoted to this task. KANT disapproved of any such attempt to obliterate given differences in the mere effort after unification. Nevertheless, he too allows knowledge to encroach upon the domains of the other two mental forces, in correlating each of them with a special faculty within the sphere of cognition. But he maintains the original diversity of cognition, feeling and desire. The faculty of knowledge comprehends the other two only in the sense that it is the legislative faculty of mind at large. It is the source both of the concepts of nature and of the concept of freedom, which contains the ground of the practical precepts of the will. It also produces the intermediate teleological judgments and judgments of taste. So we find KANT saying that understanding, in the narrower sense, legislates for the faculty of knowledge, reason for the faculty of desire, and judgment for feeling ;[1] while understanding, judgment and reason are elsewhere bracketed together as understanding in the wider sense.[2] On the other side, KANT accepts the distinction of a lower and a higher faculty of knowledge,—the former embracing sensibility and the latter understanding,—but rejects the hypothesis that they are separated by a mere difference of degree. Sensibility is, for him, the receptive, understanding the active side of knowledge.[3] Hence in his great Critique he opposes sensibility to understanding. When connected with sensibility, understanding mediates empirical concepts ; alone, it gives us pure notions.[4]

It is evident that there are three principal points to be emphasised in the course of this whole development. The first is the distinction of the three mental faculties ; the second, the tripartite division of the higher faculty of knowledge ; and the third, the relation of this to the three principal faculties. The first is, in all essentials, a legacy from the Wolffian psychology : the other two are peculiar to KANT. Previous philosophy had, in general, defined reason (λόγος) as that activity of mind which by inference (*ratiocinatio*) gives account of the grounds of things. The definition was, however, compatible with various views of the position of reason. Sometimes, just as in Neoplatonism, reason was subordinated to understanding (νοῦς, *intellectus*) ; the latter is a source of immediate knowledge, while the activity of inference implies commerce with the world of sense. Sometimes, it was ranked above understanding, as the means whereby we penetrate to the ultimate grounds of things. Sometimes, again it was considered as a special mode of manifestation of understanding. Illustrations of all three views may be found in the scholastic philosophy. The cause of this varying estimate of the place of reason is to be sought in the fact that the term *ratio* was used in two distinct senses. On the one hand, it meant the ground of a given consequence of individual truths, the 'reason for' ; on the other, the capacity of *ratiocinatio*, of inferring individual truths from their grounds of 'reasoning.' First of all, *ratio* makes its appearance among the mental faculties, in this latter significance, as faculty of inference ; later on, it appears

---

[1] *Kritik d. Urtheilskraft*, ROSENKRANZ' ed., iv. 14 ff. BERNARD's trans., 1892, 13 ff.
[2] *Anthropologie*, vii. 2, 100 and 104.
[3] *Anthropologie*, 28.
[4] *Kritik d. reinen Vernunft*, ii. 31, 55. MÜLLER's trans., 1896, 15, 40.

also as a faculty of insight into the grounds of things. And wherever the emphasis fell upon this second meaning, reason shone forth as the very organ and instrument of religious and moral truths, or as a purely metaphysical faculty contradistingished from understanding, whose concepts could never pass the bounds of outer or inner sense-experience. A definition which includes both meanings of 'reason' makes it the faculty whereby we penetrate the interconnexion of universal truths.[1] Now KANT set out from the first of the three views above mentioned, the view which regards understanding as the faculty of concepts and reason as the faculty of inference. And he might well be encouraged to attempt, by the help of logic, to carry out to its conclusion the division of the higher faculty of knowledge which this view adumbrates, seeing that he had already achieved entire success in a similar undertaking, his deduction of the categories. He accordingly assumed that, since judgment stands midway between concept and inference (conclusion), the faculty of judgment stands midway between the faculties of understanding and reason. He had, however, in his great Critique, sought to bring the two aspects of the concept of reason into a more vital relation by his doctrine of the unconditioned. In the conclusion, reason subsumes a judgment under its general rule. Now it must proceed, in the same way, to subordinate this rule to a higher condition ; and so on, until in the last resort it arrives at the idea of an unconditioned. This idea, then, in its various forms as mind, world and God, remained the peculiar property of reason in the narrower sense ; while all concepts and principles *a priori*, from which reason as faculty of inference derives individual judgments, became the exclusive property of understanding. So we find reason playing a curious double part in the Kantian philosophy. As faculty of inference, it is the handmaid of understanding, charged with the application of the concepts and principles which understanding propounds. As faculty of transcendent ideas, it ranks high above understanding. Understanding is directed merely upon the empirical interconnexion of phenomena. If it follow the idea of reason at all, it follows it only as a regulative principle, which prescribes the course that shall lead to a comprehension of phenomena into an absolute whole,— something of which understanding itself has no conception. It is, however, this regulative office of the ideas of reason that gives them their practical value. For the moral law, in KANT, is not constitutive, but regulative ; it does not say how we really act, but how we ought to act. At the same time, by the imperative form in which it demands obedience, it proves the truth of the idea of unconditioned freedom of the will.[2] In fine, then, reason legislates for the faculty of desire, just as understanding legislates for the faculty of knowledge. For feeling, which stands midway between cognition and desire, there then remains only the faculty of judgment, which in like manner stands midway between the faculty of concepts and the faculty of inference.[3] The three fundamental faculties of mind are thus referred to the three modes of manifestation of the faculty of knowledge distinguished by formal logic. And we see at once how largely this reference is the product of an artificial schematisation suggested by the logical forms. This intellectualism has also had its reactive influence upon the treatment of the mental faculties ; KANT pays attention only to the higher expressions of his three principal faculties. Now it may

[1] WOLFF, *Psychologia empirica*, § 483.
[2] *Kritik d. prakt. Vernunft*, viii. 106.
[3] *Kritik d. Urtheilskraft*, iv. 15. BERNARD's trans., 16.

be doubted whether the totality of phenomena embraced by the first faculty can properly be summed up in the word 'knowledge.' But, at all events, it is obvious that the limitation of pleasant and unpleasant feeling to the judgment of aesthetic taste, and the reference of the faculty of desire to the ideal of the good, are not suited to serve as the starting-point of a psychological consideration.

HERBART's criticism of the faculty-theory is principally directed against the form which it had assumed in the systems of WOLFF and KANT. The heart of his argumentation lies in the two following objections. (1) The mental faculties are mere possibilities, which add nothing to the facts of the inner experience. Only the individual facts of this experience, the individual idea and feeling and what not, can really be predicated of the mind. There is no sensibility before sensation, no memory before the stock of ideas which it lays up. Hence these concepts, notions of possibility, cannot be employed for the derivation of the facts.[1] (2) The mental faculties are class-concepts, obtained by a provisional abstraction from the inner experience, and then raised to the rank of fundamental forces of the mind and used for the explanation of our internal processes.[2] Both objections seem to shoot beyond the mark at which they are primarily aimed; they tell against methods of scientific explanation which have found application in practically all the natural sciences. The forces of physics, e.g., do not exist apart, by themselves, but only in the phenomena which we term their effects; and the functional capacities of physiology—nutrition, contractility, irritability, etc.—are one and all 'empty possibilities.' Again, gravity, heat, assimilation, reproduction, etc., are class-concepts, abstracted from a certain number of similar phenomena, which have been transformed on just the same analogy as the class-concepts of the inner experience into forces or faculties, to be employed for the explanation of the phenomena themselves. Indeed, if we term sensation, thought, etc., 'manifestations' of mind, the proposition that the mind possesses the 'faculties' of sensing, thinking, etc., seems to give direct expression to a conceptual construction which comes naturally to us wherever an object evinces effects that must be ascribed to causes lying within and not outside of the object. Nor has HERBART any objection to raise against the use of the concept of force at large. But he makes a distinction between force and faculty. We assume the action of a force, in all cases where we have learned to look upon a result as inevitable under given conditions. We speak of a faculty, when the result may just as well not occur as occur.[3]

Objection has been taken to this distinction, on the ground that it presupposes a concept of faculty which is found only in the most unscientific form of the psychological faculty-theory.[4] Nevertheless, it must be conceded that the discrimination of the terms is not without significance. With the development of modern natural science, the concept of force has gradually assumed the character of a concept of *relation*. The conditions which it implies are always reciprocally determinant; it is on their co-operation that the manifestation of force depends; and the removal of either side of the conditions renders it null and void. Thus the concept of force is correctly used when, e.g., the tendency to movement, that has its source in the interrelations of physical bodies, is derived from a force of gravitation, whereby these bodies determine each the

---

[1] HERBART, *Werke*, vii. 611.   [2] *Werke*, v. 214.   [3] *Werke*, vii. 601.
[4] J. B. MEYER, *Kant's Psychologie*, 116.

other's position in space. On the other hand, it is an over-hasty generalisation to refer the phenomena of falling bodies to a force of falling natively inherent in every physical body. If we thus translate the conditions of a certain set of phenomena, resident in a given object, into a force of which the object is possessed, and ignore the external conditions of the observation, we evidently have no criterion for deciding whether a variation in the effects of this object depends upon a variation in intrinsic or in extrinsic conditions. The result is confusion : disparate phenomena are brought together, and (what is of more frequent occurrence) related phenomena wrested apart. Many of the forces distinguished by the older physiology—the forces of procreation, of growth, of regeneration, etc.—are, beyond all question, nothing more than manifestations of a single force operating under different circumstances. And the same thing is pretty generally admitted of the final ramifications of the doctrine of mental faculties,— of the distinction, e.g., between space-memory, number-memory, word-memory, etc. Similarly, the older physics explained the phenomena of gravitation by appeal to a number of forces : fall by the force of falling, the barometric vacuum by the 'horror vacui,' the motions of the planets by invisible arms from the sun or by vortices. But, further, the habit of abstraction from the external conditions of phenomena may easily lead to the erroneous conception of faculty, of a force that awaits an opportunity to produce its effect : force becomes incarnate in a mythological being. It would, therefore, be unjust to psychology, were we to accuse her and her alone of this aberration. Only, she has the one great advantage over the sciences of inorganic nature, that their work has paved the way for her advance. In their hands, the general concepts that belong at once to the outer and the inner experience have been purged of the errors natural to the earlier stages of the development of thought. And along with this advantage goes the obligation to make use of it to the full.

HERBART not only realised the untenabliity of the faculty-theory ; he arrived at the positive conviction that mental processes must be considered as *unitary* processes. But he sought to satisfy the requirement of unity by raising one of the products of current psychological abstraction above all the rest. He regarded the *idea* as the real and only contents of the mind. Nay, he went so far as to declare that the idea, when once it has arisen, is imperishable, while all the other elements of mind—feelings, emotions, impulses—are merely the resultants of the momentary interactions of ideas. These opinions, as we shall see later, rest upon no better foundation than hypothesis, and bring their author, at every point, into conflict with an exact analysis of experience.[1] For the rest, it is obvious that the reduction of all mental processes to processes of ideation is a survival from the intellectualism of previous psychological systems. Nevertheless, HERBART had taken the right path in his endeavour to avoid that atomic conception of mental processes which simply repeats the mistakes of the old faculty-theory in less glaring form. Unfortunately, in escaping the one error, he was fated to fall into another. The fault of the older view is, not that it confuses unreality with reality, but that it substitutes for reality the products of our own discriminative abstraction.[2]

---

[1] Cf. ch. xix. [of the present edition].
[2] Cf. with this the essay on feeling and idea, in my *Essays*, 199 ff.

Part I
The Bodily Substrate of the Mental Life

CHAPTER I

The Organic Evolution of Mental Function

§ 1. The Criteria of Mind and the Range of the Mental Life

THE mental functions form a part of the phenomena of life. Wherever we observe them, they are accompanied by the processes of nutrition and reproduction. On the other hand, the general phenomena of life may be manifested in cases where we have no reason for supposing the presence of a mind. Hence the first question that arises, in an inquiry concerning the bodily substrate of mentality, is this: What are the characteristics that justify our attributing mental functions to a living body, an object in the domain of animate nature?

Here, upon the very threshold of physiological psychology, we are confronted with unusual difficulties. The distinguishing characteristics of mind are of a subjective sort; we know them only from the contents of our own consciousness. But the question calls for objective criteria, from which we shall be able to argue to the presence of a consciousness. Now the only possible criteria of the kind consist in certain bodily movements, which carry with them an indication of their origin in psychical processes. But when are we justified in referring the movements of a living creature to conscious conditions? How uncertain the answer to this question is, especially when metaphysical prejudice has a part to play in it, may be seen at once by an appeal to history. Hylozoism inclines to regard every movement, even the fall of a stone, as a mental action; Cartesian spiritualism recognises no expression of mental life beyond the voluntary movements of man. These are extreme views. The first is beyond all verification; the second is correct only upon the one point that the manifestations of our own conscious life must always furnish the standard of reference in our judgments of similar indications in other creatures. Hence we must not begin our search for mental function among the lower types of organised nature, where its modes of expression are least perfect. It is only by working our way downwards, from man to the animals, that we shall find the point at which mental life begins.

Now, there are a very large number of bodily movements, having their source in our nervous system, that do not possess the character of conscious actions. Not only are the normal movements of heart, respiratory muscles, blood-vessels and intestines for the most part unaccompanied by any sort of conscious affection; we find also that the muscles subserving change of position at the periphery of the body often react to stimuli in a purely mechanical and automatic way. To regard these movement-processes as mental functions would be every whit as arbitrary as to ascribe sensation to the falling stone. When, however, we rule out all the movements that may possibly go on without the participation of consciousness, there remains but one class that bears upon it the constant and unmistakable signs of an expression of the mental life,—the class of *external voluntary actions*. The subjective criterion of the external voluntary action, as directly given in introspection, is that it is preceded by feelings and ideas which we take to be the conditions of the movement. Hence a movement that we observe objectively may also be regarded as dependent on the will, if it points to similar mental processes as its conditions.

But the discovery of this criterion does not by any means remove the practical difficulties of our diagnosis of mind. It is not possible to distinguish certainly in every case between a purely mechanical reflex—or even, in the lowest organisms, a movement due to external physical causes, such as the imbibition of tumescent bodies, the change of volume from fluctuations of temperature, etc.—and a voluntary action. We have to note, in particular, that while there are characters by which we can argue with absolute confidence to the existence of a voluntary action, the absence of these characters does not always necessarily imply the absence of such action, still less the absence of psychical functions at large. Hence all that our inquiry can hope to accomplish is the determination of the lower limit at which a mental life is *demonstrably* present. Whether it does not, in actual fact, begin at a still lower level, must remain a matter of speculation only.

The generally accepted objective criterion of an external voluntary action is the reference of movement to the universal animal impulses, the *nutritive* and the *sexual*. It is only as a result of sensory excitations that these impulses can lead the animal to a change of place that shows the marks of a voluntary action; and the special character that prompts us to refer such sensorily stimulated movements to a process in consciousness is their variability. They do not appear with mechanical regularity in response to a given external stimulus, but are varied to suit varying conditions, and brought into connexion with sense-impressions previously secured. Judgment on the ground of these criteria may, in the individual case, remain doubtful; since all vital processes, even those that are entirely automatic and unconscious, evince a certain adaptation to ends, and a certain consequence in their successive stages. But sustained and attentive observation of living creatures will, as a general rule, enable us to decide with certainty whether any particular manifestation of life is intelligible only from that continuity of internal states which we name consciousness, or whether it may possibly have arisen in the absence of mind. That consciousness, in this sense, is an universal possession of living organisms, from man down to the protozoa, is beyond the reach of doubt. At the lowest levels of this developmental series the processes of consciousness are, of course, confined within extremely narrow limits, and the will is determined by the universal organic impulses only in the very simplest way. Nevertheless, the manifestations of life, even among the lowest protozoa, are explicable only upon the hypothesis that they possess a mind. Thus the amoeba, which is to be regarded morphologically as a naked cell (see Fig. 2, p. 33), will sometimes return after a short interval to the starch grains that it has come upon in the course of its wanderings, and will incept a new portion as nutritive material in the soft protoplasm of its body.[1] Many of the ciliated infusoria pursue others, which they kill and devour.[2] These are all phenomena that point towards continuity of mental processes, though in all probability to a continuity that extends only over a very short space of time. They point also, at all events in the case of the Ciliata, to a variation in the choice of means, for the satisfaction of the organic impulses, that would be unintelligible as a merely mechanical result of external influences.

We enter, of course, upon much less certain ground when we ask, further, whether the mental life really makes its first appearance at that point upon the scale of organised existence at which we notice the external voluntary action, or whether its beginnings do not reach back to a still lower level of life. Wherever living protoplasm occurs, it possesses the property of contractility. Contractile movements arise, sometimes at the instigation of external stimuli, but sometimes also in the absence of any apparent external influence. They resemble the voluntary actions of the lowest protozoa, and are not explicable in terms of external physical affection, but only as the results of forces resident in the contractile substance itself.

---

[1] ROMANES, *Animal Intelligence*, 4th ed., 1886, 18 ff. ; *Mental Evolution in Animals*, 1885, 18, 55 ; MAX VERWORN, *Psychophysiologische Protisten-Studien*, 1889, 146 ff. VERWORN's statement that voluntary actions appear for the first time in the Ciliata, and that all movements made in response to stimulus by the non-ciliated protozoa, so far as they are not of purely mechanical or chemical origin, should be interpreted as reflexes, is evidently a result not of observation, but rather of a foregone theoretical conviction that voluntary actions must have developed out of reflexes. On this theory see Part iv., below.

[2] FAMINZYN, *The Mental Life of the Simplest Organisms*, 1890 (Russian). Quoted by BECHTEREW, *Bewusstsein und Hirnlocalisation*, 1898, 6.

They cease at once with the cessation of life. We find them evinced both by the protoplasmic contents of young plant-cells and by the free protoplasm occurring throughout the animal and vegetable kingdoms. Indeed, it is probable that all elementary organisms, whether they enjoy an independent existence or form part of a compound organism, possess the property of contractility at least during a certain period of their development. Consider, e.g., the lymph corpuscles, which are found in the blood and lymph of animals, and in pus, and which occur as migratory elements in the tissues. They are not only entirely similar in bodily configuration to certain of the lowest protozoa, but they also undergo changes of form which, in outward appearance, are indistinguishable from the movements of these unicellular organisms (Fig. 1). Only, the *voluntary* character of these movements is beyond the reach of demonstration. It is true that similar structures—particularly the colourless blood-corpuscles of invertebrates—have been seen to take up solid substances, and that this action may be interpreted as an inception of food.[1] It is true, also, that movements in response to stimulus accompany the exercise of the digestive functions in certain plants. But in neither case is there any definite indication of a true impulse, i.e. an impulse determined by sensation, toward the food-stuff, or of any sort of psychological middle term between stimulus and movement.[2] The same thing holds of the movements of the lower forms of algae, fungi and swarm-spores, produced

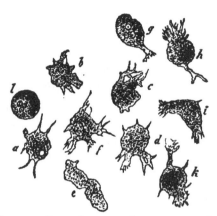

FIG. 1. Lymph-corpuscles. a—k Changes of form in the living cell; l the dead cell.

by a variable distribution of water and carbon dioxide, or by different kinds of light rays. On the other hand, the movements of certain bacteria are so suddenly affected by light and by the gases of respiration, that they at once suggest an origin in sensations. But, here again, we cannot be sure that the changes are not simply physical effects, as is undoubtedly the case with the movements evoked by hygrometric changes in the environment.[3]

---

[1] M. SCHULTZE, *Das Protoplasma der Rhizopoden*, 1863. ENGELMANN, *Beiträge zur Physiologie des Protoplasmas*, ii., 1869. VERWORN, *Die Bewegung der lebendigen Substanz*, 1892, 51 ff.; *Allgemeine Physiologie*, 1901, 363 ff. (*General Physiology*, 1899, 146 ff., 527).

[2] DARWIN, *Insectivorous Plants*, 1875, esp. ch. x. PFEFFER, *Pflanzenphysiologie*, 2te Aufl., i., 1897, 364 ff.

[3] T.W. ENGELMANN, in PFLÜGER'S *Archiv. f. d. ges. Physiologie*, xxvi. 537; xxix. 415; xxx. 95. PFEFFER, *Untersuchungen aus d. botan. Institut zu Tübingen*, i. 363, 483; ii. 582. For further details, see Ch. vii. § 3, below. On the physical causes of proto-

We must, however, always remember, in passing judgment upon this whole group of observations, that the demonstration of physical conditions, to which the phenomena of protoplasmic contraction and of the movement of elementary organisms may be referred, is by no means incompatible with the hypothesis of concomitant psychical processes. Physiology seeks to derive the processes in our own nervous system from general physical forces, without considering whether these processes are or are not accompanied by processes of consciousness. We are bidden to believe, both by theory of knowledge and by the philosophy of nature, that all manifestations of life, on the physical side, are referable to natural laws of universal validity. And physiology, acting in accordance with this requirement, has found it justified in every instance in which she has succeeded in reaching a solution of her problems. It follows, then, that the existence of mental functions can never be inferred from the physical nature of organic movements, but only from certain special conditions attending their performance. On the other hand, observation shows that the chemical and physiological properties of living protoplasm are essentially the same, whether we can prove that it manifests a mental life or whether we cannot. This holds, in particular, of the attributes of contractility and irritability. In physical regard, therefore, protoplasm maintains its identity throughout. If we add to this the fact that it is impossible to draw a hard and fast line at the point where protoplasmic movements first begin to take on a psychological character,—that there is a gradual transition from the walled-in protoplasm of the plant-cell, on through the migratory lymph-corpuscles of animals and the free-living monera and rhizopods, to the more motile ciliated and mouth-bearing infusoria—we cannot resist the conjecture that psychical life and the capacity of giving expression to it are universally represented in contractile substance.

From the standpoint of observation, then, we must regard it as a highly probable hypothesis that the beginnings of the mental life date from as far back as the beginnings of life at large. The question of the origin of mental development thus resolves itself into the question of the origin of life. Further, if physiology is obliged, by the uniformity of interaction of physical forces throughout the universe, to accept the postulate that the processes of life have their ultimate basis in the general properties of matter, psychology finds it no less obligatory to assume, in this same matter, the universal substrate of natural phenomena, the presence of conditions which attain to expression as the psychical aspect of vital phenomena. But this latter statement must not mislead us. The latent life of inorganic matter must not be confused, as hylozoism confuses it, with real life and actual conscious-

plasmic movement, cf. BÜTSCHLI, *Untersuchungen über mikroskopische Schäume und das Protoplasma*, 1892, 172.

ness; nor must it be considered, with materialism, as a function of matter. The former interpretation is wrong, because it assumes the existence of vital phenomena at a point where not these phenomena themselves are given, but only the common ground upon which they rest and whereby they become possible; the second is wrong, because it posits a one-sided dependence, where in reality we find an interrelation of simultaneously presented but incommensurable processes. We employ the concept of material substance to denote the ground of all objective phenomena. Hence it is the office of this concept to make intelligible all the various forms of physical occurrence, including the physical manifestations of life. Now among these manifestations we find movements which indicate the presence of a consciousness. Our postulates concerning matter will, then, explain the physical causation of such movements, but can never account for the concomitant psychical functions. To explain these, we must make appeal to our own consciousness.

We cannot, of course, here at the very outset of our psychology, return any final answer to the question of the ultimate objective criteria of the mental life. All that we can do, at the present stage, is to indicate in brief the position to be taken up in psychological practice. It is, however, easy to see that the wide divergence of opinion on the subject is mainly due to the intermixture of science with philosophy, or to a fixity of judgment that has its source in philosophical theory. Only in this way can we account for the fact that there may still be found, in works upon the scope of the mental life, views that range between the two extremes current in DESCARTES' day. One author will assert that the animals, if not without exception, at least as far up the scale as the higher invertebrates and the lower vertebrates, are mere reflex machines;[1] another looks upon life and mind as convertible terms, and accordingly endows plants as well as animals with consciousness.[2] The former view is evidently influenced, to some extent, by the idea that psychical and physical are antithetical terms. The alternative (physical *or* psychical) is often presented as if the one concept necessarily excluded the other,—as, indeed, it did, in the metaphysical dualism of DESCARTES. But this is misleading. The close interconnection of the phenomena of the physical life and the processes of consciousness makes the relation 'physical *and* psychical,' on the face of it, much more probable. We should, as a matter of fact, admit at once that, e.g., a sensation is a psychical quality, without meaning to deny that it is accompanied by a physical process in the sense-organ and the sense-centre. And such a coexistence of the two kinds of vital processes is, in many cases, beyond all dispute. How far it extends, over the phenomena of life at large, is again a question that, naturally, cannot be answered at the outset of our psychological investigations. But, at all events, we should be merely obscuring the facts, if we made our first approach to them with the alternative 'physical or psychical' in our hands. And the danger of misinter-

[1] A. BETHE, *Dürfen wir den Ameisen und Bienen psychische Qualitäten zuschreiben?* In PFLÜGER's *Arch. f. d. ges. Physiol.*, lxx. 1898, 15 ff. Cf. the critical remarks of WASSMANN, *Die psychischen Fähigkeiten der Ameisen*, 1899, and *Biol. Centralblatt*, xviii., 1898, 578.
[2] FECHNER, *Nanna oder über das Seelenleben der Pflanzen*, 1848; 2nd ed., 1899.

pretation is, at best, grave enough. Many movements, that may in all probability be regarded as purely automatic, are, as we said above, purposive in character; and many of them, again, are self-regulating. It is, therefore, very difficult to draw the line of division in the concrete case.[1]

We may say, then, that the mechanistic explanation of the movements of the lower animals is not the outcome of impartial and unprejudiced observation. But the rival theory, which ascribes mind and consciousness to the plant-world, is in no better case. Fechner, the chief representative of this theory, himself expressly declares that he derived it from considerations of general philosophy : he further attributes consciousness to the earth and the other heavenly bodies, making this cosmic consciousness the whole, of which the individual forms of consciousness in plant and animal are parts.[2] Hypotheses of this sort have, no doubt, a certain justification. They emphasise the intrinsic impossibility of the view that mental life may suddenly appear, at some point of time and space, as a new thing ; that we need not seek for its general conditions in the universal substrate of the vital processes. When, however, we ask how we should conceive of these conditions, we raise a metaphysical question,—a question that lies well beyond the reach of psychology and its empirical problems.

§ 2. The Differentiation of Mental Functions and of their Physical Substrate

The organic cell, in the earliest stages of its development, consists either of a naked mass of protoplasm, contractile throughout its substance, or of a denser and immotile cortex within which motile protoplasm is contained.

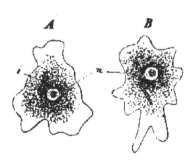

FIG. 2. An amoeba in two different phases of movement. *n* Nucleus. *i* Ingested food-particle.

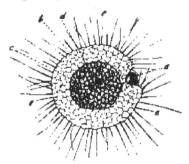

FIG. 3. *Actinosphaerium*: *a* Incepted food-particle, making its way into the soft body mass. *b* Cortical layer. *c* Central parenchyma. *d* Ingested food-particles. *e* Cilia of the cortical layer.

And the same two forms are evinced by the lowest independent organisms in which we can observe movement-processes indicative of psychical conditions (Fig. 2). The substrate of the elementary mental functions is here entirely homogeneous, and coextensive with the whole mass of the

---

[1] Cf. with this the later discussions of impulsive movement (Part iv.) and of consciousness (Part v.).

[2] FECHNER, *Zendavesta oder über die Dinge des Himmels und des Jenseits*, i., 1851, 2nd ed., 1901.

body. The only sense that is plainly functioning is the sense of touch. An impression made upon any portion of the contractile protoplasm first of all releases a movement at the place of direct impact, which may then extend to purposively co-ordinated motion of the entire body.

The beginnings of a differentiation of mental function can, however, be found even in the protozoa, wherever the cortical layer surrounding the contractile body-substance has developed special organs of movement, cilia and flagella (Fig. 3). Oftentimes this development goes hand in hand with a differentiation of the nutritive functions. An oral aperture and digestive cavity are found, and in many instances a system of open canals appears, whose fluid contents are kept in motion by a contractile vesicle. The cilia with which these infusoria are furnished render them incomparably more motile than the organisms lying at the very lowest point of the organic scale, the monera and rhizopods, which consist merely of a viscous body-mass. They are, however, more than organs of locomotion; they function as organs of touch, and sometimes appear to be sensitive to light as well. The spot of red pigment noticed in many of the infusoria may also have some connexion with light-sensation; but we have as yet no certain ground for regarding it as a primitive organ of vision.

In the compound organisms we observe a more radical differentiation of mental function and its bodily substrate. The metazoan germ-cell divides into a number of cells. These seem to be originally of the same kind, so that not infrequently all alike manifest the primitive contractility of protoplasm. In course of time, however, they become modified in matter and form; the tissues of the plant and animal body are derived from them and from the products of their growth, and the structural changes are accompanied by a more and more complete specialisation of function. The conditions which govern this process of differentiation, to which the whole of organic nature is subject, are still wrapped in obscurity. Our knowledge halts abruptly at the changes of outward form in which the internal development finds its expression.

In the plant-world we see the nutritive functions attain such a degree of elaboration that the organism (and this is true more especially of the higher plants) has, so to say, no other concern than to increase its present stock of organic substance. In the animal world, on the other hand, the process of evolution is characterised by the progressive discrimination of the animal and vegetative functions, and a consequent differentiation of these two great provinces into their separate departments. The cell-mass of the yolk, originally homogeneous, divides up first of all into a peripheral and a central layer of different structural character (Figg. 4 and 5), while the cleavage cavity gradually widens out to form the future body-cavity.[1]

[1] The relations of the various cavities, three or four in number, are in reality much

At this stage, sensation and movement appear to reside exclusively in the outer cell-layer, the ectoderm, while the nutritive functions are discharged by the inner layer or entoderm. At a higher level of evolution a third

 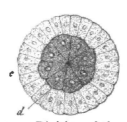 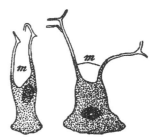

FIG. 4. Yolk in the final stage of fissiparous division.

FIG. 5. Division of the cell-mass produced by yolk-cleavage into a peripheral (c) and a central (d) layer.

FIG. 6. Neuromuscular cells of Hydra, after KLEINENBERG (epithelial muscle-cells of HERTWIG). m Muscular processes.

layer of cells, the mesoderm, forms between the two. The initial stages of development are thus identical over the whole series of forms from coelenterates to vertebrates, the differentiation of organs beginning always with the distinction of three germinal layers. The outermost layer is the source of the nervous system and sense-organs, as well as of the muscular system; the innermost furnishes the organs of nutrition; and the intermediate layer, the vascular system. In the vertebrates, the skeleton is also derived from the ectoderm.[1]

This discrimination of organs is accompanied by a differentiation of the elementary contituents of the tissues. When the separation of ectoderm and entoderm is first accomplished, the cells of the former discharge the combined function of sensation and movement. The initial step toward a separation of these two cardinal functions is apparently taken in the hydridae and medusae, where the ectoderm cells send out contractile processes into the interior of the body. The sensory and motor functions are here still united in a single cell, but are distributed over different portions of it (Fig. 6).[2] In the next stage, the properties of sensation and contractility pass to special and spatially separated cells, while connective elements

more complicated. It would be more nearly true to say that, where the change indicated in the text takes place, the body-cavity gradually replaces the cleavage-cavity. Cf. MINOT, *Embryology*, 1897, ch. ix.—TRANSLATOR.

[1] The author gives no references here. The mesoderm is now divided, by the best writers, into mesothelium, the source of the muscles and mesodermic glands, and mesenchyma, the source of connective and skeletal tissue. The derivation of the mesenchyma itself is still an open question.—TRANSLATOR.

[2] KLEINENBERG, *Hydra, eine anatomisch-entwicklungsgeschichtliche Untersuchung* 1872, 21 ff. O and R. HERTWIG, *Das Nervensystem und die Sinnesorgane der Medusen*, 1878, 157. [The cells from the epithelial layer of Hydra shown in Fig. 6 (KLEINENBERG'S 'neuromuscular' cells) are now to be regarded as muscle-cells. Later Note by AUTHOR.]

develope, to mediate the functional interconnexion of the different structures. There thus arises a third class of cells, lying in the paths of connexion between sensory and muscular cells, and acting probably as organs for the reception and transmission of stimuli. The sensory cells now become external organs, devoted to the reception of physical stimuli. At the same time, they undergo a differentiation, which fits them for excitation by various forms of movement-process in the outside world. Similarly, the contractile cells become organs for receiving and converting into external movements the excitations transmitted to them. But the psychical functions *par excellence* are discharged by the cells of the third class, the nerve-cells, which are connected by their processes with both the sensory and the muscular cells, and, as we have said, mediate the functional interconnexion of the two groups of organs. Hence the simplest scheme of a nervous system is given with a centrally situated nerve-cell, connected on the one hand with a sense-cell and on the other hand with a contractile muscle-cell, both directed towards the external world, but mediating the one the reception of sense-stimuli and the other the motor reaction upon them.

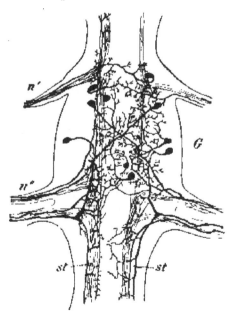

FIG. 7. Ganglion of the ventral nerve-cord of the earthworm (*Lumbricus*), after RETZIUS. G Ganglion. st Ventral nerve-cord. n', n" Nerves.

It is, however, quite certain that this simplest scheme never actually occurs. As soon as special nerve-cells are formed at all, they are formed in numbers, joined together in longitudinal and transverse series, so that a great many of them are connected only by way of others of their kind with the peripheral structures. This multiplication of the central elements means, of course, that the process of differentiation extends to the nerve-cells themselves. They assume various functions, according to the connexions in which they stand with one another and with the peripheral organs. Those lying in the neighbourhood of the terminal organs are employed in functions, auxiliary to the strictly psychophysical processes, which run their course without the participation of consciousness. Others enter into intimate relation with the mechanisms of nutrition; they sustain and regulate the physiological processes of secretion and circulation. They thus lose their place among the immediate bodily conditions of the mental life, and exert only an indirect influence upon mind. This progressive differentiation of functions and of their substrate within the nervous system finds its expression in the relative increase of the mass of the nervous elements, and in the elaboration of special nerve-centres, compact bodies of nerve-cells and their fibrillar processes. We have an instance of such centres in the ganglia of the invertebrates, which appear at the most various stages of development, from the comparatively simple nerve-rings of the cœlenterates and the lower worms and molluscs, up to the brain-like ganglionic masses of the arthropods and higher molluscs (Fig. 7).

Finally, among the vertebrates, the importance of the nerve-centres for the whole organisation of the animal is shown, from the first, in their relation to the external bodily form and to the development of the various systems of organs. Immediately after the separation of the formative materials into the two layers of the germ-primule, there appears in the ectoderm

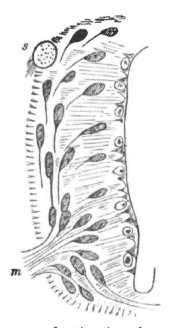

Fig. 8. Embryonic area of the rabbit, with the embryonic primule. *a* Primitive groove, containing primitive streak. *b* Embryonic primule. *c* Internal crescentic portion (area pellucida), and *d* external discoidal portion (area opaca) of the embryonic area.

Fig. 9. Transverse section through one half of the neural tube, after His. To the right, on the inner side of the tube, lie unmodified germinating cells; to the left, on the outside, are nerve-cells in process of development. *m* Ventral (motor), *s* dorsal (sensory) nerve-root.

a groove, open above, at the bottom of which is a streak of darker tissue. This is the primitive streak, whose direction corresponds with the future longitudinal axis of the embryo (Fig. 8). Presently, the groove closes and becomes the neural tube, the primule of the myel (spinal cord) and its sheaths.[1] The anterior portion of this tube gives rise, by expansion, to the primule of the brain. Concomitantly with the closure of the neural tube begins the differentiation of the germinating cells into nerve-cells. They increase in size, and send out runners, which become transformed into the various cell-processes (Fig. 9).[2]

At this point there begins a serial differentiation of function and its physical substrate, whose investigation will form the subject of the following Chapters. We shall set out with a consideration of the structural elements of the nervous system in their morphological and chemical characters. We shall next raise the question of the nature of the processes at work within those elements; in other words, we shall attack the problem of a physiological mechanics of nervous substance. This discussion will be followed by a brief description of the structural development of the nervous centres, with especial reference to the morphology of the human brain. We shall then be prepared to approach the two main problems that are presented by the co-ordination of functions in the nervous system. The first of these is the determination of the course of the paths of nervous conduction, as conditioned by the individual connexions of the nervous elements; and the second is the problem of the physiological functions of the central parts,— the last and most important question for the relation of nervous process to the processes of the psychical life.

---

[1] The myelic furrow is now known to be entirely distinct from the primitive groove. See O. HERTWIG, *Embryology*, 79 ff., 125, 416 ff.—TRANSLATOR.
[2] HIS, *Archiv für Anatomie u. Physiologie*, Anat. Abth. 1890, 95.

CHAPTER II

Structural Elements of the Nervous System

§ 1. Morphological Elements

THE nervous system is made up of three kinds of morphological elements: (1) cells of peculiar form and structure, the nerve-cells or ganglion cells; (2) fibrous structures, originating as outgrowths from the cells,—the nerve-fibres; and (3) a ground-reticulum, which in places is finely granular and in places fibrillar, and which consists of the terminal ramifications of the nerve-fibres and processes of the nerve-cells. To these must be added (4) a sustentacular substance, fibrous or amorphous in structure, which is regarded as a form of connective tissue.[1] The nerve-cells, with the fibrillar ground-reticulum that surrounds them, are essential constituents of all the central parts. In the higher nervous centres, however, they are restricted to definite areas, which, partly from their rich supply of capillary blood-vessels and partly from the presence of pigment-granules, collected both in the protoplasm of the cell-bodies and in the ground-reticulum, possess a darker coloration than the surrounding tissue. This grey substance contrasts so sharply with the white or myelinic substance that the distribution of cell-groups through the central organs may readily be followed by the naked eye. The myelinic substance itself owes its peculiar character mainly to the myelinic sheaths which enclose the nerve-fibres issuing from the grey substance. The connective tissue cement-substance occurs in three principal forms. As a soft and for the most part amorphous mass, the neuroglia, it serves to support the central nerves and cells. In the form of endoneurium and perineurium,[2] a denser tissue, showing tendon-like fibrillation, it extends among and surrounds the peripheral nerves. As the primitive sheath of Schwann, a membrane of glassy transparency and great elasticity, nucleated at intervals, it encases nearly all peripheral and a portion of the central nerve-fibres. These cement-substances form a sustentacular framework for the nervous elements. They serve, further, to carry the blood-vessels. And the perineurium[2]

---

[1] Connective tissue forms a part of the sustentacular tissue of the nervous system. But the neuroglia, which forms its larger part, is an ectodermic structure, with close relations to the neurogenetic tract. See G. A. PIERSOL, *Normal Histology*, 1893, 79.—TRANSLATOR.

[2] The text has 'neurilemma' in both instances. This is now a synonym for the primitive sheath.—TRANSLATOR.

imparts to the peripheral nerves, which have no solid wall of bone to protect them, the necessary power of resistance to mechanical injury.

(a)—The Nerve-Cells

It is probable that the nerve-cells (Figg. 10-14) are everywhere devoid of a true cell-cortex. They vary in form from spherical to irregularly angular, and differ so extraordinarily in size that some can hardly be distinguished with certainty from the minute corpuscles of the connective tissue, while others are visible to the naked eye. A clear nucleus, plainly vesicular in form, and provided with a large nucleolus, stands out in sharp

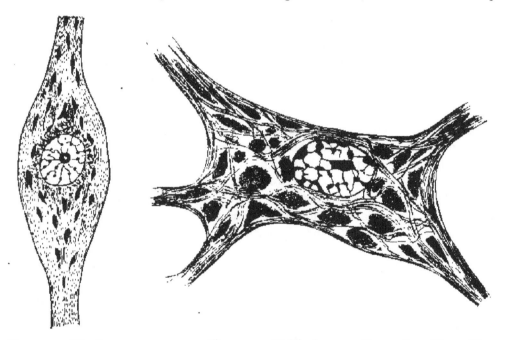

Fig. 10. Bipolar nerve-cell from the ventral cornu of the myel of the ox, unstained. After JUL. ARNOLD.

Fig. 11. Multipolar ganglion cell, with aniline staining. After BETHE.

contrast to the dully pigmented protoplasm. In the central organs the cells are embedded directly in the soft substance of the supporting tissue; in the ganglia, they are usually surrounded with an elastic sheath of connective tissue, often directly continuous with the primitive sheath of a nerve-fibre proceeding from them. The nerve-cells are characterised by their processes, one of which usually passes over directly into a nerve-fibre, while the others ramify, if not immediately, after running a brief course, into fine fibrils. The former is called the axis-cylinder, nerve-process or neurite; the latter are termed protoplasmic processes or dendrites. Secondary dendritic processes may also arise, not from the cell itself, but from its neurite (Fig. 14, c). They are then named collaterals. The two types of process are shown with special clearness in many of the larger cells of the myel (spinal cord) and brain of vertebrates.

The nerve-fibres do not form independent elements of the nervous system. They originate, as embryology teaches us (Fig. 9), in outgrowths from nerve-cells, and they remain throughout in connexion with the cells whose processes they are. We may accordingly consider the nervous system in its entirety as a vast conglomerate of nerve-cells, all woven together by fibrillar runners. Under these conditions, the only processes of the central cells that attain to any measure of apparent independence, as fibrillar elements, are those entering into connexion with the peripheral organs. But even the fibrils of the muscular and cutaneous nerves, which in many cases extend without break over large distances, are really nothing more than cell processes long drawn out. It is, therefore, the nerve-cell that is the main variable in the nervous system. Both in number and nature of its processes and in its own internal structure, the cell evinces characteristic differences, often strongly marked, from one part of the nervous system to another.[1] When highly magnified, most nerve-cells show, even without treatment by selective reagents, a fibrillated structure; clusters of granules are set, in scattered masses, between the meshes of this fibrillar network, and a special network of granules and fibrillae encloses the nucleus (Fig. 10). The granular deposits are named, from their discoverer, the corpuscles of Nissl; they are also known as tigroid bodies, or as chromophilous substance. Colour-staining brings them out with greater clearness, since they have an affinity for the dyes of the histologist, while the fibrillae and the amorphous ground-substance remain unaffected (Fig. 11). It appears, further, that these bodies stand in a peculiar relation to the different forms of cell-process; they are assembled in greater numbers at the points of origin of the dendrites, but are entirely absent from the part of the cell that gives off the neurite or axis-cylinder (Fig. 12, lower right-hand portion). Finally, besides this network of fibrillae which run their course within the substance of the cell, and whose continuity with the cell-processes evidences their nervous character, there is sometimes found a pericellular reticulum, which, basket-like, encloses the whole outer wall of the cell. Its fibrillae can, in most cases, be traced

---

[1] DEITERS, *Untersuchungen über Gehirn u. Rückenmark des Menschen u. der Säugethiere*, 1865, 53 f. HIS, *Arch. f. Anatomie*, Supplementband, 1890, 95 ff. VON LENHOSSEK, *Der feinere Bau des Nervensystems*, 2te Aufl. 1895, 36 ff. HELD, *Arch. f. Anatomie*, 1897, 204; Suppl. 273. BETHE, *Arch. f. mikroskop. Anatomie*, 1900, lv., 513. GOLGI, *Verhandl. d. anatom. Gesellschaft auf d. 14 Vers. zu Pavia*, 1900; *Anat. Anzeiger*, xviii., *Ergänzungsheft*.

into the dendrites, so that they too are, in all probability, to be looked upon as nervous structures (Fig. 13).

Nerve-cells are classified, according to the number of processes they send out, as unipolar, bipolar and multipolar. Unipolar cells are, however, always of rare occurrence; and, where they occur, have probably arisen secondarily, in course of growth from the originally bipolar form, by a fusion of its two processes,—which, we may note, divide again immediately after their emergence from the cell (see Fig. 21, z, p. 50). The bipolar cell is found more especially in the peripheral regions, e.g. in the spinal ganglia, in the retina, and [to some extent] in the ganglia of the sympathetic system. The great majority of nerve-cells are, however, multipolar. As a rule, every such cell gives off a single neurite, and an indeterminate number of dendrites. The divergent characters not only of the processes themselves, but also of the portions of the cell with which they are connected (Fig. 12) render it, in the present case, an exceedingly probable hypothesis, that the difference of structure is paralleled by a corresponding difference of function. As a matter of fact, the fibrils of the large cells of the ventral cornua of the myel, that pass over into the motor nerves, are without exception neuritic; while the processes that tend from the same cells towards the higher regions of the myel are dendritic in nature. RAMON Y CAJAL has accordingly suggested that the dendrites are devoted exclusively to cellipetal, the neurites to cellifugal conduction.[1] This scheme can, however, hardly be applied to all nerve-cells, without exception, since there are many cases in which no clear difference between the various cell-processes can be made out.

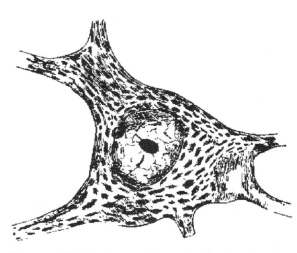

FIG. 12. Multipolar ganglion cell, showing clearly the twofold mode of origin of the fibrils (DEITERS' type). After NISSL. Neurite to the right.

For the rest, over and above their different manner of origination from the cell body, their shorter course, and their greater wealth of branches, the dendrites are morphologically distinguishable from the neurites by their character as 'protoplasmic' processes; their irregular

[1] RAMON Y CAJAL, *Les nouvelles idées sur la structure du système nerveux chez l'homme et chez les vertébrés*, 1894.

nodosity (Fig. 14) suggests the pseudopodial processes of the Rhizopoda (Fig. 2). They have also been observed, under the action of mechanical, chemical or electrical stimulation, to make amoeboid movements; though it is doubtful whether these changes are to be interpreted as vital phenomena, on the analogy of the contraction of protoplasm and of muscular

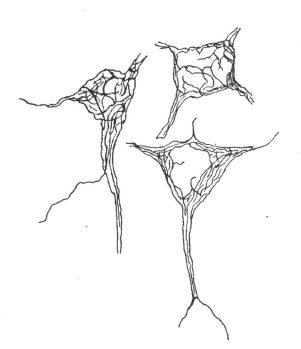
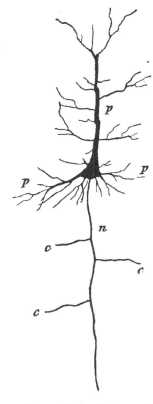

FIG. 13. Pericellular reticula of nerve-cells, stained by the silver method. After GOLGI.

FIG. 14. Pyramidal cell from the cerebral cortex, stained by the silver method. After RAMON Y CAJAL. *pp* Dendrites. *n* Neurite. *cc* Collaterals.

tissue, or whether they are not rather simply the direct physical and chemical effects of the stimuli applied.[1]

These differences between the two kinds of cell-processes are, however, as we said above, not equally well marked in all cases. In particular, the difference in length and character of course may be comparatively slight, or may even disappear altogether, the neurite, like the dendrite, dividing after a brief period into a large number of delicate branches. It is also not uncommon to find cells, especially cells of small size, whose processes show no distinct sign of difference, of whatever sort. The cells

[1] RABL-RÜCKHARD, *Neurol. Centralblatt*, 1890, 199. DUVAL, *Soc. de Biologie*, 1895. Cf. KÖLLIKER, *Verh. d. Würzburger phys-med. Gesellschaft*, 1895.

with processes of markedly different form are usually termed, from their discoverer, the cells of DEITERS (Fig. 12); cells with quickly dividing neurites are known as cells of GOLGI's type; and the cells without marked distinction of the processes are called intermediary or intercalary cells.[1]

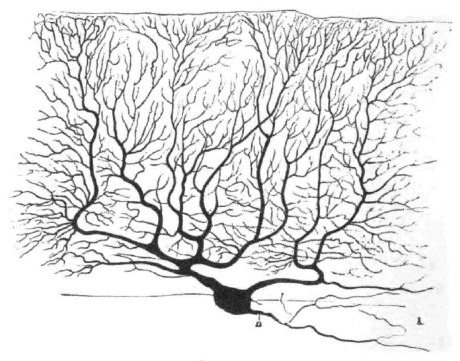

FIG. 15. Cells of PURKINJE, from the cortex of the cerebellum, with richly branching dendrites. After KÖLLIKER. *n* Neurite. *k* Collaterals.

Finally, the dendrites, like the neurite, evince certain structural differences. Sometimes, as in the pyramidal cells of the cerebral cortex (Fig. 14), they divide without much complication, their branches trending in definite directions. Sometimes, again, as in the large PURKINJE cells of the cerebellar cortex (Fig. 15), their ramifications are exceedingly complex and widely extended.

(b)—*The Nerve-Fibres*

We have seen that the nerve-process issuing from the nerve-cell forms the basis of the nerve-fibre. The main differences in the structure of the nerve-fibres depend upon differences in the character of the investing

---

[1] These intermediate cells (*intermediäre oder Schaltzellen*) appear to correspond to what are sometimes termed the GOLGI cells of the first type, and the GOLGI cells of the text to the GOLGI cells of the second type.—TRANSLATOR.

substances, which envelope the original neurite as it proceeds on its way. The constant constituent of a nerve-fibre, as follows at once from its mode of origin, is the neurite or axis-cylinder that forms the direct continuation of the nerve-process of a cell. The neurite is enclosed, first of all, in the myelinic sheath, a substance which after death breaks up by a process of decomposition into bulbous masses; later in its course, it becomes surrounded by a structureless membrane,

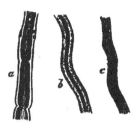

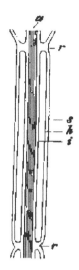

FIG. 16. Nerve-fibres. *a* Cerebrospinal nerve-fibre with primitive sheath, myelinic (medullary) sheath, and broad neurite. *b* A similar fibre, whose neurite is coagulated by collodion. *c* Sympathetic nerve-fibre without myelinic sheath; contents very finely striated; primitive sheath nucleated ('fibre of REMAK').

FIG. 17. Schematic diagram of the structure of a medullated nerve-fibre. *a* Neurite. *s* Primitive sheath of SCHWANN. *rr* Nodes of RANVIER. *hi* Corneal sheath (axilemma) of KÜHNE.

supplied at intervals with nuclei,—the primitive sheath of SCHWANN (Fig. 17). Most of the central nerve-fibres possess a myelinic sheath, but no primitive sheath; and within the grey substance the myelinic sheath itself not seldom disappears. In the sympathetic system, on the other hand, the neurite is, as a rule, enveloped directly by the nucleated primitive sheath, and lacks the intervening myelinic substance (Fig. 16, *c*). [With few exceptions,] the nerve-fibres of invertebrates evince this constitution throughout. Lastly, the terminal branches of the nerves in the peripheral end-organs often break up into arborisation, consisting simply of fine neuritic fibrils.

The two innermost of the three principal constituents of the nerve-fibre, myelinic sheath and neurite, possess a composite structure. If we trace a fibre throughout any considerable portion of its extent, we find that the myelinic substance does not afford a continuous investment of the neurite. The primitive sheath undergoes constriction at more or less regularly recurring intervals (nodes of RANVIER), and the myelinic sheath is thus divided up into cylindrical sections, separated by transverse partitions (Fig. 17). Since each section carries but a single cell-nucleus, we may suppose that it represents one of the cells of which the sheath is ultimately composed (Fig. 12). Within this internodal space (bounded by *r r* in the Fig.) there is, further, according to some observers, another double sheath, composed of a substance akin to epithelial tissue, and separating the neuritic thread from the myelinic sheath (*hi*).[1] While the myelinic sheath is thus subdivided, the neurite itself runs uninterruptedly from its point of origin to the conclusion of its course. It is made up, as was first observed by MAX SCHULTZE, of numerous primitive fibrils, which in many places, and especially where it issues from the nerve-cell, give it a finely striated appearance.[2] It is probable that these primitive fibrils pass, in the peripheral nerve-terminations, into the dendritic arborisation into which many nerve-fibres are ultimately resolved.

Putting all this together, we may infer that the neuritic thread is the constituent of the nerve-fibre essential to the conduction of nervous processes; that the myelinic sheath discharges not a nervous but a nutritive function; and that the remaining investments are merely protecting structures.[3] The inference is borne out by the fact that the formation of the myelinic sheath follows at a comparatively long interval, in the development of the nervous system, upon the appearance of the neuritic thread. At the same time, there can be no doubt of its great importance. The fibres that are to become myelinic give no clear indication of irritability, or of functional capacity at large, until myelinisation is complete.[4]

The nerve-processes and the nerve-fibres that proceed from them are, then, extremely important for the connexion of the nerve-cells with the peripheral appendages of the nervous system, the sense-organs, glands, muscles, etc. But they never mediate a direct connexion between cell and cell. Wherever such connexion occurs, it appears to be mediated solely by the contact into which dendrites and collaterals are brought with one another throughout the grey substance. This view finds support in observations made upon the peripheral terminations of the nerve-fibres.

[1] EWALD and KÜHNE, *Verhandl. d. naturhist.-med. Vereins zu Heidelberg*, N.F. i. 5. The presence of this intermediate membrane in the living nerve-fibre is denied by T. W. ENGELMANN, in PFLÜGER'S *Arch. f. d. ges. Physiol.*, xxii., 1880, 1 ff.; KÖLLIKER, *Gewebelehre*, 6te Aufl., ii., 13.
[2] MAX SCHULTZE, in STRICKER'S *Gewebelehre*, 1871, 108. POWER'S trs., i., 1870, 150.
[3] PIERSOL, *Normal Histology*, 63 f.—TRANSLATOR.
[4] See below, Ch. v. § 2.

(c)—Peripheral Nerve Terminations

The termination of a nerve in the peripheral organs may take one of two forms. Either the ends of the neuritic threads divide up into a fascicle or network of finest dendritic fibrils, that terminate freely along the elements of other, non-nervous tissues; or the neuritic thread passes directly over into a terminal cell situated within or between the organs. The terminal cell may be an original nerve-cell, pushed out towards the periphery of the body; or it may have acquired this character later on in the course of development, by the penetration of a nerve fibril into an epithelial cell. The two forms of nerve-termination occur side by side, in these their characteristic differences, in the different sense-organs, where they are evidently connected with essential differences in the mode of sensory excitation. The first form shows most plainly in the terminations of sensory nerves in the skin. The neurite, as soon as it enters the lowermost epithelial layer of the cutis, breaks up into a reticulum of delicate fibrils, whose dendritic branches surround the separate epithelial cells (Fig. 18, A). In some cases, it is true, this arrangement is so modified as to approximate more or less closely to the second form: there are cutaneous nerve-fibres whose fibrils penetrate the cells of the epidermis, or pass into or between the cells of the deeper lying connective tissue, and thus transform these originally non-nervous elements into peculiar sense-organs (touch-cells, end bulbs, touch-corpuscles, etc.). The nerve-terminations in the organ of hearing also follow, in the main, this cutaneous type.

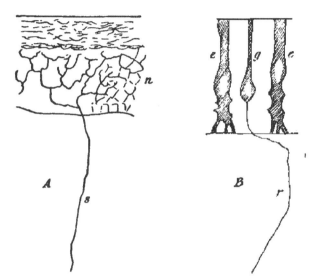

FIG. 18. Typical forms of sensory nerve-termination. *A* Free ending of a cutaneous nerve-fibre. *s* Sensory fibre. *n* Terminal reticulum between the cells of the epidermis. *B* Ending of an olfactory nerve-fibre. *r* Olfactory nerve-fibre. *g* Olfactory cell. *e* Epithelial cells.

The second form of nerve-termination is best illustrated from the organ of smell. Every olfactory nerve-fibre enters, in the olfactory mucous membrane, into a nerve-cell. This cell, which lies between epithelial cells, is drawn out at its opposite pole, i.e. at the end turned towards the free sensory surface, into a thread-like continuation (Fig. 18, *B*). The nerve-terminations in the tongue and in the retina of the eye follow this second type. In both organs, the terminal fibrils are connected with sensory cells. In their case, however, the sensory cells (taste-cells, retinal rods and cones) appear to be not true nerve-cells, but epithelial cells, which have been transformed into sense-cells by their connexion with nerve-fibres.[1]

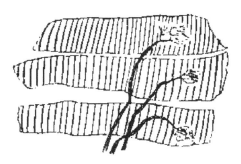

FIG. 19. Motor nerve-terminations in the cross-striated muscle-fibres of the rat. After SZYMONOWICZ.

The nerve-endings in muscle conform in all essentials to the first of these types. Here too we observe, in the first place, a more or less elaborate division of the nerve-fibres that run to the separate elements of the muscular tissue.[2] In the muscles of reptiles, birds and mammals, the terminal fibrils finally branch out in a peculiar flattened prominence, the end-plate. Most observers place this structure within the transparent elastic sheath of the muscle-fibre, the sarcolemma, though some describe it as attached to the outer surface (Fig. 19).[3]

(*d*)—*The Neurone Theory*

The facts which we have now passed in review as regards the nerve-cells, their processes, and the continuations of these processes into the peripheral organs appended to the nervous system, have led in recent years to the hypothesis that the conduction of nervous processes is mediated, in many cases, not—as was formerly supposed—by an unbroken continuity of the fibrillar elements, but rather by contact between the arborisations of the fibres of different nerve-cells. This hypothesis, it is needless to say, ascribes a greatly added importance to the nerve-cell. According to it, the functions of the nervous system are conditioned upon the spheres of function of the individual cells,—the 'cell' in this sense including as an essential constituent the fibrillar elements issuing from the cell-body. We may therefore regard the nerve-cell together with its processes as the morphological, and presumably also as the functional unit, to which we

---

[1] For a detailed account of the central and peripheral terminations of the sensory nerves, see Chs. v. vii., below.

[2] PIERSOL, *Normal Histology*, 90.—TRANSLATOR.

[3] KÜHNE, in STRICKER'S *Gewebelehre*, ii., 1871, 682. POWER'S trs., i., 1870, 219. SZYMONOWICZ, *Lehrbuch d. Histologie*, 1901, 306. MACCALLUM'S trs., 1902, 312 ff.

are in the last resort referred for an understanding of the entire nervous system. This unit of nerve-cell, with its dependent territory of fibrillar processes and arborisations, has been designated, on WALDEYER's suggestion, a neurone. In the light of the neurone theory, the whole of the central nervous system, reaching with its appended organs to the extreme periphery of the body, appears as a system of such units, set side by side or arranged in ascending series: each unit maintaining a relative independence, from the unbroken continuity of its parts, and each connected with other similar units only contact-wise, by way of the terminal arborisations of the fibrils of the individual neurones.[1] Figg. 20 and 21 illustrate this conception, schematically, for two trains of neurones, a motor and a sensory, which may be taken as typical of the systems of conduction realised in the nervous system at large. The hypothetical schema of the motor neurone train, given in Fig. 20, consists of two neurones, the one of which (N_I), as motor cell (Z_I) in the ventral cornu of the myel, is attached directly to a peripheral muscle-fibre (M), while the second (N_{II}) belongs to a higher nervous centre. The neurite proceeding from the cell Z_{II} gives off a certain number of collaterals, and finally resolves into fibrils that come into contact with the dendrites of the cell Z_I. This cell in turn sends out a neurite, whose ramose fibrillar termination stands in contact with the motor end-plate of a cross-striated muscle-fibre. The hypothetical schema of the sensory neurone train, in Fig. 21, also shows two neurones: a peripheral, N_I, that has its centre in a bipolar spinal-ganglion cell Z_I, and a central neurone, N_{II}, that belongs to a nerve-cell, Z_{II}, lying somewhere in the higher regions of myel or brain. The neurone N_I is connected by contact on the one side, through the terminal arborisation of its longer, peripherally directed fibre, with the cutaneous region H (cf. p. 47, Fig. 18 A), and on the other, through the dendrites of its second, upward trending process, with the neurone N_{II}. These bimembral chains are, naturally, to be considered only as the very simplest schemata of neurone connexion. We must suppose in general that several neurones, now all lying at the same level and now arranged in ascending order, are united in the nervous centres to form neurone chains. Where nerve-cells have been forced outward, as 'sensory cells,' into the peripheral organs, it is possible that there, too, similar arrangements may prevail. Indeed, as we shall see later on, the morphological conditions often point unequivocally to such peripheral neurone connexions (cf. below, Chs. V., VIII.).

Whether the individual cell territories are, always and everywhere, related to one another in the manner indicated by these diagrams is, we must

---

[1] WALDEYER *Ueber einige neuere Forschungen im Gebiet der Anatomie des Centralnervensystems*, in the *Deutsche med. Wochenschrift*, 1891, nos. 44–48. For the history of the theory, see M. von LENHOSSÉK, *Der feinere Bau des Nervensystems*, 2te Aufl., 1895, 103 ff.; M. VERWORN, *Das Neuron in Anatomie und Physiologie*, 1900.

admit, still an open question. So far, the neurone theory must be regarded simply as an hypothesis that brings together, in a very happy way, a large number of the data of current histology. Whether the definition of the neurone in general, and whether in particular the views of the interconnexion of the neurones promulgated especially by RAMON Y CAJAL, will prove to be tenable in all cases, cannot now be decided. Even at the present

FIG. 20. Schema of a motor neurone train. After RAMON Y CAJAL.

FIG. 21. Schema of a sensory neurone train.

day, the theory does not want for opponents. Fortunately, the settlement of these controversies among the morphologists is not of decisive importance for a physiological understanding of nervous functions. Physiological interpretation must be based, first of all, upon the manifestations of function, and these can be brought, later on, into relation to the anatomical facts. The opposite plan, of erecting elaborate physiological—not to say psychological—hypotheses upon purely anatomical foundations, is, of course, to be rejected without further argument. From this point of view, however, it must be conceded that the idea of neurones, and the view that this idea suggests of a connexion between the central elements which is relatively variable, and in certain circumstances perhaps determinable by the exercise of the functions themselves, accords better with the facts than the older view of an uninterrupted continuity of the nerve-fibres, and its dogmatic corollary of isolated conduction, were able to do. We need appeal only to the observations on the possibility of vicarious functioning, and on the substitution of new conduction-paths for others that have for some reason become impracticable. The anatomical plan of neurone connexions is evidently more adequate than this older view to the physiological results which prove that there exists, along with a certain localisation of functions, a very considerable capacity for adaptation to changed conditions. More than this,—more than an *ex post facto* representation of the course of events,—the neurone theory, naturally, cannot give us. Should that theory fall, the facts of vicarious function and of new adaptation would still all remain as they were, and would still have to be brought somehow into agreement with the properties of the anatomical substrate of the functions involved.

The morphological differences between the processes of the nerve-cells, that have formed the point of departure for the development of the neurone theory, were first pointed out by DEITERS, in his work upon the large cells of the ventral cornua of the myel. GERLACH discovered the fibrillar structure of the intercellular substance, and HIS the embryological connexion of nerve-fibres with nerve-cells. GOLGI, KÖLLIKER, NANSEN, W. HIS, G. RETZIUS, RAMON Y CAJAL and many others have made the nerve-cell a subject of special investigation.[1]

It is but natural that the results obtained should not be always in agreement. GOLGI and NANSEN supposed that the dendrites are merely nutritive elements; and GOLGI held, further, that the interlacing fibres of the ground-reticulum anastomose to form a closed system. The other observers declared for the nervous character of the dendrites, and were unable to confirm the occurrence of anastomosis in the ground-reticulum. On the side of function, GOLGI propounded the hypothesis that the neurites pass exclusively into motor nerve-fibres, while the sensory nerves take their origin from the ground-reticulum. It would follow from this, since GOLGI did not recognise the nervous nature of the dendrites, that the connexion between sensory and motor fibres is mediated not by any sort of nerve-cell, but only by the fibrillar substance of the ground-reticulum, and there, in all probability, by mere mechanical contact of the fibres. If on the other hand we admit, as the great majority of observers are now ready to do, that the dendrites are nervous in character, then we must suppose, as has been shown in particular by RAMON Y CAJAL, that while all centripetally conducting nerve-fibres first of all arborise into fibrils in the ground-reticulum, they afterwards avail themselves of the protoplasmic processes to discharge into nerve-cells. If this hypothesis be sound, the terms 'centripetal' and 'centrifugal' cannot be regarded as identical with 'sensory' and 'motor'; they are referable, in every case, only to the cells with which the fibres are con-

[1] Cf. the bibliographies in M. VON LENHOSSEK, *op. cit.* 36 ff.; KÖLLIKER, *Gewebelehre* 6te Aufl. ii. 5 ff.

nected. Centripetal, in this sense, are all conduction-paths that convey excitations to determinate nerve-cells; centrifugal, all conduction-paths that carry excitations from them. In general, therefore, the peripheral sensory nerves will belong to a centripetal, and the motor nerves to a centrifugal system. But within the central conduction-paths, i.e. those that run between different ganglionic systems, there may be fibres, centrifugal in respect of proximate cell-origin, that possibly possess a sensory character, and others, centripetal in origin, whose functions may possibly be motor. This view of the functions of the cell-processes evidently carries with it a relative independence of the territories of the individual nerve-cells,—a phase of the subject to which WALDEYER especially has called attention, and which has led him to introduce the idea of the neurone. Most recent investigators adopt the neurone theory. At the same time, there has always been a certain amount of dissent, based especially upon the oft repeated observation of the continuity of the fibrils within the nerve-cells.[1] It has even been maintained that the fibrils pursue an unbroken course throughout the entire nervous system, the nerve-cells included: an hypothesis first put forward by MAX SCHULTZE, the discoverer of fibrillar cell-structure,[2] and now revived on the ground of further work upon the same morphological phenomena.[3]

The structural schema of RAMON Y CAJAL, and the neurone theory that is based upon it, stand in the forefront of recent neurological investigation. Anatomists have also devoted much attention to the finer structure of the nerve-cell itself. There have been two remarkable discoveries in this field, that have aroused especial interest: NISSL's announcement of the tussock-like accumulations of granules (Figg. 10, 14),[4] and the observations made in many quarters on the fibrillar structure of the nerve-cells.[5] Neither of these, it is true, has passed unchallenged; both the granular masses and the fibrils have been explained as precipitates from the cell-substance, due to microchemical treatment or to *post-mortem* coagulation.[6] Nevertheless, the hypothesis that these structures exist in the living tissue is confirmed by the fact that they have been observed in fresh preparations, untreated by staining reagents (Fig. 10).[7]

NISSL's corpuscles have further been observed to undergo noteworthy changes under the action of poisons, like arsenic, or as the effect of intense fatigue or other trophic disturbances. The tussocks decrease, both in size and in number, so that in many cases they can still be observed only at certain parts of the cell-body, while the nucleus becomes farther and farther dis-

---

[1] NISSL, *Kritische Fragen der Nervenzellenanatomie*, in the *Biol. Centralblatt*, 1896, 1898. HELD, *Arch. f. Anatomie*, 1897, 204; Suppl., 273. BETHE, *Biol. Centralblatt*, 1898, no. 18. These authors believe, in general, that the neurone theory affords an adequate idea of the earlier stages in the development of the nervous system; but that, at a later period, the processes of the individual cells oftentimes grow together, so that the original independence of the cell territories is not maintained.

[2] MAX SCHULTZE in STRICKER's *Gewebelehre*, 1871, 108 ff. POWER's trs., i. 172.

[3] APATHY, *Biol. Centralblatt*, 1889 and 1898 (vols. ix. and xviii.). *Mittheilungen aus der Zool. Station zu Neapel*, xii. 1897; also in *Amer. Journ. of Insanity*, lv., 1898, 51 ff.

[4] NISSL, *Allg. Zeitschr. f. Psychiatrie*, l., 1894.

[5] FLEMING, *Arch. f. Mikrosk. Anatomie*, xlvi., 1895, 373. LENHOSSEK, *ibid.*, 345. MÖNCKEBERG and BETHE, *ibid.*, liv., 1899, 135.

[6] HELD, *op. cit.* Sometimes, as was discovered by BÜTSCHLI (*Untersuchungen über mikroskopische Schäume und Protoplasma*, 1892) and confirmed by HELD, a honey-combed appearance is presented both by the cell itself and by its nerve-process. HELD, however, regards this too as a result of coagulation.

[7] J. ARNOLD, *Arch. f. mikrosk. Anatomie*, lii., 1898, 542.

placed towards the cell-periphery, and finally disappears altogether. These changes correspond exactly to those observed in inflammatory conditions of the grey substance in the human brain, and termed homogeneous turgescence of the cells (Fig. 22 A). They suggest the idea that the tussocks discharge a specific function, intimately related to cell-nutrition. These structures are, perhaps, to be explained as accumulations of reserve material, to be drawn upon for functional purposes. If this be true, we must probably attribute to them the trophic influence which the nerve-cell exercises upon the fibres proceeding from it, and which apparently makes the cell their nutritive as well as their functional centre.[1] This influence is shown by the fact that those fibres of a transsected nerve which remain connected with the central organ persist for a long time without change, whereas the fibres of the peripheral portion of the nerve, the part that is separated from the centre, very soon show signs of degeneration. First of all, the myelinic contents of the fibre divides into clots (Fig. 23 a). Then, these clots, together with the neuritic fibrils, break up into granules (b). These in turn are slowly resorbed (c) until they altogether disappear: so that, finally, nothing is left of the nerve but its connective tissue

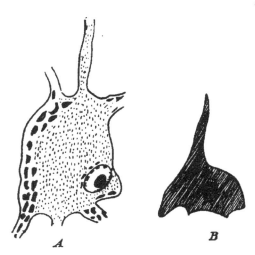

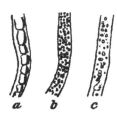

FIG. 22. Degenerated nerve-cells. A Cell in the state of inflammatory turgescence. B Atrophied cell. After FRIEDMANN.

FIG. 23. Secondary degeneration in a nerve-fibre, whose connexion with the centre has been severed. a, b, c Different stages of the degenerative process.

investments.[2] It is, however, probable that the appearance of these degenerative processes is further hastened by the arrest of function which naturally follows from the sectioning of the nerve. This view is confirmed, on the one hand, by the fact that, after a very long time, the central end of the transsected nerve also becomes atrophied, and on the other by the observation that nerve-cells, which have been thrown out of function by sectioning of a nerve-trunk or by injury to the peripheral region supplied by them, gradually shrink up (Fig. 22 B). In the case of young animals especially, this cell-shrinkage sets in comparatively quickly, after extirpation of the region of nervous diffusion. It has also been observed in man, as a secondary atrophy of the nerve-centres.[3]

[1] NISSL, *Allg. Zeitschr. f. Psychiatrie*, xlviii., 1892. MARINESCO, *Arch. f. Physiol.*, 1899, 89. VON WENDT, *Skandin. Arch. f. Physiol.*, xi., 1901, 372. M. FRIEDMANN, *Neurolog. Centralblatt*, 1891, 1.
[2] MÖNCKEBERG and BETHE, *Arch. f. mikrosk. Anatomie*, liv., 1899, 135.
[3] GUDDEN, *Arch. f. Psychiatrie*, ii., 693.

Such are the phenomena that occur as after-effects of enhancement or abolition of function in the nerve-cells and nerve-fibres. The changes observed as the results of stimulation in the dendritic processes, and interpreted by many observers as immediate manifestations of life, are of a very much more questionable nature. Amoeboid movements of the dendrites were first described by RABL-RÜCKHARD. They may possibly be explained as phenomena of imbibition and coagulation. At any rate, the psychophysical theories of sleep and waking, dissociation of consciousness, and what not, that certain authors have erected upon them, are purely imaginary psychological constructions, based on an extremely scant and more than doubtful foundation of physiological observation.[1]

§ 2. Chemical Constituents

The chemical substances of which the morphological elements of the nervous system are composed are as yet but imperfectly known. The greater portion of the investing and sustentacular tissues—the endoneurium and perineurium, the primitive sheath, and in part the neuroglia of the nerve-centres—belong to the class of collogenic and elastic substances. The only exception is the corneal sheath surrrounding the myelin, which is said to consist of a corneal substance allied to epithelial tissue, and termed neurokeratin.[2] The nerve-mass proper is a mixture of various substances, several of which resemble the fats in their solubilities, while they differ widely in chemical constitution. They have been found, not only in nerve-substance, but also in the corpuscles of blood and lymph, in egg-yolk, in sperma, and to a less degree in many other tissues. The most important of them is protagon, a highly complex body, to which LIEBREICH has assigned the empirical formula $C_{116}H_{241}N_4PO_{22}$. This formula is, naturally, intended merely to give an approximate idea of the extreme complexity of the chemical molecule of this compound.[3] From protagon are derived lecithin and cerebrin, decomposition-products which probably occur alongside of it in the nerve-substance, and together with it form the myelin of the myelinic envelope. Lecithin, it is supposed, is not a single body of stable constitution, but consists of a series of compounds that resemble the compound ethers: substances which in physical and chemical con-

[1] DUVAL, *Hypothèse sur la physiol. des centres nerveux*, in the *Comptes rendus de la société de biologie*, 1895. SOUKHANOFF, *La théorie des neurones, etc.*, in the *Arch. de neurologie*, 1897. QUERTON, *Le sommeil hibernal et les modifications des neurones*, Institut Solvay, Bruxelles, 1898.

[2] W. KÜHNE and CHITTENDEN, *Zeitschr. f. Biologie*, N.F. viii., 1890, 291.

[3] LIEBREICH, *Ann. der Chemie u. Pharmacie*, cxxxiv., 1865, 29. According to KESSEL and FREYTAG (*Zeitschr. f. physiol. Chemie*, xvii., 1893, 431), protagon further contains sulphur in its molecule. The views of these chemists, with the protagon theory at large, are sharply controverted by J. L. W. THUDICHUM (*Die chemische Constitution des Gehirns des Menschen und der Thiere*, 1901, 44 ff.). We cannot enter here into these differences of opinion. We can pass them over with the less scruple, since they are, at present, without significance for the general relations of the chemism of nerve-substance to the physiological processes.

stitution are closely allied to the fats, and in which the radicals of certain fatty acids, of phosphoric acid and of glycerin (a component of most of the animal fats) are combined with one another and with a strong amine base, cholin.[1] Lecithin has two characteristic properties. The large proportion of carbon and hydrogen which it contains gives it a high heat of combustion; and its complex nature renders it easily decomposable. Cerebrin, if boiled with acids, yields a sugar and other, unknown, decomposition products, and has accordingly been referred to the nitrogenous glucosides. Like lecithin, it is in all probability not a single body, but a mixture of several substances, which have been distinguished as cerebrin, homocerebrin and encephalin.[2] Lastly, cholesterin, a solid alcohol rich in carbon, which occurs in almost all the tissues and fluids of the body, plays a not inconsiderable part in the composition of nervous tissue. Besides these substances, which are all characterised by their high heat of combustion, nervous tissue contains substances which are classed with the proteins, but of whose composition and chemical conduct very little is understood. Finally, it must be mentioned, as a characteristic difference between the grey substance of the nerve-centres and the white myelinic substance, that the former gives a weakly acid, the latter an alkaline or neutral reaction. The acid reaction appears, like that of the muscles, to be due to the presence of free lactic acid.[3] Some observers have, in fact, maintained that this free acid increases, as a result of activity, just as it does in muscle.[4] Apart from these differences of reaction, little is known of the distribution of the various constituents in the various elementary divisions of nervous tissue. Only so much is certain, that in the peripheral nerve-fibres the neurite has all the general characteristics of a proteid, while the myelinic sheath evinces those of the myelins. In the ganglion cells, too, the nucleus would seem, from its microchemical conduct, to consist of a complex albumin-like substance, while in the protoplasm there is a mixture of albuminoid materials with protagon and its associates. The same constituents appear, further, to penetrate in part into the intercellular reticulum.

These facts render it probable that nervous substance is the seat of a chemical synthesis, whereby the complex nutritive substances carried by the blood are ultimately transformed into compounds of still greater com-

[1] The constitution of ordinary lecithin, according to DIAKONOW, is $C_{44}H_{90}NPO_9 =$ distearyl-glycerin-phosphoric acid + trimethyl-oxethyl-ammonium-hydroxide. According to STRECKER, other lecithins may be formed, in which the radical of stearic acid is replaced by some other fatty acid radical. See NEUMEISTER, *Lehrbuch der physiol. Chemie*, 2te Aufl., 1897, 91 ff.

[2] W. MÜLLER (*Ann. d. Chem. u. Pharm.* cv., 1858, 361) has worked out for cerebrin the empirical formula, $C_{37}H_{33}NO_3$. On the cerebrin series, cf. PARCUS, *Journ. f. prakt. Chemie*, 1881, 310; NEUMEISTER, *Physiol. Chemie*, 2te Aufl., 472.

[3] GSCHEIDLEN, in PFLÜGER's *Arch. f. d. ges. Physiol.*, viii., 1874, 71.

[4] MOLESCHOTT and BATTESTINI, *Arch. de biologie ital.*, viii., 1887, 90.

plexity, representing (as their high heats of combustion show) a very considerable amount of potential energy. This view of the chemism of nerve-substance is attested, first of all, by the appearance of protagon and the lecithins in such quantity that their production *in situ* is evidently far more probable than their deposition by the blood. The parent substances of protagon itself and of the bodies associated with it are to be sought, we must suppose, in the albumin-like substances of ganglion cell and neurite. There can, for that matter, be no doubt that the elementary structures of the animal body have the power of converting simpler proteids into more complex. Apart from the undisputed observation of synthetic processes within the body,[1] we have further evidence in the fact that substances containing phosphorus, which closely resemble the albuminates in their composition and chemical conduct, appear under conditions that definitely suggest their formation within the organic cell. A compound of this kind, nuclein, appears in particular to form the principal constituent of the cell-nuclei.[2] Hence we may say, tentatively, that the most important physiological result of the attempts so far made to penetrate the chemical constitution of the constituents of the nervous system is this and this only: that the chemism of nerve-substance is very particularly directed upon the formation of compounds possessing a higher heat of combustion or a larger store of potential energy. At the same time, the differences in the properties of the grey and white substance, scanty as they are, point to the conclusion that the central elements are the principal seat of the chemical processes which mediate the functions of the nervous system. These results, then, are practically all that we need bear in mind, as the outcome of chemical investigation of nervous substance up to the present time, when we approach the problems of the physiological mechanics of the nervous system.

---

[1] E. BAUMANN, *Die synthetischen Processe im Thierkörper.* Inaugural lecture. Berlin, 1878.
[2] MIESCHER, in HOPPE-SEYLER'S *Physiologisch-chemische Untersuchungen*, 4, 452; LUBAVIN, *ibid.*, 463.

CHAPTER III

Physiological Mechanics of Nerve-Substance

§ 1. General Principles and Problems of a Mechanics of Innervation

(a) —*Methods of a Mechanics of Innervation*

THE processes that run their course within the elements of the nervous system, the nerve-cells and nerve-fibres described above, have been studied in two different ways. By the one of these, investigators have sought to gain a knowledge of the internal, by the other of the external molecular mechanics of nervous substance. The former sets out from an examination of the physical and chemical properties of the nervous elements, and inquires into the changes which these properties evince as a result of physiological function, attempting in this manner to discover the internal forces at work in the nerves and nerve-centres. Inviting as this path may appear, in its promise directly to reveal the intimate nature of the nervous functions, it still takes us so short a distance towards its goal that we cannot venture to trust ourselves upon it. Apart from the scanty results of morphological investigation, mentioned above (p. 53), the study of the functional changes of the central elements is, as yet, hardly more than a programme. And our knowledge of the internal processes in the peripheral nerves is also severely limited. We know that their functioning is attended by electrical and chemical changes,—the meaning of which is still obscure: we know little more. The only road that remains open to us, therefore, is the second, that of an external molecular mechanics. In taking this, we avoid altogether the question of the special nature of the nervous forces: we set out simply from the proposition that the processes in the elementary divisions of the nervous system are movement-processes, of some sort or other, and that their relations to one another and to the forces of external nature are determined by the mechanical principles valid for motion at large. We thus take up a position akin, let us say, to that of the general theory of heat in modern physics, where the investigator is satisfied to begin with the proposition that heat is a mode of motion, from which—with the aid of the laws of mechanics—he derives all the phenomena with systematic completeness. If the molecular mechanics of the nervous system is to accomplish a like result, it must first of all reduce the phenomena that form the subject-matter of its inquiries to their lowest terms: it must investigate the physiological function of the nervous elements, first, under the simplest possible conditions, and, secondly, under conditions that can be experimentally varied and controlled. Now any outside affection of the nervous elements, that serves in some way to arouse or modify their functions, is termed in physiology a *stimulus*. In using this term, we must, of course, abstract entirely from the ideas which HALLER's theory of irritability and other modes of thought current in the older vitalistic physiology read into it. If we do this, the term retains its usefulness not only in our modern physiology of the nervous system and its auxiliary organs, but also by extension of meaning in psychology, seeing that all the multiplicity of outside affections that are embraced by it depend primarily upon a peculiar character of living substance itself, and may therefore produce identical results.

Stimuli are classified, in terms of the source from which their activity proceeds, as internal and external. Under internal stimuli are included all stimulatory influences that have their seat in the tissues and organs surrounding the nervous elements: we may instance, especially, rapid changes in the quality of the blood and of the fluids of the tissues. Under external stimuli are included, on the other hand, all the physical and chemical influences exerted upon the organism by the external world in which it lives. As regards nerve-substance, therefore, all stimuli whatsoever are to be classed as external. Whether, for instance, a chemical stimulus arises primarily in the blood in which the nerve-elements are bathed, or makes its way to them from the environment, is indifferent for the intrinsic character of the process. When, however, we desire to apply to nervous substance stimuli of a predetermined intensity and duration, we find, as a rule, that the internal stimuli (in the technical sense) are not available, since they are almost entirely beyond the range of experimental control. We accordingly have recourse to external stimuli, and most frequently to electric shocks and currents, which recommend themselves particularly both by the ease with which they destroy the molecular equilibrium of the nerve-elements, and by the extreme accuracy with which their mode of application may be regulated. In attempting an analysis of the processes in the nerve-fibres, we then begin with that peripheral effect of nervous excitation which is most open to investigation,—the muscle contraction that follows upon stimulation of the motor nerves,—and make this our measure of the internal processes. Similarly, for an understanding of the changes in the nerve-cells, we employ the simplest process, amenable to external measurement, that is released in the central organ by the stimulation of a centrally directed nerve-fibre,—the reflex contraction. In neither of these cases, however, does the muscle-contraction afford a direct measure of the processes that run their course in the corresponding nerve-fibres and at their points of central origin, or of the changes induced in these processes by any determinate outside influence; of itself, it can never furnish more than a certain measure of the processes operative in the substance of the muscle which contracts. As a rule, therefore, every change in the irritability of the nervous elements, to which we have applied artificial stimulation, may be expected to produce a change in the phenomena exhibited by the muscle: thus, if the irritability of the motor nerves is diminished, the muscular contraction will be weaker; if enhanced, it will be stronger. But we shall not be justified in arguing, conversely, that every change in contraction implies a corresponding change in nervous excitability. On the contrary, since the contractile substance has its own intrinsic irritability, which it maintains in face of stimulation whether directly applied or transmitted to it by the motor nerves, very different stimuli may possibly act upon the nerve, or upon the central structures connected with it, to release precisely the same processes in the nervous substance itself, and nevertheless, if the irritability of the contractile substance has changed in the meantime, may produce quite different effects in muscle: or conversely, may set up different processes in the nervous substance, while the contractile substance shows the same reaction. We must, therefore, never lose sight of the fact that the muscular contraction furnishes only an indirect measure of the processes of nervous excitation. If we are to argue immediately from the symptoms of altered contractility to the nervous processes, we must be sure that the observations are made under conditions which guarantee a sufficient constancy in the properties of the muscle experimented upon, or at least make such constancy highly probable. For the rest, the properties of the contractile substance itself, and the related phenomena of the course of the muscular contraction, may here be left out of consideration, as their interest is purely physiological. In no case are we concerned with the muscular contraction save as the changes which it undergoes possess a symptomatic importance for the nervous processes with which they are connected.[1]

It is the task of a physiological mechanics of the nervous substance to reduce the phenomena of nerve-stimulation, so far as they can be traced in the related mechanical phenomena evinced by muscular tissue, to the universal laws of mechanics. In essaying this problem, it must at the outset bring its subject-matter into relation with one, especially, of the great laws of mechanics,—a law which has proved pre-eminently serviceable

---

[1] A good summary of the most important facts regarding the mechanical properties of muscle will be found in TIGERSTEDT's *Lehrbuch der Physiologie*, ii., 1898, 128 ff. The reader should compare with this the recent papers of ROLLETT (PFLÜGER's *Arch. f. d. ges. Physiol.*, lxiv. and lxxi.), SCHENCK (*ibid.* lxii., lxiii., lxiv., lxv., lxvii., lxxii.) and KAISER (*Zeitschr. f. Biologie*, xxxiii., xxxv., xxxvi., xxxviii.).

in explaining the interrelations of various forms of movement-process. This is the law of the conservation of work.

(b)—*The Principle of the Conservation of Work*

We understand by work, in the most general meaning of the term, any operation that changes the position of ponderable masses in space. The amount of work done, in a given case, is accordingly measured by the change of position which it can produce in a weight of determinate magnitude. Ponderable bodies can be moved from their place by light, heat, electricity, magnetism. But all these 'natural forces,' as they are called, are simply forms of molecular motion. It follows, then, that the different modes of molecular motion can do work. The heat of steam, e.g., consists in movements for the most part rectilinear, but oftentimes interferential, of the steam particles. As soon as the steam does work,—let us say, by moving the piston of an engine,—a corresponding quantum of these movements disappears. This result is commonly expressed in the phrase, 'A certain quantity of heat has been transformed into an equivalent quantity of mechanical work.' It would be more accurate to say that a part of the irregular movements of the steam-particles has been used up, in order to set a larger ponderable mass in motion. We have, then, merely the transformation of the one form of motion into the other; and the work done, measured by the product of the moved weight into the distance through which it is moved, is exactly equal to a sum of lesser amounts of work, which could be measured by the products of the weights of a number of steam-particles into the distances traversed by them, and which now, during the performance of the external work, have disappeared. Conversely, when mechanical work disappears and heat arises in its place, by the friction or compression of physical bodies, we have the opposite transformation of mechanical work into its equivalent amount of molecular work. Not that mechanical work (in the ordinary sense of the term) appears in all cases where heat is latent: the heat is, very commonly, employed simply for the transposition of the particles of the heated body itself. It is a familiar fact that all bodies—gases most of all, liquids and solid bodies in less degree—expand under the influence of heat. Here, again, molecular work disappears. Just as it is used in the steam-engine to move the piston, so it is used in this case to alter the distance that separates the molecules. Work done in this way is termed work of disgregation. It may be transformed back again into molecular work, as the particles return to their original positions. In general, then, molecular work may be transformed either into mechanical action or into work of disgregation, and both of these in their turn may be transformed into molecular work. Now the sum of these three forms of work remains unchanged. This is the principle of the conservation of work : or, if we choose a name which will permit us, in other contexts, to abstract from that mechanical interpretation of natural processes to which we here stand committed, the *principle of the conservation of energy*.

This principle is applicable not only to heat, the most general and most widely diffused form of motion, but to other forms as well. In every case, it is always just the one term in the chain of the three interchangeable motions, the character of the molecular work, that is changed. Work of disgregation and mechanical work can be done, e.g., by electricity as well as by heat. There are, therefore, various kinds of molecular work; but there is in the last resort only one work of disgregation, as there is only one form of mechanical work. Disgregation is the name given, in every instance, to a permanent change of the distances separating the molecules, no matter what cause has produced it. When we distinguish a simple increase in the volume of a body from a change of its aggregate condition, and this again from chemical decomposition, or dissociation, we are really distinguishing nothing more than three degrees of disgregation. Mechanical work, in the same way, consists always and everywhere in the change of position of ponderable masses. It should be noted that the different forms of molecular work may also, under certain circumstances, be transformed into one another. Thus, a certain quantum of electrical work may give rise, simultaneously, to heat, disgregation and mechanical work.

It is from mechanical work that the idea of work, in the abstract, has been derived. And it is mechanical work that is selected, from the various forms of work mentioned above, to serve as a common measure of work at large. The reason is, that mechanical work can be most accurately measured, and that the only possibility of a comparison of the different forms of work is given with the reduction of all to one. This measure, now, is applied in the special case by help of the principle of the conservation of work, which lays it down that a given amount of molecular work or work of disgregation is equivalent to the mechanical work into which it is transformed or from which it is generated. In the performance of mechanical work, a ponderable body may be lifted, against the force of gravity, or moved by its own weight, or accelerated in spite of friction, and so on. In the latter event, the portion of mechanical work necessary to overcome friction is transformed into heat. Where the body is lifted, we suppose that the work employed for the lifting is stored up within it, since this work can be passed on again to other bodies, by a subsequent fall of the weight from the same height. Disgregation behaves, in this regard, just as the lifted weight does: a certain quantity of molecular work, mostly in the form of heat, is used up in its production, and this same quantity must reappear as soon as the disgregation is abolished. But a lifted weight remains lifted so long as its weight is held in equilibrium by some other form of work, e.g. by the heat-motion of expanded steam. In the same way, the disgregation of the molecules of a body persists, so long as their reunion is prevented by some form of internal work, e.g. by heat-vibrations. Hence, between the moment at which the weight is lifted or the disgregation of the molecules effected, and the moment at which the work required for these operations is reproduced by the fall of the weight or the union of the molecules, there may intervene a static condition, continuing for a longer or shorter time, throughout which just so much internal work is being done as is necessary for the maintenance of equilibrium,—so that no alteration takes place in the existing status, in the position of bodies and their molecules, in temperature, in electrical distribution. Only at the moment when this state of equilibrium is disturbed, when the weight falls or the molecules approach one another, do transformations of work set in again. The mechanical work or work of disgregation is now transformed first of all into molecular work, usually into heat, and this may in its turn pass over in part into mechanical action or disgregation of molecules; the transformations continuing, until circumstances occur that favour the reinstatement of the stationary condition. Since, now, there is a certain sum of work available, in a lifted weight or in disgregated molecules, we may consider every lifted weight and every disgregation as potential work or work of position. The amount of this potential work is always precisely the same as the amount of work that was required to effect the lift or the disgregation, and as the amount of work that may re-appear in consequence of fall or of aggregation. The law of the conservation of work may, accordingly, be expressed in other terms as follows: the sum of actual and of potential work, of work of position and work of motion, remains constant. It is clear that this is only a special way of formulating our previous law of the conservation of the sum of work; for we always mean by work of position a lift or a disgregation accomplished by expenditure of actual work, and maintained by a stationary condition of tension or motion. If we could observe the smallest oscillatory movements of the atoms as well as the motions of bodies and the permanent changes of position that they undergo, the law would hold of these atomic movements also, that the sum of actual and potential work remains unchanged. In actual fact, however, where the particles of the mass are in constant motion about approximately the same positions of equilibrium, matter appears to us to be at rest. We accordingly term the work done, invisibly to us, in a stationary condition, ' internal ' molecular work, thus distinguishing it from the molecular work which arises when there is a change in the state of equilibrium as regards temperature, electric distribution, etc., and which we call ' external ' molecular work.

These stationary conditions are continually alternating with changes of state. The stage of nature is thus occupied, in never-ending succession, with the passage from internal to external, and from external back again to internal molecular work. It will suffice here to give illustrations of the processes that have the most direct bearing upon our own problem,—illustrations of disgregation and its reversal. Differences in aggregate condition depend, it is supposed, upon different states of molecular motion. The molecules of a gas repel one another, and consequently continue to move, in rectilinear paths, until such time as they strike the wall of the containing vessel, or other molecules, from which they rebound. In liquids, the molecules oscillate about instable, in solids, about stable positions of equilibrium. If, now, we are e.g. to transform a liquid into a gas, we must increase the work of the molecules. We do this by the application of heat. So long as only the molecular work of the liquid increases, nothing results but an increase of its temperature. But if, at the same time, we allow the liquid to expand, then a part of its molecular work is further transformed into disgregation. Finally, if the application of heat is continued, and the disgregation carried to the point at which the particles of the liquid travel beyond the spheres of their mutual attraction, the liquid is suddenly transformed into gas or steam : it now enters upon a new state of equilibrium, in the production of which a large amount of molecular work, i.e. of heat, has been consumed. If heat is now withdrawn from the steam, so that its internal work is diminished, a point will be reached, on the backward path, at which the average distance between the molecules is sufficiently reduced to bring them once more within the limits of their mutual attraction. With the supervention of this original position of equilibrium, molecular work must be done, i.e. heat be liberated, as a result of the renewed activity of the forces of attraction ; and the amount of heat thus disengaged is precisely the same as that consumed in the first instance.

What holds in this case holds, in practically the same way, for the decomposition and recomposition of chemical compounds. In every substance we can distinguish between the state of physical and the state of chemical equilibrium. For every molecule, in the physical sense, consists of a number of chemical molecules or (to use the term applied to the indecomposable chemical molecule) of a number of atoms. Just, then, as the molecules may exist in different conditions of motion, varying with the aggregate state of the body in question, so may the atoms also, according to the character of the chemical compound. Modern chemistry regards all bodies as compounds ; chemically simple bodies are looked upon as compounds of homogeneous atoms. Hydrogen gas is thus every whit as much a chemical compound as is hydrochloric acid : in the former, two atoms of hydrogen are compounded together ($H.H$), in the latter, one atom of hydrogen is compounded with one of chlorine ($H.Cl$). Here again, however, what appears to be matter at rest is in reality only a stationary condition of motion. The atoms in a chemical compound oscillate, it is supposed, about more or less stable positions of equilibrium. The character of this motion is, at the same time, strongly influenced by the aggregate condition of the compound, regarded as a physical body. Thus, in gases and liquids, the state of motion of the chemical atoms is, as a rule, comparatively free; atoms are occasionally torn from their connexions, and at once compound again with other atoms that have been similarly released. In hydrochloric acid, for instance, gaseous or liquid, the average composition of all chemical molecules is HCl. Nevertheless, separate atoms H and Cl are constantly occurring in the free state, though they cannot maintain it, but are always compelled at once, by the forces of chemical attraction, to enter again into combination. From this point of view we gain a satisfactory explanation of the ready decomposability of gases and liquids in face of heat, electricity and other chemical compounds.[1]

We find, once more, in the aggregation of chemical molecules, differences analogous to those which we have noted in the aggregate states of physical bodies. There are relatively stable and relatively instable chemical compounds. In the former, the forces of attraction, in virtue of which the particles vibrate about certain determinate positions of equilibrium, are stronger; in the latter, weaker. These differences of chemical aggregation are, of course, altogether independent of the physical, since the physical molecules are always, to start with, chemical aggregates. Very stable compounds may accordingly occur in the gaseous state, and very instable in the aggregate state of solidity. In general, the compounds of homogeneous atoms, the chemically simple substances, belong to the less stable compounds; most of them, certain of the metals excepted, decompose fairly easily to form compounds with heterogeneous atoms. The same thing is true, on the other hand, of extremely complex compounds, which readily break up into simpler. Here belong most of the 'organic' substances. It follows, then, that stable chemical compounds are to be found predominantly among the simpler connexions of heterogeneous atoms. Thus, carbonic acid, water, ammonia, and many of the metallic oxides and inorganic acids are decomposed only with difficulty. Just, however, as the different aggregate states can be transformed into one another, so may relatively instable compounds be transformed into stable, and conversely. There is, as St. Claire Deville proved, no compound so stable that it cannot be dissociated by the application of heat in sufficient quantity. Here, as in the change of a liquid into a gas, a certain amount of the

[1] Clausius, *Abhandlungen zur mechanischen Wärmetheorie*, ii., 1867, 214.

internal work of the heat disappears, transformed into work of dissociation. When the dissociation is complete, the atoms are in a new state of equilibrium. In the dissociation of water, e.g., the more stable connection H_2O gives place to the less stable forms $H.H$ and $O.O$, in which the vibratory condition of the atoms differs from that in the stable compound H_2O very much as the vibratory condition of the molecules of steam differs from that of the molecules of water; that is to say, the atoms in their new, instable connexions will, on the whole, describe longer paths, and consequently do more internal molecular work. To make up this deficiency, heat is necessary. The work thus expended upon dissociation is, however, still present as potential work: for when the new state of equilibrium of the dissociated molecules is disturbed, they are able to compound again, and the work of dissociation once more makes itself apparent in the form of heat. The chemical molecules have, at the same time, passed into their former condition of equilibrium, where the stationary work which they perform in movements about their positions of equilibrium is diminished by the amount of the internal work released in the act of composition. We see, then, that the phenomena connected with composition and dissociation are identical with the phenomena observed in the alternation of aggregate states, save only that much larger amounts of work are usually required for dissociation than for disgregation, and that in the former case the exchange between work of position and work of motion attains proportionately higher values.

(c)—*Application of the Principle of the Conservation of Work to the Vital Processes and the Nervous System*

The tissues of the living organism are the seat of chemical processes which, by their great regularity of occurrence, furnish a remarkable illustration of the alternations of potential and actual, internal and external work. In the plants, we have a constant dissociation of stable compounds. Carbonic acid, water, ammonia, the nitric acid and sulphuric acid of the nitrates and sulphates, are taken up by the plant, and decomposed into less stable compounds—wood fibre, starch, sugar, albumins, etc.—in which a large amount of potential work is stored; at the same time, oxygen is eliminated. These compounds, produced by the plant, are retransformed in the animal body, by help of atmospheric oxygen (i.e. by a process of combustion), into the more stable compounds from which the plant had derived them; at the same time, the potential work stored up in the organic compounds goes over into actual work, partly in the form of heat, partly in that of external work of the contractile substance. The central station, from which all these processes of the animal body are directed, is the nervous system,

It maintains the functions that subserve the processes of combustion; it regulates the distribution and radiation of heat; it determines the activity of the muscles. In many cases, it is true, and especially in cases of muscular action, the issuance of impulses from the nervous system is itself directed by external movement-processes, the sense-stimuli. The true source of its functional capacity lies, however, not in these, but in the chemical compounds of which nerve-mass and contractile substance are composed, and which are taken over, almost without modification, from the living laboratory of plant-tissue. These contain the store of potential work, which under the influence of external stimulation is transformed into actual work.

The compounds of which the nerve-mass consists remain, so long as stimulus-processes do not intervene to modify them, approximately in that stationary condition which appears to outward observation as a state of rest. This rest is, however, here, as in all such instances of a stationary condition, only apparent. The atoms of the complex chemical compounds are in continual motion; now and again, they travel beyond the sphere of operations of the atoms with which they have hitherto been combined, and come within that of other atoms, freed like themselves. There is, therefore, in a liquid so easily decomposable as the nerve-mass, a constant alternation of decomposition and recomposition of chemical compounds; and the mass appears stationary simply for the reason that, on the average, there are as many processes of the one kind going on as of the other. In this particular instance, however, we cannot in strictness say even so much: not even during their period of rest is the state of the nervous elements really constant and unchanged. With compounds of such complexity, it invariably happens that certain of the atoms which have been removed from their former sphere of operations do not, in re-uniting, enter into their old connexions, or into connexions of the same order, but combine afresh to form simpler and more stable compounds. This process is termed intrinsic decomposition. In the living organism the disturbances arising from intrinsic decomposition are compensated by the removal of the products of decomposition, and by the intake of new materials for the renewal of the constituents of the tissues.

We may, then, consider resting nervous substance as a semisolid mass given in a stationary condition of motion. In such a mass, there is no release of external work; the work values produced by the individual atoms cancel one another. This cancellation takes place, in large measure, *within* the complex chemical molecules. As the atoms of the molecule oscillate about their positions of equilibrium, each one of them does a certain work, which, however, is counteracted by the work of other atoms, and consequently is not perceptible outside the molecule. This internal molecular work is far more considerable in an instable chemical compound, owing to the greater freedom of movement possessed by the atoms, than it is in a stable compound. It is this, therefore, that represents the potential work of the compound. For if the existing state of equilibrium be disturbed, the relatively instable may pass into a relatively stable compound; in which event the surplus of internal molecular work contained in the former is at once transformed into external. To a certain extent, however, the establishment of equilibrium takes place *without* the chemical molecule. Where atoms are continually passing from less stable to more stable connexions, work must appear; where, on the other hand, atoms are transferred from more stable to less stable connexions, work must correspondingly disappear: and in both cases it is external molecular work, generally heat, that is produced and consumed again. We may term the work that appears with the origination of the more stable compound 'positive' molecular work, and the work that disappears with the formation of the less stable compound, 'negative' molecular work. The condition of true equilibrium in a decomposable liquid like the nerve-mass will then be this: that the internal molecular work or potential work be kept unchanged, by the continual compensation of the existing quantities of positive and negative external molecular work. Or, to put the same thing in different words: the internal molecular work must be kept constant by the renewal (through retransformation into internal molecular work) of all that it loses in external molecular work. What changes, now, are brought about in this stationary condition of the nerve by the development of the process of stimulation?

§ 2. The Course of the Processes of Stimulation in the Nerve-Fibre

(a)—*Course of the Muscular Contraction following Stimulation of the Motor Nerve*

The simplest of all the external phenomena that can inform us of the nature of the processes of stimulation in nerve is the *muscular contraction* which sets in, and runs its course in time, as a result of stimulation of a motor nerve. Fig. 24 shows the course of a contraction of this kind in the

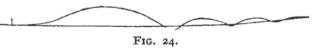

FIG. 24.

gastrocnemius of the frog; a lever with writing-point was attached to the muscle, and recorded the phases of the contraction directly upon a quickly moving smoked-glass plate, carried by a heavy pendulum. The conditions under which the tracing was obtained were made as simple as possible, in order that the course of the contraction might really be symptomatic of the stimulatory process. The muscle carried no weight beyond the light writing lever, and gave a twitch in response to stimulation. Numerous observations have shown that the loading of a muscle increases its irritability. Under the present circumstances this intensifying effect may be regarded as relatively small, and the influence that it exerts upon the various experiments whose results we are to compare, as sufficiently uniform.[1] The vertical stroke to the left indicates the moment at which the stimulus was applied to the nerve. The resulting curve, whose axis of abscissas appears by reason of the movement of the pendulum as an arc of a circle, shows that the twitch sets in perceptibly later than the stimulation, and that the contraction rises at first quickly, then more slowly, to be followed in like manner by a gradual relaxation. If the stimulus is momentary, the whole twitch is generally completed in 0·08—0·1 sec. Provided that the nerve is stimulated directly above the muscle, about 0·01 sec. of this time is lost between the application of stimulus and the beginning of the twitch; this interval is known as the stage of latent stimulation, or the latent period. The experiment makes it probable that the movement process in nerve is relatively slow. Since, however, we have not determined how much of this retardation of the processes is referable to the inertia of the muscular substance, the result obtained is not of decisive value.

We come closer to the movement in nervous substance itself when we stimulate the nerve at two different points of its course, the one remote from the muscle, the other as near to it as possible, and when the experiment is so arranged that the stimulation is timed to occur in both cases at the same point upon the axis of abscissas above which the curve of contraction is described. If the two stimuli have the same intensity, and the nerve is kept in as constant a condition as possible, the resulting curves evince a twofold difference. In the first place, as HELMHOLTZ discovered, the curve of contraction given by the more remote stimulus begins later——has

FIG. 25.

---

[1] Muscle-curves of this kind are termed, as proposed by A. FICK, 'isotonic' (curves of equal tension), and distinguished from the 'isometric' curves, described when the muscle is prevented, by over-loading, from making contractions of any considerable extent (cf. Fig. 26, p. 70). There is, of course, no such thing as a purely isotonic or purely isometric curve. In the twitch of the muscle, there must necessarily occur changes of tension, increasing in general with the amount of load, while an absolutely isometric muscle would not describe any curve whatsoever. Curves may also be obtained under the further condition that the tension increases during contraction, as when the muscle is made to pull against a spring ('auxotonic' curve), or that it is suddenly augmented during contraction by the application of a load, and so on. The different properties of the resulting curves are, however, of interest only for a mechanics of muscle.

a longer latent period—than the other. Secondly, as PFLÜGER first showed, the twitch released higher up the nerve is the stronger; its curve is higher and also, as the author pointed out, of longer duration. If, therefore, the experimenter desires to obtain two muscle-curves of the same height, he must apply a somewhat weaker stimulus to the part of the nerve that is more remote from the muscle. Even then it usually happens, provided the experiment be made on the living animal, that the corresponding contraction lasts for a little longer time. The two curves will accordingly differ in the manner indicated in Fig. 25. There is a brief interval between the starting-points of the contractions, which evidently corresponds to the time which the excitation requires for propagation from the upper to the lower point of stimulation; and the twitch released higher up, although in this case it was excited by a weaker stimulus, reaches the axis of abscissas later than its initial retardation would lead us to expect. We may, then, conclude from these experiments, first, that the movement-process of stimulation is relatively slow,—for the frog-nerve at ordinary summer temperature it averages 26, for the nerves of warm-blooded animals at normal body temperature 32 m. in the 1 sec.,—and, secondly, that it consists, in all probability, not in a simple transmission and propagation of the external stimulus movement, but in a chain of movement-processes released from one point to another within the nerve itself. This latter inference is borne out, more particularly, by the lengthening of the contractions which goes with increased distance of the point of stimulation from the muscle. The phenomenon is altogether constant, and may be observed most strikingly in the uncut nerves of the living animal.[1]

In order, now, to gain a deeper insight into the course of the phenomena of stimulation, we must endeavour to inform ourselves of the state of the nerve at each successive moment of the time following upon stimulation. We may do this, always in terms of the external effects of nervous activity, by investigating the behaviour of the nerve, at every moment of the period of stimulation, in face of a second, test-stimulus of constant magnitude.

---

[1] Cf. my *Untersuchungen zur Mechanik der Nerven und Nervencentren*, Abth. i., 1871, 177. The increase of the height of the muscle-curve with the distance of the point of stimulation from the muscle, first observed by PFLÜGER (*Untersuchungen über die Physiologie des Elektrotonus*, 140), has been referred by many physiologists, following HEIDENHAIN (*Studien des physiol. Instituts zu Breslau*, i., 1), to the effect of the section or, where connexion with the myel is retained, to the unequal decay of the nerve-tissue. If this hypothesis be correct, we must suppose that the excitability of the living nerve is the same at all points along its course. I have, however, shown, and the observation has been subsequently confirmed by TIEGEL (PFLÜGER's *Arch. f. d. ges. Physiol.*, xiii., 598), that the greater excitability of the parts more remote from the muscle obtains also in a living animal in which the circulation is maintained. I found, in particular, that the lengthening of contraction, which I had myself observed to be connected with increased length of nerve, is especially noticeable in the living nerve. This is, no doubt, the reason that it was not seen by experimenters who worked only with muscle-nerve preparations.

Here, as in the case of the simple muscle-contraction, the properties of the muscular substance itself naturally contribute their share to the total result. We can, however, eliminate their influence, very much in the same way that we did in the experiments on the propagation of stimulation. Where the conditions residing in the muscle remain constant, the observed changes must necessarily depend upon the processes taking place in the nerve.

(b)—*Excitatory and Inhibitory Processes in Nerve-Stimulation*

We must suppose, if we apply the principle of conservation to the processes in the nerve, that every process of stimulation produces two opposite effects in the nerve-fibre. The one set of operations will be directed upon the production of external work (muscular contraction, development of heat, secretion, stimulation of nerve-cells), and the other upon the recovery of the work thus liberated. We may term the former the excitatory, and the latter the inhibitory effects of stimulation. The whole course of the stimulation is then dependent upon the constantly varying play of excitation and inhibition. In order to demonstrate, by means of our test-stimulus, which of these processes, excitation or inhibition, has the upper hand, we may employ either of two different methods. We may work with stimulation-processes of so little intensity that they are unable of themselves, without the intervention of the test-stimulus, to release any muscular contraction at all; or we may eliminate the influence of the contraction itself during the time of its occurrence. We can do this, in cases where we are concerned to demonstrate an increase of irritability, by overloading the muscle, i.e. by attaching to it so heavy a weight that both the original twitch and the contraction normally released by the test-stimulus are suppressed, or at most only a minimal (what is called an 'isometric') twitch remains possible. If now, during the progress of the first stimulation, the test-stimulus nevertheless releases a more than minimal contraction, we have evidence of an increase of the excitatory effects and, in the height of the muscle-curve, a rough measure of their magnitude. Fig. 26 gives an

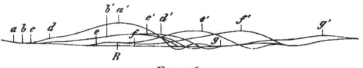

Fig. 26.

illustration of this procedure. The stimulation-process here under investigation was set up by the closing of a constant current in the ascending direction: the positive electrode, that is, lay nearer to the muscle, and the negative farther away from it. The current was closed at the point *a*. In response to the stimulation, the muscle (not overloaded) gave the twitch recorded as a'. The load was now attached, and the muscle-curve reduced by it to the minimal height R. The test-stimulus, employed to test the state of the nerve in successive phases of the stimulation-process, was the break shock of an induction-current, applied a short distance below the length of nerve stimulated by the constant current. So long as the latter was open, the twitch produced by the shock in the overloaded muscle was also minimal. A series of experiments was then performed, in which the nerve of the overloaded muscle was first of all stimulated at a by make of the constant current, and then again, after a definite period, by application of the test-stimulus. If the two stimuli were coincident (a), the height of the muscle-curve remained minimal. Where the test-stimulus came later, the successive times of stimulation b, c, d, e, f, g, gave the contractions b', c', d', e', f', g'. The course of these curves shows clearly that the stimulated nerve undergoes a change of state, which manifests itself as an increased irritability. The change begins shortly after the stimulation a; reaches a maximum that corresponds approximately with the highest points of the contractions a' and R ($e\ e'$); and then gradually decreases again,—though it persists, as is shown by the final test $g\ g'$, for a considerably longer time than the primary twitch a'.

Where it is not, as in the instance here taken, the excitatory, but the inhibitory effects that have the upper hand, the method of overloading naturally ceases to be applicable. We can, however, readily infer the presence of inhibitory influences from the magnitude of the effect produced by the test-stimulus during the progress of the contraction. If, e.g., the test-stimulus produces no effect whatever, we can argue with perfect certainty to the preponderance of inhibitions. An illustration of this state of things is given in Fig. 27. The stimulation-process here under investigation was again set up by the making of an ascending constant current; and the test-stimulus was, as before, the break shock of an induction-current applied below the portion of nerve stimulated by the constant current. A and B represent two successive experiments, in each of which the current was closed at a and the test-stimulus thrown in at b. The primary object of both experiments was to investigate, first, the effect of the current without the test-stimulus, and secondly, the effect of the test-stimulus without preceding closure of the constant current: this gave the contractions C and R, which are precisely alike in A and B. In the next place, the test-stimulus was applied, at b, immediately after the closure of the constant current at a. The results obtained in the experiments A and B were now entirely different. In A, a simple contraction C was recorded, precisely as if the test-stimulus R had not operated at all ($RC = 0$); in B, the curve of contraction was at first coincident with C, but, when the time came for the beginning of the contraction R, rose so far above C that RC is higher than the curves R and C

taken together. From this difference of result we may conclude that in A a strong inhibition persisted during the progress of the stimulation C, while in B there was either a preponderance of excitatory effects or no change of irritability at all. To decide between these alternatives, we have only to overload the muscle, in the manner indicated above, and so to reduce the contractions C and R to zero or to a minimal height. Adopting this method, we find that, as a matter of fact, in experiment B the excitatory effects had the upper hand.—Now the difference between the experimental conditions of A and B was this: that in A the test-stimulus was applied very near the part of the nerve stimulated by the constant current, while in B it lay nearer the muscle. Hence the experiments show that, in one and the same process of stimulation, the inhibitory effects may predominate in one portion of a nerve, and the excitatory in another.[1]

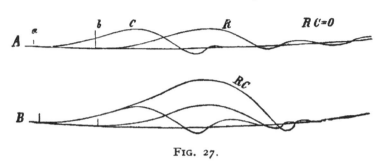

FIG. 27.

We must not omit to mention the fact that, in all these cases, it depends upon the nature of the test employed whether the one or the other of the opposed effects, the excitatory or the inhibitory, is the more clearly demonstrable. Weak stimuli are, without exception, better for the proof of inhibition, strong stimuli for that of excitation. If, however, we test the same stimulation-process with weak and strong stimuli alternately, we find in most instances that, during the greater part of its course, the excitatory and the inhibitory effects are both alike enhanced. At a phase of the stimulation-process when the effect of weak test-stimuli is wholly suppressed, the effect of strong stimuli may be increased.[2]

It follows from the above results that, if we desire to gain a quantitative expression of the relation which the inhibitory effects bear at any given moment to the excitatory, we shall best have recourse to 'isometric' contractions and to stimuli of moderate intensity, that are, on the whole,

---

[1] Experiments on the superposition of two contractions were first made by HELMHOLTZ (*Monatsber. d. Berliner Akad.*, 1854, 328). He found, in opposition to the results noted above, that there was never anything more than a simple addition of the contractions. The greater heightening of the curve of summation has, however, been confirmed by KRONECKER and STANLEY HALL (*Archiv. f. Physiologie*, 1879, Supplementband, 19 f.). The later experiments of M. VON FREY (*ibid.* 1888, 213) and J. VON KRIES (same vol. 537) also agree in all essential points with my own results.

[2] *Mechanik der Nerven*, i., 109 ff.

equally sensitive to inhibition and to excitation. Experiments made under these conditions show that the stimulation-process developing as the result of a momentary stimulus, e.g. of an electric shock or mechanical concussion, runs its course as follows. At the moment of stimulation, and for a brief period afterward, the nerve does not react to the weak test-stimulus at all; the process takes precisely the same form as it would if the stimulus had not acted.[1] If, therefore, we apply to the same point upon the nerve or to two neighbouring points, first a stimulus R (Fig. 28), then a stimulus C, and finally the two stimuli R and C together, the curve RC recorded in the third case is identical with the more intensive of the two single-stimulus curves R, C: in our illustration, with R (Fig. 28 A). We obtain the same result if we allow a very brief interval to elapse between the times of stimulation a, b. So soon as this interval becomes noticeable, however, the combined stimuli provoke a stronger contraction than either of them gives separately. Even while the time difference is less than the ordinary latent period, it not uncommonly happens that RC is greater than the sum of R and C: taken together; and the more nearly minimal the contractions, the greater does the excess become (Fig. 28 B). This enhancement of irritability increases up to a point corresponding roughly with the maximum of contraction, and then gives place to a decrease; at the same time, it can be demonstrated for a considerable period after the conclusion of the twitch. Fig. 26 (p. 70 above) gives a picture of the whole process. We may say, then, in summary, that the course of the stimulation-process is in general divisible into three stages: the stage of inexcitability, the stage of increasing, and the final stage of decreasing excitability.

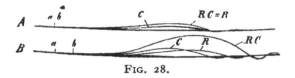

FIG. 28.

Oftentimes, however, this third stage is interrupted by a brief interval, during which irritability shows a sudden marked decrease, quickly followed by another increase. The decrease always coincides with the conclusion of the twitch. It passes so rapidly, that it can be recognised only by the increase of the latent period of the test-stimulus; and it is of regular occurrence only where the functional capacity of nerve and muscle is very high. An instance of this transitory inhibition at the conclusion of the twitch is given in Fig. 29 A. The contraction to the left corresponds to the stimulation process under investigation; the unlettered twitch to the right is the result of simple application of the test-stimulus; while RC is the twitch released by the test-stimulus under the influence of previous stimulation.

[1] *Mechanik der Nerven*, i., 63, 100.

The curves of *A* were obtained from a fresh nerve, those of *B* from a nerve that had already been subjected to repeated stimulation.[1] In this phenomenon, the period following the conclusion of the twitch forms a precise parallel to the latent period preceding contraction. In both these cases, however, it is not impossible that the result is in some measure due to

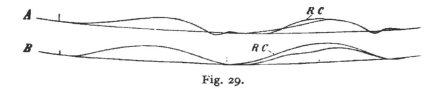

Fig. 29.

conditions residing in the muscle itself. Thus, the stage of inexcitability, which appears at the beginning of stimulation, may very possibly be attributable to the fact that the contractile substance requires a certain time to initiate a contraction. In the same way, the stage of diminished excitability that coincides with the conclusion of the twitch may be explained by the assumption that opposing influences within the muscle— already at work, perhaps, during the rapid progress of the contraction— now operate in full force. Nevertheless, the reactive effect in both stages alike must, in all probability, be regarded as a phenomenon for which nerve and muscle are jointly responsible. This view is borne out by the fact that the duration of the two stages of inhibition is largely determined by the character of the stimuli which affect the nerve. If, e.g., we apply a stimulus to a portion of nerve that lies within the sphere of operation of the anode of a constant current, the duration of the inhibitory stages is considerably lengthened.

We are now in a position to discuss the relation of the excitatory and inhibitory effects within the nerve fibre, in abstraction from the properties accruing to the reacting muscle. We may conceive of them as follows. On the occurrence of stimulation, excitatory and inhibitory effects are produced simultaneously. At first, the latter are very much the stronger. As time goes on, however, they increase more slowly, while the excitatory effects advance more quickly. Oftentimes, these last appear to maintain their ascendancy until the conclusion of the whole process. If, however, the functional capacity of the nerve is very high, the inhibitory effects may again acquire the upper hand for a brief period immediately following the conclusion of the twitch. This fact indicates, at the same time, that the process is not entirely continuous, but that the rapid result produced in contraction by the excitatory effects is always followed by an inhibitory reaction. The release of excitation thus resembles a sudden discharge, in

---

[1] *Mechanik der Nerven*, i., 86, 190, 200.

which the available forces are quickly consumed, so that for a short time the opposite effects are in the preponderance. Fig. 30 is an attempt to show this sequence of events in graphic form. Stimulation occurs at rr'. The curve ab represents the course of the excitatory, the curve cd that of the inhibitory effects; in the latter case, the intensity of the inhibition is measured by the magnitude of the downward directed (negative) ordinates of the curve cd. We assume that excitatory and inhibitory impulses are already present in the nerve, before the application of stimulus, but that they are in equilibrium. These pre-existent impulses we make proportional to the ordinates xa and xc. The curve of inhibition is char-

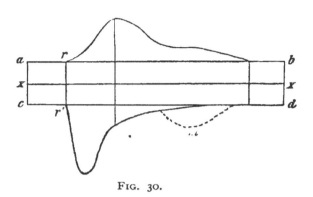

FIG. 30.

acterised by a rapid rise at its commencement, the curve of excitation by the gradual fall at its conclusion. What we term the *functional capacity* of a nerve is a function at once of excitation and of inhibition. The more functionally capable the nerve, the greater is the efficacy of both the inhibitory and the excitatory forces contained within it. In the exhausted nerve, both alike are diminished, but the inhibitory in higher degree. Here, therefore, the irritability is enhanced, and the transitory inhibitions at the conclusion of the twitch, which may perhaps be referred (as indicated by the dotted curve m) to an oscillatory repetition of the inhibitory process, are no longer observable.

(c)—*After-effects of Stimulation: Practice and Fatigue*

Our study of the changes of excitability which take place in a nerve during the process of stimulation has shown two things: that the effect produced in the nerve disappears not abruptly but quite gradually, and that it always persists for a noticeable time after the conclusion of the twitch. We have now to consider another phenomenon, which evidently proceeds from the same causes. If several stimuli are successively applied at such intervals that each falls within the period of decline of the stimulation set up by its predecessor, the irritability of the nerve is increased. Indeed, under favourable conditions this increase may be so considerable that a weak stimulus, which at first could not provoke any contraction at all, finally releases a maximal contraction. At the same time, the contractions become longer; while the longer after-effect shows further that the course of the excitation has increased not only in intensity but also in duration. These phenomena occur both with stimulation by electric shocks and with instantaneous mechanical stimuli. They are therefore bound up with the stimulation process as such; although, where electrical stimuli are employed, they undergo modification as a result of certain processes developed at the two electrodes: these processes, which we shall discuss presently, are essentially different at anode and cathode.[1] If, on the other hand, we apply the stimuli in very quick succession, so that the twitch provoked in any given case begins before the twitch released by the preceding stimulus has run its full course, we obtain the permanent contraction known by the name of tetanus, and consisting essentially of a summation of the superposed twitches.[2] This summation of contractions is here of no further interest to us; we note simply that the properties of the contractile substance have an important part to play in its origination. If we abstract from it, we may say that the phenomena of increased excitability in consequence of preceding stimuli, which we are now considering, are in the main indicative of the behaviour of the *nervous substance*; the muscle is, in all probability, concerned in their production only in so far as it resembles nerve in the general character of its irritability. This conclusion is borne out more especially by the fact that the increase of excitability by stimulation is independent of the occurrence of contraction. Where the stimulus employed is so weak that it cannot release any contraction at all, or where the muscle is so overloaded that the contraction is entirely suppressed, the increase of excitability is just as noticeable as it is when the muscle is allowed to contract. Nay more: since, under these circumstances, the phenomena of fatigue (which we discuss below) are ruled out, it becomes as a general rule still more noticeable. Taking the whole group of facts into account, we may therefore designate this increase of excitability as the elementary phenomenon of the process of *practice*. For when we speak of practice, in connexion with the function of nervous organs, we mean precisely that certain processes of excitation are facilitated: a result that can be produced most directly by an enhancement of excitability within the nerve-paths which the excitation travels. In saying this, we must, however, remember that the facts in question are facts of direct practice: that is, we must abstract from all the effects which practice can produce in other tissues,—muscles, joints, tendons, bones,—but which always make their appearance after a considerable interval; though these, in their gradual

---

[1] WUNDT, *Arch. f. Anatomie u. Physiologie*, 1859, 537; 1861, 781. *Untersuchungen zur Mechanik der Nerven*, i., 177 ff.

[2] HELMHOLTZ, *Monatsber. d. Berliner Akademie*, 1854, 328. These phenomena of summation are discussed with more accuracy of detail as regards the time-relations of the component stimuli by J. VON KRIES, in DU BOIS-REYMOND'S *Arch. f. Physiologie*, 1888, 538.

summation, constitute, of course, a very important part of the phenomena included in the usual definition of practice.

Suppose, however, that we allow the muscle to make the contractions which are the natural consequence of the stimuli applied to the nerve. We then invariably meet, after a certain lapse of time, with another phenomenon, which compensates the elementary phenomenon of practice described just now, and which presently reverses all the features of the picture. This is the phenomenon of *fatigue*. We can, therefore, observe both processes, practice and fatigue, in their simplest typical sequence, by making a muscle do work upon a weight of moderate size, which it has to lift, and by applying the stimuli at the appropriate intervals, with a brief interlude between twitch and twitch. Under these conditions, we have, first of all, the effects of practice; the functional capacity of the nerve increases, quickly at the beginning, then more slowly. Then, from a certain point onwards, the height of lift remains the same, while the duration of the contraction is quite considerably increased. After a little while, however, the height of lift decreases, and the contraction is more and more prolonged. Finally, a single stimulus shock releases a weak but very slow contraction,—similar to that provoked in the fresh muscle by the direct application of a constant galvanic current to the muscle-substance or, most markedly, by the passing of such a current through a muscle whose nervous excitability has been destroyed by curare poisoning.[1] The general character of these phenomena makes it probable that they have their principal seat, not in the nerve, but in the *muscular substance* itself. This hypothesis is, as a matter of fact, borne out by a number of different observations upon the phenomena of fatigue, which prove that they constitute, in this regard, a direct antithesis to the elementary phenomena of practice as described above. The latter can be obtained even when the muscle is entirely inactive; indeed, it is in such circumstances that they appear at their best. The fatigue phenomena, on the other hand, refuse to show themselves, so long as means are taken to prevent the contraction of the muscle during the application of stimuli to the nerve. With a sufficiently overloaded muscle, e.g., no amount of repeated stimulation will bring out the signs of fatigue. If, in this case, a test-stimulus is applied to the nerve before and after the overloading of the muscle, the resulting contraction is just the same. Similar observations have been made upon animals temporarily deprived of the use of their muscles by poisons like curare or atropin, which paralyse the terminal apparatus of the motor nerves in muscle, but leave the nerve-trunks intact. If stimuli are applied to a nerve, during the action of the poison, there is no indication of nervous fatigue.[2]

---

[1] WUNDT, *Arch. f. Anatomie u. Physiologie*, 1859, 549.
[2] BOWDITCH, *Journal of Physiology*, vi., 1887, 133. *Arch. f. Physiologie*, 1890, 505.

We must conclude from these results that the elementary phenomena of practice and fatigue are of radically different origin. The prime condition of the processes of practice is given in the nerve-substance, which is so constituted as to be very readily changed by stimulation: the change manifesting itself in a continuously increasing effectiveness of subsequent stimuli. All direct practice may be referred to this elementary phenomenon. Where it is shown by muscle, we may, in all probability, ascribe it to the nerves which the muscle contains, or to certain fundamental properties of contractile substance which nerve and muscle possess in common. With indirect practice, which appears as the result of actual, more especially of repeated exercise of function, the case is different. Here, we must admit, muscle plays a leading part: the increase of blood-supply, due to frequent repetition of contractions, means a more adequate nutrition, and consequently a higher functional capacity. These indirect effects of practice do not, however, differ in any essential respect from the changes produced in tendons, joints, bones,—increased extensibility of tendons, smoothing of articular surfaces, etc.,—by frequent repetition of the same movement. They are secondary phenomena, sharply marked off from the primary by the fact that they arise only by the mediation of changes in the blood-supply. On the other hand, the phenomena of fatigue resulting from the performance of mechanical work are as characteristic of muscle as the phenomena of practice are of nerve: they reside almost exclusively in the muscle-substance. And a like statement applies, by all analogy, to the other organs appended to the nervous system, the sense-organs and glands. Nervous substance itself seems to be, in large measure, exempt from fatigue. To explain this peculiarity, we must assume that it contains regulatory mechanisms, of a high degree of perfection, whose office is to prevent exhaustion. We have already spoken of the alternations of excitatory and inhibitory forces, evinced during the progress even of a simple process of excitation. It is these, then, we may suppose, that underlie the phenomenon of nervous inexhaustibility, guaranteeing a long period of functional activity, and protecting the nervous substance against injury of all kinds. At the same time, the inexhaustibility is, of course, a relative matter. There is good evidence that the effects of nervous exhaustion, when once it has set in, are all the more permanent, and that recuperation is all the more difficult. In view of this fact, the comparatively rapid fatigue of the peripheral organs appears in some sort as a measure of defence; it prevents any destructive consumption of nervous forces, by throwing the external instruments of nervous activity out of function before the nerves themselves are affected.

(d)—Stimulation of Nerve by the Galvanic Current

We must now devote a special paragraph to the stimulation of nerve by the constant galvanic current. We are trying to gain an idea of the processes in nerve from a consideration of the course of stimulation-phenomena at large; and the phenomena which accompany this mode of stimulation will help us to fill in various details of the picture.

In general, the galvanic current affects the nerve by way of excitation, both at make and at break; but in both cases the processes of stimulation at anode and cathode are markedly different. With currents of not excessive intensity, the processes that follow directly upon the make of the current in the neighbourhood of the cathode are of the same character as those occurring after momentary stimulation throughout the whole length of the nerve; the only difference is that the excitatory and inhibitory effects persist, with diminished intensity, so long as the current is kept closed, while at the same time the excitatory processes remain constantly in the ascendant. In the neighbourhood of the anode, on the other hand, inhibitory forces of considerable intensity make their appearance. They increase, with increasing intensity of current, far more quickly than the excitatory effects; so that with fairly strong currents, when the anode lies nearer the muscle, the inhibition there set up prevents the propagation to the muscle of the excitation beginning at the cathode. The result is that, with increased intensity of the ascending current, the making contraction very soon decreases again, and presently disappears altogether. The anodal inhibition begins at the anode as soon as the current is made, and then diffuses slowly and with gradually diminishing intensity to a considerable distance. Its rate of travel, varying with the intensity of the current, is not more than 80 to 100 mm. in the 1 sec.,—very much slower than the rate of the excitatory process, which moves with a rapidity of 26 to 32 m. It should be noted, however, that this rate increases markedly with increase in the intensity of the current, so that the inhibition finally extends into the region of the cathode. If the current is now broken, the differences present during make disappear, more or less quickly, and at the same time inhibitory effects gain a temporary ascendency at the cathode; the break-stimulation thus consists in a process of compensation. It proceeds mainly from the region of the anode, where the inhibition maintained during make is transformed into excitation,—the reversal occurring the more quickly, the stronger the current employed.

The peculiar features of the stimulation-processes released by the constant current may, then, be stated in summary as follows. The excitatory and inhibitory effects, which with other modes of stimulation are distributed uniformly throughout the nerve, here vary with the position of the electrodes: at make, the excitatory forces predominate in the neighbourhood of the cathode, the inhibitory in the neighbourhood of the anode; at break, a process of compensation sets in, which for a time exactly reverses the distribution of the two classes of effects.[1]

The phenomena of nervous stimulation are attended by other phenomena besides that of muscular work. Only the thermal and electrical changes, however, have so far been worked out in any detail. We may appeal to these to supplement, perhaps in some measure to check, the conclusions we have drawn from the phenomena of irritability. But we find, as was indicated above (p. 57), that the tale of results is exceedingly meagre. No one has as yet been able to demonstrate the occurrence of thermal changes in the nerve itself, in consequence of stimulation: but this simply means, of course, that the changes are too slight to be taken account of by our measuring instruments. On the other hand, heat is always set free when work is done by muscle, while at the same time the relation between development of heat and amount of mechanical work varies as the principle of the conservation of energy requires,—increase of mechanical energy involving decrease of the relative quantity of heat developed. This fact comes out clearly, if we so arrange an experiment that the muscle shall make maximal contractions of equal height, while lifting weights of different sizes; the greater the weight to be raised, the smaller is the amount of heat generated.[2] In contradistinction to these differences in thermal phenomena, the electrical changes accompanying the process of stimulation in nerve and muscle have been shown to be alike. In both tissues, the point of excitation always becomes negatively electrical to any other unstimulated part. These changes cannot, however, be brought at present into any intimate relation with the processes of stimulation; our knowledge of the chemical conditions upon which they depend is glaringly defective. That a certain relation exists is shown, however, by their temporal course; the rate of propagation of the current of action in the nerve-fibre coincides with the rate of propagation of the stimulation-process itself. This coincidence extends, further, to the transmission of the inhibitory processes set up by the constant current, as described above; the changes occurring at the anode also travel much more slowly than those occurring at the cathode. The latter proceed with the same rapidity as the stimulus-wave, at the rate of some 32 m. in the 1 sec.; the anodal wave of inhibition travels, as BERNSTEIN found, at the rate of only 8 to 9 m. in the 1 sec.[3]

§ 3. Theory of Nervous Excitation

The molecular state, which our general ideas of the mechanics of complex chemical processes lead us to predicate of nervous substance, was described above as a state in which there is constant performance at one and the same time of positive and negative molecular work. The positive molecular work, so soon as it gains the upper hand, will manifest itself either in disengagement of heat or in some form of external work, such as muscular con-

---

[1] PFLÜGER, *Untersuchungen über die Physiologie des Elektrotonus*, 1859. WUNDT, *Untersuchungen zur Mechanik der Nerven*, i., 223 ff.
[2] A. FICK, *Mechanische Arbeit und Wärmeentwickelung bei der Muskelthätigkeit*, 1882.
[3] BERNSTEIN, *Monatsber. d. Berliner Akademie*, 1880, 186.

traction. The negative molecular work will counteract these positive effects : heat will become latent; the progress of a muscular contraction will be inhibited. Equilibrium of the two opposed kinds of molecular work brings about the stationary condition of the nerve, during which there is no change of temperature and no accomplishment of external work. Hence, whenever we find that the action of an external stimulus releases a process which gives rise to a muscular contraction, or, for that matter, simply induces an increased irritability in presence of the test-stimulus, we may argue to an enhancement of the positive molecular work. Whenever, on the contrary, the progress of a muscular contraction is arrested, or the reaction to the test-stimulus reduced, we may be sure that the negative molecular work is in the ascendant. Whether, now, the one or the other of these effects is produced, whether, that is, the positive or the negative molecular work gains the upper hand, depends upon circumstances. We are thus led to the general conclusion that *the stimulus shock increases both the positive and the negative molecular work of the nerve.* This means, in terms of our preceding discussions, that the stimulus shock does two things : it assists the atoms of complex chemical molecules to unite in more stable connexions, while it also favours the disruption of these compounds and the return of the atoms to less stable and more complex relations. The restitution of the complex molecules corresponds to the recuperation of the nerve; the process of combustion, which ends in the formation of more stable and less readily decomposable compounds, is the source of the work which it performs, but is also the condition of its exhaustion. The only way in which the stimulus can bring about external work (muscular contraction, the excitation of nerve-cells) is by furthering the positive molecular work more effectively than the negative. The positive molecular work then becomes the source of the external work of excitation, which may be transmitted to particular organs, and so still farther transformed into other modes of work. At the same time, the positive and negative molecular work must be distributed over the course of stimulation in the sequence determined by the relation of the excitatory to the inhibitory effects. First of all, that is, there must be a storing-up of potential work, corresponding to the stage of inexcitability; the stimulus shock releases a number of molecules from their existing connexions. Thereupon begins a process of combustion, starting with the freed particles, and extending from them to the readily combustible constituents of the nerve-mass at large; during this stage a large quantity of potential is transformed into actual work. If the combustion proceeds with great rapidity, it is followed for a short time by a restitution of the complex molecules (transitory inhibitions; preponderance of negative molecular work). As a rule, however, there remains at the conclusion of the contraction a surplus of positive molecular work, which disappears only gradually; we trace it in the enhanced effect of a second stimulus supervening upon the first. It follows, then, that the same curves which we employed to illustrate the relations of excitation and inhibition (Fig. 30, p. 75) will serve here to show the relation of positive to negative molecular work. The equilibrium of the two, during the state of rest, is indicated by the equality of the initial and terminal ordinates, xa, xc and xb, xd. We must, however, suppose that the internal condition of the nerve, after the process of stimulation has run its course, is not in general precisely the same as before: there will, on the whole, have been more given out in positive work than has been acquired in negative, in potential work. Nevertheless, we must also infer, from the fact of the relative inexhaustibility of nerve, that this difference is extremely small; so that the equilibrium of forces is re-established in large measure, and in nerves of high functional capacity probably in full measure, during the actual progress of the contraction. This tendency to the *maintenance of equilibrium between positive and negative molecular work,* between loss of work-equivalents and gain of potential work, appears to be a specific property of nervous substance, founded in its chemical constitution and distinguishing it from all other tissues. It is expressed symbolically in Fig. 30, which shows the molecular processes of stimulation; the upper and lower curves each include an approximately equal area. This implies that the process of stimulation consists essentially not in a permanent disturbance of the equilibrium between positive and negative molecular work, but simply in their different distribution in time during the progress of the stimulation. The nature of this difference is given at once with the changes of irritability that can be traced from moment to moment in the figure.

We must, now, not lose sight of the fact that it is never more than a certain portion of the total sum of positive molecular work, set free in the nerve by stimulation, that is transformed into excitatory effects, or, as we may phrase it, into work of excitation; another portion may become heat, a third be changed back again into potential (negative) work. Similarly, it is only a portion of the work of excitation that is employed in the production of external stimulus effects (muscular contraction or stimulation of nerve-cells); we have seen that there is always an enhancement of irritability, both during and after the contraction. Hence a supervening stimulus will invariably find the nerve possessed of a surplus of work of excitation. If no new stimulus shock supervenes, this surplus in all probability passes over into heat. After the work of excitation has once been set up, at the point of stimulation, it exerts an influence upon neighbouring parts, where the store of molecular work is in its turn transformed in part into work of excitation, and so on. But, as we know, the process released by the momentary stimulus persists for a considerable time. Hence, while work of excitation is released, new stimulus-impulses are conveyed to the part affected from the neighbouring parts. We are in this way able to explain the heightening of excitation observable when different points of the nerve are subjected to stimulation (p. 68).

The main difference between these general stimulation-processes and stimulation by the constant current is, obviously, to be found in the uneven distribution of the sums of positive and negative molecular work which obtains in the latter case. While the current is closed, there is preponderance of negative molecular work in the neighbourhood of the anode, of positive in the region of the cathode. This difference becomes intelligible, when we remember that the resulting electrolysis must produce internal changes in the nerve-substance. At the positive electrode electronegative, at the negative electrode electropositive constituents are given off. At both places, that is, the work of the electric current produces dissociation. The immediate consequence is, that work must disappear; but as soon as the wandering partial molecules tend to enter into more stable compounds than those from which they have been separated, the positive molecular work may begin to increase, that is, a part of the work which has disappeared may be set free again. The phenomena of stimulation lead us to infer that the first of these processes takes place regularly in the neighbourhood of the cathode, the second in the region of the anode. The precise chemical changes involved are as yet unknown to us; but the phenomena of electrolysis supply an abundance of analogous instances of the interchange of forces. Thus, in the electrolysis of stannous chloride, we have at the cathode a deposition of tin, in which the work employed for its separation remains stored as potential work, while at the anode we obtain chlorine, which at once unites with the stannous chloride to form stannic chloride, liberating heat in the process. Similar results may appear in all cases where the products of electrolysis are liable to chemical interaction. At break of a current passing through a length of nerve, on the other hand, a less well-marked process of electrolytic decomposition sets in, as a consequence of its polarisation, in a direction opposed to that of the original current. This, together with the gradual compensation of the chemical differences, occasions the phenomena of the break-stimulation.

We may say a word, in conclusion, of the relation of the processes whose general mechanism we have here described to the electrical changes in the stimulated nerve. It is a noteworthy fact that the current of action which follows upon a momentary stimulation of the nerve reaches its conclusion, on the average, as early as 0·0006 to 0·0007 sec. after the application of the stimulus,[1] and therefore falls completely within the period of nervous in-

---

[1] According to BERNSTEIN's investigations, PFLÜGER's *Arch. f. d. ges. Physiol.*, i., 190; *Untersuchungen über den Erregungsvorgang im Nerven- und Muskelsysteme*, 1871, 30.

excitability.[1] It would appear, then, that the variation is connected with the inhibitory forces, or with the passage of positive into negative molecular work. We must, however, have further information, as regards the character of this connexion, before we can think of turning the electrical processes to theoretical account.

The phrases 'positive' and 'negative molecular work' are meant to suggest the general line of thought followed by the science of mechanical energy or, as we may put it more briefly, by mechanical energetics. Modern physiologists not infrequently substitute for them the words 'assimilation' and 'dissimilation,' antithetical terms borrowed from the vocabulary of metabolic phenomena, and thence transferred to that of the general mechanics of the nervous system. It is, the author hopes, hardly necessary to point out in this place that the words and phrases employed in the text are not translations back again from the language of physiological chemistry into that of mechanics; though such an idea might possibly arise, in view of the popularity of the antithesis 'assimilation-dissimilation' at the present time and the variety of contexts in which it appears. The contrary is true: the phraseology adopted in the text, and modelled upon that of a general mechanical energetics, was followed in the first edition of this work (1874) and in the still earlier "Untersuchungen zur Mechanik der Nerven" (i., 1871), before the terms 'assimilation' and 'dissimilation' had begun to play their part in physiology. Its retention in the present edition is not due to any prejudice on the author's part in favour of the original form in which his thought was cast, but rather to the objections which he feels may be urged against the alternative wording. The processes of metabolism which, for want of more precise terms, we name tentatively 'assimilation' and 'dissimilation' are, apart from the effects from which these names are derived, altogether unknown to us; and the effects themselves are simply that, in the one case, an existing tissue is reinforced by complex tissue-materials of the same order, while, in the other, existing tissue-materials are brought to disappearance. We have good ground for the assumption that, in dissimilation, the decomposition of the complex molecules, and the combustion-processes resulting from it, have the upper hand; and we may suppose that in assimilation, conversely, the chemical processes introduced are predominantly synthetic in character. But when we ask how in detail the interchange of energy is effected in the two cases, the reply is that as regards dissimilation very little, and as regards assimilation practically nothing is known. The various processes involved certainly do not conform to any simple pattern, but depend upon a series of chemical interactions so complicated that at present we have no means of tracing them. This complication is vouched for by the fact, now fairly well established for all such processes, that in dissimilation there is a constant interplay of decomposition and recomposition; existing chemical connexions are dissolved, and new compounds formed, in continual interdependence. As a rule, energy is liberated during these dissimilations, in the form of heat or of mechanical work. But, again, we cannot say which phase of the dissimilation process is responsible for this result; nor do we know if a similar interchange

---

[1] The negative variation of the muscle-current is of somewhat longer duration; it lasts approximately 0·004 sec. (BERNSTEIN, *Untersuchungen*, 64.) This time, however, also falls within the limits of the period of inexcitability.

of energy is necessarily involved in every instance of dissimilation, or if there may not be processes, whose chemical effects would lead us to class them with the others as dissimilations, but whose general and final effect is accompanied by a transformation of energy in the opposite sense. Our knowledge of the chemism of the metabolic processes is, in the author's opinion, far too defective to permit of our answering these questions. The theory of assimilation and dissimilation thus attempts to illuminate the processes in the nervous system by analogies that are more obscure than the processes themselves ; and such a proceeding can hardly inspire confidence. It is sometimes said that dissimilation is the correlate of fatigue, and assimilation of recuperation. But to say this is, after all, merely to set in place of certain complex symptoms conditions that are at least as complex, and far less open to demonstration.[1] Fatigue and recuperation are symptomatic terms whose meaning is, roughly at any rate, clear to everyone. It is, as we have seen, highly probable that the metabolic processes which give rise to both groups of symptoms are extremely complicated. When we consider, therefore, that the words 'assimilation' and 'dissimilation' used to denote these processes are words that have no chemical significance, but are in the last resort purely teleological concepts, we cannot but suspect that the symptomatic terms 'fatigue' and 'recuperation' are simply coming back to us in changed form. If we wish to analyse these latter in detail, there are, as it seems to the author, but two ways open, in the present state of our knowledge. We may, on the one hand, limit ourselves to the symptoms, but, while we do this, attempt so far as may be to reduce the phenomena, given in an extremely complicated syndromus, to their simplest components. We thus discover that every process of fatigue and recuperation contains two elementary terms, variously interrelated in the particular case,—excitation and inhibition. Or, on the other hand, we may attempt to refer the effects in question to the more general concepts furnished by mechanical energetics. We then arrive at the notion of positive and negative molecular work, in the sense in which these phrases have been employed in the text. This restriction of the hypothetical foundations of nerve physiology to straightforward physical analogies appears to the author to be especially desirable, in view of the great extension of the rival terms. We find the antithesis of 'assimilation' and 'dissimilation' in the most diverse contexts,—in the theory of visual sensations, in the theory of auditory sensations, applied to all other conceivable physiological and psychophysical phenomena. It almost seems, indeed, as if this pair of terms is gradually coming to play the part in modern physiology that was played in SCHELLING's nature-philosophy, at the beginning of the nineteenth century, by the phrase "polar opposites," which found application not only to electricity, magnetism and chemical process, but also to sensibility and irritability, light and darkness, and many other things besides.

§ 4. Influence of the Central Parts upon the Processes of Excitation

(a)—Course of the Reflex Excitation

We begin our investigation of the processes in the central nervous substance by stimulating a peripheral nerve, and endeavouring to find out how the course of stimulation is altered, if it is compelled to pass through central

---

[1] BIEDERMANN, Elektrophysiologie, 1895, 71 ff.

elements. The easiest way to perform this experiment is to avail ourselves of the phenomenon of reflex excitation. We first of all apply an electric shock of the proper intensity to a motor nerve root, whose connexion with the myel on the one hand and with its dependent group of muscles on the other is kept intact; and we then stimulate, in the same way, the central end of some sensory root. The two twitches are recorded by the muscle, and the experiment is so arranged that the times of stimulation correspond to the same point upon the axis of abscissas of the two muscle-curves. The differences in appearance and progress of the two contractions then give us a measure of the influence exerted by the intercalated central substance.

The first thing that we observe, under these circumstances, is that much stronger stimuli are required to produce contraction by way of the sensory root. If we make our shocks as nearly instantaneous as may be, e.g. by using induction-shocks, we shall frequently find it impossible to release any reflex contraction whatsoever; the currents required are of such intensity that their employment would bring with it the danger of leakage to the myel.[1] Provided, however, that the reflex irritability is high enough to permit of our making the experiment, we obtain two curves which repeat, on a greatly enlarged scale, the same characteristics that distinguish the curves obtained in a previous experiment by stimulation of a motor nerve at two points unequally distant from the muscle (cf. Fig. 24, p. 67). The reflex twitch is extraordinarily late in appearing, and is of much longer duration. Suppose, e.g., that we stimulate a motor and a sensory root which enter the myel at the same height and on the same side, and that we so regulate the stimuli as to equalise the heights of the muscle curves; we get the result shown in Fig. 31. The only marked difference between these contractions

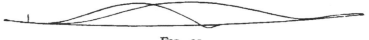

FIG. 31.

and those released from different points upon the motor nerve is that a stronger and not a weaker stimulus must be employed, to bring the reflex contraction to the same height as the other. The differences in the course of the excitation are, however, in this instance so considerable, that no increase in the intensity of stimulus is able to change their character. It is true that intensification of stimulus increases not only the height but also the duration of the contractions, while decreasing the latent period. But

[1] It is therefore advisable, in order to induce a reflex excitability that shall suffice for experimental series of some length, to help things out by minimal doses (0·002 to at most 0·004 mg.) of strychnine. I have convinced myself, by experiments specially directed upon the point, that minimal quantities of this poison do not affect the temporal course of the reflex contractions. See *Untersuchungen zur Mechanik der Nerven und Nervencentren*, ii., 1876, 9.

the weakest reflex contractions are always noticeable by their long duration, and the strongest by the length of their latent period, even when we compare the former with the strongest and the latter with the weakest direct contractions.[1] It is clear, now, that the time which the stimulation requires to pass from a sensory into a motor root is given by the interval separating the beginnings of the two contractions, the direct and the reflex. The nerve-roots are so short, that the portion of this interval taken up by the peripheral conduction may be considered negligible; and we may accordingly designate the interval, as a whole, the *reflex time*. To determine it, we must —since the latent period is dependent upon the intensity of the stimuli— have recourse once more, as we did in our measurement of the rate of propagation in the nerves, to experiments in which the muscle-curves are of the same height.

This presupposed, we may proceed to investigate the reflex time under various conditions. The simplest case is shown in Fig. 31, where the stimulation is transferred from a sensory root to a motor root belonging to the same nerve-trunk: we may term this the case of same-sided reflex excitation. Next in order comes the propagation of stimulus from a sensory root to a motor root which leaves the myel at the same height but upon the opposite side: we term this the case of crossed reflex excitation. In the third place, we may have propagation along the length of the myel, which we may call the longitudinal conduction of reflexes; as, e.g., in the transference from the sensory root of a nerve of the arm to the motor root of a nerve of the lower extremities. In no one of these three cases is the reflex time sensibly dependent upon the intensity of the excitations. It is, as might have been predicted, relatively shortest for same-sided reflex excitation, where under normal circumstances it amounts to 0·008 to 0·015 sec. It is, however, as one would be less likely to expect, relatively greater with crossed than with longitudinal conduction. Thus, if we compare the crossed with the same-sided reflex, there is an average difference to the disadvantage of the former of some 0·004 sec. If we then compare the reflex released in the thigh by stimulation of the root of a sensory nerve of the arm with the same-sided reflex, the difference between the two times is as a rule somewhat smaller.[2] Since the path travelled by the stimulation in the latter case is at least six to eight times as long as that traversed in the former, it is evident that the retardation in crossed conduction is much more serious than it is in longitudinal conduction. An explanation is, without any doubt, to be found in the fact that longitudinal conduction (as we shall see presently, in Chapter v., when we come to discuss the morphology of the myel) is sub-

---

[1] Exceptions to this rule may occur, though very rarely, in cases of maximal reflex excitation and minimal motor stimulation: *op. cit.*, 21.

[2] *Op. cit.*, 14, 30, 37.

served for the most part by the fibres of the white substance, while crossed conduction must be mediated almost exclusively by the cell-reticulum of the grey substance. We have, then, in the results of this set of experiments, a confirmation of the inference, already suggested as probable by the long duration of the reflex time, that *the central elements offer incomparably more resistance than the nerve-fibres to the progress of an excitation.* The same conclusion may be drawn from the further fact that a retardation of conduction, amounting on the average to 0·003 sec., occurs in the spinal ganglia of the frog; and again from the related observation that the sensory nerve roots are more irritable than the nerve-fibres below the spinal ganglia. It is noteworthy, in connexion with this latter result, that the ramifications of the sensory nerves in the skin are, in their turn, more easily excitable than the nerve-branches that run to the skin. Just, then, as there are mechanisms in the spinal ganglia which diminish the irritability of the incoming nerves, so must there be mechanisms in the skin which discharge a precisely opposite function. It follows from all this that the *irritability of the nerve-trunks and their branches is reduced to a minimum*: a characteristic, we need hardly say, that is eminently fitted to protect the central organs from the advent of useless sensory excitations.[1]

(b)—*Enhancement of Reflex Excitability*

The temporal relations of reflex conduction have made it appear probable that the central elements, while on the one hand they offer greater resistance to incoming excitations, are able, on the other, to develope a greater amount of stored energy. This hypothesis is confirmed by many other facts. We notice, first of all, that in almost every case, where the excitability of the myel is not enhanced by artificial means,[2] a single, momentary stimulus-shock is unable to release a reflex contraction. To obtain a response, we must repeat the stimulation; and the contraction thus set up usually takes on a tetanic character.[3] Within certain limits, the reflex makes its appearance after the same number of single stimulations, whether these be given in quick or slow succession. On the other hand, the duration of a

---

[1] *Op. cit.*, 45 f.
[2] Cf. Note 1, p. 86, above.
[3] KRONECKER and STIRLING, *Berichte d. k. sächs. Ges. d. Wissensch. zu Leipzig, math.-phys. Cl.*, 1874, 372. These observers declare, further, that the reflex twitch is invariably distinguished from the simple muscle-contraction by its more tetanic character (*Arch. f. Physiologie*, 1878, 23). I cannot follow them in this statement. It may evidently be explained by the fact that KRONECKER and STIRLING did not avail themselves of the minimal doses of poison, referred to above, and were therefore obliged to use stronger stimuli for the excitation of reflexes. I would not, however, be understood to maintain that any hard and fast line can be drawn between simple contraction and tetanus at large. On the contrary, the acceleration of the course of the simple muscle-contraction, in its ascending branch, proves that even in it several successive excitatory impulses are at work.

reflex tetanus is not directly dependent upon the duration of the stimulation, as is that of the contraction aroused by tetanic excitation of the motor-nerve. If the stimulation be of short duration, the tetanus outlasts it; if it be of longer duration, the tetanus disappears earlier than the stimulation itself.[1] Another phenomenon, that shows very clearly the differences in excitability between the peripheral and the central nervous substance, is the following. If we stimulate the motor-nerve by induction-shocks, repeated with not too great rapidity, the corresponding muscle falls, as was first pointed out by HELMHOLTZ,[2] into vibrations of the same frequency. These may be perceived as a tone, or may be recorded, by means of a fitting instrument, upon a cylinder which rotates with uniform speed. If, now, we stimulate the myel in the same way, the muscle again falls into vibrations, but the frequency of vibration is considerably diminished. Fig. 32 shows two curves of vibration obtained from the muscle of a rabbit by KRONECKER and HALL. With 42 stimuli in the 1 sec., the muscle traced the upper curve when the motor nerve was stimulated, the lower, when the stimulation was applied to the myel, which had been severed below the oblongata.[3] Closely connected with this is BAXT's observation that voluntary movements, however simple they may be made, always last a considerably longer time than simple contractions, released by the stimulation of a motor nerve. BAXT found, e.g., in experiments upon himself, that the index finger of the right hand, moving in response to stimulation by the induction current, required on the average 0·166 sec., while movement initiated by voluntary innervation required 0·296 sec.[4]

FIG. 32.

We can easily see the reason for the greater effect produced upon the myel by frequent repetition of the stimulus. Every stimulation leaves behind it an *enhanced reflex excitability*. Here, again, however, the central substance merely exhibits, on a larger scale, phenomena with which we are already familiar in the case of the peripheral nerve. On the other hand, there are certain chemical effects, that are able in some unknown way to produce a similar change of irritability, which appear to be peculiar to the central nerve-substance. The agents in these effects are termed 'reflex poisons'; the chief place among them is taken by strychnine, which brings about the changes in question with unfailing certainty. Strychnine prob-

---

[1] BEAUNIS, *Rech. expér. sur les conditions de l'activité cérébrale et sur la physiologie des nerfs*, 1884, 106.
[2] HELMHOLTZ, *Monatsberichte d. Berliner Akademie*, 1864, 307.
[3] KRONECKER and STANLEY HALL, *Arch. f. Physiologie*, 1879, Supplementband, 12. Similar observations are recorded by HORSLEY and SCHAEFER (*Journ. of Physiology*, vii. 96), and, on the human subject, by GRIFFITH (*ibid.*, ix. 39).
[4] HELMHOLTZ and BAXT, *Monatsber. d. Berliner Akad.*, 1867, 228; 1870, 184. Experiments by VON KRIES (*Arch. f. Physiol.*, 1886, Supplementband, 1 ff.) gave like results.

ably owes its power in this regard to the circumstance that its effect is limited almost exclusively to the central substance of the myel; whereas other nerve-poisons set up changes in the peripheral nerves, or in higher nerve-centres, which may serve, in greater or less degree, to counteract the effect under discussion.[1]

The action of these poisons is, in general, as follows. (1) Much weaker stimuli are sufficient to release a reflex contraction; indeed, a point is very soon reached, at which the reflex irritability becomes greater than the irritability of the motor nerve. (2) Even when the stimuli are reduced to the lowest limit of effectiveness, the contraction is higher and, in particular, of longer duration than under normal conditions; if the effect of the poison be increased, it passes over into a tetanic contraction. (3) The beginning of the contraction is more and more delayed; so that the latent period may have more than twice its ordinary duration. At the same time, the difference in the length of the latent period with strong and weak stimuli is enormously increased: when the action of the poison is at its height, the reflex tetanus hardly shows any difference of degree, whether the weakest or the strongest stimuli be applied, but in the former case sets in with extraordinary slowness. An illustration of these changes is given in Fig.

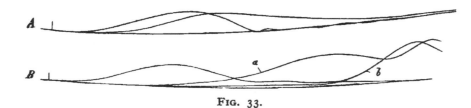

FIG. 33.

33. The curve A was taken as the action of the poison was beginning; the curves B, when it was at its full height: a was released by a strong, b by a weak momentary stimulus: in both cases a direct contraction has been recorded, for purposes of comparison. There can be no doubt that this lengthening of the latent period is directly connected with the enhancement of irritability. When the central substance is modified by the poison, the after-effect of the stimulus is prolonged, so that the excitation can be released after the initial inhibition has been overcome. The phenomenon is somewhat like that of the summation of stimulations, only that here the external stimulus is not repeated. We must, accordingly, suppose that the stimulus brings about a number of successive stimulations, whose summation presently leads to excitation. This suggests the idea that the processes of molecular inhibition are not sensibly changed by the alteration of the

[1] *Untersuchungen zur Mechanik der Nerven*, ii., 64.

nervous substance, but that the positive molecular work is seriously affected. In the normal state, it returns to the potential form, in whole or in great part, immediately after its liberation; in the present instance, it appears to be recovered but gradually. We may note that similar, though weaker, effects are produced on the myel by the action of cold.[1]

(c)—*Inhibitions of Reflexes by Interference of Stimuli*

We have spoken so far only of the influences which enhance the excitability of the central elements. Here, however, just as in the case of the nerve-fibre, the excitatory are paralleled by inhibitory effects. The fact that first drew attention to these inhibitions is a discovery of old standing in physiology: the fact that the reflex excitability of the myel is increased after removal of the brain. SETSCHENOW, starting out from this fact, found that the stimulation of certain parts of the brain in the frog,—thalamus, bigemina, medulla,—prevents or delays the appearance of the reflexes.[2] He was therefore inclined to think that the inhibitory function is confined to certain definite central parts. Further experiments showed, however, that the same effect is produced by the stimulation of other sensory nerves, or of the sensory columns of the myel;[3] so that it became necessary, in terms of SETSCHENOW's hypothesis, to suppose that these specific inhibitory centres are distributed over almost the entire cerebrospinal organ. But if any given sensory excitation may be inhibited by the stimulation of any other sensory element, the sphere of inhibition—as GOLTZ justly observed[4]—becomes coextensive with the sphere of sensory excitation; and the assumption of specific inhibitory centres falls to the ground. At the same time, while any possible sort of sensory stimulation, whether it affect other sensory nerves or sensory central parts, may arrest the progress of a reflex

---

[1] *Op. cit.*, 56 f. ROSENTHAL (*Monatsber. d. Berliner Akad.*, 1873, 104; 1875, 419) speaks of a *decrease* of the latent period in strychnine tetanus, and BIEDERMANN (*Elektrophysiologie*, 1895, 501) accepts his statement. I do not understand this result; though with a high degree of strychnine poisoning, and with stimuli of moderate intensity, the increase of the latent period is not so pronounced as to be obvious at once, without the aid of some chronometric instrument.

[2] SETSCHENOW, *Physiol. Studien über die Hemmungsmechanismen für die Reflexthätigkeit des Rückenmarks*, 1863. SETSCHENOW and PASCHUTIN, *Neue Versuche am Hirn und Rückenmark des Frosches*, 1865.

[3] HERZEN, *Sur les centres modérateurs de l'action réflexe*, 1864, 32. SETSCHENOW, *Ueber die elektrische und chemische Reizung der sensibeln Rückenmarksnerven*, 1868, 40.

[4] GOLTZ, *Beiträge zur Lehre von den Functionen der Nervencentren des Frosches*, 1869, 44, 50. That other parts of the brain, besides those designated by SETSCHENOW, are able to inhibit reflexes, was demonstrated by GOLTZ in his croak experiment. Frogs whose cerebral hemispheres have been removed may be made to croak, with almost mechanical certainty, by a gentle stroking of the skin of the back; while with uninjured animals the same procedure very frequently fails of its effect. It appears, then, that the cerebral hemispheres also have the power of inhibiting reflexes (GOLTZ, *op. cit.*, 41). Experiments made by LANGENDORFF (*Arch. f. Physiol.*, 1877, 133) and BÖTTICHER (*Ueber Reflexhemmung*, in *Sammlung physiol. Abhandl.*, ii. Reihe, Heft 3) show that the same result may be obtained by blinding the animals.

excitation, the inhibitory effect is not by any means invariably produced ; the supervening stimulation may, on the contrary, enhance the reflex,—as always happens, of course, when two excitations meet in some motor fibre, or in a motor central area. Let us term the meeting of two excitations in the same central territory, quite generally, an interference of stimulations. Then the result of such interference is dependent upon four things. It depends (1) upon the phase to which the one excitation has attained when the other begins. If the muscle contraction released by the first stimulation is still in course, or only just over, when the second arrives, we have as a rule an enhancement of the stimulus-effect. If, on the other hand, the original stimulation occurred some time before the application of the second, this latter is more easily inhibited. It depends (2) upon the intensity of the stimuli. Strong interference-stimuli inhibit a given reflex excitation more easily than weak ; sometimes, indeed, strong stimuli will inhibit the same excitation that weak stimuli enhance. It depends (3) upon the spatial relation of the nerve-fibres stimulated. Sensory fibres that enter the myel at the same height and upon the same side, i.e. that belong originally to one and the same nerve-trunk, effect a much weaker inhibition (or, in other terms, are much more ready to enhance the excitation) than fibres that come in from different sides or at different levels. Lastly, it depends (4) upon the state of the central organ. The more completely the normal functional capacity is preserved, the more certainly, other conditions being favourable, may one look for inhibition of the reflexes ; the more the functions of the organ have been impaired by cold, by strychnine or other reflex poisons, by loss of nervous force due to fatigue, malnutrition, etc., the more likely is it that an enhancement of stimulation will take the place of inhibition. This decrease of inhibition is evidenced, first of all, by the fact that stimuli of longer duration and greater intensity are required to evoke it. It always disappears first with stimulation of the nerve-fibres belonging to the same root ; but in a state of extreme functional incapacity, or of serious derangement by cold or strychnine, it disappears altogether, so that no inhibitory symptoms can be observed at all.[1]

It is, perhaps, tempting to think of these inhibitory effects due to an interference of oscillatory stimulus-motions, analogous to the interference of light and sound vibrations ; to conceive, i.e., that the stimulus-waves meet together and, in whole or part, cancel one another.[2] Such an hypothe-

---

[1] *Untersuchungen*, etc., ii., 84 ff., 106 ff. Morphine, on the other hand, seems, at a certain stage of its action, to increase the central inhibitions. For it was found by HEIDENHAIN and BUBNOFF that the contractions produced in animals by stimulation of the motor-areas of the cerebral cortex were, in the normal state, enhanced, but in morphine narcosis inhibited, by mechanical stimulation of the skin. See PFLÜGER's *Arch. f. d. ges. Physiol.*, xxvi., 137 ff.

[2] E. CYON has turned this idea to account for a theory of the central inhibitions: *Bulletin de l'Acad. de St. Pétersbourg*, vii., Decr., 1870. The facts which he adduces

sis is, however, wholly unable to explain the simple effacement of excitation that occurs, e.g., in the ventral nerve-cells of the myel, when the motor fibres issuing from them are stimulated. Moreover, it gains no support from the known facts of the course of excitation. On the contrary, the varying results of stimulus-interference indicate, quite clearly, that *in the stimulation of the central elements*, as in that of the nerve-fibre, *excitatory and inhibitory effects are released at one and the same time*. It is also clear, however, that the phenomena of inhibition are in this case much more pronounced than they are in the peripheral nerve-fibre. The special conditions under which the two opposed results of central stimulation are obtained make it probable, further, that the external effect of inhibition is produced more particularly when the stimuli are so conducted as to interfere in the same *sensory* central area; whereas summation of stimuli seems to occur whenever the excitation travels from different sensory central areas, simultaneously stimulated, to the same *motor* elements. In general, both of these effects may be produced, side by side, by the simultaneous stimulation of any different sensory elements; and it will depend upon the special circumstances whether the one or the other of them gains the upper hand.

(d)—Chronic Effects of Excitation and Inhibition : Positive and Negative Tonus

If we inquire into the nature of these special circumstances, we find as the most important, the connexions in which the various nervous elements stand with one another and with their appended organs. This conclusion is suggested at once by certain phenomena observed in nerves and muscles whose functional connexion with their central points of origin has remained intact. Thus, in the first place, a muscle which is united by its nerve to the central organ is kept permanently in a certain tension, which ceases at once, as may be observed in the slight lengthening of the loaded muscle, when the nerve is cut through.[1] This permanent tension in the state of rest is known as the *tonus* of a muscle. Its disappearance when the nerve is cut indicates that it has its ground in a chronic excitation of the nerve, transmitted to the fibre from the central elements. Its maintenance seems to depend, further, upon the connexions in which the central elements stand with one another. For the tonic excitation which travels to the skeletal muscles along the motor nerves of the myel may be abrogated, not only by section of the motor nerves themselves, but also by section of the sensory roots of the spinal nerves.[2] We must therefore

in support of it, so far as they are taken from the phenomena of vascular innervation, have been called in question by HEIDENHAIN. PFLÜGER's *Arch. f. d. ges. Physiol.*, iv., 551.

[1] BRONDGEEST, *Over den Tonus der willekeurigen Spieren*, Utrecht, 1860.
[2] CYON, *Berichte d. k. sächs. Ges. d. Wiss., math.-phys. Cl.*, 1865, 86. Cf. on the other side, G. HEIDENHAIN, in PFLÜGER's *Arch. f. d. ges. Physiol.*, iv., 1871, 435.

suppose that a portion of the forces which release the excitation reach the motor nerve-cells only by way of their connexions with sensory elements; while the related observation, often made and confirmed, that tonus persists after the severance of such sensory connexions, points us to the cells of origin of the motor nerve-fibres as a co-ordinate and independent source of excitatory forces. On the other hand, however, the central elements appear also under certain conditions, according to the circumstances in which they are placed by their nearer or more remote connexion with other like elements, to generate, and to transmit to their peripheral continuations, a surplus of *inhibitory* forces. Here, e.g., belongs the observation that increase of tonus in a determinate muscle-group is regularly followed by decrease of tension in the antagonists: so that increased excitation of the flexor muscles of a limb brings with it a decrease of excitation in the extensors, and conversely.[1] We may term this phenomenon that of negative tonicity. It then becomes evident that the two opposing forms of tonus may be brought into relation with the fundamental phenomena of excitation and inhibition, which we have seen to be observable, first in the peripheral nerve, and then, on an enlarged scale, throughout the central organs of the nervous system. We have only to add, what is shown by all these observations, that the continual shift of government from excitation to inhibition, and back again, is very largely dependent upon the influences to which the central elements are subjected, in virtue of their connexion with other like elements and with the stimulation processes which these latter convey to them.

§ 5. Theory of Central Innervation

(a)—*General Theory of the Molecular Processes in the Nerve-Cell*

The phenomena of central innervation have referred us to the same two classes of opposed molecular effects that we traced in the process of excitation in the nerve-fibre. The general view that we were led to take of this latter will, therefore, serve as our point of departure in the present instance. We begin, accordingly, by postulating for the central substance a stationary condition, similar to that which we assumed in the nerve-fibre; a condition, i.e., in which there is an equilibrium of positive and negative molecular work. The application of stimulus, here as before, means an increase in the amount of both forms of work. But everything points to the conclusion that, in the nerve-cell, there is at first a marked prepon-

---

[1] H. E. HERING and SHERRINGTON, in PFLÜGER's *Arch. f. d. ges. Physiol.*, lxviii., 1897, 222 ff.

derance in the increase of the negative molecular work; so that a momentary stimulus-shock is, as a rule, unable to release any excitation whatever. If, however, the stimuli are repeated, then, as one follows another, the amount of negative molecular work is gradually diminished, in proportion to the positive, until at last this latter attains such dimensions that excitation arises. We may therefore suppose that the typical process of stimulation in a nerve-cell is analogous to that set up at the anode in a nerve-fibre by the making of a constant current. Under the action of the stimulus, the processes which transform more stable into less stable compounds, i.e. which subserve the storage of potential work, are thrown into increased activity. There is, however, a difference. When the current is applied to the nerve, its electrolytic action introduces decomposition-processes which do not normally take place in the nerve-fibre. When, on the other hand, the nerve-cell is stimulated, we have no right to assume anything more than an enhancement of activity which, under ordinary circumstances, is directed mainly upon the formation of complex chemical molecules, i.e. upon the accumulation of potential work. This difference between nerve-fibre and central substance, whose importance is sufficiently evident, is attested by other physiological considerations. The nerve-cells are really the laboratories, in which the materials that compose the nerve-mass are prepared. In the nerve-fibres, these materials are very largely consumed, in consequence of physiological function, but—if we abstract from the inadequate and partial restitution which accompanies decomposition in every case of stimulation—cannot, obviously, be reformed. For the fibres, if we separate them from their cells of origin, lose their nervous constituents, and the renewal of these proceeds always from the central points.[1] Even in the state of functional inactivity, therefore, the interchange of materials and forces within the nerve-cell is not in perfect equilibrium. But the balance dips on the one side in the cell, on the other in the fibre. Characteristic of the nerve is the formation of definitive products of combustion, with the performance of positive work; characteristic of the cell is the production of compounds of high complexity, in which potential work is stored. It is true that the work done in the animal body, as a whole, is pre-eminently positive work, the combustion of the complex organic compounds; but it is altogether wrong to look upon this as the only means for the interchange of forces and materials within the organism. There are always going on, alongside of the positive work, reductions, dissolutions of more stable into less stable compounds, with the resulting accumulation of potential work. The nervous system, in particular, is the scene of great activity in this regard. The compounds which enter into the formation of nervous substance are, in some cases, more complex,

---

[1] Cf. p. 53, above.

and possessed of a higher combustion-value, than the nutritive materials from which they are derived; that is, are compounds in which a large amount of potential work is stored up.[1] The nerve-cells, the architects of these compounds, are in a certain sense akin to the plant-cells. These, too, accumulate potential work, which may remain latent until need arises, and then be transformed back again into actual work. The nerve-cells, in the same way, are the storehouses in which materials are laid up for future use. And the chief consumers of these stores are the peripheral nerves and their terminal organs.

Putting all this together, we may gain some idea of the relation obtaining between the central substance and the nerve-fibres that issue from it. We have, first of all, the transmission from cell to fibre of those molecular motions that we term processes of excitation. But this is by no means all. There is, further, a constant movement of material, in the direction from centre to periphery; so that the fibre is in continual receipt of substances in which potential work is stored up. Here, it is plain, we have the explanation of the *nutritive* influence which the central substance everywhere exerts upon the nerve-fibres connected with it, and, through their mediation, upon the organs which they supply. This nutritive function belongs to all nerve-centres and nerve-fibres, and is intimately connected with the general mechanics of central innervation. The hypothesis that there is a special class of nerves, specially devoted to trophic functions, seems therefore to have nothing in its favour. The conditions under which this movement of material takes place must, however, necessarily react upon the phenomena of irritability and the course of excitation. Suppose, e.g., that a certain central area has enjoyed a long period of rest, and has consequently accumulated a large store of potential work. The actual work, sensory or motor, done in this area itself and in the nerve-fibres connected with it will, in general, be more intensive and of longer duration than would have been the case under different conditions. It is, also, not improbable that the movement of material may serve to develope neurodynamic interaction between adjoining central parts, as a result of which the actual work done at any given point may be increased by the conveyance of potential work from neighbouring points.[2]

The differences in the response of the nerve-cells to the stimuli conducted to them proves, further, that every cell is divided into two distinct regions, the one of which resembles in excitability the peripheral nerve-substance, while the other shows a marked degree of divergence. We will term the former the *peripheral*, the latter the *central region of the nerve-cell*.

[1] Cf. pp. 55 f., above.
[2] Cf. the discussions in Part V. of the abnormal enhancement of excitability in the cerebral cortex, which presumably underlies certain forms of derangement of consciousness (dream, hypnosis).

The central region, we may suppose, is devoted pre-eminently to the formation of the complex compounds of which the nervous substance is composed; it is, therefore, the place of storage of potential work. A stimulus-movement conducted to it simply accelerates the molecular processes in the direction in which they are already moving, and accordingly disappears without external effect. It is different with the peripheral region. Here, too, something is done towards the transformation of actual into potential work. But, besides this, there is already a fairly rapid consumption of materials, derived in part from the central region, and a consequent production of work. If a stimulus strikes this peripheral region, its first result is, again, a relatively greater increase of the negative than of the positive molecular work. But the negative soon sinks back to its ordinary level, while the positive persists for a considerable time; so that, perhaps after an unusually long latent period, certainly if the original stimulus is reinforced by new stimulus-impulses, it is able to produce an excitation. For the rest, here as in the nerve, it is only a portion of the positive molecular work that passes over into work of excitation, and again only a portion of this that shows itself in external excitatory effects; another portion may be transformed back again into negative molecular work, and the work of excitation may be changed, in whole or part, into other forms of molecular motion. Further, when once excitation has arisen, the accumulated work of excitation is consumed very rapidly; the process suggests that of explosive decomposition. At the same time, the greater strength of the inhibition has meant the storage of a correspondingly greater amount of work of excitation; so that the stimulus-effect, when it appears, is greater than in the case of nerve-stimulation. In this respect, the irritable region of the nerve-cell stands to the peripheral nervous system in somewhat the same relation that a steam-boiler with stiffly working valve bears to a similar boiler whose valve moves easily. The expansive force of the steam must be much more considerable, in the former case, if the valve is to be opened; but, when this is done, the steam rushes out with a correspondingly greater force. It should be added that the peripheral region of the nerve-cell probably evinces a different conduct in different cases, approaching sometimes more, sometimes less nearly to the character of the peripheral nerve-substance. Thus, the sensory excitations conducted upward by the cells of the dorsal cornua of the myel are certainly less changed than the reflex excitations which are mediated as well by the cells of the ventral cornua. These differences may be conditioned upon the number of central cells which the stimulation has to traverse. But it is also conceivable that there is a continuous transition from the one to the other of the two cell-regions which we have named the central and the peripheral, and that certain fibrils terminate in middle regions, in which inhibition is not yet complete, while at the same time difficulties are placed in the path of the stimulation.

We are now in a position to interpret the peculiar enhancement of reflex excitability produced by the repetition of stimulus or by the action of poisons. Under these conditions, the positive molecular work, once liberated, can be retransformed into negative work either not at all or, at least, less completely than usual. It therefore accumulates, until excitation arises. The effect of these two modes of interference is, therefore, to prevent the restitution of the nerve-substance, and so to make it possible for comparatively weak external impulses to set up a rapidly extending decomposition, in consequence of which the stored forces are soon exhausted.

There are still two things to be explained: the phenomenon of the *mutual* inhibition of excitations conveyed to the same nerve-cells from different quarters, and the fact that the stimulation can traverse certain cells only in *one* direction, and is inhibited so soon as it attempts the other. To account for them, we must suppose that stimulations which act upon the central region of the nerve-cell serve to propagate the inhibitory processes (the negative molecular work) there in progress to the peripheral region; while, conversely, stimulations which act upon the peripheral region effect a diffusion of the excitatory processes (the positive molecular work) there released over the central region. The intrinsic probability of this hypothesis is vouched for by the well known fact that in all chemical processes, in which the state of equilibrium of complex molecules has once been disturbed, the disturbance is normally transmitted to other molecules. The explosion of the very smallest quantity of nitrogen chloride is enough to decompose many pounds of this substance, and a single blazing chip may set a whole forest on fire. There is, it is true, an apparent difficulty in the case before us: molecular processes of *opposite* character are distributed over one and the same mass, according to the direction from which the stimulation proceeds. We must, however, remember that these processes are constantly in progress, side by side, in both regions of the cell; and that, as the constant exchange of materials demands, there is a continuous and gradual transition from the one region to the other. We may again return to the illustration of the nerve-fibre under the action of the constant current. In the neighbourhood of the anode there is a preponderance of inhibitory, in that of the cathode a preponderance of excitatory molecular processes. But it may be demonstrated, by aid of test-stimuli of varying intensity, that there is increase at the anode not only of the inhibitory but also of the excitatory processes; while, on the other hand, as the strength of current is increased, the inhibitory process is propagated to the cathode and beyond (cf. pp. 97 f.). Similarly with the nerve-cell. Fig. 34 may illustrate, e.g., the behaviour of the cells of the dorsal and ventral cornua of the myel to incoming and outgoing fibres. M represents a cell of the ventral, S a cell of the dorsal cornu; c and c' are their central, p and p' their peripheral regions. In the ventral half of the myel, stimulation can travel only from m' to m; in the dorsal half, only from s to s': a stimulus proceeding from m, s' is inhibited in c, c'. A stimulation passing between S and M can travel only in the direction from S to M, and not contrariwise; for a stimulus operating at m will be arrested in c, and a stimulus applied at m' may be conducted as far as c',

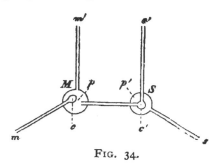

FIG. 34.

but cannot go farther. Finally, the reflex excitation proceeding from s must be inhibited by a stimulation acting at s', because the molecular motion of inhibition arising in c' tends to spread over the peripheral region, and thus destroys, in whole or part, the excitation there set up. The morphological facts put it beyond question that the part of the ganglion cell here designated the central region is the place of origin of the axis-cylinder or neurite, and that the peripheral region gives rise to the dendrites. The latter region belongs accordingly to the actual periphery of the ganglion-cell, though it may perhaps also extend some little distance into the central ground-reticulum.[1]

The results which follow from stimulation of peripheral ganglia, such as those of heart, blood-vessels, intestine, lend themselves readily to the same interpretation. Whether stimulation of the nerves which run to these ganglia produces excitation or inhibition depends likewise upon their mode of connexion with the nerve-cells. Thus, the inhibitory fibres of the heart will terminate in the central, the accelerating fibres in the peripheral region of the ganglion-cells of this organ; it is not necessary to assume the existence of separate apparatus for the two processes. The result of stimulation can be modified in only one way. The ganglia are, at the same time that they are stimulated from without, in a state of continuous automatic stimulation, so that the incoming nerves can do no more than regulate the movements made. For the rest, the nerve-cells, here as before, show the phenomena of accumulation and summation of stimuli. Intensive excitation of the inhibitory nerves of the heart will, it is true,

---

[1] See above, Ch. ii. pp. 42 ff. I may be permitted to remark that this theory of the directions of central conduction was formulated, on the ground of purely physiological considerations (*Untersuchungen*, etc., ii., 1876, 116), long before RAMON Y CAJAL used the morphological facts to develop his views of the functional significance of the twofold origin of the nerve-fibres. Cf. also p. 50.

arrest the heart-beat after a very short interval; but stimulations of more moderate intensity can produce this effect only after several beats have been executed. The phenomenon appears still more plainly in the case of the accelerating nerves, where several seconds regularly elapse after the beginning of stimulation before acceleration sets in. On the other hand, the after-effect of the stimulus always persists for a considerable time after the stimulus itself has ceased to act; the heart returns only gradually to its original frequency of beat. There is also a further point in which the conditions here evidently differ somewhat from those obtaining in the skeletal muscles. In all regions of innervation that do not stand under direct voluntary control, the mechanisms which subserve the production and accumulation of excitatory and inhibitory effects are to be found, in part, in the muscles themselves; so that, under these circumstances, the muscle-substance is endowed, within limits, with the attributes elsewhere reserved for the peripheral and central nerve-substance.[1] In view of the close relation subsisting in other respects between nervous and contractile substance, we may perhaps look upon this result as a simple enhancement of the powers possessed by muscular tissue in its own right, an enhancement due to the independence attained by the peripheral organs.

We may now turn to the elementary phenomenon of *practice* which, as will be remembered, is exhibited by the peripheral nerve-substance. The phenomenon recurs, with modifications conditioned upon the law of propagation of molecular processes within the ganglion-cell, in the central substance. Its effects are by no means simple, as may be observed in the following instances. We find, on the one hand, that co-ordinated movements, whose first performance was difficult and required continuous voluntary control, gradually become easier and, at last, altogether involuntary. We find, again, that functional disturbances, set up by the destruction of central elements, are gradually compensated, without restitution of these elements themselves. In the first of these phenomena, we have an increasing facilitation of the excitatory processes in consequence of their frequent repetition. The second suggests that, under suitable conditions, the stimulation may strike out new paths within the central substance: we may accordingly designate this latter effect of practice, in contradistinction to direct practice by repetition of function, as path-making or canalisation.[2] We are thus led to the following conclusions. First, when an excitatory process is frequently conducted through a ganglion

---

[1] T. W. ENGELMANN, PFLÜGER's *Arch. f. d. ges. Physiol.*, lvi., 1894, 149 ff.

[2] I take this very useful term *Bahnung* from S. EXNER, who first proposed it (*Entwurf einer physiologischen Erklärung der psychischen Erscheinungen*, i., 1894, 76), without meaning thereby to commit myself in any way to the views and hypotheses put forward by this author. [As the word 'facilitation' does not fit the present passage, we seem to have no better English term than 'canalisation.'—TRANSLATOR.]

cell in a given direction, the cell thereby acquires a prepotent disposition to conduct any future stimulations that may reach it in the same direction. Secondly, the processes of conduction in the central substance at large cannot be confined within fixed limits; elements in which, under normal circumstances, the excitations are annulled by concurrent inhibitions must be able, under the new conditions of practice introduced by the destruction of former conduction paths, to enter into new functional connexions. Translated into terms of the hypothesis developed above, this would mean that the frequent repetition of conduction, in a certain direction, so modifies the portion of the central substance which lies along this particular path that it takes on, more and more completely, the character normally attaching to the peripheral region. But, as a matter of fact, this sort of transformation is just what might have been predicted from the general laws of stimulation. We have seen that, in the peripheral nerve, the inhibitory forces are further and further reduced, under the action of repeated stimuli; so that at first, before functional capacity is exhausted, frequent repetition of stimulation means enhancement of irritability. Repetition of stimulus, that is, always and everywhere brings with it an alteration of the nerve-substance, which thereby loses the power of exerting the inhibitory influence connected with restoration of its internal forces. It is to this fact that we must turn for explanation of the principle of practice, in its special significance for the central functions, noting at the same time that the principle divides into two less general principles, each of importance for the understanding of these functions, and each in various ways supplementing the other: the principles of *localisation* and of *vicarious function*. We shall find, when we come to consider the functions of the central organs of the nervous system, that both alike are indispensable aids to an interpretation of the phenomena.

(b)—*Relation of Nervous to Psychical Processes*

These considerations yield, however, another and a more general result, important not only for the physiological but also for the psychological aspect of vital phenomena. We have taken, as a measure of the effects which the nervous substance can produce within itself and can transmit to other elements of the body, resembling it in certain general properties, the effects exhibited by the muscle; and we have done this, partly because the muscular effects are most easily accessible to observation, partly because they can be subsumed, with the least possible ambiguity, to metric principles of universal validity. Now we have no right to suppose that the laws which govern the transference of nervous molecular processes to the contractile substance are at all different from the laws which regulate their transmission to other substances, whose properties show them to be related to the nervous elements,—more especially, therefore, to the substances that are of peculiar import for the psychical aspect of vital phenomena, the elements of the sense-organs. On the contrary, the identity of these laws is a matter of course. It follows, therefore, that the changes set up by the action of stimulus in the sensory cells, and in the peripheral and central portions of the nervous system connected with them—whether the stimulus be applied from without or arise within the system itself—consist always in those forms of positive and negative molecular work whose general laws we have sought to trace in the symptoms presented by the muscular system. We have seen that all these forms can readily be brought under the general point of view of the principle of energy ; we have had, as illustrations of them, the decomposition and recomposition of chemical compounds, the liberation and absorption of heat, the increase and decrease of actual mechanical work. Now the processes thus analysed remain, always, physical and chemical processes. It is never possible to arrive, by way of a molecular mechanics, at any sort of psychical quality or process. If, then, experience teaches us that the molecular processes within our nervous system may have psychical concomitants, we can only say that we are here in presence of a fact which lies altogether beyond the cognisance of a molecular mechanics of nerve-substance, and consequently beyond the cognisance of any strictly physiological inquiry. It would fall within the scope of physiology only if we were able in some way to interpret the psychical processes themselves as molecular processes, i.e. in the last resort, as modes of motion or as physical energies. This, however, we cannot do: the attempt fails at once, under whatever guise it may be made. Psychical processes refuse to submit to any one of our physical measures of energy ; and the physical molecular processes, so far as we are able to follow them, are seen to be transformed, variously enough, into one another, but never directly into psychical qualities. In saying this, we do not, of course, reject the idea that psychical processes may be regularly attended by an interchange of physical forces, which as such forms a proper object of co-ordinate investigation by the molecular mechanics of the nervous system ; nor do we deny, what would naturally follow, that psychical symptoms may be taken as indicative of definite physiological molecular processes, and that these in their turn, if it ever happens that we know more about them, may be taken, under certain circumstances, as indicative of psychical conditions. But such a relation between the two departments is entirely compatible with their separate independence, with the impossibility, at any time or by any means, of the reduction of the one to the other. As a matter of fact, we can no more derive the mechanics of nerve-substance from the connexions and relations of our sensations and feelings, than we can derive the latter from molecular processes. We have, then, no choice as to the road which we shall take in the following Chapters. We must first of all occupy ourselves with the investigation of the bodily substrate of the mental life as a physiological problem ; our task being, in the main, simply to apply the principles which we have discovered in the general mechanics of nervous substance to the complex connexions of nervous elements presented in the nervous system of the animals, and more especially of man. Psychological facts will here be accorded merely a symptomatic importance, in the sense defined above : we shall depart from this rule only when the critical discussion of certain hypotheses of psychological character, which have taken shape within nerve-physiology, requires us to raise the question whether and how far these hypotheses receive adequate support from the physiological facts themselves. But the general question, as to the nature of the relations which unite the mechanics of nerve-substance and of its complex effects in the nervous system, on the one hand, and the phenomena of the mental life, on the other,—this question presupposes the analysis of both sets of facts, the physiological and the psychological : so that its investigation must, naturally, be postponed to the conclusion of the present work.

CHAPTER IV

Morphological Development of the Central Organs

§ 1. General Survey

(a)—*Object of the Following Exposition*

In the preceding chapter we have attempted to analyse, in their elementary phenomena, the vital processes conditioned upon the constitution of the nervous substance. Now in every organism which stands high enough in the scale of organic life to possess a nervous system at all, the elementary parts connect to form complicated structures, or organs; and the processes which we have been studying manifest themselves, accordingly, in co-ordinated activities of greater or less complexity. As a rule, it is far from easy to refer these complex phenomena to the relatively simple conditions laid down by a mechanics of nerve-substance that has been worked out from individual, isolated structures. We must be content to do this in the rough, and as a matter of general direction. At the same time, the more complicated and difficult the problem, the more strictly necessary is it, if our analysis of the complex physiological functions is not to go wrong from the very beginning, to keep constantly in view the general principles which our study of the simple nerve processes has brought to light. In considering, more especially, those developmental forms of the nervous system which are of chief importance for psychology, and which will therefore form the main subject of the following Chapters,—the nerve-centres of the higher vertebrates and of man,—we must remember that the elementary nerve-forces are still at work, though the manifold connexions of the elementary parts place their effects under conditions of almost inconceivable complexity. The properties of compound organs can be understood only in so far as we are able to refer them, at any rate as regards the general point of view from which they are appraised, to the properties of the elementary structures. The more firmly the physiology of the nervous system holds to this principle, which is surely beyond the need of argument, the sooner will it be competent to render service to psychology. On the other hand, neglect of the rule, combined with the adoption of a haphazard popular psychology, as manufactured on occasion by anatomists and physiologists for their own private use, has wrought havoc from the days of GALL and phrenology down to the present time. Great advances have been made in our knowledge of the morphology of the nervous system and of its complex physiological functions; GALL himself deserves credit for his investigations in anatomy. But they have failed to bear fruit for an understanding of the relations of the nervous system to the processes of the psychical life. Nay, more, under the conditions just mentioned, they have in this regard oftentimes done more to confuse than to further knowledge.

Now an inquiry concerning the bodily substrate of the mental life evidently presupposes, first of all and before it turns to the properly physiological aspect of its problem, an adequate knowledge of the morphology of the organs. This is not a merely logical requirement. Apart from the experiments on nervous elements, isolated so far as possible from their connexions, which fall within the sphere of the general mechanics of nerve-substance, both the physiological experiment and the pathological observation which serves to supplement it in various directions are conditioned upon this anatomical knowledge. When we remember the immense complexity of the structures involved, we must admit, at the same time, that as instruments of analysis they are comparatively crude: a limitation that should be steadily borne in mind in any estimate of the value of such experiments and observations. The first part of the following discussion will, then, be devoted to a general sketch of the morphology of the central nervous system. This will, of course, contain nothing that is new to the anatomist and physiologist, to whom the subject is familiar. On the contrary, it will often fail to make mention of special points that, for the time being, possess only an anatomical interest. The primary purpose of the exposition is to furnish a brief account of the structure and function of the nervous system that shall appeal especially to the psychologist and shall take account of the things that interest him. It has, however, over and above this, the secondary purpose of showing the anatomist and physiologist themselves how the familiar facts of structure and function appear when viewed, for the nonce, from the standpoint of psychology. It is true that this standpoint is not altogether neglected in the anatomical and physiological text-books. On the contrary, one cannot but admire the courage with which the anatomists and physiologists, when occasion arises, invade a difficult and (for so it really is to them) an unknown country. But the psychologist is, all the more for this very reason, in duty bound to discuss, from the point of view of a scientific psychology, the results obtained from the observation of microscopical structures, or of animals whose mind has in some way been impaired by extirpation of particular portions of the brain. He is bound to pass the facts themselves in critical review, and to estimate their psychological importance, quite apart from the more or less accidental and arbitrary reflections that are usually appended to the observational data. Now it would obviously be out of place, for the purposes of a survey specially intended, as this is, to subserve psychological requirements, to give any such detailed account of the topography of brain structure as is necessary for anatomy and pathology. We must rather lay the chief emphasis upon the morphological complexes, upon the organs as such; more particularly where structural connexions point us to co-ordination of functions. And this need seems to be most adequately met by a genetic consideration, which seeks to explain the complex conditions found in the fully developed organs from their origination in simpler forms, whether these stand lower in the scale of organic life or represent earlier stages of individual development. We shall, therefore, in this opening Chapter, say what is necessary for our present purpose of the general differentiation of the substrate of psychical functions in the animal kingdom. That done, however, we may thenceforth confine ourselves to a detailed consideration of the morphological development of the central organs in the vertebrates. Here, too, we shall make use of the lower forms of development chiefly to prepare the way for an understanding of the structural plan of the human brain.

(b)—*The Neural Tube and the Three Main Divisions of the Brain*

The first step in the evolution of the central nervous system of vertebrates is taken, as we have seen, with that primitive differentiation of the germ where a dark streak of tissue marks the place of the myel, and therefore the longitudinal body-axis of the future organism (Fig. 8, p. 37). The next stage in the development of this primule of the nervous system occurs when the outer layer of the germ disc folds on either side of the axis of the primitive streak to form two ridge-like elevations, containing a groove between them. This, the primitive groove, is the primule of the future myel. The sides at first grow rapidly upwards, and then bend inwards, so that the groove closes to form a tube, the neural tube, within which the myel arises by proliferation of the original formative cells (Fig. 9, p. 37). The primary cavity of the myel persists throughout the vertebrate series as the longitudinal central canal or myelocele. This is lined with cinerea or grey matter, which is itself invested with an envelope of alba or white matter; and from this, again, the roots of the myelic (spinal) nerves issue in a fan-shaped radiation.

The primule of the brain is formed from the anterior end of the neural tube. The rapid growth of this region leads to the formation of a bladder-like expansion, the primitive brain vesicle, which soon divides into three compartments, the fore, mid and hind brain-vesicles (Fig. 35). Both the genetic and the later functional relations of the primary vesicle suggest that this tripartite division, like the development of the brain at large, is intimately connected with the development of the three anterior sense-organs. The nervous primule of the olfactory organ grows out directly from the anterior end of the fore brain; that of the auditory organs from the lateral walls of the hind brain; while, despite the fact that the eyes would seem to represent products of the growth of the fore brain, we must, in the light of indisputable physiological facts, look to the mid brain as the ultimate source of origin of the optic nerves.

Of the three primary brain-divisions, the first and third, the fore and hind brains, undergo the greatest changes. The anterior extremity of both soon begins to outstrip the rest in growth, so that both alike divide into a principal and a secondary vesicle. The original fore brain now consists of fore brain and 'tween brain, the original hind brain of hind brain and after brain (Fig. 36). Of the five brain divisions which have thus arisen from the three primary vesicles, the fore brain or prosencephalon corresponds to the future cerebral hemispheres; the 'tween brain or diencephalon becomes the thalami; the undivided mid brain or mesencephalon

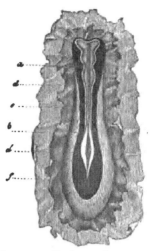

FIG. 35. Embryonic primule of the ovum of the dog, after BISCHOFF. *a* Neural tube, with the three brain vesicles at its anterior end. *a'* Extension of the neural tube in the lumbar region (*sinus rhomboidalis* or *intumescentia lumbalis*). *b* Primule of the vertebral column. *c* Primule of the body-wall. *d* Place of separation of the ectodermal and mesodermal layers of the germinative vesicle. *f* Entoderm.

developes into the quadrigemina of man and the mammals, the bigemina or optic lobes of the lower vertebrates; the hind brain or epencephalon becomes the cerebellum; and the after brain, or metencephalon, the oblongata. The diencephalon is to be considered the anterior, and the metencephalon the posterior stem-vesicle, from which the prosencephalon and epencephalon have grown out respectively as secondary vesicles. The structures developed from the three stem-vesicles (metencephalon, mesencephalon and diencephalon),—i.e., the oblongata, the quadrigemina and the thalami,—and the fibre-systems that ascend among them from the myel, are grouped together in the nomenclature of the developed brain as the caudex or brain-stem. The structures of the first and fourth vesicles, the cerebral hemispheres and cerebellum, are named, in contradistinction to the brain-stem, the pallium or brain-mantle, since in the more highly organised brains they envelope the brain-stem as a mantle-like covering.

The three brain-vesicles, then, represent expansions of the anterior end of the neural tube. With the tube itself, they form a closed system, whose parts intercommunicate by way of the continuous central cavity. But the development of the two secondary vesicles from the first and third primary vesicles brings other changes with it. The roof of the fore and hind brains divides up longitudinally; so that two slit-like apertures appear lying exactly in the median line of the body, whereby the cavities of the fore and hind stem-vesicles are exposed. The anterior roof-slit divides the prosencephalon into its two hemispheres, and leaves the diencephalon open above. The mesencephalon, which does not share the advance in organisation characteristic of the rest of the brain, merely divides by a longitudinal furrow into two halves. The posterior roof-slit appears at the place where the neural tube passes over into the brain. The cerebellum, which grows out directly forwards from this point, is at first separated into two entirely distinct halves, but afterwards grows together again in the median line. The two roof-openings serve to admit blood-vessels into the brain-cavities. These ensure the food supply requisite for further growth and for the simultaneous thickening of the brain-walls by deposition of nerve-substance from within.

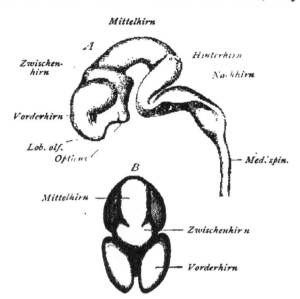

FIG. 36. Brain of a human embryo (seven weeks), magn. 3 diam. *A* Lateral, *B* dorsal view. *Vorderhirn* Fore brain. *Mittelhirn* Mid brain. *Hinterhirn* Hind brain. *Zwischenhirn* 'Tween brain. *Nachhirn* After brain. *Lob. olf.* Olfactory lobe. *Opticus* Optic nerve. *Med. spin.* Myel. After MIHALKOVICS.

The level of development now attained is practically the level of permanent organisation in the lowest vertebrates, the fishes and amphibia (Figg. 37, 38). The original prosencephalic vesicle is here divided, in most cases, into two almost entirely separate halves, the cerebral hemispheres; the only remaining connexion occurs over a small area of the floor of the vesicle. The anterior stem-vesicle (diencephalon) is split into two lateral halves, the thalami, which retain connexion at their base. The cerebellum forms for the most part a narrow unpaired lamella, from which all trace of division has disappeared. In the metencephalon or oblongata, the posterior roof-slit has formed a rhomboidal depression, on the floor of which the principal mass of the organ shows in undivided form.

(c)—*The Brain Ventricles and the Differentiation of the Parts of the Brain*

The division of the brain into five vesicles brings with it a further change : a modification in the form of the central brain cavities, whose origin as simple expansions of the myelocele we have already noticed. The brain-cavity divides, in accordance with the separation of the brain-vesicles, at first into three and then into five pockets. The division of the hemi-

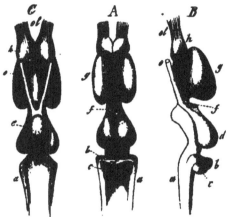
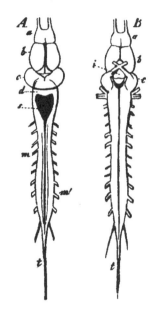

FIG. 37. Brain of *Polypterus bichir*, after J. MÜLLER. A Dorsal, B lateral, C ventral view. h Olfactory lobes. g Cerebrum. f Thalami. d Bigemina. bc Cerebellum. a Oblongata. e Hypophysis with the posthypophyses (lobi inferiores). ol Olfactory nerve. o Optic nerve.

FIG. 38. Brain and myel of the frog, after GEGENBAUR. A Dorsal, B ventral view. a Olfactory lobes. b Cerebrum. c Bigemina. A shows, between b and c, a portion of the thalami. d Cerebellum. s Fossa rhomboidalis (oblongata). i Infundibulum ; the chiasma shows anteriorly. m Myel. m' Lumbar enlargement of the myel. t Terminal threads of the myel.

spheres subdivides the first of these again into two symmetrical halves, the paraceles or lateral brain-ventricles. If, now, we set out from these on a journey through the brain-cavities, we shall traverse them in the following order (Fig. 39). The two paraceles (h), which as a rule are entirely separated from each other, open into the cavity of their stem-vesicle,—a cleft-like space, bounded laterally by the thalami, and left roofless by the anterior roof-slit (z),—the diacele or third ventricle. This leads directly into the cavity of the mesencephalon (m). In mammals the mesocele is extraordinarily reduced, so that it appears only in the form of a narrow canal, the aqueduct of Sylvius, running below the quadrigemina, and connecting the diacele with the cavity of the metencephalon. In the birds, the mesocele is more extensive, sending lateral offshoots into the bigemina (mesencephalon); and in the lower vertebrates the bigemina contain quite large cavities, which communicate with the central cavity. The two derivatives from the third primary vesicle, epencephalon and metencephalon, have originally each its own special cavity. But the cerebellum (epencephalon) is now a rounded vesicle, arching backward over the metencephalon from the point at which this borders upon the mesencephalon. The mesocele accordingly divides at its posterior end into two branches, the one of which turns upwards, and leads into the epicele (cavity of the cerebellum), while the other pursues a straight course into the cavity of the metencephalon or oblongata (Fig. 40). This latter cavity, the metacele (fourth ventricle [1]) is termed from its rhomboidal form the fossa rhomboidalis (*r* in Fig. 39). The

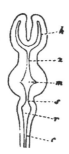

FIG. 39. Horizontal longitudinal section through the brain of the frog, partly schematic. *h* Paraceles. *z* Diacele. *m* Mesocele. *s* Canal connecting diacele and metacele (Sylvian aqueduct). *r* Metacele (*fossa rhomboidalis*). *c* Myelocele.

metacele is, therefore, not strictly a cavity, but a furrow; the posterior roof-slit has completely exposed it. It closes posteriorly to pass over into the myelocele. In mammals the epicele disappears entirely by the filling up of the epencephalic vesicle with alba. At this stage, then, the paraceles,

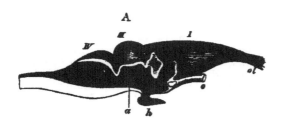
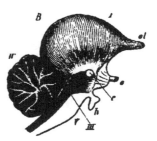

FIG. 40. Brain of a tortoise (*A*) and a bird (*B*), in sagittal section, after BOJANUS and STIEDA. *I* Hemisphere. *ol* Olfactory nerve. *o* Optic nerve. *c* Anterior commissure. *III* Bigemina: in *B* we see only the myelinic plate that connects the two bigemina, marked *a* in *A*. *h* Hypophysis. *IV* Cerebellum. *V* Behind the anterior commissure lies the diacele, which passes under the bigeminal plate into the Sylvian aqueduct (mesocele); this then continues posteriorly, upwards into the epicele, and downwards into the metacele.

[1] The 'ventriclees' are counted from before backwards, with the mesocele (Sylvian aqueduct) omitted; two lateral ventricles (paraceles), third ventricle (diacele), fourth ventricle (metacele or metepicele).

diacele, Sylvian aqueduct (mesocele) and metacele represent the whole system of brain-cavities. In the lower vertebrates, we have, further, the cavities of the thalami as extensions of the diacele ; the cavities of the bigemina as branches of the aqueduct ; and the epicele as a tributary of the metacele. In the lower orders of vertebrates, primary and secondary cavities alike are, as a general rule, more extensive in proportion to the mass of the brain,—i.e. approximate more nearly to an embryonic state. However, the different classes evince wide differences in this regard as between the various subdivisions of the brain. In the fishes, the cerebral hemispheres and cerebellum are filled with alba and become solid structures. Their growth is soon arrested, and they consequently attain to no considerable size. In the amphibia, the paraceles persist, but the cerebellum is usually solid. When we come to the reptiles and birds, we find a cerebellum with a spacious epicele ; but in all the mammals this has again disappeared. In the mammals, too, the lateral cavities of the mesencephalon (quadrigemina or bigemina) are lost ; in all the lower vertebrates, from the fishes to the birds, they not only persist but develop prominences of cinerea upon their floor (Fig. 41). Similar growths, the striata, appear in the paraceles of the avian and mammalian brain.

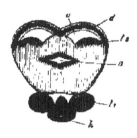

Fig. 41. Transverse section through the brain of a fish (*Gadus lota*) in the region of the bigemina. Magn. After Stieda. *d* Roof of the bigemina. *v* Mesocele. *ts* Elevation of cinerea upon the floor of the mesocele ; torus semi-circularis Halleri. *a* Sylvian aqueduct (mesocele). *li* Posthypophyses. *h* Hypophysis. Further forwards, *v* and *a* unite, to open into the diacele; new branches lead from this into the posthypophyses.

Both in the myel and in the brain (encephalon), the nervous mass is formed by proliferation of the cells constituting the walls of the original cavities. Many of these cells evince the character of the formative cells of connective tissue, and so mediate the secretion of the amorphous intercellular substance or neuroglia. Others become nerve-cells, and send out runners. In the myel, the greater part of the fibres radiate out towards the periphery, so that the cinerea is collected about the myelocele and surrounded by an envelope of alba. In the encephalon this distribution of alba and cinerea persists, practically unchanged, in the structures developed from the three stem-vesicles. In the developments from the secondary vesicles, on the other hand, the nerve-cells retain their position in the walls of the cavities, and the fibres connected with them trend towards the interior. Hence in the caudex—the oblongata, the quadrigemina and the thalami—we have a layer of cinerea lining the continuations of the myelocele and surrounded by an envelope of alba; in the pallium, a mass of alba invested with a covering of cinerea. The cinerea thus shows two distinct formations. The one, the entocinerea (tubular grey matter) belongs to myel and caudex, the other, the ectocinerea (cortical grey matter), to the pallium. The entocinerea of the encephalon undergoes still further transformation. Even in the highest region of the myel, various bundles of nerve-fibres from the myelic columns have shifted from their former position at the periphery of the cinerea, so that this is broken up by masses of alba. In the oblongata, this process has gone so far that only a comparatively small part of the cinerea holds its original place as floor of the fossa rhomboidalis, by far the greater portion being separated by the intercurrence of myelinic fibres into distinct masses. These collections of entocinerea, invested by alba, are termed nidi (nuclei). We see, then, that the entocinerea of the myel undergoes an essential modification as it passes into the encephalon;

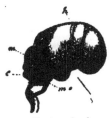

FIG. 42. Lateral view of the brain of a human embryo (3 months), after KÖLLIKER. *h* Hemisphere. *m* Mesencephalon (quadrigemina). *c* Cerebellum. *mo* Oblongata. *S* Sylvian fossa.

it is broken up by the interposition of masses of alba, and so gives rise to a third formation of grey matter, the nidal cinerea (nuclear grey, ganglionic grey). This nidal cinerea lies midway between the entocinerea and the ectocinerea. As we travel from the central cavity towards the periphery, we come first of all upon entocinerea, then upon alba, then upon the nidal cinerea, then again upon alba, and finally upon the ectocinerea.

The series of changes that we have been describing hitherto is accompanied, in all the vertebrates, by changes in the relative position of the primitive brain-divisions, as a result of which the whole brain is bent over ventralward. The various parts of the caudex are thus brought out of the straight line and set at a certain angle to one another. The bend or flexure, which in the lowest classes is but slight, approximates more and more closely to a right angle the higher we ascend in the vertebrate series (Fig. 36, p. 108). And the form of the brain is further modified by the disproportionate growth of certain divisions, especially the prosencephalon and epencephalon, which extend over and conceal the rest. Three flexures of the central nervous system can thus be distinguished. The first appears at the junction of the myel and oblongata; the second takes place in the cerebellum; and the third at the level of the mesencephalon (Fig. 42). The extent of these flexures is principally conditioned by the growth of the prosencephalon; so that degree of curvature runs practically parallel with development of the hemispheres.[1]

---

[1] HIS, *Die Formentwickelung des menschlichen Vorderhirns.* In *Abh. d. k. sächs. Ges. d. Wiss., math.-phys. Cl.,* xv., 1890, 675.

In the early stages of the development of the vertebrate brain, the prosencephalon extends anteriorly beyond the remaining brain-divisions, without covering them. But the more its growth outstrips the growth of the rest of the brain, the more opposition does the rigid attachment of the embryo to the germinative vesicle offer to its forward expansion. It must, therefore, grow out backwards, arching first over the diencephalon, then over the mesencephalon, and finally over the cerebellum itself. At the same time, it follows the curve of the mesencephalic flexure; its most posterior portion—that which covers mesencephalon and epencephalon—bends upon itself at an angle. The more vigorous the growth of the hemisphere, the farther does the bent portion of it extend back again towards its point of departure, or, in other words, the more nearly does the curve described about the diencephalon approach to a perfect circle. In this way a depression (the Sylvian fossa; s Fig. 42) is formed at the place where the hemisphere rests upon its stem-vesicle (diencephalon). In the most highly developed mammalian brains, the concavity of the curve of growth is almost entirely obliterated, and the walls of the fossa draw together, leaving between them a deep and narrow fissure.

The growth of the prosencephalon over the caudex is necessarily followed by a modification of the form of the paraceles. These are originally spherical cavities, lying within the hemispheric vesicles. As the prosencephalon grows, they extend out at first posteriorly, and then, when the curve of the hemispheric arch begins to close in upon itself, inferiorly and anteriorly as well. The central portion of the resulting cavity

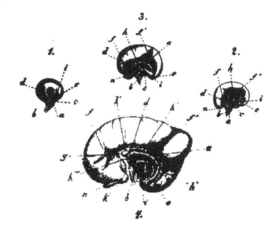

Fig. 43. Median view of human prosencephalon, showing stages of growth: partly schematic. After Fr. Schmidt. Embryos 1 of the 6th week; 2 of the 8th week; 3 of the 10th week; 4 of the 16th week. *a* Aula (foramen of Monro). *b-d* Anterior limiting lamella of aula. *c* Crus cerebri. *e* Lobus inferior of the hemisphere. *i* Posterior limit of aula. *k* Precommissure. *g* Callosum. *h* Marginal arch; *h'* external. *h"* internal division. *ff'* Longitudinal fissure of the hemisphere-vesicle, bounding the gyrus fornicatus. *n* Olfactory lobes.

is termed the cella; the extensions are the postcornu, precornu and medicornu of the paracele. While this transformation is in progress, the outer walls of the prosocele are growing more rapidly than the inner or median wall which surrounds the caudex. In this there is a narrow, originally vertical slit, the aula or foramen of Monro (*a* Fig. 23), whereby the paraceles communicate with the diacele (third ventricle). Anteriorly to the aula, the hemispheres are held together by a lamella of alba (*b–d*). As the prosencephalon arches over the rest of the brain, the aula and its anterior limiting lamella naturally arch with it. They have, therefore, in the developed brain, the appearance of a vault laid over the diencephalon. The posterior part of the aula soon closes, and only the extreme anterior portion of the original cleft remains open; this serves as a channel for vascular processes passing from the diacele into the paraceles. The lower end of the lamella of white matter, which forms the anterior boundary of the aula, becomes the precommissure (*k*); the remaining portion follows the curve of the hemispheric arch and is the primule of the fornix. Directly above this the hemispheres are united by a strong transverse band of alba, the callosum or great commissure (*g*). The portion of the median wall of the hemispheres lying above the callosum forms yet another arch, running concentrically with the fornix, and separated from the surrounding parts by a special furrow, *f f'*. This is the marginal arch, *h*. Its anterior division becomes the gyrus fornicatus; the posterior passes into a structure, continuous with the gyrus fornicatus and extending from the median wall outwards into the paracele, termed the hippocampus (cornu Ammonis). A more detailed description of these parts, which attain to development only in the mammalian brain, will be given later.

§ 2. The Myel in the Higher Vertebrates

The neural tube from which the myel developes is originally a hollow tube, filled with liquid, and lined along its interior wall with formative cells. The cells increase and multiply: some taking on the character of connective tissue-cells, and furnishing an amorphous intercellular substance, while others become nerve-cells. The processes of these last either pass directly into the fibres of peripheral nerves, or divide and subdivide to form a terminal reticulum. The main trend of all fibres is to the periphery of the neural tube, so that the cellular structures are shifted towards the centre of the myelic cavity (Fig. 44, and Fig. 9, p. 37 above). The nerve-cells, and the nerves issuing from them, are arranged, from the first, in accordance with the bilateral symmetry of the primule of the vertebrate body, in symmetrical (right and left) groups. Moreover, the connexion of the nerves with two different parts of the germ-primule carries with it the further separation of each group into two subdivisions. All nerves and fibres that enter into connexion with the corneal layer, the primule of the sense-organs and the sensitive investment of the body, arrange themselves in a dorsal group, in the near neighbourhood of the germinal structures dependent upon them.

All those nervous elements, on the other hand, that have relations to the striated muscles collect in a ventral group, corresponding to the animal muscle-plate. It results from this that the cinerea formed by the association of cells appears to right and left as a dorsal and a ventral column, surrounded by an envelope of myelinated fibres or alba. The columns are termed, from their appearance in transverse section, the dorsal and ventral cornua (horns) of the myel: a special branch of the latter is known as the lateral cornu. The dorsal and ventral cornua of each side are united at the centre. The nerve-roots issuing from the cornua are arranged, in the same way, in two series: the dorsal or sensory, and the ventral or motor (Fig. 44, *e, f*; Fig. 45, *HW* and *VW*).

Under these conditions of growth, the myelic cavity at first assumes the form of a rhombus (Fig. 44, *cm*), drawn out into a ventral and a dorsal cleft. The cavity of the dorsal cleft soon becomes almost entirely filled; that of the ventral is more plainly marked, but is closed by nerve-fibres running from side to side of the myel, and constituting the white ventral commissure. The commissure, which originally crosses near the periphery (Fig. 44 *h*), gradually reaches a deeper level (Fig. 45). Behind it, a remnant of the myelic cavity persists as an extremely narrow canal, the myelocele or central canal of the myel, around which the two collections of cinerea enter into cross-connexion (Fig. 45 *A*). The dorsal and ventral sulci (fissurae medianae post. and ant.) divide the myel into two symmetrical halves.

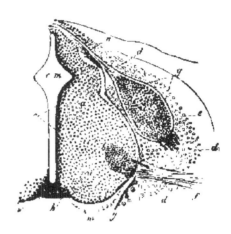

FIG. 44. Transverse section of the embryonic myel of the sheep, after BIDDER and KUPFFER. *cm* Myelocele, partly closed. *c* Epithelium of myelocele. *a* Cinerea, occupying almost the whole cross-section of the myel. *b* Place of origin of the ventral roots *f*. *e* Myelic ganglion, with the dorsal roots issuing from it. *m* Primule of the ventral and lateral tracts. *n* Primule of the dorsal tract. *h* Ventral commissure. *g* Envelope of myelic ganglion and myel. *d* Primule of vertebra.

Each of these is again subdivided by the outgoing nerve-roots into three columns (Fig. 45 *B*). The column of alba lying between the dorsal sulcus and the cell-column of the dorsal roots is termed the dorsal column (*hs*); that lying between the ventral sulcus and the cell-column of the ventral roots the ventral column (*vs*); and a third column, ascending between the cell-columns of the dorsal and ventral roots, the lateral column (*ss*). The greater part of the nerve-fibres of these white columns run their course vertically, in the direction of the longitudinal axis of the myel. An exception to the rule is furnished by the area at the central end of the ventral sulcus, occupied, as we saw just now, by the ventral commissure; here the decussating fibres follow a horizontal or oblique course; and the same directions are, naturally, taken for a short distance by the fibres which constitute the direct continuations centralward of the incoming nerve-roots. The grey cornua are of different shapes: the ventral, particularly in the lumbar region of the myel, are broader and shorter, the dorsal longer and narrower. The former contain a quantity of large multipolar ganglion-cells; the latter consist exclusively of smaller cells. A good portion of the dorsal cornua consists, further, of the nervous ground-reticulum and its interpenetrating fibrils. This gives them a peculiarly bright appearance, more especially as they approach the periphery of the myel: the region is known as the gelatinosa of Rolando.

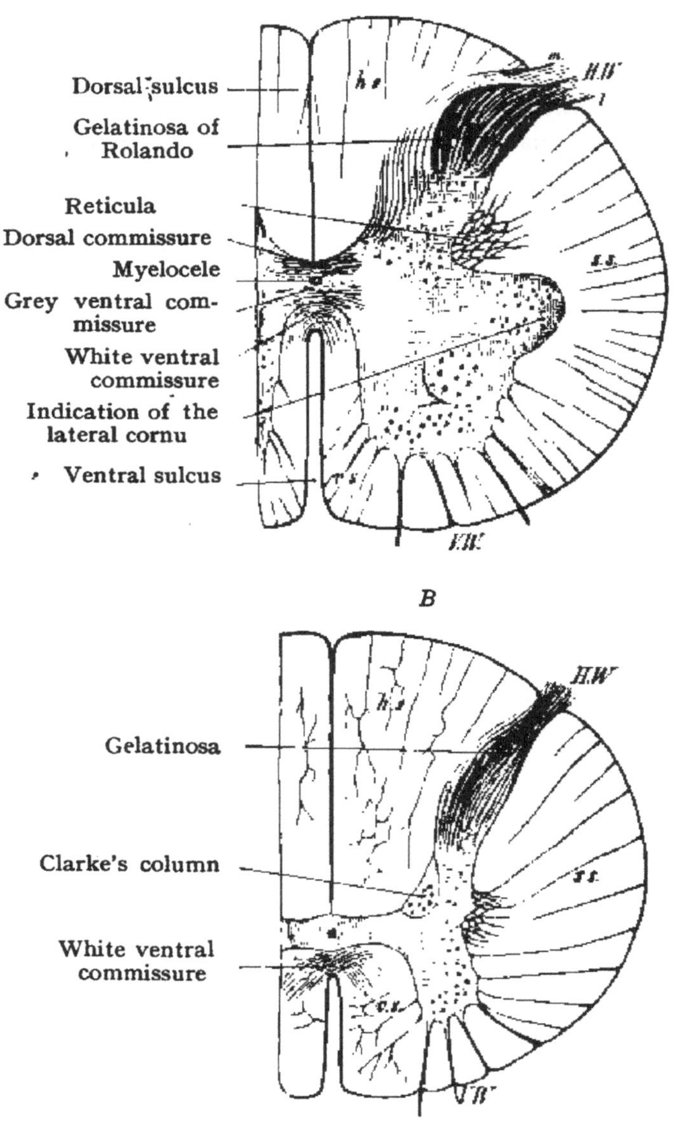

FIG. 45. Transverse section of the human myel, × 9. After GEGENBAUR. *A* from the lumbar enlargement, *B* from the thoracic region of the myel.

Passing centralward from this formation we find on either side of the central canal a compact column of alba and cinerea, Clarke's column (Fig. 45 *B*), containing a well-marked group of roundish ganglion-cells, and extending from the end of the cervical region into the lumbar enlargement. The immediate points of origin of the dorsal roots, within the myel, seem to be less richly supplied with nerve-cells than those of the ventral; but the difference is compensated later on. A cluster of large bipolar ganglion-cells is intercalated in the course of the nerve-fibres after they have left the myel, and forms with them the spinal ganglion of the dorsal roots (*e* Fig. 44). The dorsal columns are not connected, as the ventral are, by white myelinated fibres, but by a grey commissure, composed of fine fibres running transversely in the mass of cinerea behind the myelocele (dorsal comm., Fig. 45 *A*). Similar grey fibres surround the whole of the central canal; its interior is lined by a single layer of cylindrical epithelium, derived from a small remnant of the formative cells that originally invested the cavity of the neural tube (Fig. 9, p. 37 above).

So long as the development of the central organs is confined to the formation of the myel, we find, of course, a certain uniformity dominating the entire bodily organisation. The myel, over its whole length, simply repeats the same arrangement of elementary parts and the same mode of origin of nerve-fibres; and the sensory surfaces and motor apparatus that depend upon it must accordingly show a like uniformity of distribution and structure. Hence we find, as a matter of fact, that so long as the central nervous system of the embryo consists merely of the neural tube, no one of the higher sense-organs attains to development. The primules of the sensory investment of the body and of the locomotor apparatus are distributed uniformly about the central axis. A single exception occurs at the place where the nerve-mass takes on a stronger growth, for the supply of the posterior extremities; this is indicated, at an early stage, by an extension of the primitive groove, the sinus rhomboidalis or future lumbar enlargement. A similar, but less strongly marked thickening of the neural tube occurs, later on, at the point of departure of the nerves supplying the anterior extremities,—the cervical enlargement.[1] This uniformity of organisation is permanently retained in the lowest vertebrate, Amphioxus lanceolatus, in which the development of a central nervous system halts at the formation of the neural tube. The organ of vision, in this brainless vertebrate, consists of simple refracting cells, surrounded by pigment [2]; the organ of smell, of an unpaired cup-shaped depression at the anterior end of the body; the presence of an auditory organ has not been demonstrated. We see, then, that the arrest of development in this case affects just those

---

[1] In birds, the sinus rhomboidalis is not closed by proliferation of the nerve-mass, but remains permanently open. It thus resembles the fossa rhomboidalis, the continuation of the myelocele in the oblongata, which persists as an open depression in all vertebrate forms.

[2] Cf. below, Ch. vii. § 3.

organs which appear to exercise a determining influence upon the formation of the higher central parts, the vesicular differentiations of the myel.

§ 3. The Oblongata

In the lower vertebrates, the bundles of nerve-fibres take a course that is, to all appearance, but little different from their course in the myel. The only changes are that the dorsal columns split apart, disclosing the fossa rhomboidalis (Figg. 37, 38, p. 109); and that the grey cornua, as may be seen in section, have been divided off from the central cinerea and intercalated in the course of the ventral and dorsal columns. The three columns of the myel, ventral, lateral and dorsal, can still be

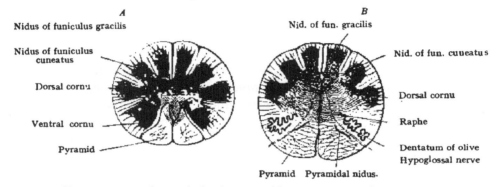

Fig. 46. Transverse sections of the human oblongata, ×2. After GEGENBAUR. *A* from the posterior, *B* from the anterior portion, just before the opening of the fossa rhomboidalis.

distinguished, but receive special names. Their fibres pursue a more tortuous course, and ganglionic nidi appear among the fibre-bundles. They thus differ very considerably from the correspondingly situated myelic columns; and, indeed, for the most part do not represent direct continuations of the myelic structure. The ventral columns are termed pyramids; their fibres decussate, in the posterior part of their course, so that the ventral sulcus is entirely obliterated (Fig. 46 *A*; Fig. 47 *p*). This decussation seems to be a repetition, on a larger scale, of the decussation of the ventral columns of the myel in the ventral commissure. At their upper end, where they enclose a ribbon-like stria of cinerea (pyramidal nidus, inner accessory nucleus of olive; pyram. nidus, Fig. 46 *B*), the pyramids are bounded on either side by the olives (Fig. 46 *B*; Fig. 47 *o*). These are well-marked prominences, which contain in their interior a large ganglionic nidus, dentate in section and therefore termed the dentatum (*nd*). The vertically ascending fibre-bundles which enclose the dentate nidus are known as the capsular columns (funiculi siliquae). The lateral columns (*s* Figg. 47, 48) grow smaller and smaller from the lower end of the oblongata upwards, until at about the point where the opening of the fossa rhomboidalis appears they disappear entirely in the interior. The dorsal columns, on the other hand, increase in external diameter. In the lower portion of the oblongata, they are divided by a shallow sulcus into inner and outer columns, the slender and the cuneate funiculi (*fg* and *fc* Fig. 48), which at the lower end of the fossa rhomboidalis carry knob-like prominences, produced by the grey nidi of the interior (*nid. grac.* and *nid. cun.*, Fig. 46). Farther upwards, the two funiculi appear to continue their course in the columns which bound the fossa rhomboidalis to right and left. These have been termed the restes (restiform bodies : *pi* Fig. 48). They are the largest columns of the oblongata, and, like the funiculi just mentioned, contain grey nidi. They are characterised by the intricate, trellis-like interlacing of their constituent fibres. Anteriorly, the restes pass entirely over into the alba of the cerebellum, forming

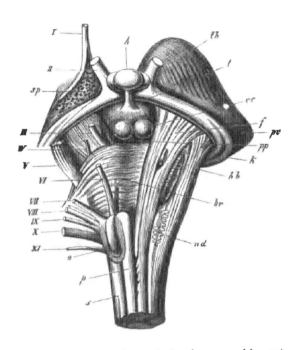

FIG. 47. Ventral view of the human oblongata, with the pons and the adjoining parts of the brain-base. On the left, the transverse fibres have been cut away, to show the continuation of the myelic columns through the pons into the crus, and the floor of the thalamus is exposed. *p* Pyramid. *o* Olive. *s* Lateral column. *nd* Dentatum of olive. *br* Pons. *f* Crusta. *hb* Tegmentum. Crusta and tegmentum are separated by a deep-lying bundle of transverse pontal fibres, cut across in the Fig. *cc* Albicantia. *t* Tuber with infundibulum. *h* Hypophysis. *th* Thalami. *pv* Pulvinar. *k* Genicula. *sp* Precribrum. *pp* Postcribrum. *I—XI*, first to eleventh cranial nerves. *I* Olfactory; *II* optic; *III* oculomotor; *IV* trochlear; *V* trigeminal; *VI* abducent ocular; *VII* facial motor; *VIII* auditory; *IX* glossopharyngeal; *X* pneumogastric; *XI* accessory.

the inferior cerebellar peduncles. Between them, on the floor of the fossa rhomboidalis and directly covered by entocinereal matter, are two further tracts, which appear to represent the continuations of the parts of the myel lying ventrally of the myelocele, i.e. the ventral cornua and the deeper-lying portions of the ventral columns. These structures, which extend over the whole floor of the fossa rhomboidalis, and are principally composed of cinerea, are known, from the arching convexity of their form, as the cylindrical columns (eminentiae teretes, *et*). Their cinerea is in connexion with most of the grey nidi of the oblongata, though some of these are forced out from the median line, and thus isolated, as a result of the splitting up of the oblongata by tracts of alba. A further and final consequence of the changes of structural conditions which we have been describing is the formation of an entirely new system of fibre-groups surrounding the oblongata in a transverse direction. Some of them enter into the ventral sulcus and the sulcus separating the pyramids from the olives; others strike across the fossa rhomboidalis. The system is known as the zonal fibre-system (stratum zonale, fibrae arcuatae, *g*).

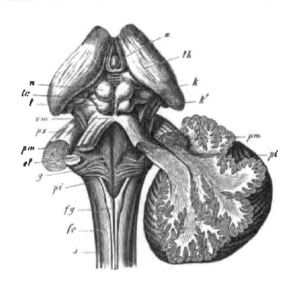

FIG. 48. Dorsal view of the human oblongata, with the quadrigemina, thalami and peduncles of the cerebellum. On the right, the radiation of the cerebellar peduncles within the cerebellum is shown. *fg* Slender funiculus. *fc* Cuneate funiculus. *s* Lateral column. The divergence of the lateral columns discloses the fossa rhomboidalis, on the floor of which may be seen the rounded prominences, *et*, divided by a median longitudinal sulcus. *g* Zonal fibres (f. arcuatae). *pi* Inferior cerebellar peduncles (restes). *pm* Middle cerebellar peduncles (crura ad pontem). *ps* Superior cerebellar peduncles (crura ad cerebrum). *n* Anterior, *t* posterior pair of quadrigemina (nates and testes). *ta* Postbrachia. *th* Thalamus. *k* Postgeniculum, *k'* pregeniculum. *z* Epiphysis (pineal body). *vm* Valvula (velum medull. ant.).

The re-arrangement of parts in the oblongata leads to a redistribution of the points of origin of the peripheral nerves. The simple rule of the myel is no longer obeyed; the nerve-roots are more or less displaced from their old positions. It is true that they still form, roughly, two longitudinal series, a dorsal and a ventral. But root-fibres that are exclusively motor issue only from the ventrolateral sulcus (twelfth cranial nerve, hypoglossal or lingual motor). The dorsolateral sulcus (or, at any rate, its immediate neighbourhood) gives rise, on the other hand, both to sensory and to motor fibres. Here begin all the other cranial nerves, with the exception of the first and second, olfactory and optic, and the third and fourth, the two anterior oculomotor nerves, whose place of origin lies further forward (cf. Figg. 47, 52).[1]

[1] These are the oculomotor and the trochlear nerves. The third oculomotor nerve, the fifth cranial or abducent ocular, arises in the most anterior region of the oblongata.

§ 4. The Cerebellum

At the anterior end of the oblongata, the structural relations of the parts are further, and very essentially, modified, owing to the outgrowth of the cerebellum from the primule of the third brain-vesicle (epencephalon). At the lowest stage of its development, the cerebellum varies but little, in outward form, from its original primule (Figg. 37, 38, p. 109); it consists of a transverse stria, bridging over the anterior end of the fossa rhomboidalis and receiving into its substance the restis of either side. Anteriorly, it is continued by a myelinated plate to the mesencephalon (Fig. 40, p. 110); laterally, it gives out tracts of transverse fibres, which run towards the lower surface of the oblongata, and decussate with each other and with the vertically ascending fibre-tracts of the pyramidal and olivary columns. These connexions remain the same later on, when the cerebellum has attained its further development. The bundles that enter it from the restes are the inferior cerebellar peduncles (crura ad medullam oblongatam, *pi* Fig. 48); the myelinated fibres issuing from it towards the mesencephalon are the superior

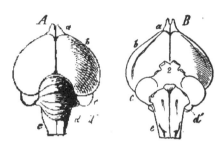

FIG. 49. Brain of the common fowl (Gallus bankiva), after C. G. CARUS. *A* Dorsal, *B* ventral aspect. *a* Olfactory bulbs. *b* Cerebrum. *c* Bigemina. *d* Cerebellum. *d'* Rudimentary pilea. *e* Oblongata. *2* Optic nerve.

cerebellar peduncles (crura ad cerebrum, *ps*). These are united by a thin myelinated plate, the valvula (velum medullare superius, *vm*), which forms the roof of the fossa rhomboidalis, and effects a direct connexion of the cerebellum with the adjoining anterior brain-division, the mesencephalon or quadrigemina.

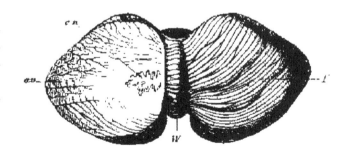

FIG. 50. Dorsal view of the human cerebellum. On the left side, the dentatum (*cn*) and the arbor (*av*) have been exposed by an oblique section. *W* Vermis. *H* Right pileum (hemisphere).

Finally, the white tracts proceeding from either side of the cerebellum form the middle cerebellar peduncles (crura ad pontem, *pm*). The structure that arises at the brain-basis by the junction of the middle peduncles and their decussations with the longitudinal myelinated fibres ascending from the oblongata is known as the pons (pons Varolii, *br* Fig. 47). It constitutes on the one hand a connecting link in the longitudinal direction between metencephalon and mesencephalon, and on the other a connecting link in the horizontal direction between the two lateral halves (pilea) of the cerebellum. The superior and inferior cerebellar peduncles are clearly visible at the very earliest stage of cerebellar development. The middle peduncles, on the contrary, do not attain to a growth that enables us to distinguish the pons as a special structure until the development of the cerebellum, and especially of the pilea, has advanced a considerable distance. Even in the birds, their place is supplied by little more than the longitudinal continuations of the ventral and lateral columns of the oblongata (Fig. 49 *B*). From the points at which the peduncles enter the cerebellar mass, above, below and sideward, myelinated fibres radiate out towards the periphery of the organ.

The morphological development of the cerebellum, the posterior section of the pallium, is completed at a comparatively early period. In all vertebrates, it is covered by ectocinerea, clearly differentiated from the radiation of myelinated fibres that occupies the interior; and even in the lowest vertebrates, the fishes, the cerebellar cortex divides into a number of layers, characterised by differences of coloration. In the cerebellum of the amphibia, we find groups of nerve-cells intercalated in the course of the myelinated fibres,—the first traces of ganglionic nidi. In the birds, these increase in number, while at the same time the layer-formation of the cortex becomes plainer, and an increase in the mass of the cortical elements is rendered possible by superficial folding (Figg. 40, 49).

The cerebellum undergoes its final stage of structural development in the mammals. Here we find, first, an unpaired median portion, the surface of which is crossed by transverse folds, and which has received the descriptive name of vermis; and, secondly, more strongly developed symmetrical lateral portions, the pilea. In the lowest mammals, it is true, the growth of the vermis exceeds that of the pilea; but in the higher forms, the pilea grow out about it in all directions (Fig. 50). The development of the pilea is accompanied by a more vigorous growth of the middle peduncles, which in the lower vertebrates are merely indicated by slender transverse fibre-tracts to the oblongata. The transverse folds of the ectocinerea increase in number, and show in cross-section the well known dendritic appearance of the arbor (arbor vitae, *av* Fig. 50). At the same time, larger ganglionic nidi appear in the radiation of myelinated fibres within the cerebellar mass. Thus each pileum contains a dentate nucleus, similar to that of the olives (nucleus dentatus cerebelli, *cn*). Other cinereal nidi, analogous in function, are scattered among the alba of the pons; their cells are intercalated between the decussations of the various fibre-bundles.

§ 5. The Mesencephalon

The mesencephalon—the division of the caudex which corresponds to the bigemina (lobi optici) of the lower vertebrates and the quadrigemina of mammals (*t, n* Fig. 48 ; *d* Fig. 37)—contains two formations of grey matter, entocinerea and nidal cinerea ; only the secondary vesicles develope the ectocinereal pallium. The entocinerea surrounds the Sylvian aqueduct in a layer of moderate thickness ; the most anteriorly situated nerve-nidi (those of the oculomotor and trochlear nerves and of the upper root of the trigeminus) are in connexion with it. Ganglionic nidi are found scattered through the bigemina or quadrigemina, and intercalated in the course of the myelinated fibre-tracts that pass below the Sylvian aqueduct. These are paired tracts of alba,

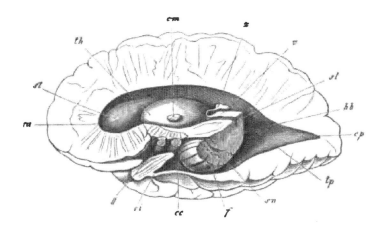

FIG. 51. Crus and paracele of the right hemisphere of man. *f* Crusta. *sn* Intercalatum. *hb* Tegmentum. *sl* Lemniscus. *v* Quadrigeminal lamina. *z* Epiphysis. *th* Thalamus. *cm* Medicommissure. *cc* Albicans. *st* Striatum. *ca* Precornu, *op* postcornu, *ci* medicornu of paracele. *tp* Tapetum of callosum. *II* Optic nerve.

united in the median line, and forming in the first place continuations of the ventral and lateral columns of the oblongata. Anteriorly, they are strengthened by the addition of longitudinal fibre-tracts, proceeding from the quadrigemina and thalami. They are termed, over their whole extent from oblongata to cerebral hemispheres, the brain crura (crura cerebri). The mesencephalic portion of the crura in the mammalian brain contains two well marked ganglionic nidi, the one of which, characterised by its dark coloration, is known as the intercalatum (substantia nigra of Soemmering : *sn* Fig. 51). It divides the crus of either side into a posterior and exterior portion, the crusta (basis pedunculi, pes cruris cerebri ; *f* Figg. 47, 51), and an anterior and median portion, the tegmentum (tegmentum pedunculi ; *hb* Figg. 47, 51). The most anterior extremity of the median portion, a band of alba which curves anteriorly into a fillet, and directly underlies the quadrigemina, is termed the lemniscus (ribbon ; or laqueus, fillet ; *sl* Fig. 51). A second tegmental nidus is named from its colour the rubrum (nucleus tegmenti ; *hb* Fig. 56). Dorsal of the crura lie the quadrigemina (*v* Fig. 51). Posteriorly, they are connected with the superior cerebellar peduncles ; anteriorly and laterally, they give out myelinated fibres, which in part mingle with the fibres of the tegmentum, in part pass into the thalami, and in part form the fibres of origin of the optic nerves. The connexion with thalami and optic nerves is mediated, in the mammalian brain, by the quadrigeminal brachia (*ta* Fig. 48). The pregemina are joined by the prebrachia to the thalami, and the postgemina by the postbrachia to the postgeniculum. In the space between the pregemina and the posterior extremity of the thalami lies the epiphysis (conarium, pineal body ; *z* Figg. 48, 51), which Descartes, in the old days, looked upon as the ' seat of the mind.' It is a highly vascular structure, which genetically represents, in all probability, a rudimentary sense-organ : it is supposed to be the central remnant of a median eye, functional in the primitive vertebrates. The mammalian quadrigemina are, as we have already seen (p. 111), completely solid. They are connected by a lamina of alba, which posteriorly forms the direct continuation of the valvula, and anteriorly passes into the post-commissure (*cp* Fig. 53) running along the boundary-line of quadrigemina and thalami.

§ 6. The Diencephalon

The diencephalon, or region of the thalami, is smaller than the mesencephalon in all the lower vertebrates (*f* Fig. 37, p. 109) ; in the mammalian brain their relation is reversed (*th* Figg. 47, 48, 51). In the fishes, however, we have an indication of the change : a paired continuation of the diencephalon extends posteriorly to the base of the brain, and there appears in the form of two hemispherical prominences, lying ventrally and somewhat anteriorly of the bigemina (lobi optici). These are the inferior lobes of the fish-brain (*li* Fig. 41, p. 111). They enclose a cavity, which stands in connexion with the diacele, the cleft-like aperture resulting from the anterior roof-slit and dividing the diencephalon into the two thalami. At the place where the inferior lobes meet in the median line, they are continued into an unpaired structure, the hypophysis (*h* Fig. 41), whose dorsal portion is an evagination of the diencephalon, while its ventral half is a remnant of embryonic tissue that originally belonged to the anterior extremity of the gullet, and remained in conjunction with the diencephalon when the base of the cranium developed. The hypophysis persists in the higher vertebrates, after the inferior lobes have entirely disappeared in consequence of the more vigorous development of the crura (*h* Fig. 52). The only point at which the ganglionic substance of the diencephalon appears, in these forms, is between the divergent crura, where we find a grey prominence, the tuber cinereum. This is continued anteriorly in the direction of the hypophysis, in a funnel-shaped prolongation, the infundibulum (*i* Fig. 38; *t* Fig. 47). The infundibulum contains a small cavity, communicating dorsally with the diacele. The entrance of small blood-vessels into the brain-mass gives the cinerea between the crura a perforated, sieve-like appearance; the region is termed the postcribrum (lamina perforata posterior; *pp* Figg. 47, 52). In the mammalian brain, two myelinated prominences, the albicantia (corpora candicantia or mammillaria; *cc*), issue ventrally from the floor of the diencephalon. Situated immediately in front of the anterior line of the pons, they bound the tuber posteriorly, as infundibulum and hypophysis bound it anteriorly. Their genetic signification is still uncertain.

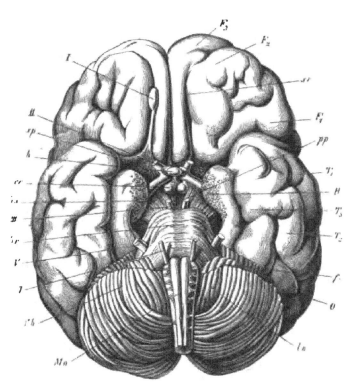

FIG. 52. Base of the human brain. *Mo* Oblongata. *Cb* Ventral surface of cerebellum. *fl* Floccule. *to* Tonsil. *br* Pons. *hs* Crus. *cc* Albicantia. *h* Hypophysis. *sp* Precribrum (olfactory area). *pp* Postcribrum (between the divergent crura). *I* Olfactory nerve with olfactory bulb (rhinencephalon): removed on the right of the Fig. *II* Optic nerve. *III* Oculomotor nerve. *V* Trigeminus. *VI* Abducent ocular. F_3 Subfrontal gyre. F_2 Medifrontal gyre. *sr* Olfactory fissure. F_1 Superfrontal gyre. T_1, T_2, T_3 Supertemporal, meditemporal and subtemporal gyres. *O* Occipital gyre. *H* Hippocampal gyre.

The diencephalon, like the mesencephalon, contains two formations of grey matter, entocinerea and nidal cinerea. In the first place, the interior of the diacele is lined with a cinereal layer, which at the same time invests a thin band of alba, joining the two thalami, and termed the medicommissure (*cm* Fig. 51). The entocinerea of the diacele extends ventrally to the brain-base, where it is directly continuous with the tuber and infundibulum. Secondly, however, a number of ganglionic nidi, separated by masses of alba, are scattered throughout the interior of the thalami (*th* Fig. 56). Similar nidi may be found in two smaller rounded prominences, which in mammals form the posterior boundary of the thalami and externally are in connexion with them, the pregeniculum and postgeniculum (*k k'* Fig. 48, p. 120). The fibres of origin of the optic nerve interlace with the fibres of both genicula, and the postgeniculum alsohreceives the quadrigeminal postbrachium. The anterior and lateral portions of the thalami show a gentle roof-slope; posteriorly, the dorsal surface is separated from the ventral by a marginal swelling, the pulvinar (*pv* Fig. 47, p. 119).

§ 7. The Prosencephalon

(a)—*The Brain Cavities and the Surrounding Parts*

In the earlier stages of its development, the prosencephalon is a vesicular structure, overlying the diencephalon. Originally simple, it is later divided by the anterior roof-slit into symmetrical halves, entirely separate save for the continuity of their floor. At the place where the roof-slit of the diencephalon is continued into the intercerebral fissure, the diencephalic cavity was primitively in open communication with the two paraceles. In all the vertebrates (except the fishes, whose hemispheres are solid structures: p. 111), the vascular trunk that penetrates the cavity of the diencephalon sends out a large number of branches from it into the hemicerebral vesicles. When the diencephalon becomes so far solid, by growth of the constituent nerve-mass, that only the diacele (third ventricle) is left, the earlier doors of communication are almost entirely closed; only two very narrow apertures are left, at the anterior end of the diacele, which permit of the entrance of blood-vessels into the hemicerebral cavities. These are the portae (foramina of Monro: *mo* Fig. 53), the remnants of the original aula (Fig. 43, p. 113). They are separated anteriorly by a septum of alba, which represents the posterior line of junction of the two prosencephalic vesicles. The floor of the septum is usually formed of large bundles of myelinated fibres, transverse in direction, termed the precommissure (*ca*). In the reptilian, and still more in the avian and mammalian brains, the hemispheres come to such a growth as to arch more or less completely over the diencephalon. As a result of this, the paraceles run out posteriorly, and the thalami, instead of lying behind the hemispheres, as they did at first, form prominences that project with the greater part of their surface into the paraceles, and show only their internal faces to the diacele.

The grey matter of the prosencephalon occurs in all three possible formations. As entocinerea, it covers the walls of the diacele, and therefore, more especially, the inner faces of the thalami and the cavity of the infundibulum, as well as the whole of the infundibular region; as ganglionic cinerea, it forms considerable masses, intercalated in the course of the continuations of the crura below the thalami; and as ectocinerea, it invests the hemicerebral pallium at large. The position of these collections of grey matter, and their relation to the radiations of myelinated fibres, are

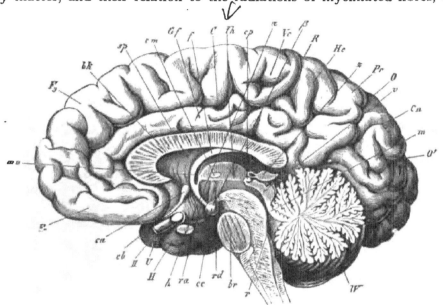

FIG. 53. Median section of the human brain. *r* Fossa rhomboidalis. *br* Pons. *cc* Albicans. *rd* Descending, *ra* ascending root of the fornix. *h* Hypophysis. *II* Optic nerve. *ca* Precommissure. *cb* Copula (lamina rostralis).[1] *mo* Porta. *bk* Callosum. *sp* Septum (septum pellucidum). *f* Fornix. *cm* Medicommissure. *th* Thalamus. *cp* Postcommissure. *z* Epiphysis. *v* Quadrigeminum. *m* Valvula. *W* Vermis of cerebellum with arbor. F_3 Subfrontal gyre. *Gf* Callosal gyre. *C* Callosal fissure. *R* Central fissure (fissure of Rolando). *Vc* Precentral gyre. *Hc* Postcentral gyre. *H* Hippocampus. *U* Uncus. *Pr* Precuneus. *O* Occipital fissure. *Cn* Cuneus. *O'* Calcarine fissure. *α, β* Lines of the transverse sections shown in Fig. 56.

the essential conditions of the structure of the prosencephalon. In all vertebrates, except the fishes and amphibia, the ganglionic nidi are placed upon the floor of the paraceles. They there form rounded prominences,

---

[1] This Figure, with several others, has been printed without change in all editions of the *Physiologische Psychologie*. The reader will observe that the line from the abbreviation *cb* is carried to what has the general position of the terma (lamina terminalis). The real copula (the *weisse Bodencommissur* of the German; Henle's commissura baseos alba) is neither designated nor even shown in the Fig. It would be waste of space to point out in detail all slips of this sort. They are, fortunately, irrelevant to the course of the author's argument. But the reader should be warned that these old figures would not pass muster with modern anatomists.—TRANSLATOR.

from which myelinated fibres radiate out towards the periphery of the hemispheres.

The lowermost stratum of the floor of the paraceles is, therefore, composed of the continuations of the ascending and diverging crura. Upon these rest, first of all, the thalami. New tracts of alba issue from the thalami, and join and reinforce the crural bundles that run forwards and outwards below them. These terminal radiations of the crus, at the anterior and external border of each thalamus, are, again, intermixed with large ganglionic nidi. The result is that the floor of the paracele rises in a rounded prominence of considerable extent, which forms the anterior and exterior boundary of the thalamus. It is termed the striatum (*st* Figg. 54, 55).

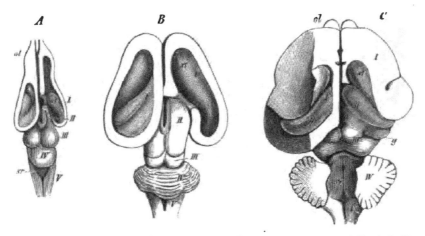

FIG. 54. Differentiation of the brain-ganglia, after GEGENBAUR. *A* Brain of tortoise, *B* of foetal calf, *C* of cat. On the left, the roof of the paracele has been removed; on the right, the fornix has also been cut away; and in *C*, on the left, the passage of the fornix into the hippocampus (cornu Ammonis) is exposed. *I* Cerebrum. *II* Thalami. *III* Quadrigemina or bigemina (lobi optici). *IV* Cerebellum. *V* Oblongata. *ol* Olfactory bulbs. *st* Striata. *f* Fornix. *h* (in *C*) Hippocampus. *g* (*ibid.*) Geniculum. *sr* Fossa rhomboidalis.

The club-like extremity, lying anteriorly of the thalamus, is called the caput; the narrower portion, surrounding the thalamus exteriorly, the cauda. Striatum and thalamus together cover the entire floor of the paracele. The surface of the striatum is invested with a tolerably thick layer of cinerea, whereas the thalamus (i.e., that portion of its surface which projects into the paracele) is covered by a lamina of alba. Along the border of thalamus and striatum lies a narrow band of alba, the tenia (stria terminalis, stria cornea: *sc* Fig. 55). The ganglionic nidi of the striatum appear in the mammalian brain, as three characteristically shaped masses. The first is directly connected with the grey investment of the striatum; it follows the arch of the peripheral surface, and so acquires a curving form, which has given it the name of caudatum (nucleus caudatus : *st* Fig. 56). It constitutes, with the myelinated masses that begin their course below it, the striatum in the narrower sense. A second and very considerable nidus, the lenticula (nucleus lentiformis : *lk*), lies to the outside of the caudatum. In vertical section it appears as a triangle, whose apex points towards the internal edge of the striatum, while its base extends far out into the alba of the hemisphere. The lenticular cinerea is divided up by intervening myelinated fibres into three groups, two external and ribbon-shaped, and one internal and triangular. The third and last nidus of the striatum lies outward from the lenticula. It, too, has the form of a narrow ribbon of tissue, and surrounds the third subdivision of the lenticula. It is named, from the closeness of its approach to the brain surface, the rampart or claustrum (nucleus taeniaeformis : *cl*). Ventrally from the claustrum, and near the cortex of the brain-base, lies yet another small nidus, the amygdala (*mk*).[1] These ganglionic nidi of the hemispheres take up many of the myelinated fibres that spring from the quadrigemina and thalami; others pass under the striatum forwards, without coming into connexion with its cinerea. Above the nidi, the myelinated bundles coming up from below radiate out from the whole extent of the striatum, in the most various directions, towards the cerebral cortex. The terminal division of the great longitudinal fibre-tract, that begins in the columns of

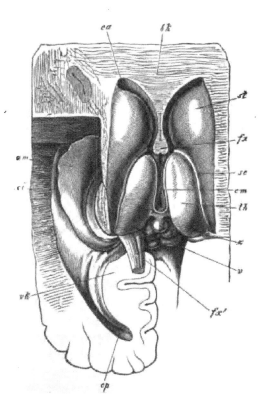

FIG. 55. Thalami and striata of man; in part after ARNOLD. On the left, the postcornu and medicornu of the paracele, with the hippocampus (cornu Ammonis) and calcar, are exposed. *v* Quadrigemina. *z* Epiphysis. *th* Thalamus. *cm* Medicommissure. *sc* Tenia. *st* Striatum. *fx* Anterior portion of fornix, *bk* anterior portion of callosum, both in section. *fx'* Posterior portion of fornix, turned back. *ci* Medicornu of paracele. *am* Hippocampus. *cp* Postcornu of paracele. *vk* Calcar. *ca* Precornu of paracele.

---

[1] Many anatomists restrict the name striatum to the caudatum alone, i.e., do not extend it to embrace the lenticula. The claustrum and amygdala must be regarded, from the form of their cells, not as true ganglionic nidi, but as parts of the cortical cinerea, from which they are separated by an intercalated lamina of alba.

the myel, then passes over into the columns of the oblongata, and thereafter takes its place among the bundles of the crura, is the corona (corona radiata; *m*). The factors which most largely determine the arrangement of its fibres are those discussed just now, as concerned in the formation of the paraceles. Since the vascular plexuses that find their way into the cavities spread over the entire floor, the coronal fibres which are to continue the crura cortexward must curve out around the vessels at the periphery, in order to attain to their goal.

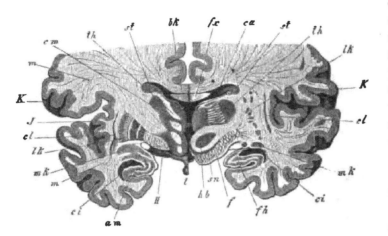

FIG. 56. Transverse section through the human cerebrum, posterior aspect; in part after REICHERT. The dorsal portion of the pallium of the hemispheres is not shown. On the left side, the section follows the line *a*, on the right side, the line *β* of Fig. 53. On the left, therefore, it passes through the medicommissure and the hypophysis; on the right, it traverses the brain a little more posteriorly, cutting the posterior portion of the thalamus and the albicans. *bk* Callosum. *fx* Fornix. *ca* Precornu of paracele. *st* Nidus of striatum (caudatum). *th* Nidi of thalamus. Three of these are distinguished: a lateral, a median (bounding the diacele), and an anterior nidus. *cm* Medicommissure. *K* Operculum. *J* Insula. *m* Radiations of the corona. *lk* Lenticula. On the left hand, the three parts of the lenticular nidus are visible. *cl* Claustrum. Between *cl* and the lenticular nidus lies the external capsule of the lenticula. *mk* Amygdala. *ci* Medicornu of paracele. *am* Cross-section of hippocampus. *II* Optic nerve. *t* Infundibulum and hypophysis. *f* Crusta. *sn* Intercalatum (substantia nigra). *hb* Tegmentum with rubrum. *fh* Cleft in medicornu of paracele, by which a vascular plexus gains access to it (hippocampal fissure).

The terminal division of the prosencephalon consists of the two olfactory bulbs or olfactory gyres (rhinencephalon). In most fishes, the rhinencephalon is so strongly developed that it not seldom surpasses in extent all the remaining portions of the prosencephalon. In the higher classes of vertebrates, and especially in the birds, it decreases in importance; but in the lower mammals it appears again as a structure of relatively considerable size (cf. Figg. 37, 38, 49, 54). In the mammalian brain it forms special gyri, which issue from the brain-base and project to a greater or less degree beyond the frontal portion of the prosencephalon. The olfactory bulbs contain cavities, the rhinoceles, which communicate with the prosocele (paraceles). In some of the mammalian orders, viz., in the cetacea and (to a less extent) in the apes and in man, the rhinencephalon degenerates.

The olfactory bulbs lie far back under the frontal regions of the hemispheres and are connected by a narrow stalk, the olfactory tract, to the middle part of the brain-base (Fig. 52, p. 125). The area which serves as point of departure for the tract, the olfactory area, presents a sieve-like appearance, due to the incoming of numerous small vessels, and is consequently termed the precribrum (lamina perforata anterior : *sp* Figg. 47, 52).

The fuller development of the prosencephalon brings with it a radical transformation of the two lateral ventricles, the paraceles. This is due, in part, to the growth of the hemicerebral masses which enclose them, but in part also to the appearance of special structures which project into the cavities. As the hemispheric vesicle of the mammalian brain arches back over the diencephalon and mesencephalon, the portion that lies behind the Sylvian fossa takes a downward turn (Figg. 36, 42, pp. 108, 112). The result is that the paracele possesses two branches, or cornua, as they are termed: a precornu, bounded on the outside by the arched wall of the hemisphere, and a medicornu (cornu inferius) whose extremity is drawn out to a point. The growth of the hemispheric vesicle over the caudex is accompanied throughout its progress (as we have already seen: p. 114 above) by a parallel growth of the aula (foramen of Monro), the original means of communication between prosocele and diacele. As the aula, then, curves over the caudex, at first posteriorly and then ventrally, what was originally its dorsal extremity coincides with the pointed end of the medicornu. The part of the aperture that now lies in the anterior wall of the medicornu forms a fissure (the hippocampal fissure, of which more presently), which is occluded by a vascular plexus from the pia (*fh* Fig. 56). In fine, therefore, the primitive aula remains open at beginning and end, but is closed over its middle portion by myelinated fibres. These belong to the fornix and callosum, structures which we shall discuss in the following section.

In the brain of the primates (the apes and man), the conformation of the paraceles undergoes yet another change, due to the large development of the occipital portion of the hemispheres. The outer wall of each paracele pushes vigorously backwards before it takes the curve downwards, so that the cavity itself is prolonged in the same direction. We thus have a postcornu (*cp* Fig. 51, p. 123), in addition to the precornu and medicornu. The backward growth of the prosencephalon stops, as it were, with a jerk, to continue forwards and downwards. This fact is attested both by the outward appearance of the occipital region, and by the shape of the postcornu, which is drawn out into an even finer point than the medicornu. In the apes, the postcornu is smaller than it is in man; in other mammals with strongly developed hemispheres, as e.g. the cetacea, it is no more than a trace or rudiment of what it is later to become.

(b)—Fornix and Commissural System

At the anterior extremity of the primitive aula, the two hemispheres grow together in the middle line. The resulting strip of alba is termed the terma (lamina terminalis: *bd* Fig. 43, p. 113). The backward curvature of the hemispheres round the transverse axis of the diencephalon naturally brings with it a corresponding curvature of the terma. Its most ventral and anterior extremity becomes a band of cross-fibres, connecting the two hemispheres, and known as the precommissure (*k* Fig. 43). In its further course it divides into two lateral halves running longitudinally from before backwards, on either side of the median fissure. We find the first beginnings of these longitudinal fibre-tracts in the birds, but they do not attain to any high degree of development until we reach the mammals, where they constitute the fornix. Closely approximated anteriorly, the columns of the fornix diverge as they pass backwards. The myelinated fibres of their anterior extremity extend ventrally to the brain-base, where they stand in connexion with the alba of the albicantia (Fig. 53, p. 127). The fibres of their posterior extremity are distributed in man and the apes into two bundles, the smaller of which comes to lie upon the inner wall of the postcornu, and the larger upon the inner wall of the medicornu of the paracele. The projection thus occasioned in the wall of the postcornu is termed the calcar (pes hippocampi minor), that in the medicornu, the hippocampus (pes hippocampi major: Fig. 55). These prominences are, however, constituted in part of other factors, which we shall discuss later. In the other mammals, which have not developed a postcornu, and which therefore cannot possess the calcar, the whole mass of fornix-fibres passes over into the hippocampus.[1]

The formation of the fornix appears to stand in intimate relation to that of another transverse fibre-system, whose appearance is even more definitely characteristic of the mammalian brain. In the monotremes and marsupials, new fibre-tracts are observed to issue from the hippocampus (cornu ammonis). They run dorsally of the incoming fornix-fibres, and pass above the diencephalon to the opposite half of the brain, where they terminate, as they began, in the hippocampus. The transverse commissure that thus arises between the two hippocampi is the original primule of the callosum. In the non-placental mammals, in which the callosum is thus restricted to a mere cross-commissure between the two hippocampi, the precommissure

---

[1] The question whether the apes have, like man, a postcornu to the paracele and a calcar (pes hippocampi minor) led to a not very profitable controversy between OWEN, who took the negative side, and HUXLEY. Cf. HUXLEY, *Evidence as to Man's Place in Nature*, 1863, 100, 113. The older writers on the ape-brain figure the postcornu. Cf. e.g. TIEDEMANN, *Icones cerebri*, 1825, 54. OWEN himself, in his later work, describes the rudiment of a postcornu in the dolphin (*Anatomy of Vertebrates*, iii. 120). In the anthropoid apes, as HUXLEY has shown, the calcar exists as well as the postcornu, only at a lower stage of development than in man.

is very strongly developed, as it is in the birds, though a free space is left between it and the callosum. In the placental mammals, the hippocampal commissure is reinforced by additional transverse fibre-tracts, which radiate out into the hemicerebral alba at large. They make their first appearance at the anterior end of the future callosum, so that the development of the callosum itself proceeds from before backwards. At the same time, the precommissure decreases in size, and enters by way of a thin and still transverse lamella of alba (Fig. 53 *ca*) into connexion with the anterior extremity of the callosum, the 'beak' or rostrum. This junction of precommissure and rostrum results in the anterior occlusion of the intercerebral fissure. Between the broad posterior extremity of the callosum, the splenium, and the dorsal surface of the cerebellum, there still remains, however, a narrow passage, by which the diacele can communicate with the surrounding space (the passage is visible in Fig. 53 as the dark space between epiphysis and splenium). This is continued laterally as a narrow cleft, leading into the paracele. We have in it the remnant of the original anterior roof-slit, whereby the vascular plexuses gain access to the three anterior brain-cavities (p. 114).

In most mammalian brains, the hippocampal commissure persists as a relatively large portion of the entire callosum (*bk* Fig. 57 *A*). Moreover, since the occipital brain is here but little developed, and the anterior brain-ganglia, the thalami and striata, also decrease very considerably in mass, the hippocampus is brought forwards to the point of origin of the fornix. The fornix itself immediately separates on either side into two divisions, the one of which forms the anterior and the other the posterior boundary of the hippocampus (*f* and *f'* Fig. 57 *B*).[1] It is, however, not until we reach the higher mammals that we find any considerable development of the fornix. Between the callosum and the deeper-lying fornicolumns are now spread two thin vertical lamellae of alba, enclosing a narrow cleft-like cavity. These are the septa (septa pellucida : *sp* Fig. 53). Fornix and septa occlude the internal openings of the paraceles; nothing is left but the beginning of the original aula, just behind the anterior place of origin of the fornicolumns (porta or foramen of Monro : *mo* Fig. 53 ; cf. *i* Fig. 43, p. 113). Between the lateral halves of the septa is the cleft-like cavity just mentioned ; it communicates posteriorly with the diacele, and is termed the pseudocele (cavum or ventriculus septi pellucidi). The callosal radiations form the roof and a portion of the outer wall of the paraceles. As external capsule, they skirt the external margin of the lenticula. On their way to the cortex, where they terminate, they interlace at all points (the posterior strands excepted) with the fibres of the corona. The posterior fibres, coming from

---

[1] In human anatomy, the portion of the callosum which connects the two hippocampi is termed the psalterium.

the hippocampi and their neighbourhood, do not receive any admixture of coronal fibres. In the lower mammals, they appear simply and solely as the hippocampal commissure (Fig. 57 *A*); in the primates, they divide into two parts; an internal, passing over into hippocampus and calcar (*am* and *vk* Fig. 55); and an external, which curves ventrally in front of the coronal fibres running to the cortex of the occipital lobe (*m'* Fig. 58), and forms the outer wall of the postcornu of the paracele. This is termed the tapetum (*tp* Fig. 51, p. 123).

We have seen that the fornix is the fibre-tract proceeding from the terma (lamina terminalis) of the aula; and we have followed the course

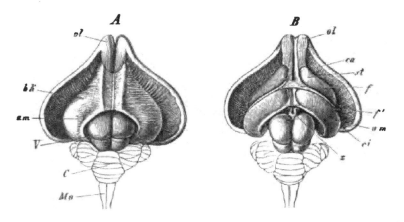

FIG. 57. Anatomy of brain of rabbit. In *A* the roof of the hemispheres has been turned back, so that the callosum is visible over its whole extent. In *B* the callosum has been removed, and the paraceles are displayed. *Mo* Oblongata. *C* Cerebellum. *V* Quadrigemina. *z* Epiphysis. In *B* the beginnings of the striata are visible to the side of *z* under the hippocampi. *am* Hippocampus. *bk* Callosum. Anteriorly to the line *bk* lies the portion of the callosum that passes into the hemicerebral alba; its interlacing with the coronal fibres can be seen in the Fig. Posteriorly to *bk* the hippocampal commissure or fornicommissure begins. *ol* Olfactory lobes. *ca* Precornu of paracele. *f* Anterior, *f'* posterior portion of fornix. *ci* Medicornu of paracele. *st* Striata.

which it takes as the outgrowing hemispheres arch over the brain-caudex. The same direction is taken by the portion of the hemicerebral wall lying immediately anterior to the terma. There is a difference, however. The floor of the hemispheres is continuous from the first, and the fornix has, therefore, no investment of grey matter. This anterior portion, on the other hand, which comes to lie dorsally to the fornix as the result of the hemispheric curvature, is not included in the original area of continuity, and is accordingly covered with a layer of cinerea over its median surface. After the callosum has forced a passage across the brain, it is separated by the callosal fibres from the fornix, and forms a longitudinal gyre running dorsal to the callosum. It is termed the callosal gyre (gyrus fornicatus or cingulum : *Gf* Fig. 53, p. 127).

In certain mammalian brains, where the frontal part of the prosencephalon is but little developed, while the callosal gyre is large, it can be traced anteriorly from a point directly behind the base of the olfactory tract. After curving over the callosum, it again emerges posteriorly at the brain-base. Here it passes over into a gyre lying behind the Sylvian and bounding the median fissure; the hippocampal gyre, the outer wall of the hippocampus (*H* Fig. 53). Where the callosum begins, the layer of cinerea ceases; the lower surface of the callosal gyre, the surface adjacent to the callosum, consists of unmixed white matter. The sole exception is a narrow stria of cinerea, isolated from the rest of the cortex, which has persisted in its posterior portion.

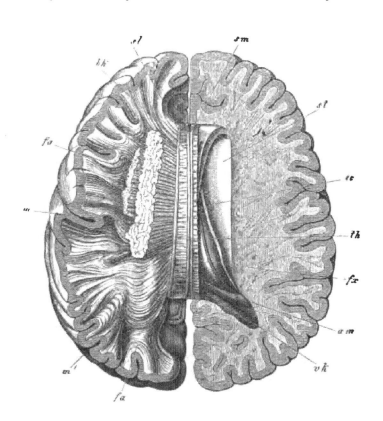

FIG. 58. Callosum and paracele of human brain. Brain hardened in alcohol. On the left side, the roof of the hemisphere has been removed, so as to expose the median portion of the callosum, and the callosal radiations into the hemicerebral alba are shown. On the right, the paracele appears in horizontal section. *bk* Callosum. *sm* Stria media (nerve of Lancisi). *sl* Stria lateralis (tenia tecta; part of callosal gyre). *m* Interlacement of callosal radiation with coronal fibres. *m'* Posterior uncrossed portion of callosal radiation. At this point the callosal tracts are reflected downwards, round the outer wall of the postcornu, to form the tapetum (*tp* Fig. 51). *fa* Fibrae arcuatae, connecting the cortical portions of neighbouring gyres. *st* Striata. *sc* Tenia (stria cornea). *th* Thalamus, for the most part covered by the following parts: *fx* Fornix; *am* Hippocampus; *vk* Calcar.

This is known as the fasciola (*fc* Fig. 59); it lies immediately above the callosum. The fasciola is free, over its whole extent, from any admixture of alba; so that the longitudinal myelinated fibres upon which it rests are entirely separated from the remaining white matter of the callosal gyre. When the gyre is removed from the callosum, these fibres, together with the fasciola which invests their posterior portion, remain attached to it; they appear as a myelinated stria, and have received a special name, tenia tecta or lateral stria (*sl* Figg. 58, 59). The importance of this separation of lateral stria and fasciola from the rest of the myelinated and cortical substance of the callosal gyre lies in the fact that the structures remain isolated at the point of transition from callosal to hippocampal gyre.[1] Alba and cortex of the callosal gyre pass directly over into alba and cortex of the hippocampal. Really, therefore, the two are but one: the only difference between the parts being that the callosal gyre is not invested with cinerea over its ventral surface, the surface adjacent to the callosum, whereas with transition to the hippocampal gyre the cortex spreads out again over the entire surface of the convolution. Now at the point where the callosal gyre leaves the splenium and becomes the hippocampal gyre,— at the point i.e. where the cortex which has previously invested the inner surface only extends over the ventral as well,—the lateral stria divides from the rest of the white matter of the gyre, and appears upon the surface of the gyrus hippocampi. This means, of course, that the fasciola, which lies just below the lateral stria, must divide from the rest of the cortex; the lateral stria forms a partition between cinerea and cinerea. The result is that we have, at the point in question, a cortical layer covered by a lamella of alba, and this again covered by a grey cortex. The two most superficial layers, lateral stria and fasciola, are, it must be remembered, strictly limited in area; they extend only over the hippocampal gyre. Indeed, they cover only a portion of that; for the white and grey areas are not coincident. The alba of the lateral stria is distributed over the entire cortex of the hippocampal gyre, as an extremely thin reticular layer of white fibres. This reticular alba is the only white layer that appears upon the cortical surface of the hemispheres (*sr* Fig. 59; cf. also *H* Fig. 53, p. 127). The fas-

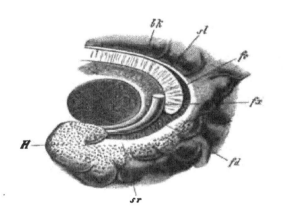

FIG. 59. Hippocampal gyre and adjacent parts of callosum and fornix in the human brain. *bk* Callosum. *sl* Stria lateralis. *fc* Fasciola (fasciola cinerea). *fd* Continuation of fasciola (fascia dentata). *fx* Lower extremity of fornix. *H* Hippocampal gyre. *sr* Reticular alba.

---

[1] The nerves of Lancisi, or striae mediae, belong not to the callosal gyre, but to the callosum itself. See *sm* Fig. 58.

ciola, on the other hand, retains its ribbon-like form; it covers, not the whole radiation of the white fibres of the lateral stria, but only a certain group of them, the group lying in the fissure which forms the interior boundary of the hippocampal gyre. From the peculiar toothed appearance that it has at this part of its course it is known as the fascia dentata (*fd* Fig. 59).

The fissure which forms the interior boundary of the hippocampal gyre corresponds to the hippocampal projection into the medicornu of the paracele. The formation of the hippocampus—to which, as we have seen, fibres from callosum and fornix contribute—is thus completed by contributions from the various regions of the callosal gyre. The white layer which invests the paracele-surface of the hippocampus is formed by the fibres of callosum and fornix (Fig. 60). It is followed by a first cinereal layer, the cortex of the hippocampal gyre (*r*); externally to that comes a second layer of alba, the continuation of the lateral stria or the reticular alba (*H*) distributed over the cortex of the gyrus hippocampi; and, lastly, beyond that follows a second cinereal layer, the fascia dentata, the continuation of

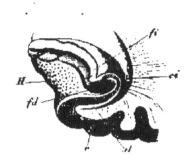

FIG. 60. Hippocampal gyre and hippocampus of human brain, in transverse section. *ci* Medicornu of paracele. *r* Grey cortex of uncus. *H* Uncus with reticular alba. *fd* External cinereal lamella of hippocampus (fascia dentata). *sl* Internal white layer of hippocampus; continuation of the lateral stria. *fi* Reflected border of this layer (fimbria).

the fasciola (*fd*). This extends, as we have said, only to the fissure which corresponds to the hippocampal projection. The same fissure forms the inner boundary of the reticular alba. Along the line at which the alba ceases, the grey matter of the fascia dentata is continuous with the cortex of the hippocampal gyre; so that here the two cinereal layers which fill the interior of the hippocampus are brought into contact. At the precise point where this transition takes place, the internal white investment of the hippocampus terminates in a free reflected border, the fimbria (*fi*).

(*c*)—*The Development of the Outward Conformation of the Brain*

We have now passed in review those divisions of the brain which appear in the general course of neural evolution. This articulation into parts is paralleled by a series of changes in outward form, the final outcome of which is dependent partly upon the degree of general development to which the particular brain has attained, and partly upon the relative growth of the individual parts. In the lowest vertebrates, the brain has gained but little upon the simplest embryonic form which is given with the separation of the primitive brain-vesicle into its five subdivisions. The whole range of structural difference is here practically exhausted by differences in the relative size of these subdivisions; the only further determinant of final brain-form is the development of the olfactory lobe as an outgrowth from the prosencephalon. A much greater variety of configuration appears as soon as the pallial structures begin to invest the brain-caudex. The covering of quadrigemina (bigemina) and cerebellum by cerebral hemispheres and of oblongata by cerebellum, and the degree of encephalic flexure, bring in their train a long series of structural peculiarities; and the list is still further swelled by differences in the outward form of the hemispheres, by the development or lack of development of the cerebellar pilea, by the corresponding appearance or non-appearance of certain nidal structures (such as the olives) on the oblongata, and by the development of a pons.

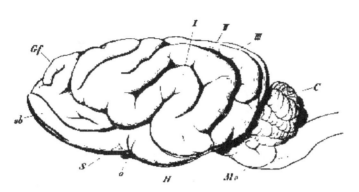

FIG. 61. Lateral aspect of brain of dog. *Mo* Oblongata. *C* Cerebellum. *S* Fissure of Sylvius. *ob* Olfactory lobes. *Gf* Callosal gyre, coming to the surface behind the olfactory lobes. *H* Hippocampal gyre. *o* Optic nerve. *I, II, III* First, second and third typical gyres of the carnivore brain.

The point where the cerebral hemisphere originally rested upon the brain-caudex is marked, in all mammalian brains without exception, by the Sylvian fossa (*S* Fig. 42, p. 112). In the higher mammals, the edges of the fossa draw together, so that we find in its place a deep fissure, the Sylvian fissure (fissura Sylvii). The fissure usually runs obliquely, from posterior-dorsal to anterior-ventral; its divergence from the vertical is determined by the growth of the occipital brain and its extension over the posterior parts of the system (Fig. 61). In the highest mammalian order, that of the primates, the Sylvian fissure undergoes a final and characteristic transformation. The frontal and occipital brains here develop simultaneously; and the fossa formed by the growth of the hemispheres over the caudex consequently appears, at the very beginning of the embryonic life, as a roughly outlined triangle, lying base upward. The edges, above, below and behind, then grow towards each other, and the fossa closes to form a Y-shaped fissure (*S* Fig. 62), dividing into an anterior and a posterior ramus (s_1 and s_2. Cf. also Fig. 65). The part of the hemisphere that lies between the two rami, and roofs in the original fossa from above, is termed the operculum (*K*). If the operculum is turned back, and the floor of the Sylvian fossa exposed, the underlying hemispheric surface proves to be bulged out and, like all the rest, divided by fissures into a number of gyres. The brain-region which is concealed and isolated in this peculiar way is known as the central lobe or island (insula Reilii; Fig. 56 *J*, p. 130). The two rami of the Sylvian fissure form the customary points of departure for the division of the hemicerebra of the primate brain into separate regions or lobes. The portion lying anteriorly of the anterior ramus is termed the frontal lobe (*F* Fig. 62); the space included between the rami, the parietal lobe (*P*); the region behind the Sylvian fissure, the occipital lobe (*O*); and the area situated ventrally of it, the tem-

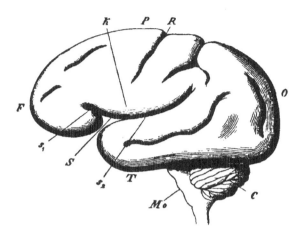

FIG. 62. Lateral aspect of brain of human foetus (7 months). *Mo* Oblongata. *C* Cerebellum. *S* Sylvian fissure. s_1 Anterior, s_2 posterior ramus. *K* Operculum. *R* Central fissure (fissure of Rolando). *F* Frontal lobe. *P* Parietal lobe. *O* Occipital lobe. *T* Temporal lobe.

poral lobe (*T*). These lobes pass into one another, on the convex surface of the brain, without any sharp line of demarcation.

Not only does the Sylvian fissure divide the surface of the hemispheres at large into a number of lobes: there are certain other and smaller areas that are marked off from their surroundings by furrows or fissures. Thus the longitudinal fibre-tract running dorsal to the callosum from before backwards, and then curving ventrally round the splenium,—the area with which we have become familiar as the callosal gyre,—may be recognised by the presence of definite fissures, separating it from the surrounding parts (*Gf* Fig. 53, p. 127). In all mammalian brains, in particular, we can trace on the median surface of the hemispheres the margin along which the investment of the inner portion of the callosal gyre is deflected into the medicornu of the paracele (hippocampal fissure: *fh* Fig. 56, p. 130); while in most of them the callosal gyre is also bounded, during its course upwards over the callosum, by a longitudinal fissure, the callosal fissure (sulcus callosomarginalis: *C* Fig. 53). In the same way, the olfactory lobe or olfactory gyre at the base of the prosencephalon is almost always set off by an inner and an outer fissure, the entorhinal and ectorhinal fissures; though in the human brain the two have fused to one (*sr* Fig. 52, p. 125).

All these fissures and furrows are occasioned, then, by the growth of the hemispheres round their point of application to the diencephalon (Sylvian fissure), by the occlusion of the external fissure of the medicornu (hippocampal fissure), or by the course of determinate bundles of myelinated fibres appearing on the ventral and median surface of the hemispheres (callosal, entorhinal and ectorhinal fissures). Since the structural relations that condition them are characteristic of the mammals as a class, they form, as soon as they can be traced at all, entirely constant features of the mammalian brain.

But there are other fissures, less uniform in their course, which give the brain-pallium of the mammals a variously convoluted appearance. The surface of cerebrum and cerebellum is split up by them into numerous gyres. The cerebellar gyres are, on the whole, arranged with more regularity than the cerebral ; they form narrow ridges, set vertically upon the underlying alba, and following for the most part a transverse direction. On the cerebrum, whose folds are not unlike the convolutions of the intestine, it is often difficult to recognise any definite law of gyre-formation. The common cause of all these ridgings and foldings of the brain-surface is evidently to be found in the disproportionate growth of the cortex and of the myelinated tracts that radiate into it. When a body increases in mass, its surface, of course, enlarges less rapidly than its volume. But the cells of the brain-surface have to take up the fibres of the interior alba ; and so surface-extent must be roughly proportional to volume, and this relation must be maintained with approximate constancy throughout the whole period of development. It is obvious, then, that the cortex has no way of keeping pace with the increase of alba except by folding. And it is for this reason that, both in the organic series and in the course of individual development, the convolution of the brain-surface increases with increase of the size of the brain.

The convolution of the cerebellum is found in its simplest form in the birds. The avian cerebellum has no pilea, and so appears, in dorsal aspect, as an unpaired structure of a more or less spherical or ovoid form. The surface of this organ is split up into transverse folds, roughly circular or elliptical in shape, all intersecting in an axis laid transversely through the centre of the sphere or ovoid : the transverse axis is, therefore, in this case the common axis of convolution for all gyres visible upon the surface of the cerebellum (Fig. 49 A, p. 121). If we bisect the organ at right angles to the direction of this axis, we find that the depth of the fissures bounding the separate prominences varies : the ridges fall into groups of two or three, marked off from one another by shallow depressions, but divided from the neighbouring groups by deeper fissures (Fig. 40 B, p. 110). In the mammals, the convolution becomes more complicated ; each of the groups of ridge-like prominences marked off by the deeper fissures contains a large number of separate gyres. Moreover, it frequently happens that several of these groups are isolated by dividing fissures, and so form still larger units, lobes. The consequence is that most of the gyres come to lie in the depth of the larger fissures, and that only the terminal lamellae appear on the surface. Hence we have in sections the well known representation of a tree, with its spreading leaves and branches, termed by the older anatomists the arbor vitae (*av* Fig. 50, p. 121; cf. also *W* Fig. 53, p. 127). Further, while this fissural differentiation is in progress, the median portion or vermis of the cerebellum is reinforced by the large, bilaterally symmetrical pilea. If the arrangement of gyres upon the pilea is fairly regular, as in man, the principal axis of convolution is again the transverse. The rule is broken, however, along the anterior and posterior margins, where the gyres gradually change their course to take an oblique or even longitudinal direction, all alike converging towards the point of attachment of pileum to vermis (Fig. 50). For the rest, many mammalian cerebella evince a great variety in the course of their gyres, more especially upon the pilear surfaces, so that no definite law of gyre-formation can be made out. This is most apt to occur in brains whose cerebellum is richly convoluted. In the human cerebellum itself there are certain divisions, isolated by important fissures,[1] in which the course of the gyres diverges more or less widely from the general trend.

An increase by convolution of the superficial extent of the cerebrum is found only in the higher vertebrate classes. And the brains even of the lowest orders of mammals show, at most, only the fissures and gyres described above (Sylvian fissure, hippocampal fissure, etc.), which are due to special causes, distinct from those that produce the remaining ridges and furrows. When once these latter have appeared, however, they persist in practically the same pattern throughout the mammalian series, up to and including the primates. The rule is that all fissures and gyres running from before backwards take a course which is approximately parallel to that of the median fissure; most of them are also reflected in a curve round the Sylvian fissure (cf. Fig. 61 *I, II, III*, p. 138). That is to say, the gyres take the same direction that the hemispheres take in their growth round the brain-caudex,—the direction from before backwards; and they are reflected round the point of application to the diencephalon in a curve which repeats the curve of hemicerebral growth. The degree of curvature is determined by the depth and extent of the Sylvian fossa or fissure. The number of longitudinal folds which thus appear on the surface of the cerebrum varies in general, in the various mammalian orders, between two and five. In many cases, one or another of them forms a junction, at some

---

[1] Here belong more especially the flocculus (*fl* Fig. 52, p. 125), a small feather like outgrowth from the posterior margin of the middle peduncle (crus ad pontem), and the amygdala or tonsil (*to*), an ovoid prominence covering the oblongata between the inferior portion of the vermis and the pileum of either side.

point of its course, with the neighbouring fold; and very frequently less well marked, secondary folds are formed, making an angle with the primary. The convolution thus appears as an irregularly meandering system, in which the general law of direction is more or less obscured. The case is very different with the formation of folds in the frontal region of the cerebrum. A little anteriorly to the Sylvian fissure, the longitudinal gyre-tract is replaced, suddenly or gradually, by an approximately transverse ridging. At the same time, the secondary cross-fissures are often disposed radially about the Sylvian fissure. In accounting for this mode of fissure-formation in the frontal brain-region, we must remember that in all mammals, except the cetacea and primates (the orders in which the olfactory gyres are to some extent degenerate), the callosal gyre comes to the surface in the frontal area, and is separated from the more posterior gyres, at its point of issue, by a transverse or oblique fissure; anteriorly, it passes directly over into the olfactory gyre, from which it is also separated, though as a rule less distinctly, by another cross-fissure (Fig. 61, Gf). The point at which the callosal gyre comes to the surface lies in some instances at a very short distance from the anterior boundary of the brain. This is the case e.g. in the carnivores, where the gyre is exceedingly broad, so that it and the olfactory gyre together occupy the entire area elsewhere taken up by the frontal brain. In other brains, the point of issue lies more posteriorly. The exposed portion of the callosal gyre is then, as a general rule, longer than it is broad; it merely fills a narrow space to either side of the anterior part of the intercerebral fissure. The cross-formation of which we are speaking is not confined, however, to the folds caused by the protrusion of the callosal and olfactory gyres; all the other fissures of the anterior brain-region take the same transverse direction. In some cases, the folds that run longitudinally in the occipital area are deflected anteriorly into a transverse course; in others, the longitudinal furrows are suddenly interrupted, and replaced by cross-fissures. We have a salient instance of the former arrangement in the brain of the carnivores (Fig. 61), which is characterised by the regularity and symmetry of its convolution; while the second type is represented by most of the other richly convoluted mammalian brains, though here, too, certain of the longitudinal fissures are not infrequently continued in the transverse direction. There are, as a rule, two principal fissures of this kind crossing the frontal brain, and the number holds, whether the fissures are completely independent or pass over posteriorly into longitudinal fissures. To these must be added, further, the posterior limiting fissure of the callosal gyre, and the fissure separating the callosal and olfactory gyres. There is thus, upon the average, a total of four transverse fissures in the frontal brain-region.[1]

[1] In the first three editions of this work, the statements of the text are illustrated by cuts of a series of mammalian brains. See 3rd ed., Fig. 48, p. 86.

All these folds, longitudinal and transverse alike, are ordinarily visible only on the upper and outer surface of the hemispheres. The base of the brain is, in most instances, entirely occupied by the gyres and fissures previously described,—anteriorly, i.e., by the olfactory gyre, and posteriorly by the hippocampal gyre (*ob*, *H* Fig. 61). If anything else can be seen, it is at most simply a narrow margin belonging to the outermost gyres of the brain-surface. Again, the greater number of brains, when viewed in median section, show only the callosal gyre and its continuations, posteriorly into the hippocampal gyre, and anteriorly into the olfactory gyre (Fig. 63); though in certain cases, where these structures are not prominent—as in the brains of the cetacea, of the apes and of man—portions of the superficial gyre-tracts may also make their appearance. But these brains deviate markedly in other respects as well from the general law of fissuration evinced by the mammalian brain. In the cetacea, whose organs of smell, peripheral and central, are completely atrophied, the callosal gyre does not come to the surface, and no olfactory gyre is present at all. The brain is extraordinarily broad; and the principal superficial fissures run over its whole length from before backwards, as they do in the occipital brain-region of the other mammals.

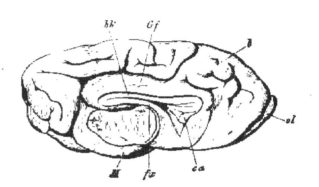

FIG. 63. Median aspect of brain of dog. Left hemisphere. *Gf* Callosal gyre. *b* Its anterior and superficial portion. *ol* Olfactory gyre. *H* Hippocampal gyre. *bk* Callosum. *fx* Fornix. *ca* Precommissure.

In the primates, the fissuration of the brain follows a special law of evolution, characteristic of the order. The olfactory gyre, which has dwindled into the olfactory bulb, lies concealed upon the brain-base. The callosal gyre appears on the surface, but only in the occipital, not in the frontal region of the brain. As the gyre curves posteriorly round the splenium, on its passage into the uncus, it sends off a branch to the surface of the occipital lobe. This divides into two lobules, the cuneus and precuneus (*Pr*, *Cn* Fig. 64). The intruding area forms a sort of island, bounded before and behind by other gyres, from which it is ordinarily divided by fissures. The cuneus and precuneus are also themselves separated by a deep transverse fissure, the occipital fissure (*O*). The same transverse arrangement of gyres and fissures obtains, further, over the entire occipital portion of the brain, from the anterior extremity of the main ramus of the

Sylvian fissure (the Sylvian fissure in the narrower sense) to the extreme posterior limit of the occipital lobe. Anteriorly, the principal fissure which runs in the transverse direction, from above downwards, is the central fissure (fissure of Rolando : *R* Fig. 65). It is bounded before and behind, in the brain of man and of the higher apes, by two transverse folds, the precentral and postcentral gyres (*VC, HC* Fig. 65). These are separated from the adjacent parts—the precentral from the frontal gyres, and the postcentral gyre from the precuneus—by shorter cross-fissures. Finally, a deep transverse fissure is found at the posterior limit of the occipital brain. This is the calcarine fissure, which separates the cuneus from the gyres extending downward to the brain-base (*O'*). We have, then, in all, on the surface of the occipital brain, five well-marked transverse fissures, three of which belong to the offshoots of the callosal gyre and the adjoining parts. On the other hand, the fissures and gyres of the frontal and temporal areas—i.e. of the region anterior to the presylvian and ventral to the subsylvian fissures—tend in general to pursue a longitudinal course, during which they are necessarily reflected in a curve round the main ramus of the Sylvian fissure. Three of these longitudinal folds can be distinguished in the frontal, and three in the temporal region; they constitute the three frontal and temporal gyres (F_1—F_3, T_1—T_3), all of which run far enough to be visible at the base of the brain (Fig. 52, p. 125). The three temporal are adjoined posteriorly to the three occipital gyres (O_1—O_3). In the area of transition from the occipital to the temporal region, the folds follow a course that lies midway between the transverse and the longitudinal; so that the three parietal gyres (P_1—P_3) show a gradual passage from the one to the other direction. There is no parallel to this in the frontal region : the three frontal gyres are interrupted suddenly and at right angles by the downward course of the precentral. The essential difference, then, between the brain of the primates

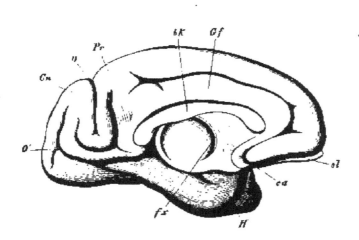

FIG. 64. Median aspect of brain of monkey (Macacus). Left hemisphere. After GRATIOLET. *Gf, ol, H, bk, fx, ca* as in Fig. 63. *Pr* Precuneus. *Cn* Cuneus. *O* Occipital fissure (parieto-occipital fissure). *O'* Calcarine fissure (lateral occipital fissure).

and that of the other mammals lies in the fact that the primates have the transverse fissures in the occipital, and the longitudinal fissures in the frontal region, whereas most of the other mammals have these relations exactly reversed. There is a corresponding difference in the course of the callosal gyre. In the primates, the callosal gyre comes to the surface in the posterior, in the lower mammals in the anterior region of the brain: a fact which can be brought out most clearly by the comparison of a primate brain and the brain of another mammal in median section (Figg. 63, 64). These differences are probably referable to the divergence of the laws of growth in the two brain-forms. In most mammals, the developing brain has a strong lateral growth in the occipital region, while the frontal area remains narrow; so that the whole organ is wedge-shaped, tapering from behind forwards. In the brain of the primates, on the contrary, the growth

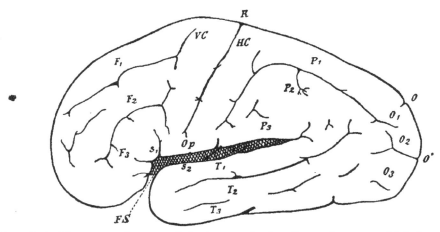

FIG. 65.[1] Fissures and gyres of the human brain. Lateral aspect of left hemisphere. *FS* Sylvian fissure: s_1 anterior, s_2 posterior ramus. *Op* Operculum, covering the insula (*J*, Fig. 56). F_1, F_2, F_3 Superfrontal, medifrontal and subfrontal gyres. *VC* Precentral, *HC* postcentral gyre. *R* Central fissure (fissure of ROLANDO). T_1, T_2, T_3 Supertemporal, meditemporal, subtemporal gyres. P_1, P_2, P_3 The three parietal gyres. *O* Occipital fissure. *O'* Calcarine fissure. O_1, O_2, O_3 The three occipital gyres.

of the occipital region is predominantly in the longitudinal, and the growth of the frontal region predominantly in the lateral direction. The organ thus assumes the form of an ovoid, whose lateral halves are closely apposed anteriorly, but posteriorly gape apart; while the lesser height of the posterior portion leaves room for the growth of the cerebellum beneath it.

Embryology tells us that the cross-fissures upon the cerebrum of man (and probably of the primates at large) represent the original foldings of the cortex.

[1] This Figure would, perhaps, be more nearly typical if the postcentral fissure were separated off from the rest of the fissural complex with which the author has connected it. Again, it is not probable that the calcarine fissure ever appears thus plainly on the lateral surface of the brain (cf. the author's remarks in the text below); though, indeed, but little is certainly known of the fissuration of the occipital lobe.—TRANSLATOR.

According to ECKER, they begin to form upon the smooth cerebral surface as early as the fifth month, whereas the first traces of longitudinal fissuration make their appearance in the course of the seventh month.[1] Four or five of these transverse fissures, disposed radially with more or less of regularity about the Sylvian fissure, may be traced upon the foetal brain. The most strongly marked among them becomes the central fissure. In the apes, the central fissure is less prominent than in man; but this defect is compensated by the greater development of the more posteriorly situated occipital fissure, which has accordingly been termed the ape-cleft (Affenspalte).[2] The calcarine fissure, lying still more posteriorly, can hardly been seen at all on the human brain except in median section (Fig. 53, p. 127, and O', Fig. 65). It is this fissure whose projection into the postcornu of the paracele forms the calcar of the primate brain (vk Fig. 55, p. 129). In man, it joins the occipital fissure at an acute angle, so that the cuneus shows as a wedge-shaped lobule, apparently isolated from the callosal gyre (Cn Fig. 53). In the apes, the calcarine fissure is shallower, and the connexion of the cuneus with the callosal gyre can accordingly be seen at once (Fig. 64). But while the portion of the primate brain that lies behind the central fissure thus developes several well marked cross-fissures, the transverse fissuration of the anterior half is much less pronounced. In place of it, we find throughout the frontal and temporal regions the longitudinal fissures and gyres which we have mentioned as appearing at a later stage of embryonic development. The three longitudinal folds that are distinguishable upon every primate brain give rise to the three frontal (super-, medi-, sub-) and the three temporal (super-, medi-, sub-) gyre-tracts (Fig. 65). These, however, do not form (as they do in many of the other mammals) a continuous convolution, arching over the Sylvian fissure. On the one hand, the three frontal gyres are interrupted by the precentral gyre. On the other, only one of the temporal gyres (the supertemporal) runs a complete course to the postcentral gyre, curving boldly upwards round the main ramus of the Sylvian fissure; the other two are deflected by the precuneus and cuneus, the two lobules bounded by the other radial fissures of the occipital brain, and then continued on the parietal brain-surface into the three parietal gyres (P_1–P_3). These latter, situated as they are at the meeting point of different gyre systems, show the least regular course of all: the third parietal gyre (P_3), which bounds the posterior extremity of the Sylvian fissure, has been named from its shape and position the angular gyre. On the median surface of the brain, the first and second parietal gyres form the boundary of the precuneus and cuneus (Pr, Cn, Fig. 53, p. 127), which here appear as direct continuations of the callosal gyre (Gf). On the brain-base, the subtemporal gyre is connected anteriorly with the club-shaped termination of the hippocampal gyre; posteriorly, it is continuous with the external ramus of an U-shaped gyre-tract which occupies the base of the occipital brain and whose inner ramus is lost in the stem of the hippocampal gyre (O Fig. 52, p. 125). The anterior portion of the brain-base is occupied by the ventral deflections of the three frontal gyres. The medifrontal and subfrontal become continuous on the margin of the Sylvian fissure (F_2, F_3, Fig. 52).[3]

[1] ECKER, *Archiv f. Anthropologie*, iii., 1868, 203. PANSCH, *ibid.*, 227.

[2] The morphological relations of the Affenspalte (fissura perpendicularis externa; Wilder's pomatic fissure) are, in reality, more complicated than the author here represents them.—TRANSLATOR.

[3] BISCHOFF, *Abhandl. d. bayer. Akad. d. Wiss.*, x., 1868. ECKER, *Die Hirnwindungen des Menschen*, 1869. PANSCH, *Die Furchen und Wülste am Grosshirn des Men-*

The law of fissuration of the brain-surface is, in the author's opinion, the resultant effect of two sets of causes : of the tensions produced by the growth of the brain itself, and of the influence upon the brain of the enclosing skull-capsule. The former condition may be appealed to in explanation of the fissures that appear at the earliest period of development. If a surface is to increase its extent by fold-formation, its ridges will of necessity follow the direction of least resistance. If the surface is more tensely stretched in the transverse than in the longitudinal direction, therefore, it will fall into transverse folds, or ridge up about a transverse axis, just like a damp piece of paper that one holds in the hands and pulls out to right and left. If, on the other hand, the tension is greater in the longitudinal direction, then the folds will be longitudinal, the ridges disposed about a longitudinal axis. Suppose, then, that the fissuration is uniform, all the folds taking a single direction : this will mean that the difference of surface-tension remained constant over the whole period of growth. Irregularity of folding will mean, on the contrary, that the line of greatest tension has varied. Now if a structure grows in different directions with varying rapidity, its surface-tensions must vary in these same directions ; and the direction of greatest tension must lie at right angles to the direction of greatest energy of growth. A growing structure, i.e., may be regarded as a coherent elastic body, in which the deformation caused by growth at any given point increases the tension at all other points, the tension reaching its maximum in the parts where the intrinsic deformation is minimal. The fissuration of the cerebellum, where the laws of growth and folding are comparatively simple, seems to confirm this principle ; and the confirmation is all the more striking, since the position of the organ may be supposed to exempt it from the influences of the skull-form. The growth of the cerebellum, during the entire period of its development, is predominantly in the longitudinal direction. Its greatest surface-tension must, therefore, lie at right angles, in the transverse direction ; and this is, as a matter of fact, the direction of its fissuration. We should expect, on the same principle, that the fold-formation of the primate cerebrum would show two stages, corresponding to two distinct periods of growth : a first, in which the direction of maximal growth is the same for the whole brain, from before backwards ; and a second, in which the energy of growth over the frontal and temporal regions is greater in the transverse direction. As a matter of fact, a comparison of embryonic brains at different stages of development shows, at the first glance, that the ratio of the two principal diameters of the human brain changes very considerably during the period of structural elaboration. In the first weeks of development, the whole brain is approximately spherical in form ; the longitudinal diameter is but little larger than the greatest transverse diameter. The line of greatest breadth crosses the brain behind the Sylvian fissure, or, more correctly, since the temporal lobes are not yet developed, behind the Sylvian fossa. As the fossa closes to form the fissure, the greatest transverse diameter is shifted anteriorly, crossing the brain at the point where the temporal lobes grow over the margin of the fissure. During this whole period, however, the longitudinal diameter of the hemispheres is gaining more and more upon the cross-diameter ; so that as early as the third month the ratio of the two is 1 : 0·9, while in the course of the fifth and sixth it has fallen to 1 : 0·7. This is the time of formation of the first permanent fissures, all of which, without exception, take the transverse direction.

schen, 1879. FLATAU and JACOBSOHN, *Handbuch der Anatomie und vergleichenden Anatomie des Centralnervensystems der Säugethiere*, i., 1899.

During the fifth month, the central, occipital, and calcarine fissures make their appearance; and in the course of the sixth, the other primary radial fissures are added to their number.[1] From the end of the sixth month, the laws of brain-growth begin to change. The total form of the brain, as expressed in the ratio of the longitudinal to the greatest transverse diameter, remains practically the same; but the growth of the various parts differs widely from the rule that has previously obtained. If we compare the dorsal aspects of foetal brains, from the sixth to the seventh month, we remark at once that the region extending posteriorly from the central fissure is increasing in length and breadth in approximately the same ratio, but that the frontal portion of the brain is growing more strongly in the transverse than in the longitudinal direction. The temporal lobe undergoes a similar modification. Even in the foetus of six months, its anterior extremity extends almost as far as the ventrally deflected margin of the frontal lobe; but it is still narrow, so that the Sylvian fossa lies wide open. In the following months, the growth of the temporal lobe is most vigorous in the upward, and comparatively slight in the longitudinal direction, and, as a result, the fossa closes to form the fissure. Now the changes here sketched are exactly coincident with the formation of the second system of folds, the longitudinal fissures. Since the growth of the frontal brain is predominantly a transverse growth, the frontal gyres must take a predominantly longitudinal direction. And since the most rapid growth of the temporal lobes is upwards, the folds formed upon them must again run from behind forwards, taking a curved path round the Sylvian fissure. Not only do the newly formed fissures follow this direction, over both regions of the brain surface, but some of those that were originally disposed radially about the Sylvian fissure have their course changed to the longitudinal or arching type. Thus the central fissure itself assumes an oblique position; and the subfrontal and supertemporal fissures, whose primules in the sixth month are radial or transverse, have their direction altered, and take their places in the longitudinal fissure system. The case is different with the portion of the brain-surface that lies between the central fissure and the posterior margin of the occipital lobe. Here the transverse fissures, while they increase in depth and extent, for the most part retain their original positions, and only gradually, as they approach the temporal lobe, pass over into a longitudinal path.[2]

The resistance of the skull-capsule is, necessarily, antagonistic to brain-growth. It is probable, however, that this influence is exerted only in the latest period of the embryonic life, and for a time after birth, before the skull has acquired its permanent form. Its principal condition is the varying rapidity of bone-growth along the various sutures, and the successive closure of these as growth advances. If the growing brain meets with an external resistance such as would be offered by the skull, it must evidently fold upon itself; and the direction of the folds will be the direction of least resistance. Where the skull is of the dolichocephalic form, the course of the fissures will thus be predominantly longitudinal, and where it is brachycephalic, predominantly transverse in direction. As a matter of fact, a connexion of this kind between skull-form and domi-

---

[1] ECKER, *Archiv f. Anthropologie*, iii., 1868, 212. Cf. the cuts of embryonic brains in the first three editions of this work. 3rd ed., Fig. 52, p. 93.

[2] In the first edition of this work (p. 101), I have cited measurements of embryonic brains, which serve to confirm the statements of the text.

nant gyre-trend has been made out by L. MEYER[1] and RÜDINGER.[2] But the actual convolution of a given brain will, of course, always be the resultant of the two sets of conditions: the intrinsic tensions of growth, and the extrinsic resistances. The former will manifest themselves most clearly in the course of the original fissures; the latter in the modifications superinduced upon the original convolution at a later stage of development.

[1] *Centralblatt f. d. medicin. Wiss.*, 1876, No. 43.
[2] RÜDINGER, *Ueber d. Unterschiede d. Grosshirnwindungen nach d. Geschlecht beim Fötus u. Neugeborenen*, 1877, 5 ff.

CHAPTER V

Course of the Paths of Nervous Conduction

§ 1. General Conditions of Conduction

OUR examination of the structural elements of the nervous system led us to conceive of the brain and myel, together with the nerves issuing from them, as a system of nerve-cells, interconnected by their fibrillar runners either directly or through the contact of process with process. Our recent survey of the morphological development of the central organs lends support to this conception. We have found a series of cinereal formations which collect the fibres running centralward from the external organs and mediate their connexion with other, especially with more centrally situated grey masses. The paths of conduction that begin in the myelic columns pass upwards first in the crura and then in the corona until they penetrate the cerebral cortex. There we have the commissures, pointing to the interconnexion of the central regions of the two halves of the brain, and the intergyral (arcuate) fibres, indicating the connexion of the various cortical zones of the same hemisphere. Hence from whichever point of view we consider the outward conformation of the central organs, we are presently met by the question as to the *course taken by the various paths of nervous conduction*. We know, of course, that the cell-territories stand, by virtue of the cell-processes, in the most manifold relations. We shall accordingly expect to find that the conduction-paths are nowhere strictly isolated from one another. We must suppose, in particular, that under altered functional conditions they may change their relative positions within very wide limits. But we may fully admit such a relative variability of functional co-ordination as is suggested by the neurone theory, and yet with justice raise the question of the *preferred* lines of conduction,—of the lines which, under normal circumstances, are chiefly concerned to mediate determinate connexions, on the one hand, between the central regions themselves, and on the other, between the centre and the peripheral organs appended to the nervous system. This answered, we may in certain cases proceed to ask a second question, regarding the *auxiliary* paths or bypaths which can replace the regular lines of transmission in particular instances of interrupted conduction or of inhibition of function.

We distinguish two main kinds of conduction-path, according to the direction in which the processes of stimulation are transmitted: the *centripetal* and the *centrifugal*. In the former, the stimulation is set up at some point on the periphery of the body, and travels inwards, toward the central organ. In the latter, it issues from the central organ, and travels toward some region of the periphery. The physiological effects of a centripetally conducted stimulation, when they come to consciousness, are termed *sensations*. Frequently, however, this final effect is not produced; the excitation is reflected into a movement, without having exerted any influence upon consciousness. Nevertheless, the paths of conduction traversed in such a case are, at least in part, the same. We therefore give the name of 'sensory' to the centripetal conduction-paths at large. The physiological effects of centrifugally conducted stimulation are very various: it may find expression in movements of striated and non-striated muscles, in secretions, in heightened temperature, and in the excitation of peripheral sense-organs by internal stimuli. In what follows, we shall, however, confine our attention for the most part to the motor and the centrifugal-sensory paths, since these are the only parts of the centrifugal conduction-system that call for consideration in psychology. The muscular movements that result from the direct translation of sensory stimulation into motor excitation are termed reflex movements; those that have their proximate source in an internal stimulation within the motor spheres of the central organ we shall call automatic movements. In the reflex, i.e., centripetal is followed by centrifugal conduction; in the automatic movement, centrifugal conduction alone is directly involved.[1]

So long as the stimulation-process is confined within the continuity of determinate nerve-fibres, as occurs e.g. in the peripheral nerves, which often traverse considerable distances, it remains as a general rule isolated within each particular fibre, and does not spring across to neighbouring paths. This fact has been expressed in the *law of isolated conduction*. The law has usually been regarded as valid not only for the periphery, but for the conduction-paths within the central organs as well; on the ground that an external impression made upon some precisely localised part of a sensitive surface evokes a sharply defined sensation, and that a voluntary impulse directed upon a definite movement produces contraction of a circumscribed group of muscles. Really, however, these facts prove nothing more than that the processes in the principal paths are, as a rule and under normal conditions, separate and distinct. It has not been demonstrated with certainty that the stimulation is strictly confined to a single primitive fibril, even during the peripheral portion of its course. And in the central parts, any such restriction is entirely out of the question, as appears both from the general

---

[1] Cf. the general discussion of reflex excitations in Chap. iii., pp. 85 ff. above.

morphological features discussed in Chapter II., and from the phenomena of vicarious function which we shall speak of presently. The only principle that can be recognised here is a *principle of preferential conduction*. There is in every case a principal path, but this is supplemented by auxiliary or secondary paths.

§ 2. Methods of Investigating the Conduction-Paths

We may avail ourselves of three distinct methods, in our examination of nervous conduction. Each one of them has certain imperfections, and must therefore be supplemented, where possible, by the other two. The first method is that of physiological experimentation; the second is that of anatomical investigation; and the third is that of pathological observation.

(1) Physiological experimentation attempts to reach conclusions as to the course of the nervous conduction-paths in two ways: by stimulation-experiments, and by interruptions of conduction due to a division of the parts. In the former case, we look as a general rule for enhancement, in the latter for abrogation of function, in the organs connected with the stimulated or divided tissue. When we come to the investigation of the central paths, however, we find that both methods alike are attended by unusual difficulties and disadvantages. Even in the most favourable instances, when the stimulation or transsection has been entirely successful, we have established but one definite point upon a path of conduction; to ascertain its full extent, we should have to make a large number of similar experiments, from the terminal station in the brain to the point of issue of the appropriate nerves. Such a task holds out absolutely no hope of accomplishment, since the isolated stimulation or section of a conduction-path in the interior of the brain presents insuperable obstacles. There are, therefore, only two problems to which these methods can be applied with any prospect of success. We may use them to determine the course of conduction in the simplest of the central organs, the myel, and in the direct continuations of the myelic columns, the crura; and we may use them to discover the correlation of definite areas of the brain cortex with definite organs upon the periphery of the body. The answer to the former question has been attempted, for the most part, by isolated transsection of the various myelic columns; the answer to the second, by experiments upon the stimulation and extirpation of definitely limited cortical areas. Even with this limitation, however, it is difficult to secure valid results. A stimulation will almost inevitably spread from the point of attack to the surrounding parts. This objection applies with especial force to the electric current, almost the only form of stimulus which fulfils the other requirements of physiological experiment, and a stimulus which the physiologist is therefore practically compelled to employ. The same thing is true of the disturbances consequent upon a division of

nervous substance. And if one is at last successful in securing the utmost degree of isolation of experimental interference, there will still be many cases in which the interpretation of the resulting phenomena is uncertain. The muscular contraction that follows upon a stimulation may, under certain circumstances, be due to a direct excitation of motor fibres, just as well as to a reaction upon the sense-impressions. And the derangements of function that appear as a result of transsections and extirpations always require a long period of observation before they can be accurately determined. This means that the certainty of the conclusions is, again, very largely impaired: the disturbances set up as the direct effect of operation for the most part disappear as time goes on, the explanation being that the principal path is functionally replaced by the secondary paths of which we spoke just now.

(2) The gaps left in our knowledge by the physiological experiment are largely filled out by anatomical investigation. The anatomist has followed two methods in the prosecution of his task: first, the macroscopic dissection of the hardened organ, and, later, its microscopic reduction to a series of thin sections. Of late years, the former of these two methods has fallen into disrepute, on the score that it runs the risk of substituting artificial products of the dissecting scalpel for real fibre-tracts. Carefully applied, however, it is a valuable means of orientation with regard to certain of the wider roads of brain-travel; while its critics are inclined, on their side, to underestimate the danger of error in the interpretation of microscopic appearances. And this danger is the more serious, the farther we are from the actual attainment of the ideal goal of a microscopic examination of the central organ,—its complete reduction to an infinite series of sections of accurately known direction. For the rest, microscopical anatomy has been brought in recent times to a high degree of perfection by the application of the various methods of staining. The advantage of these is that they permit of the more certain differentiation of nerve-elements from the other elementary parts, and thus enable us to trace the interconnexion of the nerve-elements much farther than had before been possible.[1] Anatomical investigation is, further, very materially supplemented by embryological research. Embryology shows that the formation of the myelinic sheath in the various fibre-systems of the central organs occurs at different periods of foetal development, and thus puts it in our power to trace out separately certain paths of travel that in all likelihood are physiologically interconnected. This method, however, like the others, has its limits: the systems that develope simultaneously may

---

[1] The most fruitful of these methods may find mention here. They are: GOLGI's method of impregnation by a metal, and more particularly by silver; and the methods of staining by haematoxylin and methylene blue, introduced respectively by WEIGERT and EHRLICH. For details regarding these and other methods, see OBERSTEINER, *Anleitung beim Studium des Baues der nervösen Centralorgane*, 3te Aufl., 1896, 7 ff., and EDINGER, *Vorlesungen über den Bau der nervösen Centralorgane*, 6te Aufl., 1900, 3 ff.

still include numerous groups of fibres, possessing each a different functional significance.[1]

(3) Pathological observation is equally concerned with functional derangement and with anatomical change, and so in a certain measure combines the advantages of physiological and of anatomical investigation. The observations of pathological anatomy have been especially fruitful for the study of the nervous conduction-paths. Abrogation of function over a determinate functional area means that the fibres belonging to that area undergo secondary degeneration. The pathological anatomist can, therefore, appeal to a law very similar to that upon which embryological investigation is based. Unless there are extrinsic conditions present, which render an accidental concurrence of the degeneration probable, he can assume that all fibres which suffer pathological change at one and the same time are functionally related.[2] The observation of secondary degenerations is of especial value when conjoined with physiological experimentation. The joint method may follow either of two different paths. On the one hand, a severance of continuity may be effected at some point in the central or peripheral nervous system of an animal, and the consequent functional derangement observed. Then, after a considerable time has elapsed, the paths to which the secondary degeneration extended can be made out by anatomical means. On the other, a peripheral organ (eye, ear, etc.) may be extirpated in early life, and the influence observed which the abrogation of determinate functions exerts upon the development of the central nervous organs.[3] In the former case, the nerve-fibres evince the successive stages of degeneration represented in Fig. 23, p. 53. In the latter, the parts of the brain which serve as the centres for the abrogated functions sink in, and microscopic examination shows their nerve-cells in the various stages of atrophy that lead up, in the last resort, to complete disappearance (Fig. 22 B, p. 53).

The first extensive collection of material for the investigation of the microscopical structure of the central organs was furnished by the researches of STILLING. The earliest attempts to construct a structural schema of the whole cerebrospinal system and its conduction-paths by STILLING's method, i.e. by the microscopical examination of sections, date from MEYNERT and LUYS.[4] MEYNERT, especially, rendered great services to the science; he brought to his re-

[1] FLECHSIG, Die Leitungsbahnen im Gehirn und Rückenmark des Menschen, 1876. C. VOGT, Etude sur la myélisation des hémisphères cérébraux, 1900. Cf. §§ 5, 6, below.
[2] L. TÜRCK, Sitzungsber. d. Wiener Akad., math.-naturw. Cl., vi., 1851, 288; xi. 1853, 93. CHARCOT, Ueber die Localisationen der Gehirnkrankheiten, trs. FETZER, i., 1878, 159 (Leçons sur les localisations dans les maladies du cerveau, 1875); FLECHSIG, Ueber Systemerkrankungen im Rückenmark, 1878.
[3] GUDDEN, Arch. f. Psychiatrie, ii., 1870, 693. FOREL, ibid., xviii., 1887, 162. VON MONAKOW, ibid., xxvii., 1895, 1, 386.
[4] MEYNERT, art. Gehirn in STRICKER's Gewebelehre, 1871, 694 ff. (BUCK's trans., 650 ff.); Psychiatrie, Pt. I. 1884. LUYS, Recherches sur le système nerveux cérébro-spinal, 1865. The Brain and its Functions, 1877 and later (Internat. Sci. Series).

construction of brain-structure the results of a comprehensive series of original investigations and a rare power of synthetic imagination. It is true, of course, that the schema of conduction-paths which he published was largely hypothetical, and that it has already been proved erroneous in many details. Nevertheless, it formed the point of departure for further microscopical research; so that most of the later work takes up a definite attitude to MEYNERT's structural schema, supplementing or amending. The application of the various methods of staining, and the consequent differentiation of the nervous elements, have played an important part in this chapter of scientific enquiry. Embryological investigation depends upon the fact that the myelinic sheath is formed in the different fibre-systems at different periods of embryonic development. It is this sheath which is responsible for the coloration of the alba, so that its appearance is easily recognisable. The signs of secondary degeneration consist, on the other hand, in a gradual transformation of the myelinic sheath. The tissue becomes receptive of certain colour-stains, like carmine, by which it is unaffected in the normal state. Finally, the myelinic sheath disappears altogether. At the same time, the nerve-fibres proper (neurites) change to fibres of connective tissue, interrupted by fat granules. The value of these degenerative changes for the investigation of conduction-paths lies in the fact that the progressive transformation is always confined within an interconnected fibre-system, and that the direction which it takes corresponds in all fibres with the direction of conduction (WALLER's law); so that the degeneration of motor fibres follows a centrifugal, that of sensory fibres a centripetal course. Nevertheless, this law of WALLER, like the law of isolated conduction, appears to be valid only as regards the principal direction of the progress of degeneration. In cases where the interruption of conduction has persisted for a considerable length of time, and more particularly in young animals, the deterioration of the fibres is always traceable, to some extent, in the opposite direction as well. We have, further, besides atrophy of the nerves separated from their centres, a similar though much slower degeneration of the nerve-cells which have been thrown out of function by transsection of the neurites issuing from them. This secondary atrophy of the central elements, the initial symptoms of which are the changes represented in Fig. 22, p. 53 above, is, again, especially likely to appear in young animals. It may, however, occur in the human adult, after long persistence of a defect. Thus it has been observed that loss of the eye is followed by atrophy of the quadrigemina; nay, more, in certain cases of the kind, a secondary atrophy of certain cerebral gyres has been demonstrated.

§ 3. Conduction in the Nerves and in the Myel

(a)—Origin and Distribution of the Nerves

The nerve-roots leave the myel in two longitudinal series, a dorsal and a ventral. The dorsal nerve-roots, as a simple test of function by stimulation or transsection shows, are sensitive: their mechanical or electrical stimulation produces pain, and their transsection renders the corresponding cutaneous areas anaesthetic. The ventral nerve-roots are motor: their stimulation produces muscular contraction, and their transsection muscular disability. The fibres of the dorsal roots conduct centripetally; if they are transsected, stimulation of the central cut end will give rise to sensation, but not that of the peripheral. The fibres of the ventral roots conduct centrifugally; in their case, stimulation of the peripheral cut end will give rise to muscular contraction, but not that of the central.

These facts were first discovered by CHARLES BELL, and their general statement is accordingly known as 'BELL's law.' They prove that, at the place of origin of the nerves, the sensory and motor conduction-paths are entirely separate from each other. The same thing holds of the cranial nerves, with the addition that here, in most cases, the separation is not confined to a short distance in the neighbourhood of the place of origin, but persists either throughout the whole course of the nerves or at least over a considerable portion of their extent.[1] There can be no doubt that the union of the sensory and motor roots, to form mixed nerve-trunks, finds its explanation in the spatial distribution of the terminations of the nerve-fibres. The muscles and the overlying skin are supplied by common nerve-branches. While, therefore, the two sets of conduction-paths are functionally distinct, a spatial separation throughout their entire course occurs only in certain cranial nerves, where the terminations are comparatively near to the points of origin, but the points of origin themselves lie farther apart. Under these circumstances, a separate course involves simpler space-relations than an initial union of the sensory and motor fibres, such as we find in the trunks supplying adjacent parts of the body.

Not only the origin, but also the further peripheral course of the nerves is very largely determined by the conditions of distribution. Fibres that run to a functionally single muscle-group, or to adjacent parts of the skin, are collected into a single trunk. Hence it does not follow that the mixed nerve, formed by the junction of ventral and dorsal roots, always proceeds simply and by the shortest path to its zone of distribution. On the contrary, it frequently happens that there is an interchange of fibres between nerve and nerve, giving rise to what are called the nerve-plexuses. In explaining the occurrence of these plexuses, we must remember that the disposition of the nerve-fibres, as they issue from the central organ, meets the conditions of their peripheral distribution only in a rough and provisional manner; the arrangement is by no means perfect, and requires to be supplemented later on. The plexuses are most commonly formed, therefore, at places where there are parts of the body that need large nerve-trunks, e.g. the two pairs of limbs. Here it is evidently impossible, from the spatial

---

[1] The olfactory, optic and acoustic nerves are purely sensory; the oculomotor, trochlear and abducent ocular, the facial and the hypoglossal are purely motor; and the trigeminal, glossopharyngeal and pneumogastric and accessory resemble the myelic nerves, i.e. become mixed at a short distance from their place of origin. The sensory root of these latter has a ganglion which is wanting in the sensory nerves proper.

conditions of their origin, that the nerves should leave the myel in precisely the order that is demanded by their subsequent peripheral distribution. But the plexus-formation is not only supplementary; it is, beyond question, compensative as well. The nerve-fibres that are nearest together as the nerves leave the central organs are those that are functionally related. Now functional relation does not always run parallel with spatial distribution. Thus the flexors of the upper and lower leg, e.g., are functionally related, and act in common; but those of the upper leg lie upon the ventral and those of the lower upon the dorsal side of the body, and consequently receive their nerves from different nerve-trunks, the crural and the sciatic respectively. If, then, the nerves for the flexors of the whole limb are in close proximity at their place of origin, there must be a rearrangement of fibres in the sacrolumbar plexus, in order that the two trunks may pass off in different directions. It is probable that the simpler connexions of the root-pairs are principally useful as supplementary mechanisms, while the more complicated plexus-formations are for the most part compensatory in function.

When BELL first established the law known by his name, he felt constrained by it to postulate a specific difference between sensory and motor nerves,—a difference which found expression in this fact of the difference in direction of conduction. Physiologists for a long time afterwards gave in their adhesion to this hypothesis. There was, indeed, a prevailing tendency to refer all differences of function, e.g. those obtaining between the various sensory nerves, to some unknown specific property of the nerve-fibres.[1] Later on, the belief gained ground that the nerves are simply indifferent conductors of the processes released in them by stimulation; though the only argument at first brought forward in support of it was the not very convincing external analogy of electrical conduction.[2] At the present time, we may say, with better reason, that BELL's hypothesis of a specific conductive capacity of sensory and motor nerves is not tenable. The decisive evidence is drawn from two sources. On the one hand, the general mechanics of nerve-substance has thrown new light upon the processes of conduction in the peripheral nerve-fibre (pp. 80 ff. above). On the other, the morphological facts indicate that the difference in direction of conduction depends upon the mode of connexion of the nerve-fibres at centre and periphery. Figgs 20 and 21 (p. 50 above) gave a schematic representation of the structural relations involved in the two cases. Every

---

[1] C. BELL, *An Idea of a New Anatomy of the Brain*, 1811; *An Exposition of the Natural System of Nerves*, 1824; *The Nervous System of the Human Body*, 1830.

[2] This analogy appears quite clearly as early as JOHANNES MÜLLER. Cf. his *Lehrbuch d. Physiol.*, 4te Aufl., i., 1844, 623. MÜLLER himself, however, leaves the question undecided. The first physiologist who expressed the decided opinion that the function of the nerves is determined solely by the organs with which they are connected was, as MÜLLER tells us, J. W. ARNOLD.

motor fibre, as we said in describing them, is the neurite of a nerve-cell ; and there is a certain principle of transmission of force which supposedly holds for all neurites alike. In accordance with this principle, the neurite is able to take up the stimulation-processes originated within the cell, or carried to it by its dendrites ; but the excitatory processes of which the neurite is itself the seat, though they are conducted to the cell as a result of the general diffusion that every stimulation-process undergoes in the nerve fibre, are inhibited in the central substance of the cell (p. 99). The cells of origin of the sensory fibres always lie, on the contrary, outside of the central organ : in the invertebrates, for the most part at the periphery of the body ; in the vertebrates, at any rate outside of the myel proper. Here, as we know, they form as it were little centres of their own ; the spinal ganglia, situated in the intervertebral foramens. These ganglia are composed throughout of bipolar nerve-cells ; that is to say, each cell sends out two, morphologically identical processes, which probably have the character of dendrites. In the lower vertebrates, the processes issue at different points —in the fishes, at opposite sides—of the cell. In man, the same conditions obtain in the early stages of development. As growth proceeds, however, the two processes fuse together at their point of origin, so that what were at first two distinct and separately originated processes now appear as the branches of one single process (Fig. 21, p. 50), which nevertheless retains the character of a protoplasmic process or dendrite. The two processes thus form a single neurone territory (N_1), which divides into two halves. The one lies within the myel, and after giving off numerous collaterals penetrates with its terminal fibres into a second central neurone territory (N_2). The other is continued in the sensory nerves, and is finally lost either in terminal arborisation among the epidermal cells, or in special end-organs, adapted for the support of the nerve-ramifications (H Fig. 21). We may therefore suppose, in agreement with what was said above regarding the diffusion of excitations carried by the dendrites (p. 42), that, where the peripheral and central processes issue separately from the cell-body, the process of stimulation is transmitted directly by the cell. When, as in man, the two processes unite to form one, the passage across, and then the transmission to higher neurones (N_2), may actually take place within the fibre itself. The cell Z_1 seems in this case to be cut out of the line of nervous conduction by a sort of short circuit; though this, of course, does not diminish its importance as a nutritive centre and storehouse of force. If, then, we regard the processes of conduction as conditioned in this way by the properties of the nerve-cells and the mode of termination of their processes within them, the principle of conduction in a single direction will hold only for the connexions of neurones, not for the nerves themselves ; the stimulation of any nerve, at any point of its course, must, so long as its continuity is preserved, be followed by the production of a stimulus wave which spreads out centripetally and centrifugally at one and the same time. But, as a matter of fact, there is not the slightest reason why we should hesitate to adopt this hypothesis. It is obvious that, when a sensory nerve is cut across, the excitations carried to the peripheral cut end must disappear at the periphery without effect, i.e. without arousing any sensation in our mind, just precisely as the stimuli which act upon the central cut end of a transsected motor nerve are inhibited in the cell connected with the neurite. In both cases, it is not any property of the nerve-fibres, but the character of the nerve-cells, that is responsible for the result. We can see, more especially when we consider the different modes of origin of the cell-processes, that the nerve-cell is naturally qualified to determine the direction of conduction and to regulate the mode of transmission from one neurone territory to another. For the rest, we shall presently become acquainted with facts that speak definitely for a centrifugal conduction of certain sensory excitations (pp. 182 ff.).

(b)—Physiology of the Conduction-Paths of the Myel

We have now to investigate the farther course of the nerve-paths that lead into the myel, as they are continued in the interior of this central organ. We obtain information concerning them, in the first place, from physiological experiments upon the result of stimulation, and more especially upon the effect of transsection, of certain portions of the myel. We know that the motor roots enter the ventral, and the sensory roots the dorsal half of the myel. These experiments show that the principal lines of conduction retain the same arrangement, as they take their course upwards. The effects of outside interference with the ventral portion of the myel are predominantly motor; with the dorsal portion, predominantly sensory. At the same time, they show also that even in the myel the individual fibre-systems are interwoven in the most complicated fashion. The results of hemisection of the myel, e.g., prove that not all conduction-paths remain upon the same side of the body upon which the nerve-roots enter the myelic substance, but that some of them cross over within the myel from right to left and *vice versâ*. It is true that the statements of various observers as to the kind and extent of conductive disturbance after hemisection are not in complete agreement; and it is evident, also, that the relations of conduction are not identical throughout the animal kingdom. But experiments on animals and pathological observations on man have put it beyond question that the sensory fibres, at any rate, always undergo a partial decussation. Hemisection of the myel does not lead to a complete abrogation of sensation upon either half of the body. The motor paths appear to be more variable in this respect. Experiments on animals again point to a partial decussation, though to one in which the greater part of the fibres remain upon the same side. Pathological observations, on the other hand, lead to the conclusion that in the myel of man the motor paths are uncrossed. We may, in particular, recall the well known fact that in unilateral apoplectic effusions in the brain, it is always only the one side of the body, viz., the side opposite to the apoplectic area, that is paralysed. Now there is, as we shall see presently, a complete decussation of the motor paths in the oblongata. If, then, decussation occurred to any considerable extent in the myel, the one arrangement would of necessity, so far as it went, compensate the other. We accordingly conclude that the principal motor path is situated in the ventral portion of the myel. And we are safe in affirming, similarly, that the principal sensory path lies in the dorsal portion. In the animals, it is true, we have a greater number of secondary paths, branching off to other parts of the myel, than we have in man. But even in the animals, there can be no doubt that the great majority of the fibres run their course without decussation. Impressions made upon the skin after hemisection of the myel upon the same side are not sensed, though stronger, painful stimuli will still evoke a reaction. Finally, in the lateral columns of the myel (m Fig. 66, p. 164) we have a combination of motor and sensory paths, drawn again for the most part from the fibre-systems of the same side. If the integrity of these columns be impaired, whether in man or in the animals, the resulting symptoms are in general of a mixed character.[1]

These experiments upon severance of continuity at various parts of the myel have brought to light a somewhat complicated interlacement of the fibre-systems. One of the chief factors in the resulting formation is, undoubtedly, the cinerea which surrounds the myelocele. The presence of this grey matter also explains the change of irritability brought about in the myelic fibres by stimulation-experiments. While the peripheral nerves may be readily excited by mechanical or electrical stimuli, this is so far from being the case with the myelic fibres that many of the earlier observers declared them to be wholly irresponsive to stimulation.[2] The statement, in its extreme form, undoubtedly overshoots the mark. Excitation can always be effected by summation of stimuli, or by help of poisons, like strychnine, which enhance the central irritability. At the same time, the marked change of behaviour points clearly to the intercalation of grey matter (cf. p. 86 above). If it be asked in what way this intrusion can materially affect the processes of conduction, we reply that a path coming in from

[1] LUDWIG and WOROSCHILOFF, *Ber. d. sächs. Ges. d. Wiss.*, math.-phys. Cl., 1874, 296. MOTT, *Philos. Transact.*, clxxxiii. 1892, 1.
[2] VAN DEEN, in MOLESCHOTT'S *Untersuchungen zur Naturlehre des Menschen*, vi., 1859, 279. SCHIFF, *Lehrbuch der Physiol.*, 1858, i. 238. PFLÜGER'S *Arch. f. d. ges. Physiol.*, xxviii. ; xxix. 537 ff. ; xxx. 199 ff.

the periphery will be brought into connexion, by the cinerea, not with one but with many paths of central conduction. These paths will, it is true, not be all equally permeable. Some will offer more resistance than others to the passage of excitation: in certain cases inhibitory effects, of the kind with which we have become familiar as the results of certain modes of connexion of the central elements (p. 99), may destroy or modify excitations already in progress. But there will always be various secondary paths available, over and above the principal path. The experiments upon severance of continuity call our attention chiefly to the principal path; but there are several ways—increased intensity of stimulus, enhancement of irritability, destruction of the principal path—in which the secondary paths may be thrown into function. If the white columns are entirely cut through, at any point upon the myel, so that only a narrow bridge of cinerea remains intact, sense-impressions and motor impulses may still be transmitted, provided that they are unusually intensive. And we find, similarly, that the phenomena of disability, which appear on transsection of a portion of the white columns, disappear again, after a short interval, although the cut has not healed.[1] The existence of these secondary paths or by-paths is attested, further and more particularly, by the phenomena of transference from one conduction-path to another, phenomena which prove the presence of a connecting path between different conduction-paths. They are of three kinds: the phenomena of concomitant movement, of concomitant sensation, and of reflex movement. As all alike are of importance for a right understanding of the functions of the central organs, especially of the myel, we shall be occupied with them in the following Chapter. We are interested in them here only in so far as they bear witness to the existence of determinate conduction-paths, preformed in the myel, but functioning only under certain special conditions. The place of transference from motor to motor, sensory to sensory, or sensory to motor paths must be sought, again, in the cinereal structures. Complete severance of the cinerea, with retention of a portion of the dorsal and ventral columns of white matter, abrogates the phenomena in question. Transferences within the motor paths, manifesting themselves in concomitant movements, may be made, without any doubt, either on the same side of the myel or from the one side to the other. Thus, the innervation of a finger-phalanx is transmitted both to other fingers of the same hand and, under certain circumstances, to the skin of other parts of the body. Bilateral concomitant movements of this kind are especially observable in movements of locomotion and in pantomimic movements. It is clear, on the other hand, that excitatory innervation within a definite path may be connected with inhibitory co-excitation of the cells of origin of another motor path. We have an instance of this state of things in the relaxation

---

[1] LUDWIG and WORSCHILOFF, op. cit., 297.

of tonus in the extensors that goes with excitation of the flexors of a limb.[1] This illustration, like that of co-ordinated movements, shows further that co-excitations within the motor paths may establish themselves as regular functional connexions. Transferences within the sensory paths seem, contrariwise, to be confined almost exclusively to the same half of the myel. The concomitant sensations observed after stimulation of some part of the skin are nearly always referred to cutaneous regions on the same side of the body. They are brought out most clearly by painful stimuli and by the arousal of tickling : in the latter case, more particularly when the skin is rendered unusually sensitive by enhancement of irritability. Under these conditions, stimulation of certain regions of the skin usually evokes sensations in other regions. Certain sensory parts, e.g. the external auditory meatus and the larynx, are also pre-eminently disposed for concomitant sensation.[2] We can hardly explain these facts otherwise than by the hypothesis that, on the one hand, certain preferred paths of connexion exist within the sensory conduction-paths, and that, on the other, certain sensory areas (larynx, external auditory meatus) are peculiarly susceptible to co-excitation. As regards the conditions under which conduction takes place, it is clear that concomitant movements and concomitant sensations both alike depend upon cross-conductions, that may be effected at different heights in the myel, and that differ only in direction : the motor cross-conductions extending in all directions, while the sensory, so far as we can tell, are almost exclusively unilateral, and for the most part follow the direction from below upwards. For the rest, the concomitant sensations and concomitant movements that have their ground in connexions of the myelic conduction-paths can never be certainly discriminated from those mediated by transference within the higher centres.

This statement does not apply to transferences of the third kind, reflex connexions of sensory and motor paths. The myelic reflexes may be observed for themselves alone, after the myel has been separated from the higher central parts. The conclusion to be drawn from such observation is that branch-conduction of the reflexes is effected by a large number of conduction-paths, all of which are closely interconnected. Moderate stimulation of a circumscribed area of the skin is followed, at a certain mean degree of excitability, by a reflex contraction in the muscle-group, and in that only, which is supplied by motor roots arising at the same height and on the same

---

[1] H. E. HERING and C. S. SHERRINGTON, in PFLÜGER'S *Arch. f. d. ges. Physiol.*, lxiii. 1897, 222. Cf. p. 93, above.
[2] Concomitant sensations with pain stimuli are described by LOWALEWSKY (trans. from the Russian in HOFMANN and SCHWALBE, *Jahresber. f. Physiol.*, 1884, 26) ; ' conjugate ' sensations, with arousal of tickling, by E. STRANSKY (*Wiener klin. Rundschau*, 1901, os. 24–26). In my own experience, the larynx and the external auditory meatus are especially liable to concomitant sensations.

side as the stimulated sensory fibres. If stimulus or irritability be increased, the excitation passes over, first of all, to the motor root fibres that leave the myel at the same height upon the opposite side of the body. Finally, if the increase be carried still farther, it spreads with growing intensity first upward and then downward; so that in the last resort it involves the muscles of all parts of the body which draw their nerve-supply from myel and oblongata. It follows, then, that every sensory fibre is connected by a branch-conduction of the first order with the motor fibres arising on the same side and at the same height; by one of the second order, with the fibres issuing at the same height upon the opposite side; by branch-conductions of the third order, with the fibres that leave the myel higher up; and, lastly, by branch-conductions of the fourth order, with those that emerge lower down.[1] This law of the diffusion of reflexes may, however, as we shall see in the following Chapter, be modified in two ways: by variation of the place of application of the reflex stimulus, and by the simultaneous application of other sensory stimuli (cf. Chap. VI. § 2).

(c)—Anatomical Results

The conclusions which we have reached by way of physiological experimentation regarding the course of the conduction-paths in the myel are in complete agreement with the morphological facts revealed by histological examination of this organ. In particular, the arrangement of the nerve-cells and of the fibre-systems which take their origin from the cell-processes, as shown in transverse and longitudinal sections, enables us to understand at once that every principal path is here accompanied by a large number of secondary paths, and that the most manifold connexions obtain between one line of conduction and another. We see, first of all, that the fibres of the ventral roots enter directly into the large nerve-cells of the ventral cornua, whose neurites they form; whereas the fibres of the dorsal roots, after their interruption by the nerve-cells of the spinal ganglia, divide upon entering the myel into ascending and descending systems, which there give off delicate branches at all points into the cinerea of the dorsal cornua. Here, therefore, as in the experiments with transsection, the white columns (l, m, n Fig. 66) appear in the rôle of principal paths: their ventral portions as motor, their dorsal as sensory. Secondary paths, for the conduction of unusually intensive excitations, or for the transferences required by concomitant movements, concomitant sensations and reflexes, can be mediated in a great variety of ways by the cellular and fibrillar system of the central cinerea (d, e). The interrelations of these different paths of conduction, and in particular of the two groups that in functional regard

---

[1] PFLÜGER, *Die sensorischen Functionen des Rückenmarks*, 1853, 67 ff.

stand farthest apart, the motor and sensory, are then determined by their mode of connexion with their cells of origin, and with the processes which these cells give off. We thus find, in the properties of the neurone and its area of distribution as manifested within the myel, a continuation of the differences that we meet with in the primitive forms represented in Figg. 20, 21 (p. 50). Fig. 67 shows the various morphological elements in their natural connexion. Each of the large multipolar cells *m* of the ventral cornu has direct control of some peripheral region by means of its neurite *n*, which does not break up into its terminal arborisation until it reaches the terminal plate of a muscle-fibre (Fig. 20, p. 50). On the other side, the dendrites issuing from the same cell run a very short course, to enter at once into the cinerea of the ventral cornu. The dendritic reticulum stands in direct contact with the terminal fibrils of the neurite *g* of another nerve-cell, situated as a rule high up in the brain; so that the neurones of this motor conduction cover very extensive territories. Indeed, it is probable that in most instances the entire motor conduction involves only two neurones (N_I and N_{II}, Fig. 20), the one of which extends from the cell *n* of the ventral cornu to the periphery of the body, while the other begins with some one of the fibres that run their course in the ventral or lateral column (*l, m* Fig. 66), and ends in a cell of the cerebral cortex. At the same time, still others of the dendrites belonging to the cells of the ventral cornua are in contact with the processes of the small cells *s* of the dorsal cornua, and with the small intercalatory or commissural cells *c* that lie scattered between ventral and dorsal cornua. In these latter connexions we have, presumably, the substrate of reflex conduction. The sensory nerve-paths, on the other hand, follow a very different course. In their

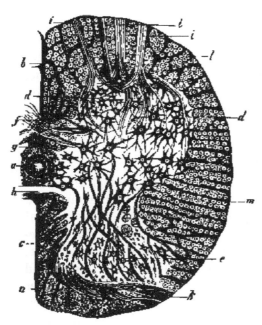

FIG. 66. Cross-section through the lower half of the myel of man, after DEITERS. For the sake of clearness, the ganglion-cells are drawn on a larger scale than the remaining parts of the figure. *a* Myelocele. *b* Ventral, *c* dorsal sulcus. *d* Ventral cornu, with the larger ganglion-cells. *e* Dorsal cornu, with the smaller ganglion-cells. *f* Ventral commissure. *g* Gelatinosa about the myelocele. Dorsal commissures. *i* Fibre-system of the ventral, *k* that of the dorsal nerve-root. *l* Ventral column. *m* Lateral column. *n* Dorsal column.

case, the spinal ganglion-cell *sp* forms the central point of a neurone territory, the one half of which extends by means of the peripherally directed processes *h* to the sensory termini of the organ of touch (Fig. 21, p. 50), while the other runs centralward in the central process *f*, which divides in the dorsal portion of the myel into ascending and descending branches (*a, d*). Both of these branches give off numerous collaterals, whose terminal ramifications stand in contact with the small cells of commissure and dorsal cornu. They themselves are finally resolved into fibrillar reticula, connected by contact with the dendrites of cells lying farther up and lower down. These structural relations seem to warrant the inference that the collaterals correspond to the various secondary paths by which transference, and especially reflex transference, is effected, and that the ascending and descending fibres constitute the principal path. The principal path of sensory conduction is, however, markedly different from the motor. As a general rule, there are several breaks in the line; the path consists of a number of neurone chains, arranged one above another. And this means, again, that the conditions of conduction in the principal path are less sharply distinguished from those in the secondary paths that begin in the collaterals. The whole morphological plan of the system of sensory conduction thus suggests a co-ordination of parts that is at once less strict and more widely variable than is the case on the motor side.

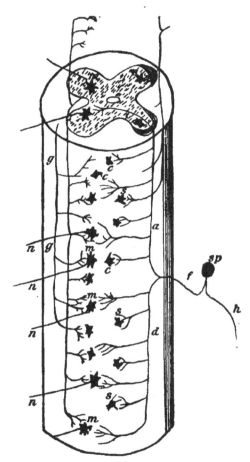

FIG. 67. Schema of the connexions of cells and fibres in the myel: combined from various diagrams of RAMON Y CAJAL. *m* Cells of the ventral, *s* cells of the dorsal cornua. *c* Commissural cells. *sp* Cell of a spinal ganglion; *h* its peripheral, *f* its central process; *a* ascending, *d* descending branch of *f*. *n* Neurites of the motor cells *m*. *g* Central continuation of the motor path.

We have spoken so far only of the general properties of the myelic conductors, properties accruing to all nerve-fibres whose mode of origin and connexions conform to a certain type. In the higher regions of the myel, other conditions are at work, paving the way for that differentiation of the conduction-paths which characterises the higher central regions. Even as low down as the thoracic portion of the myel, certain funicles divide off from the three principal columns already named, the ventral, lateral, and dorsal columns (*l, m, n* Fig. 66). The principal paths, sensory and motor, that run their course within the length of the myel, are thus split up into several separate tracts. The significance of these new funicles can best be understood from their embryological connexions and from the course of the degenerations observed in pathological cases (pp. 154 f.). It can be shown, by both lines of evidence, that the motor division of the lateral columns ascends uncrossed in their dorsal half, in a funicle which, as seen in cross-sections, encroaches from the outside upon the cinerea of the dorsal cornu. Higher up, it passes over into the pyramids of the oblongata, and is accordingly known as the path of the pyramidal lateral column (Fig. 68). In the same way, the innermost division of the motor ventral columns, the part bordering directly upon the ventral sulcus, ascends uncrossed to the oblongata, where it too passes over into the pryamids. It is termed the path of the pyramidal ventral column, and is the only division of the pyramidal tracts to remain uncrossed in the oblongata. Of the more peripherally situated funicles of the ventral column, some take a straight course upwards, while others enter the ventral commissure and cross to the opposite side of the body. The division of the lateral column which overlies the pyramidal lateral column, at the periphery of the myel, is an uncrossed and, to judge from the conditions of its origin, a sensory path: it branches off to the cerebellum by way of the postpeduncles, and is termed the path of the cerebellar lateral column. The dorsal columns, which are exclusively sensory in function, and therefore receive from below the great majority of the fibres that enter the dorsal roots, divide in the cervical region into two funicles: the slender funicles or columns of Goll (*fun. graciles*), and the more outlying cuneate funicles (*fun. cuneati*, Fig. 68).[1]

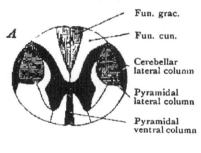
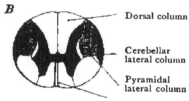

FIG. 68. Two cross-sections of the myel: *A* from the cervical enlargement, *B* from the thoracic region. After FLECHSIG.

[1] FLECHSIG, *Ueber Systemerkrankungen im Rückenmark*, 30 ff. BECHTEREW, *Die Leitungsbahnen im Gehirn und Rückenmark*, 1899, 17 ff.

§ 4. Paths of Conduction in Oblongata and Cerebellum

(a)—*General Characteristics of these Paths*

Oblongata and cerebellum, the parts of the brain stem that correspond developmentally to after brain and hind brain (p. 108), together with the pons that unites them, form in the brain of the higher mammals and of man a connected system of conduction paths. The system, as may be gathered from the general trend of the fibre-tracts that pass across it or decussate within it, is of importance in three principal directions. In the first place, this region furnishes the passage-way for the continuation of the sensory and motor conduction paths that come up from the myel. Secondly, it originates new nerves: the great majority of the cranial nerves spring from separate grey nidi in the oblongata: and, in doing this, repeats, though in much more complicated fashion, the structural patterns which we have traced, in their comparatively simple form, in the lower central organ. Thirdly, it contains a great variety of connecting paths, themselves for the most part interrupted by deposits of nerve cells, between the various paths that lead across or arise within it; while, further, in the fibre tracts that run from the main conducting trunk to the cerebellum and back again, it possesses a secondary conduction path of very considerable extent that is interpolated in the course of the principal conduction path. It will be understood that, under these conditions, the lines of travel in the region we are now to consider, as well as in the adjoining regions of mid brain and 'tween brain, are extraordinarily complicated. A complete explication of them, in the present state of our knowledge, is altogether out of the question. But more than this: it is impossible, as things are, to put a physiological or psychological interpretation upon many of the structural features that have already been made out. The functional significance of some of the most prominent conduction paths, as e.g. the entire intercalatory system that runs to the cerebellum, is still wrapped in obscurity. Hence, in most cases, the tracing out of the fibre systems is a matter solely of anatomical interest. In physiological regard it is useful, at the best, merely as illustrating the extreme complexity of the conditions which here determine conduction. We shall therefore refer, in what follows, only to certain selected instances, adapted to give a general picture of the course of the paths of conduction in the gross; and we shall enter into some detail only in those cases which appear to be of importance for the physiological and psychophysical relations of the central processes. On the score of method, we must say also that the physiological expedient of isolating the paths by transsection of individual fibre tracts, which did good service in giving us the general bearings of the paths of conduction in the myel, can hardly come into consideration here, more especially in our study of the conditions of conduction in the hind and mid brain regions. Experiments of the kind are recorded not infrequently in the older physiology. The course of the paths is, however, too complicated, and their origin too uncertain, to admit of any but an ambiguous result. The most that the method can give us is a point of view from which to appreciate the gross function of the organs or of certain of their parts; and we shall accordingly say nothing of the observations made by it until we reach the next Chapter. We may add that the method which has proved most fruitful for the problem of direction of conduction, apart from direct morphological analysis of the continuity of the individual fibre tracts, is the tracing of the course of degeneration in fibres separated from their centres of origin.

(b)—*Continuations of the Motor and Sensory Paths*

The simplest problem presented by our present enquiry is that of the further course of the paths of motor and sensory conduction that come up from the myel. The two methods just mentioned furnish us with a fairly satisfactory solution, at any rate as regards the motor paths. The principal continuation of the main path of motor conduction that runs upward in the lateral and ventral columns of the myel is, as we already know, the pyramidal path (Fig. 68, p. 166; cf. Fig. 46, p. 118). The course of this path in detail has been made out, with some degree of completeness, by help of the descending degeneration which appears in it after destruction of its terminations in the brain. It is the continuation of that division of the motor principal path which lies in the myel in the dorsal portion of the lateral columns and along the inner margin of the ventral columns (Fig. 68 B). The branch of this path that belongs to the ventral columns decussates in the cervical region of the myel. Now the larger branch, from the lateral columns, also undergoes a complete decussation, clearly visible on the external surface of the oblongata (p, Fig. 47, p. 119). The central continuation of the path then runs to the cerebral cortex, without interruption by cinerea. Fig. 69 gives a schematic representation of the course of these paths, the longest and so far the best known of all lines of central conduction. After they have traversed the pons, the fibres of the pyramidal path enter the crusta (f, Fig. 56, p. 130) between lenticula and thalamus, and then trend upwards in the space between lenticula and caudatum to pass into the corona, where their principal branches constitute the fibre-masses that terminate in the region of the central gyres and the surrounding area (VC, HC, Fig. 65, p. 145).[1] The path is thus fairly well defined. Part of it, as is proved by the paralyses following lesion of the pyramids

---

[1] CHARCOT, *Leçons sur les localisations*, etc., 145 ff. FLECHSIG, *Ueber Systemerkrankungen*, 42 ff. EDINGER, *Vorlesungen*, 6te Aufl., 86, 358.

and their continuation in the crus, undoubtedly subserves the conduction of voluntary impulses. In the animal kingdom, the pyramidal path affords a better measure than any other of the fibre systems collected in the brain stem of the general development of the higher central organs. In the lower vertebrates, the pyramids are altogether wanting. In the birds, they are but little developed. They steadily increase in importance in the mammalian series, up to man; while at the same time the tract from the lateral columns, which passes to the opposite side of the body in the pyramidal decussation, grows constantly larger as compared with the tract from the ventral columns, which decussates in the myel. A branch of the motor path which is forced inward by the pyramids, and which remains intact after removal of the pyramidal fibres, may be traced in part to the mesencephalon. It consists mainly of divisions of the ventral columns (*mf*, Fig. 70). Finally, certain of these remains of the ventral columns are collected in the interior of the rounded prominences to form the dorsolongitudinal bundle (*hl*, Fig. 72), which in its further course through the pons makes connexions with the pontal nidi and more especially, as it appears, with centres of origin of the oculomotor nerves and with the cerebellum.[1] We may accordingly suppose that these branches of motor conduction which run to the mesencephalon serve to mediate co-excitations in that region. The connexions of the dorsolongitudinal bundle, in particular, seem to point to connexions of the motor innervation of the eye and of the skeletal muscles, such as are involved in locomotion and in the orientation of the body in space.

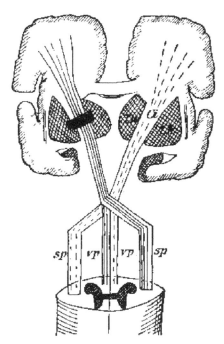

FIG. 69. Course of the pyramidal paths in man, after EDINGER. The fibres to the left half of the brain are indicated by continuous, those to the right half by interrupted lines. The diagram also illustrates the course of secondary degeneration, when the area of disease is situated in the left capsula. *sp* Branch of the pyramidal path derived from the lateral, *vp* branch derived from the ventral column. *Th* Thalamus. *Lk* Lenticula. *Ci* Course of the pyramidal fibres through the capsula of the lenticula. Cf. the cross-section of the brain shown in Fig. 56, p. 130.

[1] EDINGER, *op. cit.*, 317. RAMON Y CAJAL, *Beitrag zum Studium der Medulla oblongata*, 1896, 52 ff.

The course of the sensory path through the oblongata has not been made out as fully as that of the motor. The main reason for this defect in our knowledge lies in the difference of structure to which we referred above. It is characteristic of sensory conduction in the myel that the path does not pass upward in unbroken continuity, but consists of a chain of neurones. This structural complexity is not only continued but increased in the oblongata, where large numbers of cells, grouped together to form separate nidi, are interposed in the line of conduction. We may suppose that these nidi serve for the most part as transmitting stations—points at which a path, whose course has so far been single, splits up into several branches that diverge in different directions. The main divisions of the sensory path pass in this way, within the oblongata, first of all into the grey masses deposited in the slender and cuneate columns (Fig. 68 A, and Fig. 46, p. 118). Further on, the sensory path continues in a bundle lying close under the pyramids (l, Fig. 70), which appears on the ventral surface of the oblongata directly above the pyramidal decussation (p, Fig. 47, p. 119), here in its turn suffers decussation, and then passes on in the lemniscus of the crus, a structure lying in the outer and upper portion of the tegmentum. The lemniscal decussation (formerly known as the superior pyramidal decussation) thus forms yet another continuation of the decussations of myelic fibres which begin within the myel itself. Other sensory fibres (ci, Fig. 70), drawn from the dorsal columns, pass into the tegmentum proper, which thus brings together portions of the motor (mf) and of the sensory path. All these sensory fibres terminate in the grey masses of the region of the quadrigemina and thalami, from which, finally, further continuations of the sensory path proceed to the cerebral cortex.

(c)—*The Regions of Origin of the Cranial Nerves and the Nidi of Cinerea in the Oblongata*

The general sketch of the course of the sensory and motor paths, given in the preceding paragraphs, makes matters much simpler than they really are. There are two facts, not yet mentioned, that are chiefly responsible for the complications actually found. The one of these consists in the origination of a large number of new sensory and motor paths, which are derived from the cranial nerves, and in their further course either join the paths formed by the myelic nerves or strike out special lines of their own; the other, in the appearance of large groups of central nerve cells, which serve either as transmitting stations for the conductions coming up to the cerebrum from below, or as junctions for the important branch-conduction to the cerebellum, here opened for travel. The difficult questions concerning the origin of the cranial nerves, questions that have not yet in every case received their final answer, are of interest for psychology only in so far as they involve that of the paths followed by the sensory nerves. Since these belong in large part to the mesencephalic region, we may postpone their consideration until later. It will suffice for our present purpose to refer to Fig. 72 (p. 176), as an illustration of the conditions of origin of the cerebral nerves at large. The Figure shows how the funicles of origin of these nerves spring from isolated grey masses, the nerve nidi; how they then again and again strike across the longitudinal fibre tracts; and how they finally follow the general trend of the ascending paths. Most of the fibres of origin, however, enter into still further connexions with

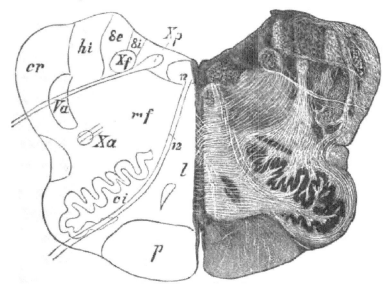

FIG. 70. Cross-section through the oblongata, × 4. After WERNICKE. *p* Pyramid. *ci* Olive. *l* Lemniscal tract (tract of the fillet) with fibres from the olives and from the funicles of the ventral column. *mf* Motor field (funicles from the ventral columns, joining the tegmentum later on). *hi* Remains of the dorsal column (also passing into the tegmentum). *cr* Restis and cerebellar peduncle. *12* Nidus and root of the hypoglossus. *Va* Ascending root of the trigeminus. *8e* External, *8i* internal nidus of the acusticus. *Xf* Mixed root of the glossopharyngeus. *Xp* Dorsal, *Xa* ventral nidus of the pneumogastric.

other nidal structures scattered throughout the oblongata. This statement applies in particular to the fibres of the oculomotor nervous system, to which we return below, when we come to discuss the conduction paths of the sense of sight, and to the mixed nerves, among which the pneumogastric, trigeminus and facialis are of especial importance by reason of their manifold functional relations. The nidi just mentioned are, we may conjecture, centres of excitation and transmission for the great functions regulated from the oblongata,—heart beat, movements of respiration and articulation, mimetic movements. Our knowledge of the mechanics of innervation in these cases is, however, still very incomplete.[1]

[1] Cf. RAMON Y CAJAL, *Medulla oblongata*, 43, 122 ff. EDINGER, *op. cit.*, 86 ff.

We turn now to the grey nidi of this region of the brain. We have already mentioned the nidi of the dorsal columns, interposed directly in the sensory path. Very much more complicated are the functions of the largest nidi of the oblongata, the olives (Fig. 46 B, Fig. 47, pp. 118 f.) whose principal office seems to be the giving off of branch-conductions. On the one hand, the neurites of the cells give rise to a fibre system, the further course of which is uncertain : it is supposed to connect partly with the cerebellum, partly with the lateral columns of the myel. On the other hand, the dentata give rise to two fibre systems. The first of these covers the outer surface of the olivary nidus, in the form of zonal fibres (g Fig. 48, p. 120), and then bends round into the restes and their continuations, the cerebellar peduncles (cr Fig. 70). The second issues from the interior of the nidus and crosses the median line, to decussate with the corresponding fibre-masses of the opposite side. Other fibres from the olives enter the longitudinal fibre tract that lies between them, and then run within the pons to the lemniscus of the crus (l Fig. 70) ; they thus appear to join the sensory principal path to the cerebrum. Putting the facts together, we may say that the olives are structures which stand in intimate relation with the branching off of conduction paths towards the cerebellum. Another ganglionic nidus, lying higher up—in man concealed by the pons, in the lower mammals projecting on its posterior border—the trapezium or superior olive, forms, as we shall see presently, a nodal point of great importance in the conduction of the acoustic nerve.

(d)—Paths of Conduction in Pons and Cerebellum

The conduction paths that branch off from the oblongata to the cerebellum, and there turn back again to join the caudex in its course through the pons, bear a striking external resemblance to a shunt interposed in the main current of an electrical conduction. And it seems, as a matter of fact, that this obvious comparison fairly represents the actual relations of the nerve paths, as they are shown schematically in Fig. 71. The sensory and motor principal paths, just described, have also been included in this diagram, in order that the reader may obtain a rough idea of their relation to the branch path leading to the cerebellum. The mammalian cerebellum contains, as we have already said, two formations of cinerea : the one appearing in the ganglionic nidi, the other in the cortical layer investing the entire surface of the organ (pp. 121 f.). Our present knowledge of the relations between the fibres that enter into and issue from the cerebellum and these grey masses may be summarised as follows (cf. Fig. 48, p. 120). The fibres of the restes are deflected round the dentatum, more especially over its anterior margin. They do not appear to connect with the cinerea of this nidus, but radiate from its upper surface towards the cortex, where they terminate and are lost. From the cortex itself comes a system of transverse fibres, which cut across the more longitudinal radiations of the restes, and draw together in stout fascicles to form the medipeduncles (brachia of the pons). The interior of the dentata gives rise, further, to the funicles which pass into the prepeduncles (crura ad cerebrum). And, finally, there is a connexion between the dentata and the cerebellar cortex. This path, together with the radiation of the restis and the medipeduncle, occupies the outer division of the alba, while the innermost portion is constituted by the prepeduncle. It is therefore probable that all the fibres running through the postpeduncles of the cerebellum from the oblongata have their termination in the cortex. The cortex itself gives rise to two fibre systems: the one passes directly over into the medipeduncles, the other appears first of all to connect the cortex with the dentatum, which then gives off the vertically ascending fibres of the prepeduncles. These run upwards, with the continuations of the myelic columns, converging as they proceed; just anteriorly to the upper end of the pons they reach the middle line, and undergo decussation. Besides the two divisions of this system of ascending fibres, we find, lastly, further radiations, whose fibres subserve the interconnexion of more or less remote cortical areas. Some of the longer lines cross from the one side to the other in the vermis.

The further course of the paths leading from the cerebellum to the cerebrum is as follows. The path which is continued in the medipeduncles appears, first of all, to terminate in grey masses in the anterior region of the pons. From these masses arise new, vertically ascending fibres, some of which can be traced to the anterior brain ganglia, the lenticula and striatum, while others proceed directly to the anterior regions of the cerebral cortex. The fibres collected in the prepeduncles find their proximate termination in the rubrum of the lemniscus (*hb* Fig. 56, p. 130). A small number of the fibres issuing from this point probably enter the thalami; but the greater portion pass to the internal capsule of the lenticula, and thence in the corona to the cerebral cortex, ending in the regions posterior to the central gyre, and more especially in the precuneus. The valvula (*vm* Fig. 48, p. 120), which joins the prepeduncles at the beginning of their course, serves in all probability to supplement the connexions of the cerebellum with the brain ganglia, by mediating a conduction to the quadrigemina.

We must believe, in view of these results of anatomical investigation, that the concurrence of conduction paths in the cerebellum is extremely complicated. Let us consider these paths as a branch conduction, interposed in the course of the direct conduction from myel to cerebrum as mediated by oblongata and pons. We have two divisions, a lower and an upper. The lower division of the branch conduction carries sensory fibres from the dorsal and ventral columns (olivary path of the dorsal columns, and cerebellar path of the lateral columns), which connect the myel with the cerebellum; and motor funicles, which branch within the pons to enter the restes. The upper division makes two principal connexions, by way of the medipeduncles: the one with the cerebral cortex direct, the other with the anterior brain ganglia (lenticula and striatum). At the same time, there is a connexion, mediated by prepeduncles and valvula, with the posterior brain ganglia (thalami and quadrigemina). The most extensive of these conductions, that to the cerebral cortex effected by the medipeduncles, radiates out to all parts of this organ, but is principally directed forwards to the frontal brain and the adjacent regions.

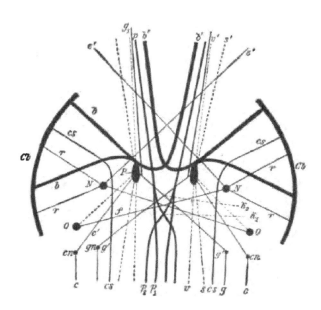

FIG. 71. Schema of the paths of conduction through pons and cerebellum. *Cb* Cerebellar cortex. *N* Dentatum of the cerebellum. *P* Grey masses of the pons. *O* Olive. *gn* Nidi of the slender funicles. *cn* Nidi of the cuneate funicles. p_1 Ventral column of the pyramids (uncrossed). p_2 Lateral column of the pyramids (crossed). *vv'* Remains of the ventral columns. *ss'* Remains of the lateral columns. *g* Slender funicles or columns of GOLL. *c* Cuneate funicles. *g'*, *c'* Central continuations of these funicles. g_1 Lemniscal path. *f* Conduction from olive to cerebellar nidus. *cs* Direct cerebellar path of the lateral columns. *r* Conduction from cerebellar nidus to cerebellar cortex. *bb'* Path of the medipeduncles. *e'* Path of the prepeduncles. k_1 Pyramidal decussation. k_2 Lemniscal decussation.

The schema given in Fig. 71 shows the main features of this conduction system. The reader will recognise, first of all, the pyramidal path, with its crossed branch from the lateral and its uncrossed branch from the ventral columns, running directly between myel and cerebral cortex (p_1 p_2, p). He will next notice the other motor paths, derived from the ventral columns, and interrupted in the mesencephalic region by masses of cinerea. Some of these paths are continued in a new neurone chain, and extend to the cerebral cortex; other fibres of the same system probably terminate in the mesencephalic region itself (*vv'*). A considerable division of the sensory path (*gg'*), drawn from the dorsal columns, passes in the lemniscal decussation (k_2) to the opposite side: part of it is lost in the grey masses of the pons, part continues in fibre tracts which, interrupted by grey nidi, run to the anterior brain regions and so finally to the cortex. There is also an uncrossed sensory path (*cc*), derived from the dorsal and lateral columns, which passes into the tegmentum of the crus and finds its proximate terminus in the tegmental grey nidi. Another path, also sensory in origin, is the uncrossed branch conduction (*cs*) carried to the cerebellum from the restes in the postpeduncles; it terminates in the cerebellar cortex, for the most part in the vermis. Finally, there is a crossed conduction (*f*), issuing from the grey nidi of the olives, which, unlike the former, enters into the nidal structures (*N*) of the cerebellum. These are all incoming paths. The outgoing lines, leading to the cerebrum, are two in number: the prepeduncles, which start from the cerebellar nidus, and may be traced partly into the prosencephalic ganglia, partly to the cerebral cortex (*e'*); and the fibres of the medipeduncles (*bb'*), which run direct from the cerebellar cortex to the cerebrum. These latter enter, first, into the grey nidi of the pons, and are by them brought into connexion, in some measure, with the brain ganglia, but most extensively with the cerebral cortex, and in that principally with the frontal region. The system is completed by the paths of connexion between nidal structures and cortex (*rr*) which belong exclusively to the cerebellum.

The general relations of these incoming and outgoing paths suggest that the cerebellum brings into connexion with one another conductions of different functional significance. This inference finds further support in the peculiar structure of the cerebellar cortex. The characteristic constituents of this region are, as we saw above (Fig. 15, p. 44), the cells of PURKINJE, easily distinguished by their large size and the manifold arborisation and reticulation of their protoplasmic processes. If, now, the cerebellar cortex serves to connect fibres of different function, sensory and motor, as is suggested by the relations of the incoming and outgoing paths, it is clear that we may look upon these cells of PURKINJE as elementary centres of connexion between functionally different fibre elements. We should then have to assume, on the analogy of the large cells in the ventral cornua of the myel, that the dendrites mediate centripetal, the neurites centrifugal conductions: in other words, that the chief office of the former is to take up the excitations carried in the postpeduncles, while the latter collect to form the paths of conduction that continue in the medipeduncles to the cerebrum and there, as it appears, are chiefly connected with the centres of innervation of the prosencephalon.

The pons is chiefly important as receiving the paths to be carried up from cerebellum to cerebrum, and associating them to the vertical ascending fibres of the crus. Its development in the animal kingdom thus keeps even pace with the development of all these paths of conduction, and especially of the pyramids and medipeduncles. The fibres that cross over from the one side to the other in the median line of the pons (at R Fig. 72) are decussating fibres belonging in part to the direct continuations of the myelic columns through the pons, in part to the medipeduncles of the cerebellum. The decussation of these latter has been established by pathological observations: atrophy of a cerebral lobe is ordinarily attended or followed by a wasting away of the opposite half of the cerebellum. The fibres of the medipeduncles, probably without exception, pass through internodes of grey matter before they are deflected into the vertical paths; and small grey nidi are also strewn in the path of the directly ascending prepeduncles (ba Fig. 72). These presently decussate, and come to an end in the rubrum of the tegmentum. In this way, by collection of the myelic columns that come up from below, and of the continuations from the cerebellum that join them from above and from the side, there forms within the pons that entire fibre tract which connects the lower-lying nerve centres with the structures of the cerebrum,—the crus. At the same time, the pons is broken through by the root bundles of certain cranial nerves, which take their origin higher up. The nidi of origin of these nerves are situated partly upon the cinereal floor of the highest portion of the fossa rhomboidalis (metacele), partly in the neighbourhood of the Sylvian aqueduct (mesocele), which forms a continuation of the central canal.

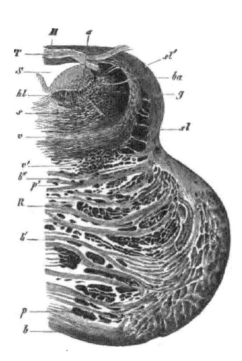

Fig. 72. Cross-section through the pons of man, at the level of the root of the trochlearis, after STILLING. *M* Valvula. *T* Root of trochlearis. *S* Sylvian aqueduct. *5* Cells of origin of the fifth cranial nerve in the grey floor of the aqueduct. *hl, v, v', sl* Continuations of the ventral columns. *hl* Dorsolongitudinal bundle. *v* Median remains of the ventral columns on either side of the raphe. *v'* Anterior remains of the ventral columns adjoining the lemniscus. *sl* Lemniscus; continuation of the divisions of the ventral columns that surround the olives (capsular columns, fun. siliquae). *sl'* Passage of the lemniscal fibres into the roof of the Sylvian aqueduct. *s* Remains of the lateral columns, and formatio reticularis. *g* Gelatinosa, and continuations of the dorsal columns. *ba* Prepeduncles. *R* Raphe. *b* Ectal, *b'* intermediate, *b''* ental cross-fibres of the pons. *p-p'* Continuations of the pyramidal tracts, intermixed with cinerea and with the ascending continuations of the medipeduncles issuing from it.

As a result of its cleavage by cinerea and by the cross fibres of the medipeduncles, the crus divides into two parts, distinguishable in the gross anatomy of the brain, and known as crusta and tegmentum. A third division, the lemniscus, belongs to the tegmentum so far as regards the direction of its course, but in all other respects is clearly differentiated from it. Neither of the two principal parts constitutes a complete functional unit; on the contrary, each of them includes conduction paths of very diverse character. Nevertheless, the twofold division of the crus seems to represent a first, even if a rough classification of the numerous paths of conduction to the cerebrum. Thus the inferior portion or crusta (p—p^1 Fig. 72) is principally made up of the continuations of pyramids, remains of the dorsal columns, and medipeduncles. Its outermost portion carries that continuation of the dorsal columns which passes in the lemniscal decussation to the opposite side of the body (k_2 Fig. 71). The intercalatum (substantia nigra of SÖMMERING: Sn Fig. 73) is a ganglionic nidus, belonging to the conduction paths of the crusta, which separates crusta from tegmentum. The portion of the crus which lies above the intercalatum, the tegmentum (v'—hl Fig. 72), is at first composed of the remains of the lateral and dorsal columns, and of a part of the remains of the ventral columns. In its further course, beyond the point at which the rubrum appears in cross sections of the tegmentum (R Fig. 73), these are reinforced by the prepeduncles (mf, hi, cr Fig. 70). Finally, the lemniscus, which we have recognised as a separate subdivision of the tegmentum (sl—sl' Fig. 72), also carries fibres from the dorsal columns, as well as fibres from the ventral columns and the cerebellum. Taking the origin of all these tracts into consideration, we may designate the crusta as that part of the crus which, so far as it derives directly from the myel, is especially devoted to the conveyance of motor paths; the tegmentum and lemniscus are of mixed, and mainly, as it seems, of sensory origin. At every point, however, these direct continuations of the myelic systems are augmented by intercentral paths, the conductions from the cerebellum. In this way, as may be seen from Fig. 72, which shows a cross section taken approximately through the middle of the organ, the structure of the pons becomes extraordinarily complex. We may add that it contains, crowded together in a comparatively small space, the whole number of conduction paths, many of which in their later course are widely divergent. It is, therefore, a remarkable coincidence that, besides the epiphysis, which is not a nervous centre at all (see p. 124, above), the pons should have been regarded with especial favour by the metaphysical psychology of past times as the probable 'seat of the mind.' HERBART himself accepts this view. If, on the contrary, one were asked to lay one's finger upon a part of the brain that by its complexity of structure and the number of elements it compresses into a small space should illustrate the composite character of the physical substrate of the mental life, and therewith show the absurdity of any attempt to discover a simple seat of mind, one could hardly hope to make a happier choice.

5. Cerebral Ganglia and Conduction Paths of the Higher Sensory Nerves

(a)—*The Cerebral Ganglia*

If we look at the series of cerebral ganglia, we see at once that those of mesencephalon and diencephalon, the quadrigemina and the thalami, serve as intermediate stations on the line of conduction: peripherally, they receive sensory and motor fibres; centralwards, they stand in connexion with the cerebral cortex. They lie, as their function requires, directly upon the crura, whose fibre masses partly run beneath them straight to the prosencephalon, partly curve upwards to enter into the grey nidi of the ganglia. There is a difference, however: the thalamus takes up comparatively few fibres from below, and sends out very considerable bundles to the cerebral cortex; the quadrigemina do just the reverse. Both ganglia, as we shall see in detail later, are of especial importance as nodal points in the optic conduction. Fig. 73 shows a section taken through the middle region of this whole area, and will assist in some degree towards an understanding of the structural relations.

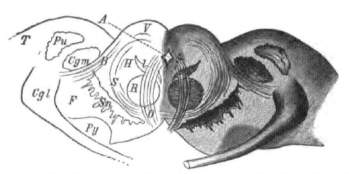

FIG. 73. Vertical section through the caudex in the region of the pregemina; in part after EDINGER. *A* Aqueduct. *B* Prebrachium. *V* Pregeminum. *T* Thalamus. *Pu* Pulvinar. *H* Tegmentum. *F* Crusta. *S* Lemniscus. *Cgm* postgeniculum. *R* Rubrum. *Sn* Intercalatum. *Py* Pyramid. *I* Dorso-longitudinal funicle. *O* Oculomotor (third cranial) nerve.

The position of the prosencephalic ganglia, the striata with their two subdivisions, caudatum and lenticula, is more obscure. The incoming and outgoing fibres tell us but little of their function. Both divisions receive fibres from the periphery, derived for the most part from the diencephalic and mesencephalic ganglia. The crural fibres, on the other hand, pass below and between the prosencephalic ganglia, without entering them (Fig. 74). The grey masses of the ganglia send no further reinforcements to the coronal radiation. It would appear, then, that these structures are terminal stations of conduction, analogous to the cerebral cortex, and not intermediate stations like the thalami and quadrigemina.[1]

(b)—Conduction Paths of the Nerves of Taste and Smell

An important place is filled in the system of conductions that falls within the region we are now considering (prosencephalon, diencephalon, mesencephalon) by the paths of the sensory nerves. Fortunately, these are among the conductions that have so far been most fully investigated, and whose

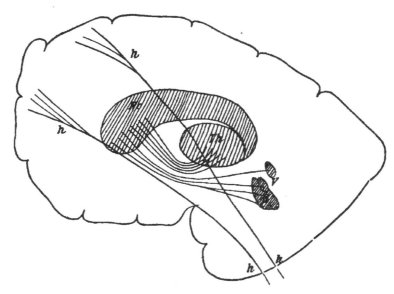

FIG. 74. Schema of the paths of conduction to the striata; after EDINGER. *Nc* Caudatum. *Th* Thalamus. *V* Quadrigemina. *B* Grey masses of the pons (intercalatum). *hh* Fibre masses passing directly from the crura to the corona. The connexions to the lenticula (not represented in the Fig.) are to be thought of as running straight out from the *Th* to the observer.

functional significance is at the same time relatively easiest of interpretation. In view of their great importance for psychology, we shall, therefore, depict their principal features in some little detail. We begin with the conduction paths of the nerves of taste and smell; putting these together not so much because the peripheral sense organs are closely related, both in spatial position and in function, as rather because the two lines of conduction may in a certain sense be regarded as prototypes of the much more complicated conditions that obtain in the cases of sight and hearing. The

[1] EDINGER, *op. cit.*, 272. BECHTEREW, *Leitungsbahnen im Gehirn und Rückenmark*, 439.

gustatory path approaches very closely to the type familiar to us in the sensory paths of the general sense. When the conducting fibres have left the central organ, they pass only once more, and then in the near neighbourhood of the centre, through bipolar cells, analogous to the cells of the spinal ganglia; they then break up at the periphery of the organ in a reticulum, which is distributed between non-nervous epithelial elements. The olfactory path, on the other hand, is a pronounced instance of the second type of sensory conduction, characterised by the outward displacement of central nerve cells to the peripheral organ, which accordingly represents, in all essential particulars, a portion of the central organ: cf. above, p. 47.

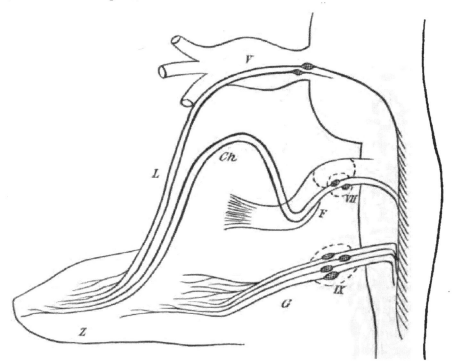

FIG. 75. Schema of the origin of the gustatory nerves, after EDINGER. *V* Trigeminus (fifth cranial nerve). *L* Lingual branch of the trigeminus (lingualis). *F* Genu of the nervus facialis. *G* Glossopharyngeus. *Ch* Chorda tympani. *VII.* Geniculate or facial ganglion. *IX* Glossopharyngeal ganglion. *Z* Tongue.

There is, however, a further point, in which the path of the gustatory nerves differs from those of the other nerves of special sense. The gustatory fibres, in consequence, we may suppose, of their distribution over a functional area of some considerable extent, run their course in two distinct nerve trunks: those destined for the anterior portion of this area in the lingualis (*L* Fig. 75), and those intended for the posterior portion in the glossopharyngeus (G). This division appears, however, to be simply external. Both of the gustatory nerve paths take their origin from the same masses of nidal cinerea on the floor of the metacele. At first, however, the gustatory fibres that run to the anterior portion of the tongue join the facialis, at the genu of which (F) they pass through the cells of a small special ganglion. Thenceforward they are continued in the chorda tympani (Ch) side by side with the lingual branch of the trigeminus. The glossopharyngeus, on the other hand, which supplies the posterior portion of the tongue, passes through its own ganglion. At the periphery, as we shall see when we come to consider the peripheral sense apparatus (Ch. VIII., § 4), the two nerves break up into terminal fibrils, which end in and among the taste beakers, without, as it appears, coming into contact with other than epithelial terminal structures. The course of the fibres, as shown synoptically in Fig. 75, accordingly corresponds in all details with a general sensory conduction, such as is represented

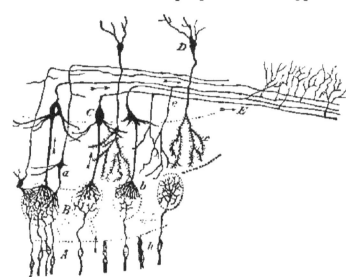

FIG. 76. Origin and termination of the olfactory nerves in man, after RAMON Y CAJAL. A Peripheral olfactory cells. h Epithelial cells lying between them. a Small intermediary nerve cells. B Dendrites of the glomeruli. C Central olfactory cells, with b their dendrites in the glomeruli. D Cells of the (probably) centrifugal path, with c their terminal arborisations. E Fibres of the olfactory tract, with f collaterals. e Free nerve terminations.

in Figg. 21 and 67 (pp. 50, 165) for the myelic nerves: the ganglia VII. and IX. may be regarded as analogues of the spinal ganglia.

The paths of the olfactory nerves follow a radically different course. Their point of origin lies furthest forward of all the sensory nerves, so that they border directly upon certain cortical regions of the cerebrum. This is the reason that the olfactorius, from the outset, is not a single nerve, but appears in the form of numerous delicate threads, which issue direct from a part of the brain that belongs to the cortex, the olfactory bulb (Fig. 52, p. 125). Conduction begins at the periphery in the cells of the olfactory mucous membrane (*A* Fig. 76), which are set between epithelial cells, and have themselves the character of nerve cells that send their neurites centralward. These neurites, in their course to the olfactory bulb, break up into delicate fibrils, which for the most part come into contact with the dendrites of small nerve cells: the two sets of processes together forming a compact ball of tissue (*a, b*). Each of these cells, in its turn, sends out a principal process, which passes into one of the large nerve cells of the bulb (*C*). Here we must place the proximate cortical station of the olfactory path. The dendrites issuing laterally from the cell bodies represent, in all probability, ramose secondary conductions; while the main path of centripetal conduction is continued, in the direction of the arrows, in the neurites, which leave the cell upon the opposite side, and pass into the olfactory tract. This, the principal path, accordingly extends over a peripheral and a central neurone territory. There is, now, a second group of central olfactory cells which, if we may judge from their connexions and the direction of their processes, are probably to be regarded as nodal points of a system of centrifugal conduction. These cells (*D*) send out a single peripherally directed neurite, which breaks up within the glomeruli in a delicate reticulum of terminal fibrils (*c*). The olfactory path thus shows a marked divergence from the type of sensory conduction represented by the cutaneous nerves. The peripheral organ itself appears as a peripherally situated portion of the cerebral cortex, and the olfactory fibres, by a natural consequence, resemble central rather than peripheral nerve fibres. Another novel feature is introduced in the probable existence of a secondary path of centrifugal conduction,. And, lastly, we must note the central connexion of the olfactory regions of the two sides by the precommissure (*ca* Fig. 53, p. 127). The connexion is presumably to be interpreted as an olfactory decussation, by which the centripetal paths are carried to the opposite hemisphere, and the neurones *D c* are also enabled to mediate co-excitation, in the centrifugal direction, of the peripheral cells *A* of the opposite side of the body.

(c)—*Conduction Paths of the Acoustic Nerve*

In man and the higher vertebrates, the cochlea of the auditory organ is, in all probability, the only part of the labyrinth of the ear that subserves auditory sensation. If we may judge from the character of the cochlear nerve terminations, the peripheral starting-point of the acoustic conduction conforms in all respects to the conduction type represented by the cutaneous nerves. The terminal fibrils of the acusticus extend among the epithelial and connective tissue structures of the basilar membrane (cf. Ch. VIII., § 4, below), and then, in the auditory canal of the cochlea (*S* Fig. 77) traverse groups of bipolar ganglion cells (*g*) which resemble the cells of the spinal ganglia and are termed in common the spiral ganglion. The cells of this ganglion, which accordingly corresponds to an outlying spinal ganglion, give off neurites which run centralward, and finally break up into terminal arborisations within various accumulations of cinerea, more especially in two large nidi in the region of the metacele, with the processes of whose cells they are

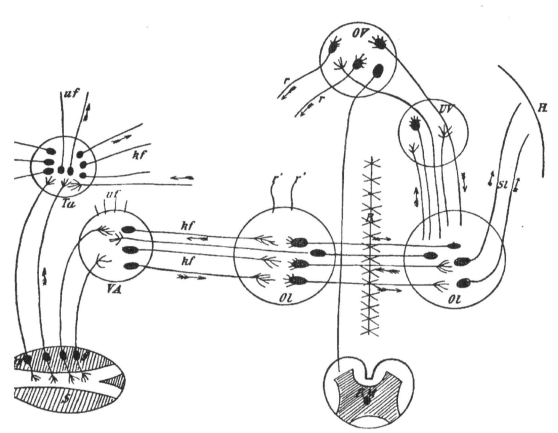

FIG. 77. Schema of conduction by the acoustic nerve, combined and simplified from HELD's diagrams. *S* Cochlea. *g* Bipolar ganglion cells of the spiral ganglion. *Ta* Tuberculum acusticum. *Cb* Cerebellum. *VA* Anterior acoustic nidus. *Ol* Superior olive. *R* Median line of the oblongata and pons, with decussating fibres: raphe. *RM* Myel. *UV* Postgeminum. *OV* Pregeminum. *Sl* Lemniscus. *H* Cerebral cortex. *rr* Reflex paths to the motor nidi of muscles of eye and face. *r′r′* Reflex paths from the superior olives to the muscles of the body. *uf* Uncrossed fibres. *kf* Crossed fibres.

thus brought in contact. The nidi in question are a somewhat smaller anterior nidus, the anterior acoustic nidus (*VA*) and a larger posterior nidus, the tuberculum acusticum (*Ta*). Both of these ganglia send off a small number of fibres, which pass upwards on the same side (*uf*), and a larger number, which ascend on the opposite side of the body (*kf*). The former run partly to the postgemina, and partly, having joined the lemniscus, direct to the cerebral cortex. There is also, in all probability, a branch path from the tuberculum acusticum, which proceeds with the postpeduncles to the cerebellum (Cb). The great majority of the fibre tracts issuing from the two nidal masses cross, however, to the opposite side, either directly or by way of the superior olives (Ol); in each of which the conduction is transferred to new neurone territories. After decussation, they continue in the same direction as the uncrossed fibres: some to the postgemina (UV), some in the lemniscus to the acoustic area of the cerebral cortex (H). Still other neurites ($r'r'$), which take their origin from cells in the superior olives, follow a shorter road, running crossed or uncrossed, to nidi of motor nerves. This latter path must accordingly be regarded as a reflex path. The branch conduction to the postgemina is continued, with interruption by their cell masses, to the pregemina (OV), from which again a centrifugal fibre system (rr) runs to motor nidi, and more especially to the nidi of the oculomotor nerves. It would seem, therefore, that this quadrigeminal path is also, in part, a reflex path; though the quadrigemina serve at the same time as a transmitting station, from which a further centripetal conduction is continued to the anterior brain ganglia. To the sensory conductions already described must be added, finally, a path between the same cell stations in the quadrigemina (OV, UV) and the acoustic nidi (VA, Ta), which, if we may judge from the peripheral direction of its neurites, conducts in the opposite direction to that marked in the Figure, and would therefore represent a centrifugal path. Like the centripetal path which it accompanies, it consists of a large number of crossed and a small number of uncrossed fibres. It is indicated by the downward pointing arrows. We thus have, in summary, the following paths of conduction: (1) the primary path, conforming in type to the path of the spinal nerves, which runs from the peripheral end-fibres of the acoustic nerve to the ganglion spirale (the equivalent of a spinal ganglion) and thence to the acoustic nidi (VA, Ta) in the oblongata; (2) the principal centripetal path, beginning in these nidi, which divides into a smaller uncrossed and a larger crossed bundle and runs, with interruption by the superior olives or by other masses of nidal cinerea, to the cerebral cortex; (3) a branch path, beginning in the same nidi of the oblongata, which also divides into crossed and uncrossed portions, and runs to the quadrigemina and thence in all probability to the anterior brain ganglia; (4) reflex paths, which lead across to motor nidi as low as the superior olives and as high as the pregemina, and which include, more particularly, the paths of the oculomotor nerves and of the facial muscles concerned in the movements of speech; (5) a branch path to the cerebellum, which again begins in the primary acoustic nidi; and, finally, (6) a centrifugal sensory path, which issues from the quadrigeminal nidi, and is associated in its peripheral course with the corresponding centripetal path.[1]

This list shows us how extraordinarly complex is the network of relations into which the auditory organ is brought by its central paths. Apart from its twofold crossed and uncrossed connexion with the cerebral cortex, the following facts should be noted as of especial significance. First, there is a reflex path connecting the acoustic centres with the points of origin of muscular nerves, and among them with the centres for the movements of articulation and for the movements of the eyes, which latter are extremely important in the spatial orientation of the body. Secondly, we find that the conduction system, like that of the olfactory nerve, includes centrifugal paths, whose office is, perhaps, to transmit the excitations of the auditory organ of the opposite side, or other sensory excitations that find their nodal points in the mesencephalic region, in the form of concomitant sensation.

We remark, in conclusion, that the acoustic nerve proper, which comes from the cochlea, is connected over a part of its peripheral course with the nerve that comes from the vestibule and canals. This, the vestibular nerve, is a branch of the eighth cranial, and is commonly accounted, like the cochlear, to the acoustic nerve. In its central course, however, it appears to follow a different road. It passes through special nidal structures, and finally, as its secondary degenerations prove, terminates in separate areas of the cerebral cortex.[2]

(d)—Conduction Paths of the Optic Nerve

The principal difference between the optic and acoustic conductions is that the optic surface itself, like the olfactory surface, is an outlying portion of the central organ, displaced to the periphery of the body. It is natural, therefore, that the optic fibres too, when they emerge from the retina, should at once appear, as by far the great majority of them do, in the character of central nerve fibres. The cells that give visual sensation its specific quality, the rods and cones (S and Z Fig. 78)—usually termed, on this account, visual cells—are sensory epithelia which, like the gustatory cells, are connected only by contact with the terminal fibrils of the optic conduction. In the retinal layers that cover them are several strata of nerve cells, easily divisible by their marked differences of form into two main groups: the large multipolar ganglion cells (G_2), which may be regarded, from the relations of their neurites and dendrites, as proximate points of departure for the optic conduction running centripetally from the retina to the brain; and bipolar ganglion cells (G_1,) to which may be added stellate intercalary cells, found far forward in the neighbourhood of

---

[1] This exposition follows HELD, *Arch. f. Anatomie*, 1893, 201 ff.
[2] BECHTEREW, *Die Leitungsbahnen*, 169 ff.

the elements S and Z, and not represented in the Figure. These last two classes constitute together a neurone territory, intervening between the last terminal fibrils of the peripheral optic conduction and the large ganglion cells (G_2), which may be considered as the extreme peripheral member of the centripetal optic conduction. Between its limits we find, further, terminal arborisations of neurites (e), derived not from cells of the retina itself but from more central regions,—probably from the pregemina, since these, as we shall see in a moment, form important nodal points in the optic conduction at large. There is thus a further point of resemblance between the outlying central area represented in the retina and the olfactory surface; here as there, the structural relations indicate the existence of a centrifugal secondary path, running alongside of the centripetal principal path.[1]

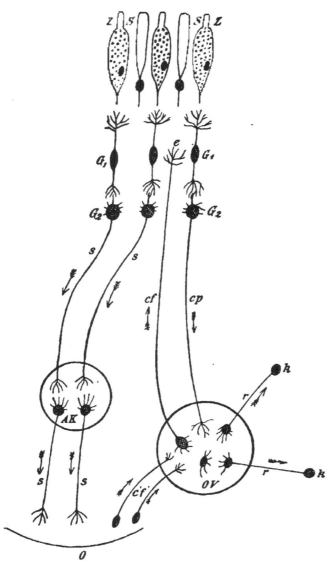

FIG. 78. Schema of the optic conduction, in part after VON MONAKOW. S, Z Rods and cones of the retina. G_2 Large nerve cells of the layer of ganglion cells. G_1 Bipolar nerve cells. e Terminal arborisations of centrifugal optic fibres. OV Pregeminum. AK Pregeniculum. O Occipital cortex. ss Direct optic radiation. c'f' Centrifugal optic conduction to the pregeminum. cp Centripetal, cf centrifugal sensory mesencephalic path. rr Reflex paths to the nidi (kk) of the oculomotor nerves.

[1] For a detailed account of the terminal nervous apparatus of the retina, cf. below, Ch. VIII. § 4.

The fibres collected in the optic nerve conduct, then, for the most part centripetally; though there is, in all probability, a small admixture of centrifugal conductors. Following its course, we come upon the decussation of the optic nerves, the chiasma, where a distribution is made of the optic fibres, to the paths running further towards the central organ, that is obviously of extreme importance for the co-operation of the two eyes in binocular vision. It is instructive, in this regard, to trace the phylogenetic stages through which the mode of distribution in the human chiasma has gradually been attained. In the lower vertebrates, up to the birds, there is a complete decussation of the paths, the right half of the brain receiving only the left optic path, and conversely. In the mammalian series, from the lower orders onwards, direct paths play a larger and larger part alongside of the crossed fibres; until finally, in man, the distribution has become practically equal; so that the one (the temporal) half of the retina passes into the optic tract of the opposite side, and the other (the nasal) into the tract of the same side.[1] We owe our knowledge of this fact less to direct anatomical investigation, which finds great difficulty in the tracing of the detailed course of the optic nerve, than to pathological observations of the partial loss of sight resulting from destruction of the visual centre of one hemisphere or from the pressure of tumours upon the optic tract of one side. The main results of these observations are brought together, in schematic form, in Fig. 79. It will be seen that the corresponding halves of retina and optic nerve are cross-hatched in the same direction. The temporal halves of both retinas have a crossed (tt), the nasal halves a direct path (nn). Before decussation, the crossed path lies on the outside, the uncrossed on the inside of the optic nerve; after decussation, the crossed changes to the inside, the uncrossed to the outside of the optic tract. In contradistinction to the retinal halves, which thus receive only a one-sided representation in the brain, the central area of the visual surface, or macula lutea, where the retinal elements are set most thickly, is favoured with a bilateral representation. Destruction of the central optic fibres of one side is accordingly followed by half-blindness (hemianopsia) or limitation of the field of vision to one-half of each retina (hemiopia), with the exception of the area of direct vision around the fixation point, which becomes blind only when the central disturbance affects both sides of the brain.[2] We return later (pp. 229 ff.) to the relations which this peculiar mode of distribution sustains to the function of vision.

The conduction of the optic tract of either half of the brain is thus composed of temporal paths from the opposite retina, nasal paths from the

---

[1] RAMON Y CAJAL, *Die Structur des chiasma opticum.* Trans. J. BRESLER, 1899.
[2] GUDDEN, *Arch. f. Ophthalmologie*, xxv., 1. VON MONAKOW, *Arch. f. Psychiatrie*, xxiii., 1892, 619; xxiv., 229. GILLET and VIALET, *Les centres cérébraux de la vision*, 1893.

retina of the same side, and macular paths from both retinas. It divides again, on both sides—as is shown schematically in Fig. 78, where abstraction is made from the decussations which we have just been discussing—into two paths : the one of which runs first of all to the pregenicula (*AK*), while the other passes to the pregemina (*OV*). The two paths appear to have no connexion with each other, despite the proximity of quadrigemina and genicula (see Fig. 48, p. 120). In the same way, the optic path to the pregeminum runs direct to this through the prebrachia, without coming into contact with the postgeminum. The first of these two paths, that which travels to the pregeniculum, forms the direct optic radiation (*ss*)

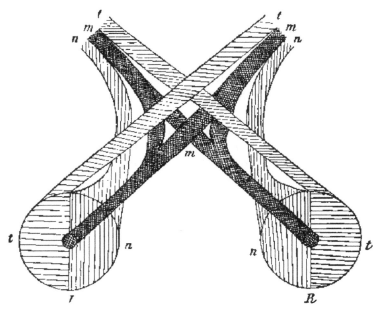

FIG. 79[1] Schema of the optic decussation in man, after VIALET. *L* Left, *R* right retina. *t* Decussating fibres of the temporal half. *n* Uncrossed fibres of the nasal half. *m* Fibres of the centre of the retina, running to both sides.

to the cortex of the occipital lobe. It passes over, in the grey nidi of the pregeminum, into a new neurone terrritory, whose neurites break up into terminal fibrils in the brain cortex. On the other hand, the large pyramidal cells of the cortex send out neurites, which apparently join the coronal

[1] It should be said, with regard to Fig. 79, that the schema there given simply shows the relative positions of the optic fibres in the nerve and optic tract, with reference to the various parts of the retina, as they are to be inferred from the investigations of HENSCHEN (*Brain*, 1893), VIALET (*Les centres de la vision*, 1893), and others. The central arrangement of the fibres corresponds to this peripheral schema only in so far as the bundles proceeding from the macula lutea find representation in the occipital cortex of both hemispheres. Cf. the account of the whole matter in BECHTEREW, *Die Leitungsbahnen im Gehirn und Rückenmark*, 209 ff. On the other hand, the definitive

fibres that enter the pregemina, and thus constitute a centrifugal conduction extending to that point ($c'f'$). The pregemina themselves, which contain terminal arborisations of fibres, first beginnings of neurites from ganglion cells, and various forms of intercalary cells, and which send out fibres both to the peripheral sense organ and to the nidi of the oculomotor nerves, appear accordingly as intermediary stations of great complexity. While, on the one side, they receive the central conduction coming from the brain cortex, they serve, on the other, towards the periphery, as points of departure for sensory and motor fibres,—the sensory paths conducting in part centripetally to them, and in part centrifugally away from them. If, then, we abstract from the facts of decussation, described above, we may say that the fibres of the optic tract make up the following paths: (1) the centripetal sensory principal path (ss), which in the large multipolar ganglion cells of the retina (G_2) receives the excitations pouring in from the periphery; has an intermediary station, again interrupted by ganglion cells, in the pregeniculum (AK); and finally reaches the cerebral cortex in the optic radiation of the corona: (2) a centripetal sensory mesencephalic path (cp), which runs to the pregemina; here, in its turn, enters a new neurone territory; and finally, as it would appear, passes into the centrifugal paths (rr) that go to the nidi of the oculomotor nerves — the whole path $cprr$ thus representing a reflex path, which connects retina and oculomotor nerves in the mesencephalon: and lastly: (3) a path which, if we may judge from the mode of connexion of its elements, conducts centrifugally, and which divides into two parts: a central branch $c'f'$, running from optic cortex to mesencephalon, and terminating in the pregemina; and a peripheral branch cf, beginning in the pregemina and

position of the lateral and median bundles in the cortical centres is, as we show below (pp. 206, 235), for the most part the precise opposite of their position in these proximate conduction paths; experiments on animals and pathological observations on man prove that the lateral portions of the retina are represented on the same, the median on the opposite side of the brain. In seeking to explain this fact, we must bear in mind that the proximate termination of the optic paths lies in the mesencephalic centres of the genicula, and that it is accordingly from this point that the final assignment of fibres to the cortex is made. In view of the complexity of the relations involved, and of the somewhat ambiguous symptoms which follow from injury to the cortex, many investigators, like HENSCHEN, and, to some extent, VON MONAKOW, have recently taken the position that the connexion of the various parts of the retina with the cortical centres at large has not yet been finally settled; and HENSCHEN is further inclined to restrict the visual centre to a limited area within the calcarine fissure (O' Fig. 65, p. 145), instead of allowing it the fairly extended region in the occipital cortex (Fig. 89, p. 206) to which it is usually referred. VON MONAKOW, however, while admitting that he is in doubt as regards the definitive correlation of retina and cortex, does not hesitate to express his conviction that the central representation of the various parts of the retina is, in any event, based upon their relation to the centres of ocular movement (*Ergebnisse der Physiol.*, 1 Jahrg., 1902, 2 Abth., 600). This statement is, as the reader will see, in full agreement with what is said below (pp. 229 ff.) of the theory of decussations in general, and of the decussations of the optic paths in particular, as against the simple copy-theory of RAMON Y CAJAL.—Later note by AUTHOR.

ending, as we saw above, in the retina. In view of all these connexions we can readily understand that reactions to light impressions can be released in the mesencephalon, without any participation of the principal path: released as reflexes to the oculomotor system, by way of the transferences effected in the quadrigemina, and as reflexes to other muscles of the body, by way of the other connexions. The paths which, from the direction of their neurone connexions, must in all probability be regarded as centrifugal conductors may be supposed to serve, on the one hand, as the vehicle of direct reflections of central excitations to the nervous structures at the periphery, and, on the other, as lines of transmission, by help of which excitations in the one retina mediate centrally coexcitations of the other.[1]

6. Paths of Motor and Sensory Conduction to the Cerebral Cortex

(a)—General Methods for the Demonstration of the Cortical Centres

We have now traced, as accurately as may be, the course of the fibre systems that run to the cerebral cortex, whether directly from the crura, or indirectly from the cerebellum and the brain ganglia. We have made use, in this enquiry, both of the results of anatomical investigation and of the degenerations set up by severance of the fibres from their centres of function. But we have not been able to say anything at all definite of the final distribution of the central fibre systems in the cortex itself. As a matter of fact, there are still certain mazes of interlacing fibres to which anatomists have not yet found the clue; and our two methods fail us, when we seek to determine by their aid the precise relations in which the various regions of the cerebral cortex stand to the deeper lying nerve centres and to the peripheral parts of the body. We therefore ask assistance at this point from two other sources, physiological experiment and pathological observation. The former supplies us with a certain correlation, in the animal brain, between definite cortical areas and the various motor and sensory functions of the peripheral organs. The latter attempts the same problem for the human brain, by a comparison of the functional derangements recorded during life with the results of post-mortem examination. The conclusions drawn from experiments on animals may be transferred to man only, of course, in so far as they answer the general question

---

[1] MONAKOW, *Arch. f. Psychiatrie*, xx., 1889, 714 ff. BECHTEREW, *Die Leitungsbahnen*, 199 ff. RAMON Y CAJAL, *Les nouvelles idées sur la structure du système nerveux*, 1894; *Studien über die Hirnrinde des Menschen*, i. *Die Sehrinde*, 1 00. Besides the reflex path *rr* to the nidi of the oculomotor nerves, there is another, which mediates the reaction of the pupil to light stimulation. Its course has not yet been fully made out; but it seems to be altogether divergent from the other, since the pupillary reaction is not abrogated by destruction either of the pregemina or of the genicula. Cf. BECHTEREW, *op. cit.*, 215.

of the representation of the bodily organs in the cerebral cortex. When we attempt to map out, on the human brain, the terminal areas of the various paths of conduction, we have to rely solely upon pathological observations. These possess the further advantage that they allow us to make more certain tests of the behaviour of sensation than do the experiments upon animals. On the other hand, they have the disadvantage that circumscribed lesions of the cortex and pallium are of comparatively rare occurrence, so that the collection of data proceeds but slowly.

Experiments on animals fall into two main classes: stimulation experiments and abrogation experiments. Under the latter heading, we include all experiments which are intended to abrogate, temporarily or permanently, the function of some cortical area. In stimulation experiments, the symptoms to be observed are phenomena of movement, twitches or contractures in the muscles; abrogation experiments bring about abrogation or disturbance of movements or sensations. Both forms of experiment are of value for the definition of the terminal areas of the motor paths; for the sensory areas, we must have recourse in most cases to abrogation experiments. There are, however, many regions of the cerebral cortex which form the terminal areas of intercentral paths from the cerebellum and brain ganglia, paths which are connected only in a very complicated and roundabout way with the lines of sensory or motor conduction, or with both. We shall, therefore, expect a priori that not every experimental or pathological change, induced over a limited area, will be followed by noticeable symptoms; and that, even where such symptoms appear, they will not, as a rule, consist in simple phenomena of irritability and disability such as arise from the excitation or transsection of a peripheral nerve. This expectation is amply confirmed by experience. At many points, stimulation may be applied without producing any symptoms whatsoever. Where it does produce a result, the muscular excitations often have the character of co-ordinated movements. The symptoms of abrogation, on the other hand, are for the most part simple disturbances of movement or impairments of sense perception; it occurs but seldom, and in general only where the lesion is of considerable extent, that there is complete abrogation of function, sensory or motor. It is well, therefore, in speaking of experiments upon the cerebral cortex, to use expressions that in some way indicate this ambiguity of result. We shall accordingly distinguish between *centromotor* cortical areas, whose stimulation produces movements of certain muscles or muscle groups, and whose extirpation is followed by a derangement of these movements, and *centrosensory* areas, whose removal brings in its train symptoms of loss or defect upon the sensory side.[1] These terms must

[1] I avoid the use of the simpler terms 'motor' and 'sensory,' in order to indicate from the outset, the essential difference that obtains between the conditions of conduc-

not, however, be interpreted at the present stage of the enquiry as implying any hypothesis whether of the significance of the phenomena of stimulation and abrogation or of the function of the cortical areas to which they are applied. The only question to be discussed here is that of the termination of the paths of conduction in the cerebral cortex; and all that we require to know, in order to answer it, is the functional relation obtaining between the various regions of the cortex and the peripheral organs. How these functional relations are to be conceived, and in what manner the different cortical areas co-operate with one another and with the lower central parts,—these are questions that we do not yet need to consider. There is, however, one point, so important for the right understanding of the conditions of conduction that it should, perhaps, be expressly mentioned in this place; a point that follows directly from the extreme complexity of interrelation which we have found to prevail in the central parts. It is this: that, for anything we know, there may exist several centromotor areas for one and the same movement, and several centrosensory areas for one and the same sense organ; and that there may quite well be parts of the cortex which unite in themselves centromotor and centrosensory functions. Suppose, then, that we are able to demonstrate certain results of stimulation and abrogation. They will simply indicate that the particular area of the cortex stands in some sort of relation with the conduction paths of the corresponding muscular or sensory region. The nature of the relation can be conjectured only after a comprehensive survey has been made of the whole body of central functions. All questions of this kind must, therefore, be postponed until the following Chapter.

The extreme complication of the course of the conduction paths, and the unusually complex conditions that govern the central functions, in face of which the formation of a critical judgment becomes a matter of serious difficulty, make us realise all the more keenly the comparative crudeness and inadequacy of all, even the most careful, experimental methods. In stimulation experiments, it is never possible to confine the stimulus effect within such narrow limits as is desirable, if we are to establish the relations of conduction obtaining between distinct cortical areas. Moreover, the central substance, as we have seen, has its own peculiar laws of excitability, which make negative results practically worthless as data from which to draw conclusions. Physiologists are therefore inclining more and more to attribute the higher value to abrogation experiments. But here, again

---

tion here and in the peripheral nerves. The other terms in current use, 'psychomotor' and 'psychosensory,' seem to me to be objectionable, for the reason that they suggest a participation of consciousness or of mental functions which, to say the least, is hypothetical. It must also be remembered that there are many central parts besides the cerebral cortex, e.g. the brain ganglia, that are also endowed in certain measure with the properties under discussion.

there are difficulties, as regards both the performance of the experiments and the interpretation of their results. The shock given by the operation to the whole central organ is usually so violent, that the immediate symptoms cannot be referred to any definite cause; they may be due to functional disturbance in parts of the brain widely remote from the point of injury. Hence almost all observers have gradually been led to agree that the animals must be kept alive for a considerable period of time, and that only the later, and more especially the chronic symptoms may be made the basis of inference. Even so, however, various sources of error are still possible. Thus, as GOLTZ pointed out, inhibitory influences may continue to be exerted, either upon the entire central organ or upon distant regions, particularly if but a short interval has elapsed after the operation. Or, if a longer time has passed, the injured part may have been functionally replaced by other cortical areas: numerous pathological observations on man have put the efficacy of such vicarious function beyond the reach of doubt. Or, finally, as LUCIANI remarked, the cortical lesion may, on the contrary, set up a secondary degeneration of deeper lying brain centres, so that the abrogation of functions may be extended far beyond its original scope. In view of these difficulties, which mean that the experimental result may be obscured by sources of error of the most various kinds and of opposed directions, it is obvious that conclusions in which we are to place any measure of confidence must be drawn without exception from a large number of accordant observations, made with due regard to all the factors that might affect the issue. And when these precautions have been taken, it is still inevitable that the conclusions, in many cases, attain to nothing higher than a certain degree of probability. In particular, they will as a general rule fail to carry conviction, until they are confirmed by pathological observations upon the human subject.

(b)—Motor and Sensory Cortical Centres in the Brain of the Dog

Centromotor areas in the cerebral cortex may easily be demonstrated, as HITZIG and FRITSCH were the first to show, by experiments with electrical or mechanical stimuli. The simplicity of the structural plan of the carnivore brain (Fig. 61, p. 138) makes it comparatively easy to rediscover the irritable points, when they have once been found. In Fig. 80 there are marked upon the brain of the dog the principal points about which the statements of the different observers are in general agreement.[1] Besides these superficial areas, there appear to be other cortical regions in the same neighbourhood, lying concealed in the depth of the central fissure, which

---

[1] FRITSCH and HITZIG, *Arch. f. Anat. u. Physiol.*, 1870, 300 ff. HITZIG, *Untersuchungen über das Gehirn*, 1874, 42 ff. FERRIER, *The Functions of the Brain*, 2nd ed., 1886.

are mechanically excitable: their exact localisation is, however, impossible, owing to their inaccessible position.[1] The motor areas are all situated over the anterior portion of the brain, between the olfactory gyre and the Sylvian fissure. With stimuli of moderate intensity, the effect of stimulation is produced on the opposite side; bilateral symptoms are observed only in the case of movements in which there is a regular functional connexion of the two halves of the body, e.g. in ocular movements, movements of chewing, etc. With stronger stimuli, the effect is confined as a rule to the muscles of the same side of the body. The stimulable areas are seldom more than a few millimetres in extent, and excitation of points lying between them is, if the stimuli are weak, unaccompanied by any visible effect. If the stimulus is made more intensive, or is frequently repeated, contractions may, it is true, be set up from these originally indifferent points; but it is possible that such results are due to diffusion of currents (in electrical stimulation) or to an enhancement of excitability brought about by the preceding stimulation. There can, indeed, be no doubt that repetition of stimulus is able to induce this enhancement; for it is often found that, under such conditions, the excitation spreads to other motor areas, so that the animal is finally thrown into general spasms, the phenomena of what is called cortical epilepsy.[2] For the rest, the contractions set up by cortical stimulation are always distinguished from those released by electrical stimulation of the coronal fibres by a much longer duration of their latent period, the expression of that retardation of the stimulation processes which is of universal occurrence in the central elements.[3]

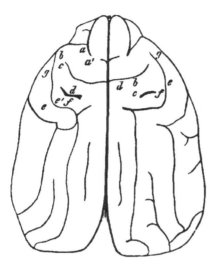

FIG. 80. Centromotor areas on the surface of the brain of the dog. The areas on the left are given, in part, according to FRITSCH and HITZIG; in part, according to the author's own observations; on the right, some of FERRIER's results are shown for purposes of comparison. *a* Neck muscles. *a'* Back muscles. *b* Extensors and adductors of the fore leg. *c* Flexors and pronators of the fore leg. *d* Muscles of the hind leg. *e* Facialis. *e'* Superior facial region. *f* Eye muscles. *g* Muscles of mastication.

The phenomena of abrogation, observed after extirpation of definite portions of the cerebral cortex of the dog, differ in two respects from the

---

[1] LUCIANI, *Arch. ital. de biologie*, ix., 268.
[2] FRANCK, *Les centres motrices du cerveau*, 1887.
[3] FRANCK and PITRES, *Arch. de physiol.*, 1885, 7. 149. BUBNOFF and HEIDENHAIN. Pflüger's *Arch. f. d. ges. Physiol.*, xxvi., 137.

results of the experiments with stimulation. In the first place, they show that the removal of a stimulable area is usually followed by disturbances of movement in other groups of muscles, which were not excited by stimulation of the same area. Thus, extirpation of the area *d* in Fig. 80 is likely to produce paralytic symptoms in the fore leg as well as paralysis of the hind leg; and, conversely, extirpation of the area *c* is attended by a partial paralysis of the hind leg; again, destruction of the centres of neck and trunk *aa'* involves both the extremities; and so on. At the same time, the paralysis of the stimulable areas is always more complete than that of the areas sympathetically affected. In the second place, the extirpation of parts of the cortex that are irresponsive to stimulation may also give rise to phenomena of paralysis; and this statement holds not only of points of the cortex lying between the stimulable areas, within the zone of excitability, but also of more remote regions. It can thus be demonstrated that the entire anterior portion of the frontal lobe, and even the superior portion of the temporal region as well, are in the dog centromotor in function. Only the occipital and the larger, inferior portion of the temporal region can be removed

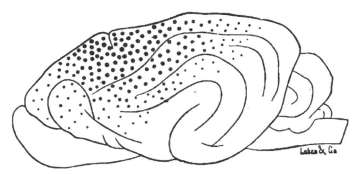

FIG. 81. Centromotor region of the surface of the brain of the dog. After LUCIANI.

without producing symptoms of abrogation on the motor side. Fig. 81 gives a graphic representation of these facts. The sphere of centromotor abrogation is dotted over; the size and number of the points in any given area indicate the intensity of the phenomena of abrogation appearing (always on the opposite side of the body) after extirpation of that particular zone.[1] The character of these disturbances, and more especially the regularity with which definite muscle groups are affected by the extirpation of definite parts of the cortex, render it improbable that the results obtained from non-stimulable areas are the outcome of transitory inhibitions, propagated as simple sequelæ of the operation from the point of injury to other, uninjured parts. We may more reasonably explain the differences between the phenomena of stimulation and those of abrogation

---

[1] LUCIANI and SEPPILLI, *Die Functionslocalisation auf der Grosshirnrinde*, 289 ff. (*Le localizzazioni funzionali del cervello*, 1885). HITZIG, *Berliner klin. Wochenschrift*, 1886, 663.

by supposing that the excitable zones stand in closer relation to the peripheral conduction paths than do the others, whose centromotor influence can be demonstrated only by way of the inhibition of function which follows upon their removal. For the rest, it is a significant fact for the theory of these phenomena of centromotor abrogation that they do not consist by any means in complete muscular paralyses. In general, there is inhibition of voluntary movement only: the muscles involved will still contract reflexwise upon stimulation of the appropriate points upon the skin, and may be thrown into sympathetic activity by the movement of other muscle groups. Further, all symptoms of abrogation, save where very considerable portions of the cortical investment of both hemispheres have been removed, are impermanent and transitory; the animals will, as a rule, behave, after the lapse of days or months, in a perfectly normal way, and the restoration occurs the more quickly, the smaller the extent of the cortical area destroyed.[1]

The demonstration of the centrosensory areas, if it is to be accurate and reliable, must, as we said above, be undertaken by help of the phenomena of abrogation. This limitation of method, and more especially the uncertainty which attaches to sensory symptoms, place serious obstacles in the path of investigation. There are, however, two points in which the disturbances of sensation set up by extirpations of the cortex in the dog appear to resemble the motor paralyses which we have already passed under review. First, the cortical regions correlated with the various sense departments are, evidently, not well-marked and circumscribed; they always cover large areas of the brain surface, and even seem to overlap. Secondly, the disturbances, here as before, do not consist in any permanent abrogation of function. If the injury is restricted to a comparatively small area, they may be entirely compensated. If it affects a larger portion of the cortex, there will, it is true, be permanent sensory derangements, but they will express themselves rather in an incorrect apprehension of sense impressions than in absolute insensitivity to stimulus. Thus, dogs whose visual centre has been entirely removed will still avoid obstructions, and others, whose auditory centre has been extirpated, will react to sudden sound impressions, although they can no longer recognise familiar objects or the words of their master. They take a piece of white paper, laid in their path, for an obstacle which they must go round; or confuse bits of cork with pieces of meat, if the two have been mixed together.[2] All these phenomena indicate that the functions of perception have in such

---

[1] On this point, cf. in particular GOLTZ, *Ueber die Verrichtungen des Grosshirns*, 1881, 36, 119 ff.

[2] GOLTZ, PFLÜGER'S *Arch. f. d. ges. Physiol.*, xxvi., 170 ff.; xxxiv., 487 ff. LUCIANI and SEPPILLI, *op. cit.* (German), 50 ff.

cases been abrogated or disturbed, but that the removal of the centro-sensory areas is by no means and in no sense the equivalent of destruction of the peripheral sense organs. There is, further, one respect in which the terminations of the sensory conduction paths differ from those of the motor: while the derangements of movement point to a total decussation of the motor nerves, the disturbances of sensation, or at least of the special senses, are bilateral, and accordingly suggest that the fibres of the sensory paths undergo only a partial decussation in their course from periphery to centre.

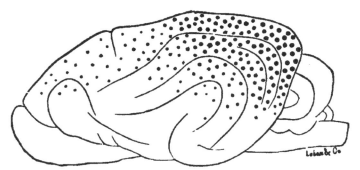

FIG. 82. Visual centre of the dog. After LUCIANI.

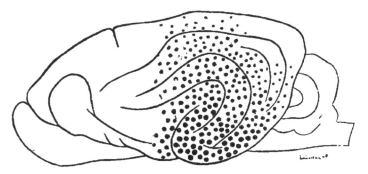

FIG. 83. Auditory centre of the dog. After LUCIANI.

Figg. 82, 83 and 84 show roughly the extent of the visual, auditory and olfactory areas in the cortex of the dog, as determined by the method of abrogation. The frequency of the dots indicates, again, the relative intensity of the disturbances which

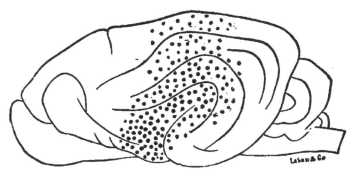

FIG. 84. Olfactory centre of the dog. After LUCIANI.

follow upon extirpation of the area in question; the black dots correspond to crossed, the hatched dots to uncrossed abrogation symptoms. We notice that the visual centre is situated for the most part in the occipital lobe, though less marked disturbances may be caused from a part of the parietal lobe and probably also from the hippocampus; the temporal lobe, on the other hand, is practically exempt. The auditory area has its centre in the temporal lobe, from which it appears to extend over a portion of the parietal lobe, as well as the callosal gyre and the hippocampus. The olfactory area has its principal centre in the olfactory gyre. Besides this, it seems to occupy the uncus and the hippocampus, while its share in the parietal region is but small. In the visual and auditory spheres, the crossed fibres have an undoubted preponderance; in the olfactory area, the uncrossed appear to be in the majority. The gustatory area cannot be made out with certainty: it probably lies on the two opposite surfaces of the intercerebral fissure in the anterior region of the parietal lobe.[1] On the other hand the area whose extirpation affects the sense of touch and the sensations of movement—the two cannot be distinguished in this group of symptoms—occupies a broad space on the convex surface of the brain. It has its centre, in the brain of the dog, in the anterior parietal region, and extends from that over the whole frontal portion, and downwards and backwards to the margins of the temporal and occipital lobes. The centrosensory area for the sense of touch has, that is, precisely the same extent as the centromotor area for the general muscular system of the body; it can accordingly be illustrated from Fig. 81, which we have already employed in our previous discussion. This coincidence suggests the hypothesis that a distribution into smaller, overlapping centres for the various parts of the body will obtain in the case of sensations as we have found it to obtain in the case of movements. For the rest, the phenomena of abrogation which make their appearance after removal of the touch sphere run precisely parallel to the disturbances of the special senses described above: the permanent symptom is always the derangement of perception, and never the insensitivity sometimes observed as the direct consequence of operation.

(c)—Motor and Sensory Cortical Areas in the Monkey

The brain of the monkey so closely resembles the brain of man (cf. Fig. 64, p. 144), that the discovery of its cortical centres is a matter of peculiar interest. It was therefore natural that the attempt should be made, soon after the establishment of the centromotor points on the brain of the dog, to determine the corresponding points on that of the monkey. Experiments were carried out by HITZIG[2] and FERRIER,[3] who found, in agreement with the course of the pyramidal paths, that the stimulable centres lie for the most part in the region of the two central gyres, whence

---

[1] SCHITSCHERBACK, *Physiol. Centralblatt,* v., 1891, 289 ff.
[2] HITZIG, *Untersuchungen über das Gehirn,* 126 ff.
[3] FERRIER, *The Functions of the Brain,* 1886, 235 ff.

they extend as far as the superior portion of the subfrontal and medifrontal gyres. More exact determinations of the points were then made in further investigations by HORSLEY and SCHÄFER,[1] and by HORSLEY and BEEVOR.[2] Fig. 85 gives the results obtained by the two latter writers on a Bonnet Monkey (*Macacus*). They show in general that the cortical centres for the trunk and the hind limbs lie principally on the superior surface; those for the fore limbs somewhat lower down; and lastly, those for the muscles of face, larynx and eyes still lower, towards the Sylvian

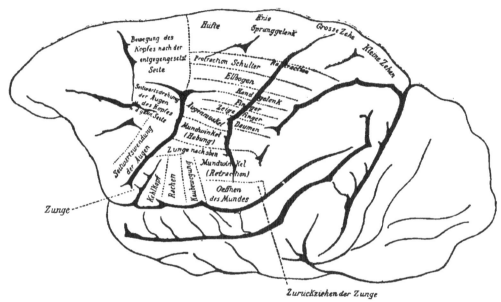

FIG. 85. Centromotor cortical areas in the brain of a Bonnet Monkey (*Macacus sinicus*). After HORSLEY and BEEVOR.
The index follows the Figure in two vertical columns, beginning on the left, and reading from above downwards. Where a column sub-divides, the titles run from left to right within it. Movement of head to opposite side; Turning of eyes and head to same side; Turning of eyes; Tongue; Hip; Knee; Hallux; Small toes; Ankle; Shoulder, protraction and retraction; Elbow; Wrist; Fingers; Index finger; Eye muscles; Thumb; Angle of mouth, elevation; Tongue protruded; Angle of mouth, retraction; Larynx; Pharynx; Mastication; Mouth open; Tongue retracted.

fissure; while the centres for movements of head and eyes are situated forwards from the main centromotor area, the two central gyres, in the region of the frontal brain. It was further found in these observations, as it had been found in the corresponding experiments on the dog, that weak electrical stimulation simply produces movements of a circumscribed muscle group upon the opposite side of the body, whereas a somewhat more intensive stimulation evokes movements on the same side as well,

[1] SCHÄFER, *Beiträge zur Physiologie*, C. LUDWIG gewidmet, 1887, 269 ff.
[2] HORSLEY and BEEVOR, *Philos. Transactions*, 1890, clxxix., 205; clxxxi., [129.]

together, more particularly, with concomitant movements of other, functionally co-ordinated muscle groups upon the opposite side. Thus, stimulation of the cortical centre for the shoulder is very apt to affect, besides the shoulder itself, the muscles of the arm and fingers; or conversely, stimulation of the finger centres will set up, besides movements of the fingers, movements of the upper and lower arm; and so on. On the brain of the orang-utan, whose structural development brings it still nearer the human brain, HORSLEY and BEEVOR found an arrangement of centromotor points that precisely parallels that found in the macacus. The only difference is, that they are more clearly separated by small inexcitable areas. In all cases, the regions lying beyond the parts specified, i.e., in particular, the anterior portion of the frontal brain and the temporal and occipital lobes, proved to be inexcitable on the motor side.

These results of stimulation are, on the whole, borne out by the results of extirpation of various regions of the cortex, if we allow for the greater margin of uncertainty which the abrogation method always leaves (p. 191). It is noteworthy, also, that the disturbances are apparently less quickly compensated in the more highly organised brain of the monkey than they are in the dog, so that the symptoms of abrogation and stimulation are here more nearly in accord. Nevertheless, according to the observations of HORSLEY and SCHÄFER, it is impossible to induce an approximately complete paralysis upon the opposite side of the body, even in the interval immediately following the operation, unless the whole centromotor zone is extirpated. If the area of injury is more limited, the muscles involved show only a weakening, not a total abrogation of movement.

The determination of the centrosensory centres is, again, far less certain; the interpretation of the symptoms presents very much greater difficulties. Hence for the brain of the monkey, as for that of the dog, the results may be regarded as reliable and assured only in so far as they refer to the general delimitation of the various sense departments. With this proviso, we may conclude from the experiments of HERMANN MUNK, with which those of other observers agree on these essential points, that the cortical surface of the occipital brain constitutes the visual centre, and that of the temporal lobe the auditory centre. The area for touch, taken as inclusive of all the organic sensations, coincides in position with the centromotor regions for the same parts of the body, i.e. is situated in the neighbourhood of the two central gyres and of the superfrontal gyre.[1]

We have, in the above discussion, left the question of the nature of the cortical functions untouched, save in so far as it is connected with the problem of the termination of the paths of conduction in the cerebral cortex. The

---

[1] H. MUNK, *Ueber die Functionen der Grosshirnrinde*, 2te Aufl., 1890. *Berichte der Berliner Akademie*, 1892, 679; 1893, 759; 1895, 564; 1896, 1131; 1899, 936.

question cannot come up for consideration in its own right until the following Chapter, when we review the central functions in their entirety. Even with this limitation, however, the experiments upon the terminations of the conduction paths still leave room for differences of interpretation. At the same time, physiologists are on the road to an agreement: it cannot be disputed that the ideas of the moderate party, ideas which compromise between the hypothesis of a strictly circumscribed localisation, on the one hand, and the denial of any local differences whatsoever, on the other, have gradually gained the upper hand. It is this middle course that we have followed, on the whole, in the preceding paragraphs. It may be that the lines of the various motor areas will, in the future, be drawn somewhat more closely or somewhat more widely; but the fundamental assumption that the functional areas extend from definite and narrowly circumscribed centres, and that at the same time they frequently overlap one another, has established itself more and more firmly, as the most probable view, in the minds of impartial observers. GOLTZ has protested with great energy against the hypothesis of sharply defined localisations. His work has done a great deal, both by its positive contents and by the stimulus it has given to other investigators, to clear up our ideas upon the subject.[1] But the results which GOLTZ has obtained in his later papers do not differ in any essential respect from those of most other observers; and he himself has now come to accept a certain dissimilarity of central representation, which in its general features resembles the account given above. Cf. also Ch. VI., pp. 281 ff. below.

More serious are the differences of opinion regarding the functional significance of the various regions of what is called the sensory sphere. As regards the position of the centrosensory areas, Munk has concluded, on the basis of numerous experiments with dogs and monkeys, that we must distinguish between cortical areas in which the fibres of the sensory nerves directly terminate, and areas in which sensations are raised to the rank of perceptions. The phenomena which make their appearance after destruction of the former, he names, in the case of the two higher senses, cortical blindness and cortical deafness; the disturbances which result from extirpation of the centres of the second order, he terms mental blindness and mental deafness. According to Munk, the visual centre in the dog includes the portion of the brain lying posteriorly to the Sylvian fissure, and covered by the parietal bones; in the monkey, the whole surface of the occipital lobe (A Figg. 86, 87). This visual centre is then subdivided into a central area (A' Fig. 86), and a peripheral area which surrounds the central on all sides (A). The centre is supposed, on the one hand, to correspond to the spot of clearest vision of the eye of the opposite side, and, on the other, to contain the elements in which memory images are deposited. Its destruction accordingly means loss of clear vision and, at the same time, of a correct apprehension of sensations. The peripheral portion, A, according to the same author, is on the contrary merely a retinal centre. Every point within it is correlated with corresponding points upon the two retinas, each half of the brain representing the same-sided halves of the retinas of the two eyes. Hence, if one occipital lobe is extirpated, the animal becomes hemianopic; it is blind to all the images which fall upon the same-sided halves of its retinas. Further, in dogs the correlation is symmetrical. The central visual area of

[1] *Ueber die Verrichtungen des Grosshirns*, Abth. i.-vii. In PFLÜGER'S *Arch. f. d. ges. Physiol.*, 1876–1892.

each hemisphere corresponds to the smaller, lateral division of the retina of the same side, and to the larger, median division of that of the opposite side; so that, e.g., extirpation of the central visual area of the right hemisphere produces blindness over the extreme edge of the right retina, and over the

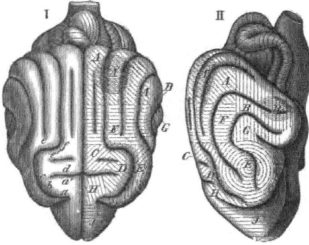

FIG. 86. Sensory regions on the surface of the brain of the dog. After MUNK. *I.* Dorsal view. *II.* Lateral view (left hemisphere). *A* Visual area. *A'* Central region of the visual area. *B* Auditory area. *B'* Region for the perception of articulate sounds. *C—J* Tactual area. *C* Region for the fore leg, *D* for the hind leg, *E* for the head *F* for the eyes, *G* for the ear, *H* for the neck, *J* for the trunk. *a—g* Points of motor excitability (see the explanation of Fig. 80).

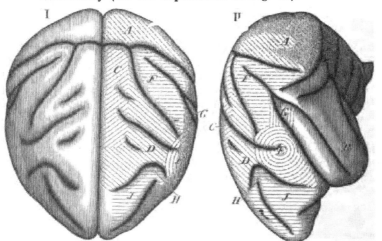

FIG. 87. Sensory regions on the surface of the brain of the monkey. The letters have the meanings given under Fig. 86.

whole surface of the left retina with the exception of its extreme edge. This distribution accords, as will be seen at once, with that which has already been shown to exist in the mesencephalon in consequence of the partial decussations in the chiasma.[1] MUNK found, also, that these results of extirpation were con-

[1] Cf. p. 188, above.

firmed by experiments with local electrical stimulation, which regularly induced movements of the eyes, interpreted by him as movements of fixation due to visual sensations. Thus, stimulation of the posterior portion of the visual centre causes the eye to turn upwards; stimulation of the anterior portion causes it to turn downwards; while stimulation of the central area A' leaves the eye unaffected or, at most, occasions slight movements of convergence. It thus appears that stimulation of the posterior portion of the visual centre is the equivalent of stimulation of the lower half of the retina, that of the anterior portion the epuivalent of stimulation of the upper half of the retina, and that of the middle portion A' the equivalent of stimulation of the fovea centralis: for every light-excitation in indirect vision produces a movement, whereby a correspondingly situated objective light-stimulus is transferred to the centre of the retina.[1] Similar eye movements were also observed by E. A. SCHÄFER as a result of stimulation of a particular point in the tactual area of the cerebral cortex; and BAGINSKY found that stimulation of the auditory area of the dog aroused movements of the ears and, sometimes, of the eyes.[2] Movements of this kind, following upon stimulation of central sensory surfaces, may be interpreted in two ways. We may regard them as reflexes, released in the nidi of the motor nerves or in the mesencephalic centres; or we may look upon them as stimulus movements, running their course in the paths which subserve the conduction of voluntary movements. The latter view finds support in the fact that there exist in the mesencephalic centres special organs of reflex transmission, whose function is left wholly unimpaired by removal of the brain cortex. The visual centre is bounded, below and on the outside, by the central apparatus of the sense of hearing. The area, whose extirpation in the dog is followed, according to MUNK, by abrogation of auditory sensations, occupies the lateral border of the parietal and the entire temporal lobe; in the monkey, it is confined to the temporal region, which in the primates is more strongly developed (B). Destruction of a limited area B' lying at the centre of this larger area (Fig. 86, *II.*), with retention of the surrounding parts, is said to abrogate only the perception of articulate sounds, i.e. to occasion mental deafness; while removal of the whole region B induces total deafness. A similar distinction between the different functional areas is carried through by MUNK for the centres of the sense of touch. Thus, the ocular sensations of touch and movement are referred by him to a region which forms the direct anterior boundary of the visual centre (F); and the cutaneous centre for the region of the ear is situated in the same way with regard to the auditory centre. We then have, anteriorly, the other central areas of the general sense of touch, placed one after another in the order: fore leg, hind leg, head (C, D, E), the series ending with neck and trunk (H, J). These regions, in agreement with the results of other observers, coincide with those described above as the centro-motor areas for the same parts of the body. The relation of the two is shown on the right half of the dorsal aspect of the brain of the dog represented in Fig. 86, *I.*, to which the motor areas of Fig. 80 (p. 194) have been transferred.

MUNK's statements, and more especially those that relate to the distinction between direct sensory centres and what he calls mental centres, have, however, been challenged from many quarters. The physiological and psycho-

---

[1] On the relation of eye movement and retinal sensation, see below, Ch. XIV. § 2.
[2] E. A. SCHÄFER, *Proc. of the Royal Soc.*, 1887, 408. BAGINSKY, *Arch. f. Physiol.*, 1891, 227 ff.

logical assumptions which underlie this division of functions are hazardous in the extreme. That apart, there are two principal points in which MUNK's conclusions are negatived by the facts as otherwise ascertained. In the first place, it is evidently incorrect to assert that the removal of any cortical area of the animal brain is followed by total blindness or absolute insensitivity to sound stimuli. There are many observations which show that rabbits, and even dogs, will react appropriately to impressions of light and sound after removal of the entire cerebral cortex. They avoid obstacles placed in their path, perform complex expressive movements, and so on.[1] In the second place, the symptoms consequent upon lesions of the cortex correspond in all cases to what MUNK terms mental blindness and deafness; they are, as GOLTZ puts it, symptoms of cerebral weakness. The removal of a cortical area is never the equivalent of destruction of the peripheral organ, or of a part of it.[2] LUCIANI conjectures, further, that the more profound sensory disturbances noticed by MUNK some time after the operation may perhaps be due to a propagation of descending degeneration to the lower centres of the thalami and quadrigemina. Only the relations of definite parts of the visual centre to definite regions of the binocular field of vision have found confirmation in the experiments of other observers:[3] a result which, as we shall see below, is also in agreement with the defects of the field of vision observed in man, after partial destruction of the visual cortex.

(d)—Motor and Sensory Cortical Centres in Man

The disturbances observed in man, as a result of lesion of the cerebral cortex, may take the form either of stimulation phenomena or of symptoms of abrogation. The former, which appear sometimes as epileptiform contractions, sometimes as hallucinatory excitations, hardly come into account for the question of localisation of functions, since they rarely accompany local and circumscribed injury of the cortex. We have, therefore, to rely upon the symptoms of abrogation; and these are the more valuable, the more limited the range of function which they involve. Nevertheless, it requires great care to separate them from the affections of surrounding parts, which are seldom absent at the beginning of the disturbance, and from the phenomena of restitution of function, which make their appearance after the lapse of time.[4] The observations which have been brought together, with due regard to these precautions, lead to results, more especially as regards the centromotor areas of the human cortex, which agree in their principal features with the experimental results obtained on the brain of the monkey. This will be seen at once from a comparison of Figg. 88 and 85

---

[1] CHRISTIANI, *Zur Physiologie des Gehirns*, 1885, 31 ff. GOLTZ, in PFLÜGER's *Arch. f. d. ges. Physiol.*, li., 570 ff.

[2] GOLTZ, in PFLÜGER's *Arch. f. d. ges. Physiol.*, xxxiv., 459, 487 ff. CHRISTIANI, *op. cit.*, 138 ff.

[3] FERRIER, in *Brain*, 1881, 456; 1884, 139. LOEB, in PFLÜGER's *Arch. f. d. ges. Physiol.*, xxxiv., 88 ff. LUCIANI and SEPPILLI, *op. cit.* (German), 145.

[4] For the criteria to be applied, cf. NOTHNAGEL. *Topische Diagnostik der Gehirnkrankheiten*, Einleitung.

(p. 199), the former of which gives a schema of the localisation areas in man, based on pathological observations, while the latter shows the centromotor points of the brain of *Macacus*. It is evident that, in the cortex of man as in that of the monkey, the areas whose lesion produces motor paralysis are grouped in a comparatively small region of the cortex, viz., in the two central gyres and the adjoining superior divisions of the three frontal gyres. Here, as before, that is, they lie within the region which

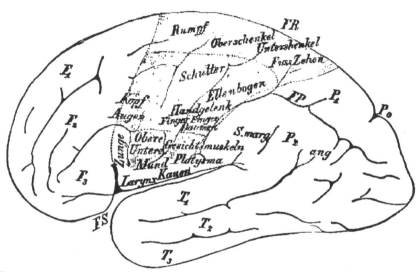

Fig. 88. Motor cortical areas of the cerebral hemisphere of man. After von Monakow. *FS* Sylvian fissure. *FR* Central fissure. F_1, F_2, F_3 Superfrontal, medifrontal and subfrontal gyres. T_1, T_2, T_3 Supertemporal, meditemporal and subtemporal gyres. *S. marg.* Marginal gyre. *ang.* Angular gyre. P_1, P_2 Parietal and subparietal gyres. *FP* Interparietal fissural complex. *Po* Occipital fissure. The remaining names are to be read across, from left to right, and from above downwards. Trunk ; upper leg ; lower leg ; foot ; toes. Shoulder ; elbow. Head ; wrist. Eyes ; fingers ; thumb. Tongue ; upper and lower facial muscles. Mouth ; platysma (a muscle lying beneath the skin, at the side of the neck, and extending from chest and shoulder to face). Larynx ; mastication.

corresponds to the pyramidal path. The centres for trunk and lower limbs, situated in the highest part of the central gyres, extend further into the portions of these gyres that bound the intercerebral fissure.[1] On the other hand, destruction of the cortex of the temporal and occipital lobes, or of the anterior portion of the frontal lobes, occasions no impairment of bodily movement. The paralyses appear always on the opposite side of the body, and consist in abrogation or derangement of the voluntary

[1] NOTHNAGEL, *Topische Diagnostik*, 438 ff. H. DE BOYER, *Études cliniques sur les lésions corticales*, 1879. EXNER, *Untersuchungen über die Localisation der Functionen in der Grosshirnrinde des Menschen*, 1881. VON MONAKOW, *Gehirnpathologie*, 1897, 282 ff.

movements, to which may be added, later on, contractures due to the action of muscles not affected by the lesion.[1] It is clear, from the relative positions of the centres, as shown in Fig. 88, that on the one hand paralyses of arm and leg, and, on the other, paralyses of arm and face may very easily occur together, but that leg and face cannot well be involved while the arm remains free : a conclusion that is fully borne out by pathological observation.

The phenomena of abrogation observed in pathological cases of partial destruction of the cortex inform us, further, of the position of the principal centrosensory areas in the human brain. First and foremost, the

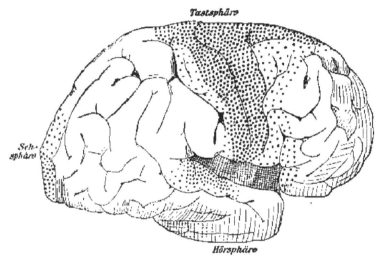

FIG. 89. Sensory areas on the outer surface of the human brain, after FLECHSIG. *Tastsphäre*. Tactual area. *Sehsphäre*. Visual area. *Hörsphäre*. Auditory area.

central terminations of the optic paths, constituting what is called the visual centre, have been definitively localised in the cortex of the occipital lobe. The *visual* centre covers the whole inner surface of this lobe, and includes as well a narrow marginal zone on its outer surface (Figg. 89, 90). The phenomena indicate, at the same time, that each half of the brain is correlated with the nasal half of the opposite and the temporal half of the same-sided retina, in accordance with the decussations of the optic fibres in the chiasma mentioned above (Fig. 79, p. 188). Further evidence is given in support of this arrangement by cases in which a partial atrophy of both halves of the occipital brain has been observed after a long-standing blindness of the one eye, and by others in which a partial degeneration

---

[1] FERRIER, *Localisation der Hirnerkrankungen*, 12 ff. (*Localisation of Cerebral Disease*, 1878). NOTHNAGEL, *Topische Diagnostik*, 549. VON MONAKOW, *Gehirnpathologie*, 376 ff.

of the pregeminum and geniculum of the opposite side has followed upon destruction of the one occipital lobe.[1] The course of the degenerated fibres in the latter instance shows, in accordance with the anatomical facts, that all the optic fibres pass through these mesencephalic ganglia before they reach the central visual areas.[2] The main difference between visual disturbances of this kind and those due to peripheral causes, e.g. destruction of a retina, lies in the fact that they always affect both eyes. In still other cases, lesions of the same cortical area give rise to symptoms that speak yet more decisively for the central character of the derangement: sensitivity to light may remain intact, at all points of the field of vision, while the

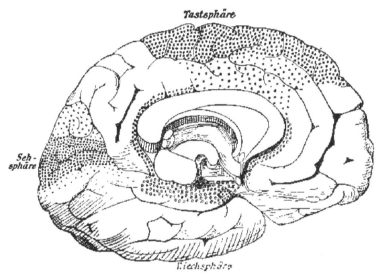

Fig. 90. Sensory areas on the median surface of the human brain, after FLECHSIG. The conjectural limits of the olfactory area are indicated by small open circles. *Tastsphäre*, *Sehsphäre*, as before. *Riechsphäre*, Olfactory area.

discrimination of colours, or the apprehension of forms, or the perception of the third dimension is seriously impaired. In some such cases, however, it is found that other parts of the brain, more especially the frontal and parietal lobes, are involved; occasionally, indeed, the seat of injury resides in these alone, while the posterior portions of the cerebral cortex are left comparatively unaffected.[3] We may therefore suppose that symptoms

[1] NOTHNAGEL, *Topische Diagnostik*, 389. LUCIANI and SEPPILII, *op. cit.* (German), 167 ff. VON MONAKOW, *Gehirnpathologie*, 445 ff.

[2] VON MONAKOW, *Arch. f. Psychiatrie*, xxiv., 229 ff. Cf. also the conditions found to obtain in the brain of LAURA BRIDGMAN, a deaf-mute, who became blind in early childhood. It may be remarked, further, that the whole development of this brain suggests an elaborate system of vicarious functioning, especially in the sensory region. DONALDSON, *Amer. Journal of Psych.*, iii., 1890, 293; iv., 1892, 503 ff.

[3] Cf. the cases described by FÜRSTNER (*Arch. f. Psychiatrie*, viii., 162; ix., 90) and REINHARD (*ibid.*, 147), and by VON MONAKOW, *Gehirnpathologie*, 468 ff.

of the kind are always to be referred to disturbances of a more complex order, implicating more than one region of the brain. A like judgment must, undoubtedly, be passed upon the word-blindness which we consider in the following Chapter. It must always be remembered, in a discussion of these phenomena, that the formation of visual ideas is an extremely complicated process, not confined to the region of the direct terminations of the optic paths, but involving the co-operation of numerous other cortical areas as well.[1]

A similar complication obtains in the case of the *auditory* area of the human cortex. Pathological affection of the terminal areas of the acoustic nerve is shown, primarily, by abrogation or impairment of the power of hearing; but this is invariably accompanied by a profound modification of the faculty of speech. The connexion of the two is not surprising, since the motor and sensory areas of the sense of hearing lie side by side in the cortex (see Fig. 88, and Figg. 89, 90), and may therefore easily be involved in the same lesion. There is, however, a further factor that introduces a peculiar complication into the phenomena: in all affections of what we suppose to be the cortical terminations of the acoustic nerve, derangement of the direct motor and sensory terminals is, apparently, always accompanied by disturbances of connective paths or centres. Hence most of the derangements of the faculty of speech—those ordinarily distinguished by their symptoms as aphasia, word-deafness, agraphia, word-blindness, etc.—are of extremely complex character. And we must accordingly assume that, besides the direct auditory centre, there are always involved other central areas which, like the corresponding motor centre, lie in its near neighbourhood. We shall recur to the probable conditions of these derangements of speech in our consideration of the complex functions of the central organ (Ch. VII.). As regards the boundaries of the direct auditory centre, we cannot speak with complete assurance; its connexion with other central areas, which co-operate in the auditory functions, leave a margin of uncertainty. There can, however, be no doubt that the principal terminus of the acoustic path (Fig. 89) is the posterior section of the supertemporal gyre (T_1 Fig. 88), the part that borders the end of the Sylvian fissure. That is, this region lies directly opposite to the motor areas of the subfrontal gyre, which are brought into activity in the movements of speech (Fig. 88).[2]

The demonstration of the centres for the fibres of the gustatory and olfactory nerves presents considerable difficulty, though for other reasons.

---

[1] Cf. the following Chapter, and the account of visual ideas given in Ch. XIV.
[2] WERNICKE, *Der aphasische Symptomencomplex*, 1874. KAHLER and PICK, *Beiträge zur Pathologie und pathologischen Anatomie des Centralnervensystems*, 1879, 24, 182. LUCIANI and SEPPILLI, *op. cit.* (German), 217 ff. VON MONAKOW, *Gehirnpathologie*, 506, ff.

The method of abrogation here fails us : the ambiguity of the symptoms, whether in man or in the animals, renders it practically impossible to determine the effects of cortical lesion. In this instance, therefore, we must still rely entirely upon the results of direct anatomical investigation of the course of the conduction paths. These results indicate that the *olfactory* area occupies the space marked in Fig. 90 by small open circles ; i.e., that it extends on the one hand over a narrow strip on the posterior margin of the frontal lobe and over the callosal gyre, and on the other over the superior and inner margin of the temporal lobe, adjoining the posterior extremity of the callosal gyre. The parts in question, and especially the callosal gyre, are, as we know, much more strongly developed in certain animal brains, e.g. in the carnivores (Fig. 63, p. 143) ; so that the area of distribution accords with the relatively low development of the sense of smell in man. The *taste* area is supposed to lie somewhere in the neighbourhood of this olfactory centre. So far, however, it has not been definitely localised, either by anatomical or by functional methods.[1]

We return to safer ground when we seek to determine the central areas for the sensations of the *general sense*, i.e. more particularly for tactual and common sensations. Numerous observations go to show, in agreement with the results of operation on animals, that the centrosensory regions of the sense of touch coincide with the centromotor regions for the same parts of the body. Disturbances of tactual and muscular sensation are found to follow upon injury to the posterior portion of the three frontal gyres, the two central gyres, the paracentral gyre, and the parietal and subparietal gyres ; i.e. to the whole region indicated in Figg. 89 and 90. The reference of special areas to the different parts of the body, and the separation of touch from common sensation, are matters of less certainty. On the former point, we can only say that, despite the general coincidence of the sensory and motor regions, it is still possible that the two kinds of centres are not wholly identical, but simply bound together by a close relationship of structure and function. On the latter, we have a few observations that point to a central differentiation of internal and external tactual sensations. Cases occur in which the sensation of movement is abrogated, while cutaneous sensation and motor innervation remain intact ; and these isolated disturbances of articular and muscular sensations seem to be induced more especially by affections of the parietal and subparietal gyres.[2] But, after all has been said, the results so far obtained with regard to the localisations of the general sense leave us still in doubt upon many

---

[1] FLECHSIG, *Gehirn und Seele*, 2te Aufl., 1896, 61 ; *Die Localisation der geistigen Vorgänge*, 1896, 34.
[2] EXNER, *op. cit.*, 63 ff. LUCIANI and SEPPILLI, *op. cit.* (German), 321 ff. On disturbances of the sensations of movement, consult further NOTHNAGEL, *Topische Diagnostik*, 465 ff. VON MONAKOW, *Gehirnpathologie*, 362 ff.

points of detail. In particular, all statements concerning the relation of these centrosensory cortical areas to the centromotor must be regarded, at present, as altogether hypothetical. They rest, not upon reliable observations, but for the most part upon some foregone psychological or physiological assumption.

If, in conclusion, we compare the whole group of results derived from pathological observation of the relations of the cerebral cortex to the several conduction systems with the outcome of the experiments made upon animals, we see at once that, where the facts are at all securely established, there is a large measure of agreement between the two methods. Thus, the position assigned to the centromotor areas in man and the animals is practically the same. In particular, the motor points of the central gyres are arranged in a similar order upon the human and monkey cortex. The same thing holds of the localisation of visual excitations in the occipital lobe. In the acoustic area, it is true, we find differences. The development in man of the cortical region connected with speech is offset, in most of the animals, by the greater bulk of the olfactory centres. There is thus a more pronounced dissimilarity in the structure of the anterior portion of the brain, and a consequent lack of correspondence of the cortical areas. According to the observations of FERRIER, MUNK and LUCIANI, the auditory centre of the dog, e.g., is forced, by the development of the olfactory gyre, relatively far back, into the posterior part of the temporal lobe. This apart, however, the auditory area appears, to all intents and purposes, to occupy an analogous position in the human and animal brain. And the same statement may be made, finally, with still greater confidence, of the cortical areas for tactual and common sensations, whose localisation refers us, in all cases, to regions which either coincide or interfere with the corresponding centromotor areas. So far, then, there is a general agreement between the results. The only difference of any considerable moment is that the derangements of function resulting from cortical lesions are as a rule more serious in man than they are in the animals. And this difference itself has only a relative significance, since it appears in the same way between various classes of animals, e.g. between dog and rabbit, or still more markedly between monkey and dog. It would seem, then, that the phenomena in point are simply illustrations of the general fact that the subcortical centres have a higher value, as centres of independent function, the lower the organisation of the brain to which they belong.[1] Lastly, having allowed this difference its due weight, we have again to say that the character of the disturbances produced by local lesions of the cortex is the same for man and for the animals, in so far as the derangement never amounts to an absolute abrogation of function, and is therefore by no

[1] On this point see below, Ch. VI., §§ 5 and 6.

means equivalent to the interruption of a peripheral conduction path. The nearest approach to such a result is given in the paralyses which follow upon destruction of the centromotor zones. Even these, however, are definitely distinguished by the possibility of comparatively rapid restoration of function.

We have made mention, in the preceding paragraphs, of all the areas of the human cortex that can lay claim, chiefly on the ground of pathological observations, to be considered as the termini of motor and sensory conduction paths. The motor area, shown in Fig. 88, and the visual centre of the occipital lobe were the earliest of these 'cortical centres' to be discovered, and are at the present day the two whose lines can be most sharply drawn. Much more precarious, for the reasons given in the text, is the status of the acoustic area: and this despite the fact that the derangements of speech, which stand in intimate connexion with it, have been under observation for a long period of time.[1] Finally, the correlation of the central gyres and the adjoining region (as mapped out in Figg. 89 and 90) with the sensations of the general sense (external and internal sensations of touch, pain, and organic sensations) may be regarded as sufficiently well established. The localisation was first suggested by TÜRCK, who noticed that lesions of these coronal fibres and of the crural fibres in the region of the capsula of the lenticula produced unilateral sensory disability.[2] In these cases, and still more in cases of destruction of the central gyres themselves, the symptoms are, however, invariably complicated by the simultaneous appearance of motor paralysis in the corresponding regions of the body. For the rest, the hemianæsthetic disturbances are usually distinguished from such hemiplegic accompaniments by their more irregular character; they may be confined to certain factors of the general sensitivity—muscular sensations, pain, sensations of temperature, etc.—or they may be combined with other sensory disturbances in the departments of special sense, and more especially with amblyopia.[3]

All these sensations of the general sense, sensations derived from the organ of external touch, as well as from joints, muscles, tendons and other bodily organs, have been grouped together by certain authors under the indefinite name of 'bodily feeling.' In accordance with this usage, the area ascribed to the general sense in Figg. 89 and 90 was termed by H. MUNK the 'area for bodily feeling.' The title has become current; and its employment is generally connected with various psychological hypotheses, which play an important part in the interpretation of the centromotor symptoms induced by lesions of this region. Thus, SCHIFF propounded the theory,[4] which has been accepted by MEYNERT,[5] H. MUNK,[6] and many other anatomists and pathologists, that the centromotor innervations are direct concomitants of the *ideas* of the respective movements. This means that the cortical region assigned to the 'area for bodily feeling' is to be regarded as a sensory centre, analogous to

---

[1] See below, Ch. VI., § 7.
[2] CHARCOT, *Leçons sur les localisations*, etc. (*Vorlesungen über die Localisation der Gehirnkrankheiten*, 120 ff.). NOTHNAGEL, *Topische Diagnostik*, 581 f.
[3] VON MONAKOW, *Gehirnpathologie*, 364 ff.
[4] *Arch. f. experimentelle Pathologie*, iii., 1874, 171.
[5] MEYNERT, *Psychiatrie*, 1884, 145.
[6] *Arch. f. Physiol.*, 1878, 171; *Ueber die Functionen der Grosshirnrinde*

the centre of sight or hearing. The volitional process is then explained as a reflex transference, occurring, possibly, in the cortex itself, or, perhaps, in deeper-lying parts. This aspect of the theory is rendered especially plausible by the belief that 'will' is nothing else than an 'idea of movement,' and that consequently the 'cortical function' underlying voluntary action consists simply and solely in the excitation of a movement idea, i.e. in a sensory process. Now the assumption that 'will' is equivalent to idea of movement is, of course, a purely psychological hypothesis; it can be demonstrated or refuted, not by anatomical and physiological facts, but only by a psychological analysis of the voluntary processes themselves. Hence we cannot enter upon its examination in this place, though we shall take it up in due course. The physiological investigation of the conduction paths is properly concerned with the single question, whether the cortical areas under discussion are exclusively centrosensory in function, or whether they also evince centromotor symptoms. If the question is put in this way, and we repeat that this is the sole way in which, from the physiological standpoint, it can be put, then the only answer possible, in the light of the observations, is the answer given in the text. But it need hardly be said that that answer gives us no warrant for speaking of a 'localisation of the will' in the brain cortex. To do so would be as absurd as to say, e.g., that the subfrontal gyre and its surrounding parts are the seat of the 'faculty of speech.' The removal of a screw may stop a clock; but no one will be found to assert that the screw is what keeps the clockwork going. The will *in abstracto* is not a real process at all, but a general concept, gained by abstraction from a large number of concrete facts. And the concrete individual volition, which alone has actual existence, is itself a complex process, made up in every case of numerous sensations and feelings. There can be no doubt, therefore, that it involves a number of different physiological processes. The hypothesis that a complex function, like speech or volition, is conditioned solely upon certain individual elements may accordingly be pronounced *a priori* as improbable in the extreme. Besides, all that follows from the observations is that those parts of the brain cortex which we claim as centromotor contain transmitting stations, which are indispensable for the transference of voluntary impulses to the motor nerve paths: the anatomical facts making it further probable that the regions in question contain the *proximate* stations of transmission from brain cortex to central conduction paths.[1]

There is one other fact that we may mention, in conclusion, as of importance for the psychogenetic interrelations of the different sense departments. According to the investigations of FLECHSIG, the fibre systems that radiate from the mesencephalon to the various cortical centres obtain their myelinic sheath at very different stages of embryonic (partly also of postembryonic) development, and therefore, we may suppose, assume the functions of conduction at these same intervals. In man, the fibres that ascend to the tactual centre from the sensory dorsal columns of the myel, together with a few others that enter the optic radiation, are the earliest of the coronal bundles to attain to full development. They are followed, at a somewhat later period, by fibres which in part supplement this pre-existing system, and in part trend towards the olfactory and visual centres. The myelinisation of the fibre system of the acoustic path is completed last of all, to some extent after birth. At the same

---

[1] Cf. with this WUNDT, *Zur Frage der Localisation der Grosshirnrinde*, in *Philos. Studien*, vi., 1891, 1 ff.

time, it does not appear that the animal series presents any thorough-going parallelism in this regard; the investigations of EDINGER prove that the olfactory radiation is developed very early in the lower vertebrates, while in man it belongs to the systems of later development.[1] And in the human brain, this general course of development divides into a large number of separate stages, each corresponding to the completion of some smaller fibre system. FLECHSIG himself has thus been led to distinguish no less than forty fibre tracts, running in developmental succession to definite regions of the cortex. He finds, in general, that the conduction paths of the 'association centres,' discussed in the following Section, are the latest to reach maturity.[2] It should be said, further, that FLECHSIG's statements have been called in question from many quarters. Some authorities altogether reject the idea that the myelinic sheath developes system by system; others at least dispute the regularity of the development.[3] Moreover, it cannot be denied that the greater the number of the cortical centres that we are called upon to distinguish by the order of their completion in time, the smaller becomes the probability that each single centre possesses a peculiar functional significance. Nevertheless, the general result is noteworthy, that the conduction paths whose cortical centres receive special elaboration in the human brain are apparently also the latest to attain to individual development.[4]

§ 7. Association Systems of the Cerebral Cortex

The whole group of fibres that pass upwards in the myel and, reinforced by additions from the posterior brain ganglia and the cerebellum, finally radiate into the corona of the cerebral cortex, is ordinarily termed the *projection system* of the central organs. The name was first employed by MEYNERT, and is intended to suggest the idea that the system in question represents the various peripheral organs in determinate regions of the cerebral cortex. In metaphorical language, the periphery is 'projected' upon the brain surface. The fibre masses of this projection system, some of which enter the coronal radiations as direct continuations of the crura, while others are derived from the mesencephalic ganglia, quadrigemina and thalami, and yet others issue from the cerebellum, are crossed at every point of their path to the cerebral cortex by foreign fibre masses, which connect various regions of the cortex with one another. This second group is known (the term was again coined by MEYNERT) as the *association system* of the cerebral cortex.[4] Both names, as employed here, have, of course, a purely anatomical significance. The projection system has nothing at all to do with what, e.g., is called in physiological optics the outward 'projection' of the retinal image, and the association system, similarly,

---

[1] FLECHSIG, *Die Localisation der geistigen Vorgänge*, 13 ff. EDINGER, *Vorlesungen*, 6te Aufl., 161 ff.
[2] FLECHSIG, *Neurol. Centralblatt*, 1898, no. 21.
[3] Cf. DÉJERINE, *Zeitsch. f. Hypnotismus*, v., 1897, 343; O. VOGT, *ibid.*, 347; SIEMERLING, *Berliner klin. Wochenschrift*, xxxv., 1900, 1033. See also p. 217, below.
[4] MEYNERT, in STRICKER's *Gewebelehre*, 117 (POWER's translation, ii., 481 f.); *Psychiatrie*, 40.

has nothing to do with the psychological 'association of ideas.' The point must be sharply emphasised, because, as a matter of fact, confusions of this sort, due to obscurity in psychological thinking, have often played —nay, continue to play—a part in discussions in which the terms are employed. Now, as regards the projection system, the anatomical facts are sufficient to prove that, if it represents a sort of projection of the peripheral sensory surfaces upon the brain cortex, it can at best be accredited with but a partial performance of this duty. For, on the one hand, the various sensitive areas of the bodily periphery appear, in most cases, to be connected at the same time with several points upon the cortex; and, on the other, the different fibre systems which terminate in a given area of the cortex may correspond to distinct external organs. All this means that the projection system is at least as deeply concerned with the central *connexion* of the bodily organs as it is with that central *representation* of them from which it takes its name. As regards the association system, there is not the slightest reason for bringing it into any kind of connexion with the associative processes of psychology. The only hypothesis that we have the right to make about it, on the score of function, is that its fibres serve in some manner to effect the functional unity of separate cortical areas.

The association system like the projection system, may be divided into various component systems, distinguished in this case partly by the direction of connexion, partly by the distance separating the connected regions of the cortex. We thus obtain the following subordinate systems of association fibres:

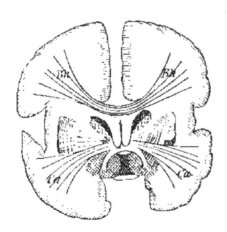

FIG. 91. Systems of transverse association fibres; schematic cross-section through the prosencephalon in the region of the precommissure. After EDINGER. *Bk* Callosal radiations. *Ca* Fibres of the precommissure.

(1) The system of *transverse* commissures. This is principally composed of the callosum or great commissure, but is supplemented as regards the temporal lobes by a portion of the precommissure, which also contains the decussation of the olfactorius fibres (Fig. 91; cf. above, p. 132, and Fig. 53, p.127). The callosum represents a strongly developed cross-connexion; its fibre masses connect not only symmetrical, but also, to some extent, asymmetrically situated cortical regions of the two hemispheres. The callosal fibres cut across the coronal radiations at all points except in the occipital region, where the two sets of fibres separate into

distinct bundles (*m'*, Fig. 58, p. 135; cf. also Fig. 57, p. 134). The connexion effected by the callosum between symmetrical parts of the cortex is fullest, as might be conjectured from its marked increase of size in transverse section as we proceed from before backwards, for the cortex of the occipital region. This is why a defective development of the callosum, as observed in cases of microcephaly, is accompanied by a marked atrophy of the occipital lobes.

(2) The system of *longitudinal* connective fibres (Fig. 92). This system takes an opposite direction to the foregoing; its fibres connect remote cortical areas of the same hemisphere. Dissection of the brain reveals

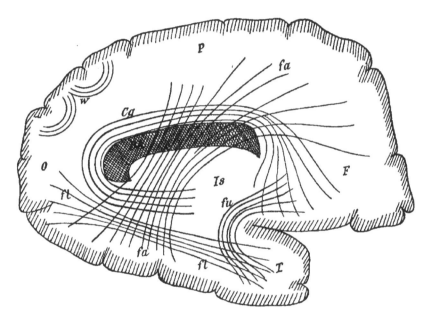

FIG. 92. Systems of longitudinal association fibres. After EDINGER. *F* Frontal *P* parietal, *O* occipital, *T* temporal lobe. *Bk* Callosum. *Is* Region of the insula. *Cg* Londitudinal fibres of the callosal gyre (cingulum). *fu* Uncinate fascicle. *fl* Longitudinal fascicle. *fa* Arcuate fascicle. *w* Intergyral fibres (fibræ propriæ).

several compact bundles of this kind, devoted more especially to the connexion of the frontal with the temporal lobe (uncinate and arcuate fascicles) and of this latter with the extremity of the occipital lobe (longitudinal fascicle).

(3) The system of *intergyral* fibres (fibræ propriæ, Fig. 92). This system serves to connect adjoining cortical areas. The fibres are for the most part deflected round the depressions of alba formed by the cerebral fissures (cf. also *fa*, Fig 58, p. 135).

The association systems that thus connect the various regions of the cerebral cortex may be again divided into three classes, according to their mode of origin and termination. They may (1) connect different areas of the projection system, i.e. centromotor or centrosensory regions, with one another. They may further (2) connect determinate areas of the projection system with other areas, in which no projection fibres directly terminate. Finally, (3) it is probable that in certain parts of the cortex associative fibres of different origin run their course together; so that these areas are connected with the projection system only indirectly, by way of the association fibres that issue from them and terminate in other cortical regions. Areas of this sort, which must be regarded exclusively as terminal stations of association fibres, have been termed by FLECHSIG 'association centres.'[1] They occupy, according to this investigator, practically the whole region of the cerebral cortex which is not taken up by the sensory centres: i.e., in the human brain, the parts which are left unmarked in Figg. 89 and 90. If, then, we consider every continuous surface of this sort as a separate central area, we shall have to distinguish three association centres: an anterior or frontal centre, which covers the larger part of the frontal brain; a middle or insular centre, which extends over the cortex of the insula and its immediate neighbourhood; and a posterior, parietotemporal centre, of wide dimensions, taking in a considerable portion of the parietal and temporal lobes. Between these association centres and the projection centres there lie, still according to Flechsig, intermediary areas and marginal zones, in which projection fibres, either intermixed with the others or grouped in distinct bundles, terminate along with the association fibres. The validity of this distinction of special centres, wholly deprived of direct connexion with the projection system, is disputed by many authorities; and the statements made with regard to the boundary lines and dimensions of the fields in question, and more especially with regard to the extent of the marginal zones and mixed areas, are open to doubt on many points. Nevertheless, it appears to be an established fact that certain areas of the human cortex are supplied for the most part by association fibres, and that these are, in general, the areas whose destruction shows itself not so much in direct centromotor or centrosensory symptoms as in more complicated anomalies of function. On the other hand, it must not, of course, be forgotten that the 'direct' motor and sensory centres themselves cannot possibly be regarded as simply projections of the peripheral organs upon the brain surface. The symptoms of abrogation are decisive: the disturbances set up are of a complicated nature, and their compensation may later be effected, within wide limits, by vicarious functioning of other parts. This result is in harmony with the further fact that there is no region of the brain surface

---

[1] FLECHSIG, *Gehirn und Seele*, 2te Aufl., 1896; *Neurol. Centralblatt*, 1898, no. 21.

that does not receive association fibres as well as projection fibres : indeed, it is probable that the former constitute the large majority of the coronal fibres in all parts of the human brain. On this count, therefore, it would seem that the search for specific differences is altogether in vain. But if any and every derangement of function due to central interference, in whatever part of the brain it may occur, is of a more or less complicated character, it follows that there can be no question of contrast or antithesis as between the functions of the various areas. The difference is always a difference of degree; we have to do, in the particular case, with a closer and more direct or with a remoter and more indirect relation between a given cortical area and certain peripheral functions. This fact should be kept in mind, further, in all attempts to put a functional value upon the different distribution and relative dimensions of the projection and association centres. It has been found, e.g., that the association centres, together with the main bundles of association fibres that run between the different parts of the brain (Figg. 91, 92), attain very much larger dimensions in the human than in the animal brain : in many cases, indeed, their presence in the animal cortex cannot be demonstrated at all. This statement holds more particularly of the frontal association centre, whose high degree of development determines in large measure the peculiar conformation of the primate, and more particularly of the human brain. Finally, it is worth remark that the cortical area which contains the most extensive representation of peripheral organs, the region in the neighbourhood of the central gyres correlated with bodily movements, the sense of touch and organic sensations, also evinces the most extensive connexions with the association centres.

The existence of 'association centres,' as defined by FLECHSIG, has in recent years been the subject of animated discussion among the students of brain anatomy and brain pathology. RAMON Y CAJAL, EDINGER, and HITZIG (the latter with certain reservations) declared themselves in favour of the hypothesis; while DÉJERINE, VON MONAKOW, SIEMERLING, O. VOGT and others pronounced the distinction altogether impracticable.[1] There are no cortical areas, say these authorities, to which projection fibres cannot be traced; just as there are, by general admission, none which are not supplied with association fibres. The question as such is, of course, a question in anatomy pure and simple. We can here do no more than point out that its settlement can hardly be of such importance, from the physiological point of view, as it might, perhaps, appear to us from the anatomical. The occurrence of cortical areas which, in all probability, are connected with peripheral organs only indirectly, by way of the conduction paths that lead to other centres, may, no doubt, be con-

---

[1] RAMON Y CAJAL, *Die Structur des chiasma opticum*, 56. EDINGER, *Vorlesungen*, 6te Aufl., 228. HITZIG, *Les centres de projection et d'association*, Rapport lu au xiii. Congrès internat. de Med. à Paris, *Le Nevraxe*, i., 1900 (criticism by FLECHSIG, *ibid.*, ii., and reply by HITZIG, 1900). VON MONAKOW, *Monatsschrift f. Psychiatrie*, viii., 1900, 405. O. VOGT, *Journ. de physiol. et pathol. gén.*, 1900, 525. See above, p. 213.

sidered as evidence on the one hand of the extremely complicated structure of the particular brain, and, on the other, of the peculiarly complex function of these areas themselves. But the conditions do not, surely, warrant us in ascribing to them a specific function, and setting them off, as 'psychical centres,' from the 'projection' or 'sensory centres.' As a matter of fact, there is nothing to indicate that the structure of the cerebral cortex conforms to any such simple design as that certain parts shall be, so to say, reflections of the peripheral organs, while others shall be reserved as centres of a higher order, serving to bring the direct centres into mutual connexion. On the contrary, it is an essential characteristic of every part of the central organ that it brings together elements which, while spatially separate at the periphery, nevertheless co-operate for the unitary discharge of function. In the case before us, it is first of all the lower central parts, and then, in the last resort, the whole body of the cerebral cortex, that mediate connexions of this kind. What is called the 'visual centre,' e.g., is by no means a repetition of the retinal surface within the cortex. The retina itself is, as we know, nothing else than a part of the cortex that has been displaced far forwards; so that, in this instance, the central duplication would really be a piece of quite needless self-indulgence on the part of Nature. It is because the visual centre contains, along with the conduction paths that connect it with the retina, other paths, whereby it is able to connect the retinal excitations with further functional areas, e.g. the motor, concerned in the act of vision,—it is for this reason that the visual centre is a true 'centre,' and not a mere duplicate of the peripheral organ. If, now, there are portions of the cerebral cortex whose elements stand in no sort of direct connexion with the conduction paths that run to the periphery, then we must simply say that these areas are possessed, in an unusually high degree, of an attribute which determines the character of the central organ at large, and which must therefore be predicated in some measure of all the other areas, whose connexions with the periphery *are* more or less direct. To speak of a number of 'psychical centres,' one must have made assumptions that are equally impossible whether from the standpoint of physiology or of psychology. There is, in reality, but one psychical centre; and that is the brain as a whole, with all its organs. For in any at all complicated psychical process, these organs are brought into action, if not all together, at any rate over so wide a range and in such various quarters as to forbid the delimitation of special psychical centres within the functional whole.

§ 8. Structure of the Cerebral Cortex

The investigation of the fibre systems by physiological experiment, by pathological observation, and by anatomical dissection comes to a natural end at the point where these systems pass over into the cerebral cortex itself. If we wish to inquire further regarding their mode of termination within the cortex, and more particularly regarding the mutual relations of the different parts of the projection and association systems that run to one and the same cortical area, we must gather up the results of the histological examination of the *structure of the cerebral cortex*. Now our knowledge of this extraordinarily complicated formation has, it is true, not advanced so far that we can establish, beyond the reach of doubt, the terminations of all the various paths of conduction that have been traced to it. Nevertheless, there is a certain body of fact that may, without

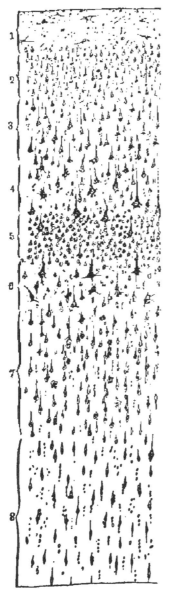

FIG. 93. Section through the postcentral gyre. After RAMON Y CAJAL. 1 Plexiform layer. 2 Small, 3 intermediate pyramidal cells. 4 Large pyramidal cells of the outer layer. 5 Small pyramidal and stellate cells. 6 Large pyramidal cells of the inner layer. 7 Layer of spindle-shaped and triangular cells. 8 Deeper-lying portion of this layer.

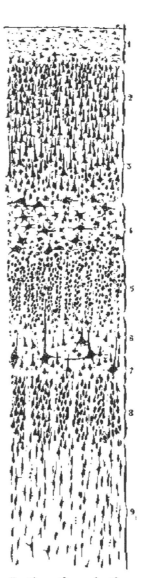

FIG. 94. Section through the occipital cortex of man. After RAMON Y CAJAL. 1 Plexiform layer. 2 Small, 3 intermediate pyramidal cells. 4 Layer of large stellate cells. 5 Small stellate cells. 6 Small pyramidal cells, with ascending neurites. 7 Giant pyramidal cells. 8 Pyramidal cells with deflected ascending neurites. 9 Spindle cells.

hesitation, be turned to account for the physiological and psychological appreciation of the individual conducting systems.

We notice, first of all, that in certain structural outlines the cerebral cortex shows uniformity of design over its whole extent. It consists throughout of several strata of nerve cells. In the human cortex we can distinguish, according to the size, direction and position of the cells, eight or nine distinct layers. The order in which these strata are arranged is, on the whole, the same for all regions, though their relative thickness and the number of the elements characteristic of each layer differ very considerably from part to part. Figg. 93 and 94 show the structural relations obtaining in two typical cases. Fig. 93 gives a microscopical transsection through the postcentral gyre, i.e. through a part of the centromotor region of the cerebral cortex; Fig. 94 gives a similar section through the occipital cortex of the human brain. In these, as in all other sections, from whatever part of the brain they may be taken, the outermost and innermost layers are practically identical in constitution: they are characterised by spindle-shaped cells, in the former set crosswise in a fibrillar reticulum whose general trend is in the horizontal direction, and in the latter placed lengthwise among longitudinally directed fibre masses. There are, on the other hand, well-marked differences in the depth of the layers of large and small pyramidal cells, and of those composed of large and small stellate cells. In the centromotor regions, the pyramidal cells form the great majority of all the cell elements. This may be clearly seen in the section from the postcentral gyre shown in Fig. 93, whose formation lies midway between that of the typical 'motor' and the typical 'association' cortex (superfrontal, subtemporal, etc. gyres); but it is still more apparent in the precentral gyre, where the pyramidal cells ('giant' cells) are especially large and extend far down into the seventh layer of spindle and triangular cells. In the visual cortex, on the contrary, the pyramidal cells, and particularly those of the larger class, are greatly reduced both in bulk and in range of distribution, while there are large accumulations of stellate cells, that send out dendrites in all directions (4 and 5, Fig. 94).

These differences in the representation of characteristic cell forms are paralleled by differences in the arrangement of the cortical fibre systems. Where the pyramidal cells are the prevailing type, the fibres in general take a longitudinal course, ascending vertically from the alba to the cerebral surface. A large number of these longitudinal fibres issue directly from the pyramidal cells: the neurites of the larger cells (*A* Fig. 95), in particular, are continued without break to the myelic columns. We have, then, in these longitudinal fibres of the centromotor region, the direct point of departure of the pyramidal path. All the other processes of the pyramidal cells are dendritic in character. The stoutest of them leaves the cell body on the side opposite to the neurite and runs, still longitudinally, to the periphery of the cortex, where it is broken up in the nervous reticulum of the outermost layer. We thus have, in all probability, a direct centrifugal conduction, as indicated by the arrows in the Fig., beginning in the peripheral layer of the cortex and continuing through the pyramidal cells into the motor paths. This system is, however, cut across by other longitudinal fibres, some of which issue from smaller cells whose neurite runs a brief course and then splits up into terminal fibrils, while others ascend in more connected fashion from the alba, and again break up in the fibrillar reticulum of the outermost cortical layer. The former (B) constitute, it is supposed, links in the association system, which, as we know, sends fibres to every cortical area; the latter (D) are probably centripetal neurites of deeper lying cells, situated in the mesencephalon. Putting these facts together, we may describe the structure of the motor cortex as follows. (1) Its most characteristic constituent is the centrifugal path (A), mediated by the pyramidal cells. It contains further (2) a centripetal fibre system (D), probably connected with the path (A) in the nervous reticulum of the outermost cortical layer, and representing the terminal sphere of a neurone territory which belongs to deeper lying portions of the brain; and (3) an association path (B) mediated by intercalary cells,

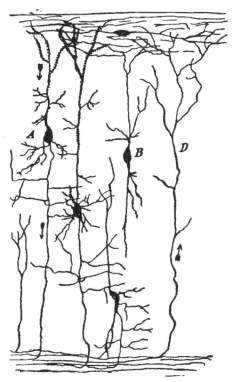

FIG. 95. Individual cells and fibre connexions from the centromotor region. After RAMON Y CAJAL. A Large pyramidal cells, with upward trending dendrites and downward trending neurites. B Intercalary cells, representing, perhaps, links in the chain of association fibres. D Terminal ramifications of upward trending neurites.

which, like the other two, takes in general a longitudinal course and discharges into the fibrillar reticulum of the outermost layer. The direction of conduction in this path is indeterminate; it may possibly vary with the direction of the incoming excitations. Finally, we must mention (4) the plexus of stellate cells, which, while it plays but a small part in the centromotor regions, is never entirely wanting. This, if we may judge by the character that attaches to it in the occipital cortex, is to be regarded as the terminal station of paths of sensory conduction. Its position in the motor cortex is, as we have said, comparatively insignificant. It may be distinguished from the other constituents by its plexiform structure, the fibres running in all possible directions. The presence in the centromotor region of a formation which is characteristic of the sensory centres, may, perhaps, be taken to mean that this region is sensory too, as well as motor. Such an interpretation would be in accordance with the fact that physiological experiment and pathological observation place the centre for the general sense in this part of the cortex.

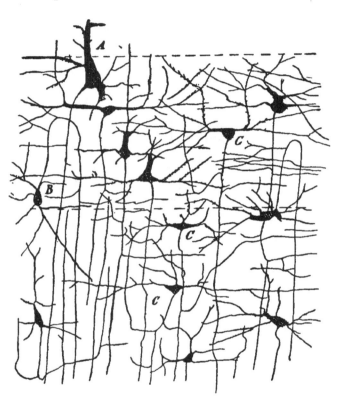

FIG. 96. From the layer of stellate cells of the visual cortex. After RAMON Y CAJAL. *A* Pyramidal cell. *B* Intercalary cell. *C* Stellate cells.

We now turn, by way of contrast, to the 'visual' cortex, as a typical illustration of a pre-eminently sensory region. We are at once struck by the marked difference in the course of the fibres. Plexiform formations, with fibres running in all directions — horizontally, therefore, as well as vertically and obliquely — are very strongly preponderant, while the longitudinal fibre masses characteristic of the terminal areas of the pyramidal paths find but scanty representation (Fig. 96). These plexuses, *C*, are constituted of the large and small stellate cells, sending out processes in all directions, which appear conspicuously in the section of Fig. 94; in all probability, they consist simply of interlocking neurones, of relatively limited range. The characteristic systems of the motor area also appear, only in lesser numbers, in the visual cortex; just as the formations which we connect with the sensory functions are present, in some degree, throughout the centromotor region. We notice, in particular, the longitudinal centrifugal fibres, connected with the pyramidal cells (*A*). There are, further, the centripetal fibres, ascending to the cortex from deeper lying cell groups ; and, lastly, the supposed association fibres with their intercalary cells (*B*). We must accordingly infer that the visual cortex discharges centromotor, as well as centrosensory functions. The muscles that can be innervated from it are, we may suppose, more especially the muscles of the eye, though it is possible that other motor organs, correlated with the ocular muscles, are also under its control. H. MUNK has observed movements of the eyes, in animals, as a result of stimulation of the visual cortex.[1]

Such are the differences that obtain between the two main types of cortical structure, the sensory and the motor. Minor differences are found in the various parts of the motor cortex, and again between the visual area and the other predominantly sensory regions. The former have already been discussed. As regards the latter, we notice that in the olfactory cortex of man the pyramidal cells are even rarer than in the visual ; the smaller pyramidal cells are altogether wanting. The auditory cortex is characterised, on the other hand, by its great wealth of stellate cells and by the extent of its sensory fibrillar reticula. In the 'association cortex,' finally, these plexuses become less conspicuous, and the granular layers, containing for the most part intercalary cells of varying form, play the leading part.

Putting all this together, we may sum up as follows the general outcome of investigation into the structural peculiarities of the cerebral cortex. Not only are the essential morphological elements the same, for all divisions of the cortex, but their general arrangement also presents no really significant differences. At the same time, there are several layers which, with their characteristic elements, attain to very different degrees of development according to the special functions of the various parts of the cortex. Two kinds of cellular elements, in particular, with the arrangement of fibrillar processes that goes with them, appear to be of symptomatic importance in this regard : the pyramidal cells, with their longitudinally directed fibres, and the stellate cells, with their fibrillar reticula,—the former characteristic of the centromotor regions, and therefore, we may suppose, serving in the main as points of departure of the great centrifugal conduction paths ; the latter characteristic of the sensory regions, and therefore, in all probability, serving in the main as terminal stations of paths of centripetal conduction. To these we must apparently add, as a third characteristic constituent, varying greatly in extent of development, certain

---

[1] RAMON Y CAJAL. *Studien über die Hirnrinde des Menschen*, German trans. by BRESLER. Heft 1 : *Die Sehrinde* ; Heft 2 : *Die Bewegungsrinde*, 1900. *Comparative Study of the Sensory Areas of the Human Cortex*, in *Decennial Volume of the Clark University*, 1899, 311 ff.

cells with limited neurone territory, set longitudinally and connected with longitudinal fibre systems, which may perhaps be looked upon as the substrate of the 'association' paths. Lastly, in all regions of the cortex, the outermost layer with its reticular fibre arborisations seems to form a meeting-place, in which conduction paths of the most various kinds come into contact with one another.

The question whether the different regions of the cerebral cortex possess a specifically different structure, which may at the same time serve as the basis for the discrimination of functions, or whether their constitution is, in essential features, the same throughout, has often been under discussion in recent years. MEYNERT, in his epoch-making studies of the human cortex, declared himself for uniformity of structure;[1] and he has been followed by GOLGI[2] and KÖLLIKER.[3] Other investigators, and more especially RAMON Y CAJAL,[4] to whom we are at the present time most deeply indebted for our knowledge of the structural conditions here prevailing, uphold the hypothesis of specific differences. This divergence of opinion seems, however, when closely examined, to be much less radical than its phrasing indicates; it hinges, apparently, upon the different interpretation put by the parties to the controversy upon the term 'specific,' as applied to structural peculiarities. RAMON Y CAJAL'S enquiries have themselves furnished conclusive proof of the extraordinary degree of similarity obtaining in the structure of the various regions, and have shown that the differences are in every case merely relative differences in the number of particular elements and in the development of the layers. Nay more: since they have made it probable that the different centromotor, sensory and 'associative' functions are bound up with definite cell and fibre systems which, as a general rule, are found in *all* parts of the cerebral cortex, and that these functions are in the main conditioned simply upon differences in direction of conduction, which in their turn depend upon differences in mode of connexion with peripheral organs and with other cortical areas, they have really done away with any possibility of the correlation of specific elementary substrates with the 'specific' functions of the various departments of the cortex. They rather force us to the conclusion that the different modes of cortical activity are founded not upon the specific character of the structural elements, but solely upon their different modes of connexion. Nevertheless, as we shall see in what follows, modern brain anatomy presents us with the very curious spectacle of a science that holds with extreme tenacity to the hypothesis of specific functions, while its own results are constantly rendering this hypothesis less and less practicable, and indeed, if the evidence of structural relations is to count at all, bear striking testimony *against* the specific nature of the elementary nervous functions.

[1] MEYNERT, *Vierteljahrsschrift f. Psychiatrie*, i., 97, 198; ii., 88. Also in STRICKER'S *Gewebelehre*, ii., 704 ff. (POWER'S trans., ii. 381.)
[2] GOLGI, *Sulla fina anatomia degli organi centrali*, 1886.
[3] KÖLLIKER, *Gewebelehre*, 6te Aufl., ii., 809 ff.
[4] RAMON Y CAJAL, *Studien über die Hirnrinde des Menschen*, Heft i., 5 ff. Cf. also FLECHSIG, *Die Localisation der geistigen Vorgänge*, 82 ff.

§ 9. General Principles of the Processes of Central Conduction

(a)—*The Principle of Manifold Representation*

It is almost inevitable that the student who is tracing the course of the conduction paths, and their concurrence and interrelation in the various divisions of the central organs, should be led into hypotheses concerning the functions of these different parts. Hence it is not surprising to find that, as a matter of fact, physiological conclusions have often been based upon anatomical data. The value of such inferences must, of course, always remain problematical, seeing that they always need to be supplemented by direct physiological analysis of the functions themselves. At the same time, it is evident that we may look to the conditions of conduction to indicate points of departure for functional analysis. They will, at any rate, warrant us in ruling out certain ideas, from the outset, as inadmissible, and in accepting others as more or less probable; and they will do this altogether apart from any functional reference or physiological knowledge. Thus, in view of the complicated character of the acoustic conduction, as represented in Fig. 77 (p. 183), it will be granted without hesitation that an hypothesis which should explain the process of tonal perception as due merely to sympathetic vibrations of some sort of graded nervous structures within the brain must be pronounced wholly improbable. In the same way, the idea that the act of spatial vision is effected by a direct projection of the retinal image upon elements of the visual centre, arranged in mosaic on the analogy of the rods and cones of the retina, could hardly be reconciled either with our knowledge of the relations of the optic conduction to other, and more especially to motor paths, or with the observations made upon the structure of the visual cortex. In this sense, then, the argument from anatomy to physiology forms a useful preparation for the considerations of the following Chapter. Now that we have concluded our discussion of the conduction paths which are of particular importance for the psychological functions of the nerve centres, we may, accordingly, pause to point out the main lines of interpretation suggested by the general results of the preceding enquiry, and to attempt their formulation in certain laws or principles.

We head our list with the principle of *manifold representation*. This first and most general principle was formulated long since by MEYNERT, himself the first to make a systematic study of the microscopical structure of the brain. It declares that, as a general rule, every region of the bodily periphery which is controlled by the central organ has not one but several means of representation at the centre. In other words, if we have recourse to the analogy of a mirror and its images—an analogy, however, which, as we shall soon see, cannot really be carried through—it says that every sense organ and every organ of movement, together with every least part of such an organ, every sensory or motor element, is reflected not once only, but several times, in the central organ. Every muscle, e.g., has its proximate representation in the myel, from which (under the right conditions) it may be stimulated, or its excitation inhibited, without the interference of higher central parts. It is then represented a second time in the regions of the mesencephalon, the quadrigemina or thalami; and again, a third time, in the centromotor regions of the cerebral cortex. Finally, we must assume that it is indirectly represented in the parts of the cerebellum, and in the association centres, with which these regions stand in connexion. Now it is by no means necessary that the whole group of central representatives shall co-operate in every discharge of function by the peripheral elements. On the contrary, there can be no doubt that the lower centres are often able to exercise an influence upon the peripheral organs, in which the higher representations are not involved at all. When, however, the peripheral effect is the result of activity in the higher neurones, the excitation, under ordinary circumstances, is either mediated directly by lower centres, or at least arouses concomitant excitations in them. In this sense, therefore, the principle of manifold representation appears as an immediate consequence of the complex nature of all central functions. At the same time, it shows that there is an ascending progression in the co-operation of the various central representatives of one and the same peripheral region, and thus leads at once to the following second principle.

(b)—*Principle of the Ascending Complication of Conduction Paths*

The central organs of the higher vertebrates are, very evidently, subject to a law of ascending complication. The number of branch paths, and therefore of the relations mediated by them between centres which, while functionally distinct, are still somehow interrelated by the needs of the organism, increases rapidly as we pass from below upwards. In the myel, the main lines of conduction are brought together compactly in the peripheral nerves; and the connection between principal path and secondary paths is of a comparatively simple and limited character. In the oblongata and the mesencephalon, these connexions begin to show a considerable increase, both in number and complexity. In the mesencephalic portion of the acoustic and optic paths, for instance, we find that the connexions with motor and with other sensory centres, which in the myel were arranged on a relatively simple pattern, are repeated in a very much more elaborate and complicated form. This ascending progression of conductive connexions reaches its final term in the cerebral cortex. Every part of the cortex, however diverse its proximate connexions and however distinct its proper function, is the meeting-place of conductive systems of the most varied kinds; so that what we term a 'visual' centre, e.g., always possesses something of the 'motor,' and something even of the 'associative,' along with its sensory character. It is, therefore, a corollary from this law of increasing complexity of representation in the ascending direction, as bearing more particularly upon the functions of the cortex, that every cortical area in the brain of man and of the higher animals is, in all probability, itself the seat of a manifold representation. Every portion of the visual cortex, that is, will contain, besides the representation of a part of the peripheral retina, further representations of motor areas connected with the function of sight and, possibly, of other, functionally related sensory areas; and finally, in all likelihood, indirect representations, mediated by the association fibres, of more remote functional centres that are again in some way concerned in the act of vision. Hence the idea that a sensory centre is, in essentials, nothing more than a central projection of the peripheral sensory surface,—the visual centre, e.g., a projection of the retina, the auditory centre a projection of the 'resonance apparatus' of the labyrinth,—even if it were admissible on physiological and psychological grounds, could hardly be held in face of the grave objections arising from the anatomical facts.

This principle of increasing differentiation in the ascending direction enables us to explain a further fact, suggested by the results of the gross anatomy of the brain, but brought out with especial clearness by histological examination of the conduction paths and by the phenomena of function that we describe in the following Chapter. This is the fact that many, perhaps most of the functions which in man and the higher mammals are finally integrated and co-ordinated in the cerebral cortex, appear in the lower vertebrates to be completely centralised in the mesencephalic ganglia: so, more especially, certain sensory functions, such as sight and hearing. Even in the lower mammalian orders, e.g. the rodents, the cortical representations of these organs do not attain anything like the extent and the functional importance that they possess in man. That is to say, the central organ provides itself with new representations, only in proportion as a more complicated co-ordination of functional units becomes necessary. When this happens, there is a relative reduction of the existing central stations in the same degree. This accounts for the comparative insignificance of the mesencephalic region in the brain of the higher animals and of man.

(c)—*The Principle of the Differentiation of Directions of Conduction*

At this point the question naturally arises, whether or not the investigation of nervous conduction has furnished any evidence of specific differences in the functions of the central elements and of their conductive processes. We answer it by saying that one, and only one such difference may probably be inferred from the anatomical and physiological relations of the conduction paths. This is the difference in direction of conduction, connected with the twofold mode of origin of the nervous processes, which was first suggested from the anatomical side by RAMON Y CAJAL, and which receives confirmation from certain elementary facts of nerve mechanics (p. 99). In the older physiology, the establishment of determinate directions of conduction was ascribed to the nerves themselves, though it could hardly be brought into intelligible connexion with the properties of the nerve fibre. We are now able to refer it to a peculiar process of differentiation in the nerve cell. The explanation has been given above, in Ch. III. Every cell, as we there set forth, is the seat of excitatory and inhibitory processes, which under the influence of this differentiation are distributed in different proportions to definite cell regions. Originating in this way, however, the principle of different directions of conduction can hardly be looked upon as a law of universal validity. It is rather a principle of development, entirely compatible with the persistence of an undifferentiated condition in certain of the central elements. We have, as a matter of fact, found this condition to obtain in various types of cells, in which the twofold mode of origin of the conduction paths is neither anatomically proved nor physiologically probable. And it is noteworthy that these cells always occur in situations where the functional requirements do not include a differentiation of the directions of conduction, or rather—for this is really the more correct expression—where there is no demand for inhibitions of an excitation that has come in from a given direction. Thus, the differentiation is more or less doubtful in many cells of the sensory system, from those of the spinal ganglia onwards; and there are many intercalary cells, some lying within the central organs, some displaced far outwards in peripheral sense organs, which physiologically give no ground whatever for the assumption of a definite direction of conduction, and morphologically offer no sign of a twofold mode of origin of their processes. Cf. above, pp. 158 f.

The differentiation of the directions of conduction is, then, the result of a process of differentiation peculiar to the nerve cell, and apparently connected with an especial modification of the cell structure. It is, at the same time, the sole form of functional difference that the investigation of the conduction paths has brought to light; and, we must add, the sole form that a simple determination of these paths can ever reveal to the investigator. For the enquiry has, of course, its definite limits. It can tell us where, between what terminal stations, and (under favourable conditions) in which directions the processes are conducted; but it cannot tell us anything of the nature of the processes themselves. Nevertheless, it is a point of importance for the physiology of the central functions that, apart from this differentiation of the directions of conduction, no qualitative differences in the central elements can be demonstrated by morphological methods or inferred from the mechanics of innervation.

(d)—The Principle of the Central Colligation of Remote Functional Areas. Theory of Decussations

We have yet to mention a circumstance from which, in very many cases, the principle of the manifold representation of peripheral areas undoubtedly derives its peculiar significance: the fact that bodily organs which lie more or less widely apart, but yet function in common, are oftentimes brought into spatial as well as into functional connexion in their central representations. This means, of course, that the integration of functions may be mediated with the least possible circuity by conduction paths running directly between the central stations. Thus, the nerve paths that are brought into action in the locomotor movements of man and the animals issue from the myel at very different levels. But there are several places in the central organ (mesencephalon and cerebral cortex) where the centres for these movements lie close together; so that a suitable co-ordination can be effected, for voluntary as for involuntary, purely reflex movements, along well-trodden paths of cross connexion between neighbouring centres. In the same way, the intimate relation that obtains between the rhythm of auditory ideas and the rhythm of bodily movements becomes intelligible when we remember the number and variety of the connexions, at comparatively short distance, between the acoustic and the motor centres. It would seem, then, to be one of the most important features of conduction within the central organ at large that it serves, literally, to *centralise*: it unites the various functional areas, and thus renders possible an unitary regulation of functions that are separated in space but belong together in the service of the organism. And this means, further, that all the separate functions distinguished by us, since they are known solely in this their centralised form, must in reality themselves consist of an union of many functions, distributed over different, in many cases over widely remote peripheral organs. We may, therefore, reject without discussion any such view of the conductive connexions of the central organ as maintains, e.g., that there is a central act of vision, independent of motor innervations and of the mutual relations of different retinal elements: for the central organ of vision is not a mere projection of the retina upon the cerebral surface, but an extremely complicated structure, in which all the partial functions concerned in the visual function find representation. And we may reject, similarly, any theory that proposes to isolate the rhythmical form of successive auditory impressions, as a form of excitation peculiar to the auditory centre, and thus to separate it from the associated motor impulses. Every psychophysical function that falls under our observation is already, in point of fact, a centralised function, i.e. a synergic co-operation of a number of peripheral functions. What the retina or the peripheral auditory organ could contribute of itself to the formation of our perceptions, we do not know, and we can never find out: for the functions of eye and ear and of all other organs come under our observation always and only in this centralised form, i.e. as related to the activities of other functional areas.

Among these combinations of remote peripheral organs for unitarily centralised, synergic functions, a place of special importance is taken by the connexions dependent upon *decussation of the paths of conduction.* In their case, the separation and rearrangement of the paths are carried, by their passage to the opposite half of the brain, to the highest conceivable point; and, as a result of this, the functional significance of such central rearrangement is shown with the greatest possible clearness. Among the decussations themselves, that of the optic nerve, which appears in well-marked developmental sequence through the whole animal kingdom, shows the most obvious relations to the visual function. Where the compound eye occurs in its earliest stages of development, as in the facetted eyes of the insects, the retinal image forms a rough mosaic whose spatial arrangement—since every facet represents a relatively independent dioptrical structure—corresponds to that of the external object; what is above and below, right and left, in the object has precisely the same position in its image. Such an eye, therefore, if it has a muscular apparatus at its disposal, does not move about a point of rotation situated within itself, but is seated upon a movable stalk, i.e. turns (like a tactual organ) about a point lying behind it in the body of the animal. Under these conditions, it does not appear that the optic paths undergo any appreciable decussation; indeed, it is characteristic of the invertebrates at large that the great majority of the nerve paths remain upon the same side of the body. When, on the other hand, we turn to the lowest vertebrates, we are met at once by a complete reversal of the picture; the optic paths are now entirely crossed, so that the retina of the right eye is represented exclusively in the left, that of the left eye in the right half of the brain. RAMON Y CAJAL conjectures, with great acumen, that this arrangement may serve to compensate the inversion of the retinal image effected by the dioptrical apparatus of the vertebrate eye: he reminds us that the eyes of the lower vertebrates are, as a general rule, set laterally in the head, and that they accordingly cannot furnish a common image of the objects seen, although their two images may supplement each other in the sense that the one eye sees parts of an extended object which remain invisible to the other. The hypothesis also furnishes an explanation of the fact that the decussation changes from total to partial in proportion as the eyes, placed in front of the head, acquire a common field of vision,—as they do in many of the higher mammals, and more especially in man. RAMON Y CAJAL, however, bases his interpretation of these facts upon the assumption that the retinal image is directly projected upon the visual cortex. Suppose, e.g., that the eyes are so situated, laterally, that the right eye images precisely the half ab, the left the half bc of the object abc (Fig. 97). It follows at once, from the fact of inversion, that the two retinal half-images $\alpha\beta$ and $\beta\gamma$ are out of their right positions: for if we regard $\beta\gamma$ as the direct continuation of $\alpha\beta$, β should be joined to β, and not γ to α. If, now, the optic fibres undergo a total decussation, this incongruity will disappear in the projection on the central visual surface; the two halves of the image can be put together as half-images in just the same relation that they sustain in the external object ($\alpha'\beta'$, $\beta'\gamma'$).

RAMON Y CAJAL believes that the decussation of the optic nerves, thus necessitated by the optical construction of the eye, has formed the point of departure for all the further decussations of conduction paths; that it was followed, first of all, by the crossing of the motor paths of the ocular

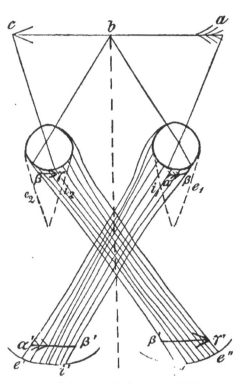

FIG. 97. Schema of the act of binocular vision in a vertebrate with laterally placed eyes and total decussation of the optic nerves.

muscles, and then by that of the other, sensory and motor paths, correlated with these.[1] The hypothesis is ingenious in the extreme; and it is entirely probable that optic decussation and binocular synergy are closely interrelated. Nevertheless, the theory cannot be carried through in its present form. It is based upon assumptions that conflict not only with everything else that we know of the nature of the act of vision, but also, in the last resort, with everything that we know of the character and course

[1] RAMON Y CAJAL, *Die Structur des chiasma opticum*, 22 ff.

of the conduction paths and of their terminations in the brain cortex. The retina itself is, as we have remarked above, a part of the central organ that has been pushed outwards to the periphery. It is, then, first and foremost, somewhat surprising that the disorientation of the image on the retina should be of no consequence, and its derangement on the cortex seriously disturbing. Those who hold such a view evidently rest it upon the belief that consciousness resides directly in the cortex, and there takes cognisance of an image of the external world, which must therefore, at this point, exactly repeat the real position of the external objects. That certain difficulties arise from the presence of the cortical gyres is admitted by RAMON Y CAJAL himself. To meet them, the further hypothesis must be made, that the disorientation of the images produced in each individual brain by the convolution of its outer surface is compensated by a remarkably accurate adaptation in the distribution of the crossed fibres. But then there is still another difficulty. If the image on the central visual surface corresponds exactly to the spatial properties of its object, then we must expect not only that the asymmetry arising from inversion of the image is binocularly compensated by the decussations in the chiasma, but also that, in each separate eye, there is an analogous compensation with regard to the vertical dimension. What in the retinal image is above, must in the visual centre be below, and conversely. The right and left decussation of the optic fibres would then be accompanied, in every optic nerve, by a second, vertical decussation. But this has not been demonstrated. Even in cases of what is called cortical hemianopsia in man, its existence has never been suspected. On the other hand, it is noteworthy that this cortical hemianopsia is much more obscure in its symptoms than the hemianopsia observed in cases of interruption of the fibres in the optic tract and thalami; minor defects, in particular, may pass without symptoms of any kind, or may be connected simply with a diminution, not with complete abrogation of sensitivity to light.[1] This, however, is just the opposite of what we should expect, if an undisturbed reproduction in the visual cortex of the space relations of the object were the one thing necessary for the act of vision. Moreover, we must remember that there is a very much simpler and more plausible explanation of the fact that we see objects upright, despite the optical inversion of their images, than would be given with this hypothesis of a vertical decussation. Wherever the visual organ has become a dioptrical apparatus, involving inversion of the image, the point of ocular rotation lies, not behind the eye in the body of the animal, as it does in the stalked eyes of the invertebrates, but in a point d within the eye itself (Fig. 98). Hence, when the central point of vision in the yellow spot moves in the retinal image from below upwards

---

[1] VON MONAKOW, *Gehirnpathologie*, 45͡.

in the direction $\alpha\beta$, the external point of fixation in the object moves from above downwards, in the direction $a\,b$. That is to say, the displacement of the point of rotation to the interior of the eye brings with it a direct compensation of the inversion of the image. For we estimate the space relations of objects in terms of the position and movement of the line of fixation before the point of rotation, not behind it, and not either in terms of the retinal image—whose position is really just as little known to us as are the space relations of the hypothetical image in the visual centre : and of that we do not even know whether or not it exists at all. Intrinsically, it is, without any question, far more probable that we should assume in place of such an image a system of excitations, corresponding to the various sensory, motor and associative functions simultaneously concerned in the act of vision.

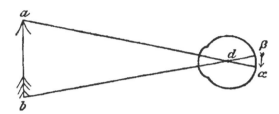

FIG. 98. Relation of the position of the image on the retina to the movements of the eye.

This compensation of the inversion of the retinal image by the motor mechanism of the single eye evidently furnishes the nearest analogy for the reciprocal orientation of the right and left retinal images as it occurs in binocular vision. Here, too, we must suppose, the motor mechanism has not adapted itself, after the event, to the relation obtaining between the two hypothetical images in the visual centre, but has from the first exercised a determining influence as regards orientation within the common field of vision. Now for the visual organ with laterally placed eyes, the fundamental characteristic of the field of vision is that it consists of two entirely different halves ; in the ideal form of such an organ, the separate fields will just meet in the middle line. Vision of this sort may fitly be termed, with RAMON Y CAJAL, 'panoramic' (as opposed to 'stereoscopic') vision. It covers a wide range ; but it mediates only a superficial image, and gives no direct idea of the third dimension. Further, a correct orientation of the two halves of the panoramic image is possible only if an object that travels continuously from the one half of the field of vision to the other shows no discontinuity in its movement ; and this condition, again, is fulfilled only if similarly situated eye muscles are symmetrically innervated as the movement continues. If the object has been followed, e.g. by the line of regard of the right eye in Fig. 97 from a to b, then the movement must be carried on, without interruption, from b to c, by innervation of the line of regard of the left eye ; that is to say, the innervation of the left *rectus internus*, whose direction of pull is indicated by the dotted line i_2, must be so co-ordinated with the innervation of the right *rectus internus*, i_1, that it promptly relieves its predecessor, to give way in its own turn to the innervation of the left *externus*, e_2. Now there is, as we have said, no ground for supposing that the visual centre is the scene of any kind of pictorial projection, even remotely resembling that which we have on the retina. It is, however, not improbable that the mechanisms of release, by means of which sensory are transformed into motor impulses, are here arranged in a certain symmetry: in such a way, that is, that if e.g. the road to the *rectus internus* is thrown open in the visual cortex of the right hemisphere at a definite point e', it must in the left hemisphere be thrown open at a point e'', functionally co-ordinated with e' and lying symmetrically with it to the median plane. This arrangement will, naturally, come about by process of development. Let us take, as the first term of the series, a state of affairs where the eyes of the two sides stand in no sort of functional relation to each other: the condition seems, as a general rule, to be actually realised, e.g. in the visual organs of the invertebrates. Here, we must imagine, these mechanisms of release, like all the other central elements, will in each optic ganglion be arranged symmetrically to the median plane: whatever lies farthest to the right on the right-hand side of the body will do the same on the left side, and conversely. Suppose, again, that the development is carried a step further, and that the eyes are to co-operate for a panoramic vision of the kind described above. The symmetrical arrangement would now be insufficient; it would prevent the regular sequence of the movements of the two eyes, required for an adequate apprehension of objects. The arrangement in the visual centre of the hypothetical mechanisms of release is, of course, unknown to us, apart from the probability of their symmetry with reference to the median plane; fortunately, it is also, for our present question, a matter of indifference. We will assume, for simplicity's sake, that the points of release lie inwards for the *interni* and outwards for the *externi*. Then, if the object is followed in fixation from a to c, the *externus* e_1 will first be innervated from a central point e'. As the *internus* i_1 comes into action, the central innervation will move from e' to i'. Next, upon the entrance of the object into the visual field of the left eye, it will pass without interruption to i_2, i'', and thence, finally, to e_2, e''. If there were no decussation, the central point of release corresponding to a point upon the nasal half of the retina would, on the contrary, lie inwards, and the point of release corresponding to a point upon the temporal half lie outwards, on both sides of the median line. The arrangement of the points, from right to left, would then be i' e' e'' i'', and the innervation would first of all travel on the right, from within outwards, and then shoot across to the left visual centre, to execute a similar movement there. We must add that the arrangement which controls movement naturally determines as well the localisation of the resting eyes ; so that *bc* is seen as the direct continuation of *ab*. The reason, once more, is not that this is the order in which images of the separate points are projected upon the brain, but that it is the order in which there is congruity of the sensory and motor functions that work together in every instance of spatial perception. Presumably, therefore, the total decussation of the visual organ with panoramic function does not represent an arrangement which was first found good on the sensory side and later extended to the motor. It must rather be regarded as an arrangement which, from the outset, applies to both sensory and motor areas, and which mediates their co-operation.

We are, then, justified in positing an organisation that extends over the entire sensorimotor system and is determined by the necessary co-ordination of particular sensory and motor points. The hypothesis has the further advantage that it, and it alone, can adequately explain the obvious connexion between the change from total to partial decussation of the optic fibres, on the one hand, and the passage from panoramic to stereoscopic vision on the other. Suppose that we have reached the stage at which the eyes are set so far forward that their fields partially overlap, to form a common field of vision, embracing the same objects. The

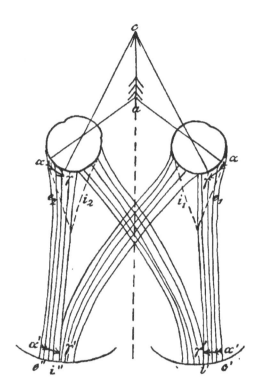

FIG. 99. Schema of the act of binocular vision in man and in animals with a common field of vision.

conditions are now very different from those obtaining in panoramic vision. The synergy of the eye movements, in so far as it is controlled by the nearer objects in the common field of vision, is no longer laterally symmetrical, no longer such, i.e., that right corresponds to right and left to left upon the two sides, but has become medianly symmetrical, so that those points are homologous that lie on either side at the same distance from the median plane. Stated directly in terms of eye movement, this means that the synergy in panoramic vision is that of parallel, in stereoscopic vision that of convergent movement of the lines of sight. The difference will be clear at once from a comparison of Fig. 99 with Fig. 97. In Fig. 97, where we have a representation of the limiting case in which the two fields of the laterally placed eyes pass into each other without break, the point of contact b is the sole point seen in common by both halves of the visual organ. If the object is given the direction in the third dimension indicated in Fig. 99, only this one point upon it remains visible to the two eyes. For the visual organ with a common field of vision (Fig. 99) the case is different. Here the object, despite its position in the third dimension, remains entirely visible to both eyes; the image $a\gamma$ upon each retina corresponds to that side of it which, as it recedes in space, is turned towards the eye in question. Along with this change in scope of vision goes, further, a change in the conditions under which the eyes must move in order to bring all parts of the object upon the yellow spot. The movements are not touched off successively, as in the previous instance,—the left eye taking up the movement at the point where the excursion of the right eye reaches its limit,—but have become simultaneous: right and left eye range over the object, from a to c and back again from c to a, both at once. And the muscles co-ordinated for the purposes of these movements are muscles placed symmetrically not as regards external space, but as regards the median plane of the body and, consequently, as regards each separate eye : *internus* and *internus*, *externus* and *externus*. This means, once more, that there is a radical change in the conditions under which the movements are touched off centrally by light stimuli. The farther inward, towards the median plane, a retinal point lies in either eye, the farther out, in the third dimension of space, lies the corresponding point of the object situated in the common field of vision. If, therefore, a point is stimulated upon the nasal halves of the two retinas, the *interni* are brought into action at i' and i'', and a movement is produced by symmetrical increase of convergence in the direction ca. If, on the other hand, a retinal point is stimulated on both sides that approximates to the near limit of the field of vision, the binocular organ will traverse the object with symmetrically decreasing convergence; the two *externi* are brought into synergic action at e' and e''. Recurring to our hypothesis that the elements in the central organs are arranged upon a principle of median symmetry, we may say, therefore, that the requirements of symmetrical convergence will be fulfilled if the mechanisms for the release of motor impulses by light stimuli are distributed symmetrically to the median plane in the visual centre of the same side. Since distant points in space correspond to retinal points that lie nasalward, and near points in space to retinal points that lie temporalward, the arrangement of the mechanisms of release will be in conformity with the medianly symmetrical disposition of the parts of the brain if the *musculi interni* are represented in the brain, too, on the inside, nearer the median plane, and the *musculi externi* on the outside. Let us assume that this arrangement actually holds. Then the inversion of the image, due to the dioptrical structure of the eye, is precisely the position that will satisfy the needs of stereoscopic vision and of the mechanism of convergence. It is, accordingly, a condition of the adaptation of the visual organs to these needs that *the optic paths remain uncrossed for the whole extent of the common field subserving stereoscopic vision.* But the common field is only a part of the total field of vision. In man himself and in the animals with a like visual endowment each eye has, besides, its own particular field, represented by the inner portions of the retinas, and governed, of course, by the conditions of panoramic vision and the special laws of eye movement that they bring in their train. Here, then, the two visual organs are laterally symmetrical, and the necessary decussation of the optic paths —and, with them, of their centromotor releases—is effected on the pattern of Fig. 97. In this sense, therefore, the partial decussation of the optic paths gives an accurate picture of the state of affairs resulting on the one hand from the co-operation of the two eyes in binocular vision and on the other from the co-ordination of their independent functions. We may add that, in all probability, the decussation in the chiasma possesses this functional significance not only for the terminations of the optic paths in the visual cortex, which we have had primarily in mind in the foregoing discussion, but also for the terminations in the mesencephalic region. According to the plan of the *opticus* conduction laid down in Fig. 78 (p. 186), the two centres are similarly disposed in the essential matter of sensorimotor connexions.

There are many other instances of the decussation of conduction paths, recurring at all levels from the myel upward. In no case, however, is the functional interpretation of the phenomenon as obvious as it is in that of the *opticus* crossing. Nevertheless, we have no right to conclude that all the other decussations are simple consequences of this transposition of the optic fibres. On the contrary, the same synergy that is apparent here obtains also for the other organs of sense and of movement, and more particularly for the relations between sensory excitation and motor reaction, and may therefore lead independently at any point to analogous results —though the results, once produced, may very well reinforce and support one another. This relative independence of the different decussations is further suggested by the fact that in the lower vertebrates, where the optic decussation is total, other decussations, as e.g. that of the motor paths of the skeletal muscles, are much less complete than they are in man. Moreover, in all the vertebrates up to man, the myel evidently retains the character of a central area in which the conduction paths remain for the most part upon the same side of the body, whereas the oblongata shows at once a large number of partial decussations, due to the correspondingly large number of motor functions of bilaterally symmetrical nature—movements of respiration, of mastication, of swallowing; mimetic movements—that have their centres in this region. Similar decussations occur also in the olfactory and acoustic areas, where they are again, in all probability, connected with motor synergies.

There is, finally, a further circumstance, affecting those cerebral areas which, as seats of the more complex functions, receive association paths from various sensory and motor centres, that presumably stands in intimate relation to the phenomenon of decussation: the circumstance that certain centres, which exist potentially in both hemispheres, are preponderantly developed upon one side. This applies especially to the 'speech centre,' which we discuss in the following Chapter. In the great majority of cases, the speech centre has its principal seat in certain frontal and temporal areas of the left hemisphere. Since this left side, in consequence of the decussations of the motor paths, contains the centres for the motor innervation of the right half of the body, we may suppose that the arrangement is connected with the disproportionate development of the muscular system on the right and, more particularly, with the right-handedness of the ordinary man. The latter phenomena may themselves be referred partly to the character of human movements, which involve a preference for the one side, and partly to the asymmetrical position of other bodily organs, especially the heart.

The study of the conduction paths has been dominated, up to the present time, by the view, natural to the adherents of a strict localisation theory, that every bodily organ must find its representation at some point of the brain cortex. The other and at least equally tenable idea, that all parts of the brain and, very especially, all parts of the brain cortex are intended to mediate the interconnexion of different conduction paths, has, in consequence, been forced unduly into the background. The strict localisation theory, as held by H. MUNK and by other physiologists and pathologists, assumes that the surface of the brain is made up of a number of sensory centres, which are in reality simple reflections or copies of the peripheral sensory surfaces; so that e.g. every point upon the retina has a corresponding point in the visual cortex. Secondarily, it is true, recourse is had to the subsidiary hypothesis (mentioned above, pp. 201 ff.) that the immediate neighbourhood of these direct sensory centres is taken up with special ideational centres, to which the direct sensory impressions are in some way transferred: this hypothesis is to explain the origination of memory ideas. The point of view persists, practically unchanged, in FLECHSIG's and RAMON Y CAJAL's theory of specific 'association' centres. For it appears to be the opinion of these authorities that, if the more complicated functions are thus handed over to independent centres, the sensory centres proper are for that very reason all the more securely established in their character as direct reflections of the bodily periphery. As a matter of fact, however, this view is sufficiently refuted, even apart from the complex nature of the disturbances consequent upon cortical lesion, by MEYNERT's principle of manifold representation. It is unjust to what is by far the most important aspect of central organisation, the combination into an unitary resultant of component functions that are oftentimes separate at the periphery. GOLTZ has been, from the first, its earnest opponent; and in so far as it leaves altogether out of account the true character of the central functions, his opposition is justified. On the other hand, he and his school have plainly gone too far in denying localisation of function outright. Localisation, in a certain sense, is a direct corollary from the fact that centralisation is never universal, but is always confined primarily to the integration of a limited number of components. Within these limits, the course and distribution of the conduction paths point, without any question, towards a certain localisation, though they and, in the last resort, the structure of the cerebral cortex itself, point not less clearly to an interconnexion of functions at all parts of the organ. If we look at the facts as a whole, we may safely say—while abstracting entirely from functional derangements, whose interpretation is oftentimes doubtful—that modern brain anatomy has furnished overwhelming proof that the older idea of the brain cortex, as a reflection or copy of the totality of the peripheral organs, supplemented at most by a few special areas reserved for higher psychical needs, is altogether untenable.

The problem of the decussation of conduction paths, in the strict sense of the term, is less difficult of solution than that of the unilateral representation of function, such as has been demonstrated, in particular, for the functions involved in speech. Originally, it would seem, the function in these cases was symmetrically disposed upon both halves of the brain, but practice has for some reason been predominantly unilateral, and the one half has consequently gained the ascendancy. It is natural to connect this difference of development with the right-handedness of the majority of mankind. And the connexion is sustained by the fact that, in various instances, derangements of speech have been observed in left-handed persons as a result of apoplectic effusions in the right half of the brain.[1] Now it is not difficult to explain this relation, if we once accept the possibility of unilateral development. In civilised man, who is right-handed, writing is a function of the right hand; and the associations that colligate the various speech functions are so many and so varied that the unilateral development of writing alone might bring with it a corresponding unilateral localisation of the related factors. But since men write, as a rule, with the right hand, and are in general more practised in the mechanical control of the right hand than of the left, the left half of the brain must, by reason of the decussation of the motor conduction paths, receive a larger measure of practice than the right. This practice will, of course, be shared by the speech centre. The numerous instances of restoration of the speech functions, with persistence of the central lesion, may then be referred, along with all the other possible forms of vicarious function, to the substitution under special conditions of the right for the left half of the brain. We have a similar substitution in the case of the external organs: a patient who is paralysed on the right side is able, by practice, to use his left hand for actions previously performed by the right, e.g. for writing; and the change of habit at the periphery naturally carries with it a new course of practice at the centre. But when all this is granted, the initial question still calls for answer; the question why the right-hand side of

[1] OGLE, *Medico-chirurgical Transactions*, liv., 1871, 279.

the body should ever have been preferred at all. In seeking to answer it, we must bear in mind that most mechanical functions, to a certain extent even that of walking, make a heavier demand upon the one side of the body than upon the other ; and that, under this condition, the right side is naturally marked out for special favours by the general asymmetry in the position of the organs of nutrition in the higher animals. Here again, the plan of arrangement is, as we all know, governed by the close interdependence of the individual organs. The placing of the liver on the right means that the great reservoirs of venous blood also lie on the right, so that the arterial system is necessarily relegated to the left. In the rare cases in which this disposition is reversed (cases of what is called *situs transversus viscerum*), it is the rule that *all* the asymmetrical organs are involved in the rearrangement of parts. Now the central organs that stand in greatest need of protection are the circulatory organs. Consequently, most mammals in combat with their enemies are apt to put their right side in the forefront of the battle ; and this habit must react favourably, by way of stronger development, upon the muscles of the right side of the body. In man, the upright position brings with it a special need for the protection of the central organs of circulation, and at the same time helps to render this protection easy and efficient. On the other hand, it is probable that the left-handed situation of the circulatory organs has furthered the development of the left-hand side of the brain.[1] Since, then, the more developed half of the brain must correspond to the more developed half of the body, it is on the whole intelligible that the peripheral paths of the right side should in the main be represented in the left half of the central organ, and those of the left side in the right. On this assumption, it is possible that the decussation of the pyramidal paths in man and the mammals may itself be a simple consequence of the asymmetrical practice imposed by outside conditions upon the bodily organs and their central representatives.

---

[1] According to GRATIOLET, the frontal gyres develop more rapidly on the left than on the right ; in the occipital brain, the reverse order appears to obtain (*Anatomie comparée du système nerveux*, ii., 242). GRATIOLET'S results are, however, questioned by ECKER (*Arch. f. Anthropologie*, iii., 215). W. BRAUNE (*Arch. f. Anatomie*, 1891, 253) has also failed to find confirmation of OGLE's statement that the left hemisphere is, almost without exception, heavier than the right. On the other hand, it is a fact easily verified that, in all primates, the fissures are more asymmetrically arranged in the anterior than they are in the posterior part of the brain. Moreover, the left frontal gyres, according to BROCA, are usually more complicated than the right. These observations accord with those made by BROCA and P. BERT upon the differences in temperature found in man at different parts of the head ; the left half of the frontal region is on the average warmer than the right, and the frontal region as a whole warmer than the occipital (P. BERT, *Soc. de biologie*, 19 Janv., 1879).

CHAPTER VI

The Physiological Function of the Central Parts

§ 1. Methods of Functional Analysis

EVEN if we knew the course and the interconnexions of all the paths of nervous conduction, there would still be one thing needful for an understanding of the physiological function of the central parts: a knowledge of the influence exerted upon the processes of innervation by the central substance. And there is but one possible way of determining this influence: we must attempt to ascertain the function of the central parts by means of direct observation.

Under this limitation, two roads are open to the investigator who would gain an insight into the complicated functions of the nerve centres. He can arrange the phenomena in order of their physiological significance; or, accepting the lines of division drawn by the anatomists, he can examine into the separate function of each individual central region. It is obvious that the former of these procedures is to be preferred: not only because it lays the chief emphasis upon the physiological point of view, but also because, when the investigation of the conduction paths is over and done with, a doubt must still remain whether every one of the principal parts distinguished by anatomy represents a similarly well-defined functional area. In the present state of our knowledge, however, it is impossible to carry out the physiological programme with any sort of completeness. The method can be applied, with any hope of success, only to the two lowest central organs, myel and oblongata, where the phenomena may be referred without exception to two basal physiological functions, reflex and automatic excitations: the latter oftentimes deriving directly from nutritive influences exercised by the blood. We may well suppose that these same two basal functions are the source of the physiological activities of the higher central parts. At the same time, the interrelation of the phenomena is here so complicated, and their interpretation in many cases so uncertain, that it seems wiser, for the present, to examine each individual central area for itself with a view of discovering its physiological properties. We shall, accordingly, preface our enquiry by a general discussion of reflex and automatic action, in the course of which we shall have opportunity fully to consider the functions of the lower central regions; and we shall then proceed to investigate the brain and its parts in regular sequence from below upwards. We may, however, omit structures which, like pons, crura and corona, are intended in the main simply for the conduction of processes of innervation, and have therefore been sufficiently dealt with in the preceding Chapter.

The methods employed in the functional examination of the central organs are, in general, the same as those which find application in the study of the conduction paths, save that anatomical investigation, which there holds the first place, must naturally play a merely subordinate part now that we are concerned with the activities of the organs. We shall ask assistance, where possible in combination, from physiological experiment and from pathological observation; and we shall pay attention, under both headings, to symptoms of stimulation and symptoms of abrogation. The special conditions of the phenomena are such that stimulation experiments must for the most part be employed in the general study of the reflexes and of automatic excitations, whereas the functional analysis of the various departments of the brain must rely almost exclusively upon symptoms of abrogation.

§ 2. Reflex Functions

(a)—Spinal Reflexes

The simplest mode of central function, and the mode that still approximates most nearly to a simple conduction of processes of stimulation, is the reflex movement. In so far as the reflex process is a special form of conduction, we have discussed it in the preceding Chapter. But it is more; it is a form of conduction modified in various ways by the influence of the central substance. In the first place, the reflexes are not, like the processes of stimulation, conducted in both directions in the nerve fibres, but only in the one direction, from sensory to motor path: a fact which, as we explained above, is in all probability connected with the twofold mode of origin of the nervous processes in the motor cells.[1] Secondly, the reflexes clearly show, in their dependence upon the stimuli that release them, the effects of the peculiar conditions of excitability obtaining in the grey substance. Stimuli that are weak and of brief duration fail, as a rule, to evoke a reflex movement: but the movement, once it appears, may far surpass in intensity and duration the direct muscular contraction set up by the same stimulus. Lastly, the central character of these processes is evinced by the dependence of the reflex centres upon other central areas with which they stand in connexion. Thus, it has been observed that the reflex excitability of the myel is enhanced by removal of the brain.

[1] See above, pp. 43, 99.

It appears, therefore, that inhibitory influences are continually proceeding from the higher central organs, and lessen the irritability of the lower lying reflex centres. These are, in general, still more strongly inhibited if other sensory central parts, with which they are connected, are stimulated along with them. The reflex, e.g., released by excitation of a sensory myelic root or of its peripheral radiation is inhibited by simultaneous stimulation of the dorsal myelic columns, of quadrigemina and thalami, of another sensory root, or finally of peripheral organs within which sensory nerves are distributed. It is not improbable that the influence of the cerebral hemispheres belongs to the same group of phenomena; for this too proceeds, in all likelihood, from the terminations of the sensory conduction paths in the cortex. It has been observed that the inhibition of reflexes in mammals is especially strong if stimuli are applied directly to the centro-sensory areas of the cerebral cortex.[1] The mechanism of reflex inhibition would thus appear to be the same throughout: reflexes are inhibited, when the sensory cells that should transfer their excitation to motor cells are simultaneously excited with a certain degree of intensity from other sensory areas. This inhibitory effect is, however, limited to the condition that the areas whose stimulations interfere lie at a sufficient distance from one another in space. If adjacent sensory parts, or the nerve paths corresponding to them, are stimulated, the result resembles that of summation of stimulations within the same sensory area: that is to say, the interference gives rise not to inhibition but to intensification of the excitatory processes. Lastly, reflex excitations may also suffer inhibition from central elements interpolated in their own proper path. This is the interpretation of the fact that stimuli applied to the cutaneous radiations of the sensory nerves are more effective than stimuli applied to the nerve trunks, and that contrariwise the nerve roots become more irritable after their passage through the spinal ganglion. We must suppose, that is, that the subdivision of fibres in the sense organ serves, on the one hand, to increase irritability, and that, on the other, the excitation which arrives at a spinal ganglion cell there undergoes a certain inhibition: a combination of circumstances which, naturally, brings it about that the nerve trunk possesses a relative minimum of reflex excitability.[2] The general lines to be followed, in an attempt to explain all these phenomena, are laid down by the principles of nerve mechanics that govern the reciprocal relations of excitatory and inhibitory effects, and by that morphological differentiation of the central elements which, in all probability, runs parallel with them.[3]

[1] H. E. HERING and SHERRINGTON, in PFLÜGER's *Arch. f. d. ges. Physiol.*, lxviii., 1897, 222.
[2] See above, p. 88.
[3] See above, Ch. iii., pp. 80, 94, ff.

There are, further, many phenomena which show, still in accordance with the general principles of nervous activity, that the individual reflex excitation aroused by a sensory stimulus does not by any means come upon the scene as interrupting a state of absolute non-excitation in the nervous elements. On the contrary, the state which we term the 'state of rest' is really a state of oscillation—as a rule, of oscillation about a certain position of equilibrium—in which the excitatory and inhibitory forces counteract one another. It is a state in which, on the average, there is a slight preponderance of permanent excitation, though this may be transformed, under special conditions, and more particularly under the influence of antagonistic effects, into a preponderance of permanent inhibition. In this way, the single transient reflex process is superinduced upon a reflex tonus, whose effects become apparent whenever there is interruption of the sensory paths in which the permanent innervation of reflex excitation is conducted. Thus, transsection of the sensory roots of an extremity is followed, in animals, by an atonic, quasi-paralytic state, which however neither abrogates the influence of voluntary impulses upon the atonic muscles nor prevents their action by way of concomitant movements.[1] As regards intensity and distribution, these tonic reflex excitations appear, further, to stand under the regulative influence of all the manifold conditions imposed upon the organs by the nature of their functions. Reflex stimuli, which release transient reflex movements, may accordingly produce radically different results, according to the state of the pre-existing tonus and of the relative distribution of excitatory and inhibitory forces. Thus SHERRINGTON found, in observations upon animals whose myel was cut through in the cervical region, that extensor reflexes appeared if the leg was in the position of flexion, and flexor reflexes, if it was extended. We may also appeal to this influence of the variable conditions of permanent tonic excitation upon the individual reflex movement for explanation of the fact that the law of diffusion of reflexes with increasing intensity of stimulus (discussed above, p 162) admits of exception; the general and relatively constant conditions of reflex conduction are cut across by the more variable influences arising from the reciprocal regulation of sensations and movements.[2]

(b)—*Metencephalic (Oblongata) and Mesencephalic Reflexes*

The reflexes that have their seat in the oblongata are, in general, of a more complicated character than the spinal reflexes. This organ is, in particular, the seat of a number of compound reflexes, which play an important part in various physiological functions. We may mention the

---

[1] MOTT and SHERRINGTON, *Proc. of the Royal Soc.*, lvii., 1895, 481. C. BASTIAN, *ibid.*, lvii., 89.
[2] SHERRINGTON, in THOMPSON YATES' *Labor. Reports*, i., 45, 175.

movements of inspiration and expiration, with the closely related processes of coughing, sneezing, vomiting ; the muscular changes involved in the act of swallowing ; the mimetic movements ; vascular innervation and the movements of the heart. Many of these reflexes stand in an intimate relation of interdependence, as is indicated by the fact that their peripheral paths are oftentimes laid down in the same nerve trunks. Some of the above-named processes, such as the movements of respiration and the heart beat, result from a plurality of causes, and therefore continue after interruption of the reflex paths ; in such cases, the reflex is but one of several determinants, and its influence is correspondingly restricted. Others, again, like the movements of swallowing, appear to be pure reflexes ; they are abrogated by interruption of the sensory conduction to the reflex centre, even though the motor conduction to the muscles governing the movement have been left intact. All these reflexes alike, however, differ from the spinal reflexes on the point that, as a general rule, their sensory stimuli pass at once to a large number of motor paths. Many of them are essentially bilateral, and do not require the action of strong stimuli for their extension from the one to the other side of the body. Thus the respiratory movements, which are released by excitation of the pulmonary radiation of the tenth cranial nerve, involve motor roots that issue on both sides from the oblongata and from the cervical and thoracic portions of the myel. These movements furnish, at the same time, an illustration of a self-regulating reflex, which contains within it the impulse to continued rhythmical repetition. While the collapse of the lungs in expiration serves reflexly to start the movement of inspiration, their distention with inspiration serves conversely to excite the muscles of expiration. If the reflex impulse given to the expiratory muscles in inspiration is too weak to bring them into active exercise, it simply inhibits the antagonistic inspiratory muscles. This is the case in ordinary quiet breathing, in which inspiration alone, and not expiration, is connected with active muscular exertion. In the movements of swallowing, the regular sequence is apparently maintained by a different mode of self-regulation. The act of swallowing consists of movements of the larynx, pharynx and œsophagus : movements that succeed one another in regular order, on the application of a stimulus to the mucous membrane of the soft palate. The succession of movements in this instance is, perhaps, regulated in the way that stimulation of the soft palate releases, first of all, simply the movement of the palatal muscles, and that this in turn acts as a stimulus for the reflex elevation of the larynx and contraction of the pharyngeal muscles. In fine, then, it is probable that all these oblongata reflexes, whose detailed description belongs, of course, to physiology, are characterised by the combination of movements for the attainment of definite effects,—the manner of combination being determined, oftentimes, by a mechanism of self-regulation, itself conditioned upon the reciprocal relation of a number of reflex mechanisms A second noteworthy property of these reflexes is the following. The motor path of a given reflex movement sometimes stands in connexion with a second sensory path, from which, accordingly, the same movement may be aroused. Secondary sensory paths of this kind are connected, in particular, with the respiratory centres, so that the combined activity of the muscles of respiration becomes available for other purposes than those of inflation and emptying of the lungs. There is, e.g., a connexion of the sensory nerves of larynx and œsophageal mucous membrane (i.e. of the superior and, in part, of the inferior laryngeal nerves), and of the branches of the fifth cranial nerve distributed to the nose, with the centre of expiration. Stimulation of these sensory areas produces, first, inhibition of inspiration and then violent expiration. The latter is, however, preceded by a strong inspiration, the immediate consequence of the establishment of inhibition, due to the persistence of the influence of automatic excitation which we discuss below. Coughing and sneezing are, accordingly, reflexes of expiration ; but they are not excited from the sensory area of pulmonary radiation of the vagus, from which the impulse to expiration ordinarily proceeds. They are distinguished by the fact that stimulation of the nasal branches of the trigeminus arouses not only the respiratory muscles but also the motor nerve of the face, the *facialis*, to reflex activity. The sneezing reflex consequently affords a direct transition to the mimetic reflexes of laughing, crying, sobbing, etc., in which again the muscles of the face unite in conjoint function with the muscles of respiration.[1] Further : the secondary sensory path from the expiratory centre to the mucous membrane of the air passages is paralleled by a similar path from the inspiratory centre to the cutaneous investment of the body. We are thus able to account for the movements of inspiration produced by intensive stimulation, especially cold stimulation, of the cutaneous surface.

It may, then, be taken as a matter of common occurrence that in the oblongata a given motor reflex path is connected with a number of different sensory paths. But more than this : one and the same sensory path may enter into connexion, conversely, with several reflex centres, so that its stimulation arouses coincidently various kinds of reflex movements. Here belong, e.g., the mimetic reflexes, mentioned above, in which movements of respiration are combined with facial movements. A similar arrangement of connexions is in part responsible for the interaction of respiratory movements and heart beat. The heart is supplied by two sorts of nerve paths, which affect the sequence of beats in opposite ways : accelerating nerves,

---

[1] These and the other mimetic reflexes are of great psychological importance, and are accordingly discussed under the heading of expressive movements in Part IV., Ch. xvii.

which increase the rapidity of heart beat, and inhibitory nerves, which diminish it, or bring the organ to a complete standstill. Both may be reflexly excited; but the centre for the accelerating fibres is intimately connected with certain sensory paths that run to the heart in the spinal nerves for the last cervical and first thoracic ganglion of the sympathetic; and the centre for the inhibitory fibres with others, that take their course for the most part in the cardiac branches of the vagus. Hence stimulation of the great majority of sensory nerves, and in particular of the cutaneous, laryngeal and intestinal nerves, produces inhibition, and stimulation of the sensory fibres that enter the muscles produces acceleration of the heart beat: this latter fact explains the increased action of the heart that accompanies general muscular exertion. Similar results follow from the movements of the lungs: their inflation accelerates, their collapse reduces the frequency of heart beat. The respiratory movements are therefore regularly accompanied by fluctuations of the pulse, whose rapidity increases in inspiration and decreases in expiration. On the whole, that is, the movement of the blood is accelerated by enhancement of the movements of respiration. Again, we find the same kind of interaction between the reflex connexions of cardiac and vascular innervation. The vessels are governed, like the heart, by motor and inhibitory nerves, both of which may be reflexly excited. Stimulation of most of the sensory nerves releases the motor reflex, i.e., acts upon the nerve fibres which constrict the small arterial blood vessels and thus produce an increase of blood pressure in the larger arteries, and which are therefore termed pressor fibres. The only exception to this action is in the vessels of the part of the skin to which the stimulus is applied: these vessels usually dilate, either immediately or after a brief stage of constriction, and thus occasion the hyperæmia and redness of the stimulated parts. There are, however, various sensory areas which stand, conversely, in direct reflex connexion with the inhibitory or depressor fibres of the blood vessels, and whose stimulation leads accordingly to a widespread dilatation of the smaller vessels. Here belong, in particular, certain fibres of the vagus, which radiate within the heart itself and form its sensory nerve supply: fibres which, in all probability, are exclusively devoted to this reflexly mediated interaction between cardiac and vascular innervation. For their stimulation must be effected, in the normal course of physiological function, by increased action of the heart; this, in turn, is produced by increase of blood pressure and of the amount of blood contained in the arterial system; and this, once more, can be compensated only by a dilatation of the small arteries, which permits the outflow of the blood into the veins, and thus at the same time reduces the arterial blood pressure. We see, in fine, that all these reflexes of the oblongata stand in relations of interdependence, such that the functions discharged by this central organ mutually regulate and support one another. An intensive cold stimulus applied to the surface of the skin produces, reflexly, a spasm of inspiration and an arrest of heart beat. But the danger which thus threatens the life of the organism is avoided, since the expansion of the lungs serves, again reflexly, to excite expiration and acceleration of cardiac movement; while at the same time the stimulation of the skin brings about, by way of yet another reflex, a constriction of the smaller arteries, and so prevents any excessive emptying of the arrested heart. In many of these cases, as in a certain number of the reflexes proceeding from the myel, the central transmissions have simply a regulatory significance. The peripheral organs are the seat of direct innervation effects, due perhaps to special ganglion cells lying within them, perhaps to the excitomotor properties of the muscle fibres themselves; and the addition of the system of spinal and oblongata reflexes can do no more than modify these effects by way of excitation or of inhibition.[1]

In all probability it is the nerve nidi of the oblongata, with their intercurrent central fibres, that we must consider as the principal reflex centres of this organ. The complicated character of the metencephalic reflexes appears to find its sufficient explanation in the anatomical conditions of these nerve nidi. They are, upon the whole, more strictly isolated than are the centres of origin of the spinal nerves. But, as an offset, certain nidi are closely connected by special central fibres both with one another and with continuations of the myelic columns. These two facts, taken together, explain the relative independence and singleness of aim of the oblongata reflexes. Myelic fibres are involved in these reflexes to a very considerable extent; and it is therefore probable that they are brought together, first of all, in some cinereal formation, and only after leaving this enter into connexion with the nerve nidi to which they are assigned. Thus, the respiratory motor fibres are, perhaps, collected in a special ganglionic nidus, which stands in connexion with the nidus of the vagus nerve. We may fairly suppose that this significance attaches to several of the grey masses scattered in the reticular substance. On the other hand, it is not probable that movements so complicated as the mimetic movements, or the movements of respiration and swallowing, possess each a single ganglionic nidus as their special reflex centre. Apart from the fact that centres of this sort, for complicated reflexes, have never been demonstrated, their existence is negatived by the nature of the movements themselves. The respiratory movements, e.g., evidently require us to posit two reflex centres, the one for inspiration, the other for expiration. Various mimetic reflexes, like laughing and crying, can be much more easily explained on

---

[1] For the relative autonomy of the cardiac movements, see especially T. W. ENGELMANN, in PFLÜGER's *Arch. f. d. ges. Physiol.*, lvi., 1894, 149; for the autonomous functions of the movements that fall within the sphere of the spinal reflexes, see GOLTZ and EWALD, *ibid.*, lxiii., 1897, 362.

the assumption of a reflex connexion, joining certain sensory paths at one and the same time with the respiratory centres and with determinate parts of the nidus of the facialis, than on that of an especial auxiliary ganglion, serving directly to initiate the above complex group of movements. In the same way, the movements of swallowing must be derived, like the respiratory movements, from the principle of self-regulation; we must suppose that the first movement of the entire process gives, as it is made, the reflex stimulus to the second, this the stimulus to the next following, and so on.

Of the four 'specific' sensory stimuli, two only are concerned, to any great extent, in the arousal of reflexes by way of sensory nerves: impressions of taste, and light stimuli. The former stand in reflex relation to the mimetic movements of expression; to reflexes, i.e., some of which (as we remarked above) readily combine with reflex respiratory movements, and thus lead us to infer a close connexion of the corresponding reflex centres. Light stimuli regularly evoke a twofold reflex response: first, closure of the eyelid, with a direction of the two eyes inward and upward, and secondly contraction of the pupil. Both reflexes are bilateral, though with weak excitations the movement is more pronounced upon the stimulated side. The reflexes released by way of the auditory and olfactory nerves appear in the neighbourhood of the external sense organs; if the stimuli are extensive, appropriate movements of the head may also be induced. In man, the proximate auditory reflexes are for the most part confined to contractions of the tensor tympani, which presumably accompany every sound stimulation: but in many animals reflex movements of the external ear are clearly observable.

If the stimulus is extensive, or the degree of irritability unusually high, the sphere of reflex activity may be extended beyond the limits of the direct reflex connexions. This phenomenon of diffusion is more definite and uniform for the cranial than it is for the spinal nerves. In the case of the optic nerve, e.g., the reflex to the muscles that move the eye-ball is connected, in extensive stimulation, with contraction of the corresponding muscles for movement of the head; and the facialis reflex to the orbicularis palpebrarum may be accompanied by concomitant movements of the other mimetic muscles of the face. Reflexes touched off from the gustatory nerve fibres may cover a wider territory; they are apt to involve, not only the facial nerves, but the vagus centre as well. Stimulation of the sensory nerves of respiration is confined, as a rule, within the limits of its original reflex area. The strongest excitation of the central trunks of the pulmonary branch of the vagus has no reflex effect beyond the tetanus of inspiration. The reflex connexions of the expiratory fibres are more far-reaching. Stimulation of the sensory laryngeal nerves, and especially of their peripheral ends, is likely to involve the muscles of the face and of the upper extremity. But the fullest and most extended reflex relations are those of the trigeminus, the largest of the sensory cranial nerves. Stimulation of the trigeminus affects, first of all, its own motor root, which supplies the masseter muscles; and passes from this to the nerves of the face, the respiratory nerves, and finally to the whole muscular system of the body. There are two evident reasons for this range of reflex effect. First and generally, the trigeminus controls the largest sensory surface of all the sensory nerves, so that its nerve nidi also occupy a wide area, and opportunity is thus given for manifold connexions with motor centres of origin. Secondly and particularly, the position of its nidi is favourable. The superior nidi are situated, above the oblongata proper, in the pons; i.e. in the organ in which the ascending columns of alba are grouped together, by the interpolation of cinerea, to form the various bundles of the crus. We see, therefore, why it is that lesion of the oblongata and pons in the neighbourhood of the nidi of the fifth cranial nerve is followed by general reflex spasms. The result need not, of course, be attributed solely to these nidi: the stimulation in such cases may affect other sensory roots of the oblongata as well.[1]

(c)—*Purposiveness of the Reflexes. Extent of Reflex Phenomena*

The reflex phenomena bear upon them the mark of purposiveness. As regards the oblongata reflexes, this characteristic appears at once from the above description of their conditions and of their orderly co-operation. But the spinal reflexes also show, for the most part, a certain degree of the same quality. Thus, if a stimulus be applied to the skin, the animal makes a movement of arm or leg that is obviously directed upon the removal of the stimulus. If the reflex becomes stronger, the arm or leg of the opposite side will make a similar movement, or the animal will jump away, apparently to escape the action of the stimulus. Only when the movements take on a convulsive character, as they do with extremely intensive stimuli or in states of unusual excitability, do they lose this expression of purposiveness. These facts have suggested the question whether the reflexes may properly be regarded as mechanical consequences of stimulation and of its diffusion in the central organ, or whether they are actions of a psychical kind, and as such presuppose, like voluntary movements, a certain amount of consciousness. Worded in this way, however, the question is evidently misleading. There can be no doubt that the arrangements in the central organ can produce purposive results with mechanical necessity; we have the same phenomenon in any perfected form of self-regulating machinery. Moreover, the oblongata reflexes are highly purposive, and nevertheless

---

[1] NOTHNAGEL, in VIRCHOW'S *Archiv.*, xliv., 4. BINSWANGER, *Arch. f. Psychiatr.*, xix., 759.

dependent upon definite mechanical conditions. Again, there is no reason whatever why a sensory stimulus should not release a reflex movement and arouse a sensation or idea at one and the same time : so that we cannot take the absence of all conscious process as the direct criterion of a reflex movement. On the other hand, the definition of the reflex would, it is true, be indefinitely extended, and the term would cover practically the whole range of organic movement, were we to apply it to any and every movement released in the central organ by the action of sensory stimuli. Suppose, e.g., that I make a voluntary movement, in order to grasp some object that I see before me : this, which is indubitably an act of will, still falls under the general heading of a movement released by sensory stimulation. It lacks, however, and conspicuously lacks, an attribute which is specifically characteristic of the reflex ; the attribute, indeed, that first gave rise to the distinction between reflex and voluntary action, and without which the distinction loses all meaning. A movement mediated in the central organ by way of response to sensory stimulation, if it is to be denominated a reflex movement, may not bear upon it the marks of *psychical causation* ; i.e., the idea aroused by the stimulus may not constitute, for the agent's own consciousness, the *motive* to the external movement. My involuntary reaction to a sensed stimulation of the skin is, therefore, a reflex, so long as the sensation remains a mere accidental concomitant of the movement, so long, that is, as the movement would be made in precisely the same way without such a concomitant sensation. On the other hand, reaction is not a reflex, if I voluntarily put out my hand to seize the stimulating object that is pressing upon the skin ; for in this instance the movement is conditioned, for the agent, upon the conscious process. In the individual case it may, naturally, be difficult to decide, especially if the observations are made from the outside, whether a given movement is or is not a reflex. But this practical difficulty does not justify our setting aside altogether the criterion that distinguishes the reflexes from other forms of action, and leaving out of account the fact that, while related by their purposiveness to psychically conditioned movements, they differ from them, clearly and definitely, in the lack of conscious intermediaries. It is precisely this criterion that makes the reflexes an easily distinguishable and characteristic class of organic movements. We may also mention a further aspect of reflex action, closely connected with the criterion just discussed, though naturally of less universal application : the fact that reflexes follow *immediately* upon the operation of sensory stimuli, while psychically conditioned movements admit of a longer or shorter interval between stimulus and movement. What holds of this holds also of other objective characteristics, as e.g. that of the possibility of choice between different means. Such criteria are not always applicable : partly, because the characteristics do not attach at all generally to psychically mediated movements, but partly, too, because the purposive nature of the reflexes leaves a certain amount of room for difference of interpretation.

If we admit that these criteria are adequate to the empirical delimitation of the reflexes, as a readily distinguishable group of organic movements, we must also accept the conclusion that the central reflex area, in man and in the higher animals that resemble him, probably does not extend higher up than the mesencephalic region. In all cases where a sensory stimulus is conducted to the cerebral cortex, and there for the first time transformed into a motor impulse, the central transference appears, without exception, to involve the interpolation of psychophysical intermediaries; so that the action is presented to the agent's own consciousness as psychically conditioned. Many authors, it is true, speak of 'cortical reflexes' as of an established fact. But they are using the term reflex in a wider sense, in which any and every movement that results from sensory stimulation is denominated a reflex, whether psychical intermediaries are brought into play or not. From this point of view, the voluntary action is sometimes defined as a 'cortical reflex.' It is clear that such an expression deprives the word 'reflex' of all special significance. It is also clear that the retention of the term in its stricter meaning is extremely important; for the origin of a class of movements that are at once purely physiological and yet purposive in character is a real and distinct problem. We cannot, of course, enter upon this question of origin at the present time; we can answer it only when we come to examine the various forms of animal movements. We may, however, point out, in view of the following discussion of the functions of the different central regions, that what holds of man in this connexion does not necessarily hold of the animals. We may lay it down as a general proposition that, in man, the centre at which the idea of the reflex gives way to the idea of the psychically conditioned action is the cerebral cortex. But the law is not universally valid; not even valid for all the vertebrates. It is a result of that progressive centralisation in the ascending direction, of which we have spoken in the preceding Chapter, that the mesencephalic areas which, in man, function simply and solely as reflex centres, appear in the lower vertebrates still to be centres for psychically conditioned movements. Indeed, the facts suggest that in the lowest vertebrates, where the cerebrum as a whole is of very minor importance, even the oblongata and the myel may possibly, up to a certain point, mediate movements of this psychical kind. Lower yet, in the invertebrates, they may proceed from any one of the peripheral ganglia; and in the protozoa they evidently have their seat in the general sensorimotor protoplasmic substance of the body. The centralisation of the psychical functions in the brain, that is, goes *pari passu* with their decentralisation in the bodily organs; and this decentralisation corresponds to an extension of the reflex functions. Hence, in the lowest animals, all movements possess the character, not—as is sometimes maintained in the interest of certain ingrained dogmas—of reflexes, but rather of psychically conditioned movements.[1]

§ 3. Automatic Excitations

(a)—*Automatic Excitations in Myel and Oblongata*

The phenomena of 'automatic function' are in so far parallel to the phenomena of reflex action that they are processes of a purely physiological character, and accordingly have nothing in common with processes which, like voluntary actions, recollections, etc., present themselves to us in direct experience as 'psychically conditioned.' In this purely physiological sense, the automatic functions are therefore nearly allied to the reflexes. But they differ from them in the point that the automatic stimulation processes take their origin in the nerve centres themselves, and are not released by a stimulus conducted to the centre from without. As a general rule, the motor areas that evince reflex phenomena are also susceptible of automatic excitation. The results of these automatic stimulations need not be muscular movements, or inhibitions of particular movements, but may also take the form of sensations. Hence it is not always easy to discriminate them from reflex excitations, or from the direct effects of external stimuli. For all our senses are continually affected by weak stimuli, which have their ground in the structural conditions of the sense organs themselves, and, so far as the sensory centres are concerned, these weak excitations, such e.g. as are aroused by the pressure exerted in the eye upon the retina, in the labyrinth of the ear upon the sensitive membranes, are, of course, the equivalent of stimulation from the outside. If we rule out cases of this kind, it appears that the sole source of automatic excitation is to be looked for in sudden changes in the chemical constitution of the nervous substance, caused for the most part by alteration of the blood.

As regards the myel, the effects of automatic excitation are shown most clearly by the muscles of certain organs of the nutritive system: e.g. the circular muscles of the blood vessels, whose lumen becomes enlarged after transsection of the myel,[2] and the sphincter muscles of bladder and intestine, where similar results have been observed.[3] The tonic excitations of the skeletal muscles appear, on the other hand, to be exclusively reflex in character (cf. p. 93, above), since transsection of the muscle nerves produces

---

[1] See above, Ch. i., pp. 29 ff., and below, Chs. xvii., xviii., on Will and Consciousness.
[2] GOLTZ and FREUSBERG, in PFLÜGER's *Archiv. f. d. ges. Physiol.*, xiii., 1876, 460.
[3] MASIUS, *Bulletin de l'académie de Belge*, xxiv., xxv., 1867, 1868.

no change in muscular tension, apart from the concomitant twitch and its elastic after-effects.[1] Automatic excitations seem, however, to occur, alongside of reflex excitations, in the peripheral organs that are separated from the central organs proper and provided with independent centres, e.g. in the heart and intestinal muscles (cf. p. 248, above).

The automatic excitations that proceed from the oblongata are of especial importance. Here, too, the reflex centres appear, without exception, to be automatic centres as well. The movements that arise in them are consequently continued, after the sensory portion of the reflex path has been interrupted. Here belong the movements of respiration and heart beat, and the innervation of the blood vessels. All of these processes are connected with two centres, distinct not only in function but also in locality: the respiratory movements with centres of inspiration and expiration, the cardiac movements with centres for acceleration and inhibition of the heart beat, the vascular innervation with centres for constriction and dilatation of the blood vessels. Under such circumstances it seems to be the rule that the one centre acts reflexly while the other combines automatic with reflex functions, or even gives the preference to automatic stimuli: so the inspiratory centre in the case of respiratory movements, the centre for inhibition of heart beat in that of cardiac movements, and the centre for vaso-constriction in that of vascular innervation. It may be that the position of these nerve nidi, and the way in which their blood supply is distributed, render them especially liable to automatic excitations. The normal physiological stimulus to the production of such excitations is, in all probability, that state of the blood which is induced by arrest of breathing or, indeed, by any circumstance that prevents the elimination of the oxidised constituents of the tissues. The presence in the dyspnœic blood of oxidation products in general, whether of the final product of combustion, carbonic acid, or of lower stages of oxidation as yet unnamed, appears accordingly to constitute it a source of nervous stimulation. The accumulation of these materials excites the inspiratory centre: an inspiration is made, which causes the lungs to distend and thus, in its turn, serves reflexly to excite the centre of expiration (p. 245). This automatic stimulation completes the circle of self-regulating functions, whereby the process of respiration is kept in perpetual activity. The first impulse is given by the change in the constitution of the blood: this acts as an internal stimulus to excite inspiration. The beginning once made the further periodic course of the whole process continues of its own accord. The expiratory reflex excited by distention of the lung is followed, as the organ collapses, by the inspiratory reflex and at the same time, in consequence of the renewed accumulation

[1] HEIDENHAIN, *Physiol. Studien*, 1856, 9. WUNDT, *Lehre von der Muskelbewegung*, 1858, 51 f.

of products of oxidation, by renewed automatic stimulation of the inspiratory centre.

We may suppose that the same changes in the composition of the blood condition the automatic innervation of the inhibitory centre for the heart and of the pressor centre for the blood vessels. It is ordinarily assumed that the excitations in these two cases are not, as they are in the case of respiration, subject to a rhythmical rise and fall, in consequence of the self-regulation of the process of stimulation, but hold throughout to a uniform level of intensity. This is inferred from the facts that severance of the inhibitory nerves of the heart, the vagus trunks, produces a persistent acceleration of the heart beat, and that severance of the vascular nerves effects a permanent dilatation of the small arteries. But these facts are not incompatible with the theory that the automatic excitation in both cases oscillates between certain upper and lower limits. There are, in reality, numerous phenomena that tell in favour of such a theory: e.g., the alternate constrictions and dilatations that may be observed in the arteries, and that usually disappear after transsection of the nerves; or the connexion between rapidity of pulse and respiration, a connexion which, as we have seen, depends in part upon the changes of volume in the lung and is therefore explicable in reflex terms, but in part also suggests a different origin, seeing that a long-continued arrest of breathing, whether it occur in the position of inspiration or in that of expiration, arrests the heart as well. Moreover, in death by suffocation we always find, besides intensive excitation of the inspiratory muscles, constriction of the blood-vessels and inhibition of the heart beat. We may accordingly conjecture that the automatic excitation of all these oblongata centres depends upon analogous changes in the constitution of the blood. The observed differences may very well have their ground in the relations of the peripheral nerve terminations; for the inspiratory centre stands in connexion with ordinary motor nerves, whereas heart and blood vessels are characterised by the independence of their peripheral innervations. The heart continues to pulsate, though with change of rhythm, when separated from all nerves whatsoever; and the vascular wall remains capable, under the same conditions, of alternate constrictions and dilatations. The causes which determine these peripheral excitations are, in all probability, similar to those which regulate the respiratory innervation in the myel and, like the latter, are compounded of automatic and reflex processes: while the rhythmical function of the heart and the equilibrium between excitation and inhibition in the vessels are also maintained by some self-regulative mechanism. That is to say, the innervations of lungs, heart and blood vessels are, probably, in so far related to one another that the automatic excitations from which they spring may be referred to one and the same source of origin. The centres for these movements appear to offer especially favourable conditions for the action of the internal stimuli; for no other central area reacts so sensitively to fluctuations in the composition of the blood. In other quarters of the central nervous system, we may suppose, the influence of the blood becomes effective only if the blood supply has been modified from these centres of respiratory, cardiac and vascular innervation, and the changes thus set up form a source of central stimulation. Thus, excitations of the vascular centre, which inhibit the circulation of blood in the brain, are probably, in many instances, the cause of general muscular convulsions. Under such circumstances, the external symptoms are, for the most part, initiated in the pons; sometimes, perhaps, in a more anteriorly situated motor brain-region.[1] The dyspnœic blood may, however, occasion muscular convulsions of the same kind, though less widely diffused, by stimulation of the myel.[2]

(b)—*Automatic Excitations in the Brain Cortex*

Of the parts lying beyond the pons, the centrosensory and centromotor regions of the brain cortex seem to be the principal centres from which, under the appropriate conditions, automatic excitations may proceed. In their case, however, we are never in presence of purely automatic processes, in the physiological sense defined above. The relations of the cerebral cortex to the psychical functions are such that the automatic excitations are connected, in every instance, with conscious processes,—processes that may, in general, be subsumed under the rubric of psychical association, and that refer us to psychophysical conditions of a very complicated kind. Nevertheless, the part played by automatic stimulation is far from unimportant. It serves to *modify the excitability of the cerebral cortex;* and the state of cortical excitability largely determines the appearance and course of these psychophysical processes. Among its results, we must mention, in the first place, those phenomena of stimulation that may almost be termed the normal accompaniments of *sleep*. They show themselves usually, and oftentimes exclusively, as sensory excitations. So arises the customary, sensory form of the *dream*, in which automatic enhancement of excitability in the sensory centres produces—always, probably, under the influence of external sense stimuli—ideas of hallucinatory character. Sometimes motor excitations are also involved: muscular movements occur, ordinarily in the mechanisms of speech, more rarely in the locomotor apparatus, and combine with the phenomena of sensory excitation to form a more or less coherent series of ideas and actions. In all these phenomena, sensory and motor alike, the automatic change of excitability is simply

---

[1] KUSSMAUL and TENNER, in MOLESCHOTT'S *Untersuchungen zur Naturlehre des Menschen*, iii., 1857, 77.
[2] LUCHSINGER, in PFLÜGER'S *Arch. f. d. ges. Physiol.*, xiv., 1877, 383.

the foundation, upon which the complex psychophysical conditions of the dream consciousness and its outward manifestations are built up. The point of departure of these central changes, which follow the oncoming of sleep, is again to be sought, most probably, in the innervation centres of the oblongata. Mosso has shown, by observation of cases in which a portion of the skull had been removed, that at the moment of falling asleep the flow of blood to the brain is reduced; and, further, that the supply may, in most instances, be temporarily increased by the application of external sense stimuli, even if these are too weak to arouse the sleeper.[1] The general reduction of the blood flow is, in all probability, the cause of the marked diminution in the excitability of the brain centres, and of the corresponding obscuration of consciousness, that characterise the approach of sleep. Very soon, however, this inhibition of the central functions spreads still further, involving to a certain extent the centres of respiration and heart beat; so that the phenomena of dyspnœa not infrequently make their appearance during sleep. The enhanced excitability of particular central elements of the brain cortex, vouched for by the phantasms of dreaming, may accordingly be ascribed to the direct excitatory influence upon the cortex of the dyspnœic modification of the blood. It is also possible, in view of the reciprocal relations sustained by the various central areas, that stimulations accidentally set up in a given region of the cortex will produce the more intensive result, the greater the degree of latent excitation in the adjacent parts.[2]

Similar excitations of the cerebral cortex may occur in the waking state; but they are then invariably the result of *pathological* changes. Here, again, investigation frequently refers us to an abnormal state of the circulation as their ultimate condition. The abnormality may be of local origin, proceeding from the vessels of the meninges or of the brain itself. Local lesions, in particular, set up in the neighbourhood of the sensory centres, are ordinarily attended by corresponding hallucinations. These, however, may also be due to general disturbances of circulation, which appear sometimes as the consequence, sometimes as the cause of psychical derangement;[3] for changes in the innervation of heart and vessels are frequently observed in cases of mental disease.[4] Now all the chronic forms of insanity are connected with more or less serious modifications of

---

[1] Mosso, *Ueber den Kreislauf des Blutes im menschlichen Gehirn*, 1881, 74 ff.

[2] Cf. with this the discussion of the psychology of dreams, Part V., Ch. xx. The excitatory influence of the dyspnœic blood, mentioned in the text, is confirmed by the fact that other forms of automatic or reflex stimulation—dyspnœic spasms, epileptiform twitches, and the like—are especially apt to occur during sleep.

[3] WERNICKE, *Lehrbuch d. Gehirnkrankheiten*, ii., 10. KRAEPELIN, *Psychiatrie*, 6te Aufl., i., 54.

[4] WOLFF, *Allg. Zeitschr. f. Psychiatrie*, xxvi., 273. ZIEHEN, *Sphygmographische Untersuchungen bei Geisteskranken*, 1887.

the brain cortex; and diffuse affections of the vascular membrane with which the cortex is invested are the most frequent causes of acute psychical disorder. But the phenomena of stimulation accompanying such disorder closely resemble those that normally appear in sleep. They belong, as the latter also belong, partly to the sensory, partly to the motor sphere. The sensory excitation manifests itself in sensations and ideas of the different senses, oftentimes equal in intensity to those that can be caused by external impressions, and therefore indistinguishable from them. These hallucinations are accompanied by changes in the subjective sensations, muscular and organic, upon which the affective disposition largely depends. Motor stimulations show themselves in the form of imperative actions, which are likely to impress the observer by their unwonted energy. Here too, however, as in dreams and dream movements, the enhancement of excitability due to automatic stimulation is combined with further psychophysical processes, which are responsible for the specific contents of the phenomena.[1]

§ 4. Functions of the Mesencephalon and Diencephalon

(a)—Functions of the Mesencephalon and Diencephalon in the Lower Vertebrates

It is evident from mere inspection, and without recourse to histological methods, that the mesencephalic and diencephalic region, which in man and the higher mammals, more especially in the nearly related primates, cannot compare with the mass of the overarching cerebral hemispheres, forms in the lower vertebrates the most highly developed part of the central organ. Even in the birds and the lower mammals, where the prosencephalon has already attained a considerable size, its relative development is still greater than that of the superior parts (cf. Fig. 54, p. 128). These salient facts of the gross anatomy of the brain are paralleled throughout by functional differences; so that it is far more dangerous in the case of mesencephalon and diencephalon than it is in that of myel and oblongata to argue from symptoms observed in the lower animals to the organisation of the higher, and in particular of man. Yet another difficulty in the way of a functional analysis of this region, whether in the animals or in man, lies in the circumstance that experimental interference and pathological disturbance rarely affect a definite and definitely circumscribed area, but are apt to spread to adjacent parts,—experimental interference, more especially, involving the crural and coronal fibres that pass upward below and between the thalami and quadrigemina. Hence most of the results of the earlier

[1] For this psychological aspect of mental derangement, and for an account of sleep and of similar states (hypnotism), see Part v., Ch. xx.

experiments upon the transsection of these centres leave us uncertain whether the motor derangements observed were really the consequence of the destruction of the parts themselves, or not rather of the interruption of the neighbouring conduction paths.[1] Indeed, the whole method was at fault. The symptoms of stimulation and abrogation do good service in the investigation of conduction paths, and especially of their beginnings in the myel and of their terminations in the cerebral cortex. But in the present case, where the separation of the parts under examination from their surroundings presents extreme difficulty, they can hardly be employed with any prospect of success. As the stimulus method is here, for obvious reasons, practically out of the question, physiology has accordingly come more and more to substitute for the direct an *indirect* form of the method of abrogation. Instead of asking what functions remain intact after removal of the mesencephalic and diencephalic centres which he has under investigation, the modern physiologist inverts the question, and asks what functions are still left when all the prosencephalic parts that lie above and beyond them have been cut away. He then makes a series of similar observations upon animals of the same species in which the entire central organ has been removed with the exception of oblongata and myel; and, by recording the difference of result in the two cases, is able to reach a conclusion with regard to the functional significance of the intermediate central region. This method was employed long since by FLOURENS upon birds,—though employed, at first, rather with a view to the determination of the importance of the prosencephalon itself, whose extirpation it involved.[2] It was then applied, systematically, by GOLTZ, in work upon the frog;[3] and has been used by CHRISTIANI[4] and, still more recently by GOLTZ[5] again for mammals, and finally by J. STEINER[6] for vertebrates of all classes. It evidently guarantees a somewhat more reliable result, if not for each individual centre included in the mesencephalic and diencephalic region, at least for this region as a whole.

The observations taken on the lines here laid down prove that the functional importance of the mesencephalic and diencephalic centres through-

---

[1] Here belong more particularly the experiments of LONGET (*Anatomie et physiologie du système nerveux*, 1842; German trans. by HEIN, i., 385); SCHIFF (*Lehrbuch d. Physiol.*, i., 342); VULPIAN (*Physiol. du système nerveux*, 658), and others. These experiments will always retain a place of honour in the history of the experimental physiology of the central organs. But, from the modern point of view, they must be pronounced antiquated; if only for the reason that they attempt to ascertain the functions of the parts by a purely symptomatic method, from the phenomena of abrogation and stimulation, without regard to morphological relations and the course of the conduction paths.
[2] FLOURENS, *Recherches expér. sur les fonctions du système nerveux*, 2nd ed., 1842.
[3] GOLTZ, *Beiträge zur Lehre von den Functionen der Nervencentren des Frosches*, 1869.
[4] CHRISTIANI, *Zur Physiologie des Gehirns*, 1885.
[5] GOLTZ, *Der Hund ohne Grosshirn*, in PFLÜGER'S *Arch. f. d. ges. Physiol.*, li., 1892, 570.
[6] J. STEINER, *Die Functionen des Centralnervensystems*, Abth. 1-4, 1885-1900.

out the vertebrate series keeps practically even pace with the development of the parts as revealed by gross anatomy. This development is not uniform for the two regions: in the lower orders, the mesencephalon (bigemina or optic lobes) has the preponderance, and the diencephalon (thalamus) is relatively insignificant. Thus, in the entire class of the fishes, with the exception of *Amphioxus lanceolatus* which stops short at the myel, the mesencephalon appears as the dominant central organ. So long as it remains uninjured, the essential psychical functions are hardly modified. In particular, the animals react quite normally to optical and tactual impressions, and move spontaneously and appropriately. Smell alone is abrogated: the olfactory nerves are, naturally, removed with extirpation of the prosencephalon: and the inception of nourishment, in so far as it is governed by impressions of smell, may in consequence be more or less seriously deranged.[1] Passing to the amphibia, we find at once a marked difference of behaviour in animals whose cerebrum has been removed. One function is, unquestionably, retained by them, and must therefore depend for its effectiveness upon the integrity of the mesencephalon: the function of progression, and the regulation of co-ordinated movements of the whole body. The decerebrised frog sits upright, like the uninjured animal; if made to change its place by the action of cutaneous stimuli, it avoids obstacles laid in its path; and so on. It presents but a single abnormality: that, at first, it neither moves nor takes food of its own accord.[2] At the same time, its behaviour shows two noteworthy features. On the one hand, the functional separation of mesencephalon and diencephalon is becoming clearer; on the other hand, we observe the influence of practice upon the formation of new habits. If the diencephalon is intact, the frog, as SCHRADER remarked, slowly recovers: it begins to catch flies again of its own accord, and continues to improve until at last it is altogether indistinguishable from a normal animal.[3] A bird deprived of the prosencephalon behaves in very much the same way. It, too, as FLOURENS observed many years ago, at first remains motionless: it stands upright, breathes regularly, swallows if it is fed, and reacts to stimuli by co-ordinated movements of flight; but it makes no movements of its own initiative. Here again, however, there is a gradual change of behaviour, if the animal is kept alive for any length of time: it makes restless movements from side to side, avoids obstacles as it moves, and so forth.[4] CHRISTIANI, who was the first to make observations on mammals, found that the rabbit, after removal of all the parts of the brain anterior to the mesencephalon and diencephalon, is similarly capable of reacting appropriately to light stimuli, of avoiding

---

[1] J. STEINER, *Die Functionen des Centralnervensystems*, ii., 211 ff.
[2] GOLTZ, *Die Functionen der Nervencentren des Frosches*, 65.
[3] SCHRADER, in PFLÜGER'S *Arch. f. d. ges. Physiol.*, xli., 1887, 75.
[4] SCHRADER, in PFLÜGER'S *Arch. f. d. ges. Physiol.*, xliv., 1888, 175.

obstacles when stimulated to movements of escape, and of occasionally executing what appear to be spontaneous movements.[1] Finally, a still more thorough-going restoration of function was seen by GOLTZ, in the case of dogs that he had kept alive for a considerable period of time after complete extirpation of the cerebrum.[2] As usual, the animals were entirely passive in the interval immediately following the operation : only the vegetative functions (heart beat, breathing, movements of swallowing upon the introduction of food into the gullet) went on without disturbance from the beginning. The progress of time brought with it, however, a much more complete recovery of active function ; and at last the animals moved about in an almost normal manner, reacted to tactual stimuli by barking, got on their feet again if they had fallen down, alternated between sleep and waking, and could be aroused from sleep by sound stimuli. Smell had, it is true, been entirely abrogated with the extirpation of the olfactorius ; nevertheless, the dogs fed of their own accord when food was held against their muzzles. Bad-tasting morsels they spat out again. On the other hand, there was never any expression of pleasurable feeling, of attachment, and never any act that could be interpreted as a sign of personal recognition. These were permanently lost.

From these results we must conclude that the mesencephalic and diencephalic region plays a very considerable part in the whole vertebrate series up to the carnivores. It contains a group of important central stations for the colligation of sense impressions with their appropriate movements,— stations which, like the reflex mechanisms of the myel, continue to function after their severance from the higher central parts. But more than this : its integrity is the condition of the integrity of the simpler psychical functions. The mental loss that the animal suffers by operation is twofold. It loses, on the one hand, the functions connected with determinate sensory nerves that are involved in the lesion caused by removal of the prosencephalon : so the reactions to smell impressions. It loses, on the other hand, the functions which presuppose a manifold connexion of present impressions with past experiences : so the recognition of persons, the feelings of attraction and repulsion, of joy, etc. Some authors, it is true, disregarding the results obtained from decerebrised dogs, and relying on observations made upon anencephalic monsters, localise the feelings and emotions, in man as well as in animals, in the mesencephalic and diencephalic region. But they are guilty of an obvious error in reasoning. They ascribe the response to gustatory stimuli—mimetic reflexes, which in these pathological cases are left intact—to concomitant feelings. It is, of course, no more allowable to argue in this way than it would be to interpret any other reflex movement,

---

[1] CHRISTIANI, *Zur Physiologie des Gehirns*, 25.
[2] GOLTZ, in PFLÜGER'S *Arch. f. d. ges. Physiol.*, li., 570 ff.

on account of its apparent purposiveness, as of necessity a conscious and voluntary action.

We see, then, that these middle brain regions are, for the animals in general, something more than centres of complicated reflexes. In the light of the phenomena described above, we must consider them also as centres for the simpler psychically conditioned functions. A more detailed comparison shows, now, that as regards the time of their appearance these phenomena present very striking differences. In the lowest vertebrates, the fishes, removal of the prosencephalon produces no marked change of any kind in the psychical behaviour of the animals. At a somewhat higher level, in amphibia, reptiles and birds, there is, at first, an interruption of the psychical functions; and those that remain intact, since there is no trace of any lasting after-effect and but very slight indication of adaptation to new conditions, might if needs were be interpreted as complicated reflexes. It is, however, evident that in course of time the animal makes a fairly complete functional recovery. The same picture, only with its lines more strongly drawn, may stand, finally, for the mammal. The lapse of psychical functions after the operation is here more pronounced; a longer period is required for recovery; the permanent mental defect is more clearly observable. Nevertheless, the injury is compensated within wide limits. If we are rightly to interpret these phenomena, we must of course remember that all the functions which are permanently lost in the higher mammals— recognition, expressions of pleasure and attachment—do not exist at all in the lower animals. Now this gradual return of the expressions of mental life, in animals endowed with a fairly well developed prosencephalon, admits, if looked at simply by itself, of two explanations. It may be that the operation gives rise to some sort of inhibitory effects, perhaps conditioned upon the injury to the parts, which must be gradually overcome; or it may be that the uninjured remnant of the brain gradually takes on a share of the functions discharged in the normal organism by the prosencephalon. According as we incline to the one or the other of these interpretations, will our estimate of the functional significance of the mesencephalic and diencephalic regions vary. If we accept the former, these parts will be responsible, throughout the vertebrate series up to the carnivores, for a very considerable proportion of the functions of the brain at large; the animal's recovery will mean, for them, simply a restoration of their original rights. If we accept the latter, their functional activity after recovery will be abnormally increased, because partly vicarious. Now it cannot be denied that there are many facts which tell in favour of the effect of operation, as at least a joint factor in the general result. Radical interferences by operation, and especially interferences with the central organs, are known to affect the functions for a certain period of time. Still, it is hardly probable that the effect of operation is the determining factor in the case before us. The contrast between the proximate effects of the loss and the subsequent state of the animal is too striking and too uniform. Besides, there would be nothing to explain the graduation of phenomena in the animal kingdom: the fact, e.g., that in the frog—to say nothing of the mammals—a considerable period of time elapses before complete compensation is observable, whereas in the fishes recovery sets in at once. And lastly, there are numerous phenomena, drawn from all kinds of sources, which prove that injury or loss to the central parts, whether in man or in the animals, may within very wide limits be offset by the vicarious functioning of uninjured organs. We shall see presently that this law of functional substitution is indispensable, if we are to explain the reciprocal relations of the various cerebral areas. It is, then, only natural, in the absence of evidence to the contrary, that we should posit its validity in the present instance for the interrelations of the various parts of the brain. We may add that the general possibility of such vicarious function is inherent in the nature of the quadrigemina and thalami, as intermediate stations upon the direct lines of conduction between the peripheral organs and the cerebral cortex,—stations in which all the sensory paths, and a large proportion of the motor, are interrupted by the interpolation of neurone chains. Putting all these facts together, we arrive at the following genetic conclusions, as a general point of view from which the various phenomena observable in the vertebrate series may be classified and explained. At the lowest stages of brain development, the mesencephalic and diencephalic region—especially the former, since the diencephalon is as yet comparatively insignificant—appears as the principal central organ. Subordinate to this, on the one side, are oblongata and myel. Adjoining it, on the other, as an appendicular structure, is the prosencephalon; originally, we must suppose, an outcome of the separate development of the olfactorius. As we proceed upwards through the vertebrate series, further representations of the conduction paths brought together in the bigemina gradually make their appearance, as superior centres, in the prosencephalon. In proportion as the latter advances, the mesencephalon and the diencephalon—the latter conditioned in its own development upon the formation of the prosencephalon—take on the function of intermediate centres, where excitations from the periphery touch off complicated reflexes, and excitations from the prosencephalon evoke reactions depending upon a more extended colligation of impressions. Nevertheless, the possibility remains, up to the higher stages of development, that on the removal of the superior regulatory mechanisms the lower centres may gradually recover some measure of the autonomy of which at a lower level they were in complete possession. Hence it may well happen that in the normal interplay of the central organs,—so long, that is, as they stand under the dominance of the prosencephalic region.—these parts of the brain may have no other function than that of complex reflex centres ; but that in the absence of the higher regulatory organs they may once more assume the character of independent centres, whose co-operation involves the appearance of psychical functions.

We conclude, therefore, that this part of the brain possesses, under all circumstances, the importance of a centre whose office it is to bring into connexion the principal organs of sense and of movement. Such a view of its functions is, upon the whole, confirmed by the symptoms which ordinarily follow upon its direct removal or impairment. The most striking of these, upon the sensory side, is the *blindness* which, in mammals, in accordance with the course of the opticus paths, is correlated in particular with the pregemina, including the pregeniculum. Disturbances of movement appear, on the other hand, provided that the lesion does not extend beyond the quadrigemina, to be confined, at least in the mammals, to the muscles of the eyes ; the general muscular system of the body is unaffected.[1] If, however, the diencephalon is injured, the general motor derangement is very pronounced. It consists, where the injury is unilateral, in peculiar imperative movements, in which the animal, instead of going straight forwards, turns round in a circle. These *circus movements* (Reitbahnbewegung, mouvement de manège) are also observed after injury to other parts of the brain, more especially the crura and the cerebellar hemispheres, and after unilateral extirpation of the semicircular canals of the internal ear. In the lower veterbrates, e.g. the frog, the circus movements are invariably made towards the uninjured side. In the invertebrates, too, the principal ganglia behave, in this matter of motor disturbance and its direction, in precisely the same way as the mesencephalon of the lower vertebrates.[2] In the mammals, on the other hand, the rule is that movement is directed towards the injured side, if the anterior portion of the thalamus has been divided, towards the uninjured side, if the section has been made in its posterior portion. Abnormalities have also been observed in the tonicity of the muscles of the body, so that the animal when at rest is not extended, but bends upon itself, the direction of curvature corresponding to that of the circus movements.[3] These movements may take on various forms, according to the special conditions of the injury : they may appear as rolling movements about the longitudinal axis of the body, as ' clock hand ' movements, or finally as circus movements proper. They are, we may suppose, occasioned in all cases by an asymmetrical innervation, which however may itself be due to a number of causes : to unilateral increase

---

[1] BECHTEREW, in PFLÜGER'S *Arch. f. d. ges. Physiol.*, xxxiii., 413.
[2] STEINER, *Die Functionen des Centralnervensystems*, iii., 79 ff.
[3] SCHIFF, *Lehrbuch d. Physiol.*, ii., 343.

or decrease of motor innervation, or to the asymmetrical release of reflex movements connected with disturbances of sensitivity. Which of these conditions, or what combination of them, is actually at work cannot, at present, be certainly determined.

The operation never fails to set up this motor derangement. In the higher mammals, we find, further, symptoms of abrogation or diminution of cutaneous sensitivity upon the uninjured side of the body. Such symptoms are always ambiguous, and the results are correspondingly doubtful.[1] On the whole, however, if we look at the phenomena in their entirety, and take into consideration at the same time the defects observed shortly after removal of the prosencephalon and the known facts regarding the course of the conduction paths, we may conclude that the mesencephalic and diencephalic region constitutes, in all the higher vertebrates, an important intermediate station on the road from the deeper lying centres to the prosencephalon; a station for the release, on the one hand, of compound reflexes, more especially of reflexes to visual and auditory stimuli, in which the prosencephalon is not concerned; and, on the other, of centrifugal excitations from the cerebrum, whose components are here co-ordinated in such a way as best to subserve the needs of the organism. In view of the anatomical relations and of the results of experiments with partial extirpation, it is probable that the postgemina represent, in the main, intermediate stations for the acoustic area; the pregemina and pregenicula similar stations for the sense of sight; and the thalami proper stations for the extensive area of the sense of touch. We thus have, in this whole region, a group of nodal points for the function of all the sense departments (with the exception of smell) and of the movements correlated with them. It follows that the mesencephalon and diencephalon, in proportion to their degree of development as compared with that of the prosencephalon, are able between them, after the lapse of the prosencephalic functions, to undertake in their own right the unitary regulation of the processes of the animal life; although certain functions, conditioned exclusively upon the cerebrum, are of course permanently lost. This physiological status implies a concomitant development of psychical processes: the persistence of impressions of sense for a certain time after the cessation of stimulus, the formation of complex perceptions, mediated by associative processes, and the conduct of movements in accordance with impressions received in the more remote past. In other words, centres that originally subserved reflex action and the transmission of impulses have, under pressure of novel conditions, become transformed into independent centres of direction. They are still centres

---

[1] FERRIER, *Functions of the Brain*, 1886, 412. NOTHNAGEL was unable to discover any marked symptoms whatsoever, even after extensive lesions of the thalami. See VIRCHOW's *Archiv*, lviii., 429 and lxii., 203.

of the second order; but their lesser functional value, as compared with the higher centres whose substitutes they are, depends essentially upon the degree of development attained by these higher centres themselves.

For a long time, the physiology of the mesencephalic and diencephalic region suffered from a misconception. It was insistently held that the functions of these parts were not only analogous, but in the main actually equivalent throughout the vertebrate kingdom; so that, in particular, what held of the animals must also hold of man. The older method, of experiments with direct abrogation, was not competent to remove this error. The necessary change of view has been brought about, gradually, by extirpation experiments on the prosencephalon itself; experiments which, as we remarked above, have really attained in this way a different purpose from that upon which they were originally directed. Physiologists, from FLOURENS to GOLTZ, made these experiments with the primary intention of deriving from the resulting symptoms of abrogation a more exact knowledge of the function of the prosencephalon. But it became more and more evident—especially, as it happened, in the course of investigations pursued by GOLTZ and his pupils—that this direct end could be accomplished but very imperfectly, if at all, on account of the direct and indirect consequences that follow the operations, and that make the comparison of the injured with the normal animal anything rather than a problem in simple subtraction. At the same time, it became evident that all such experiments yield most important information regarding the functions of which the uninjured brain remnant is capable. Extirpation experiments are, therefore, still valued by the modern investigator, but they are valued for a different reason. They are not expected to reveal anything of moment concerning the functions of the parts destroyed, but rather to illustrate the possible functions of those that are left intact. It need, however, hardly be said, after the discussion in the text, that these functions are not to be identified forthright with those discharged by the same parts in the normal interplay of the organs. In this connexion, the differences that we find throughout the animal kingdom, the very differences that were formerly overlooked, are of great significance. First and foremost, the differences between the various vertebrate classes, but secondarily and within certain limits—despite the radically divergent position of the central organs, from the genetic point of view—the differences among the invertebrates as well, have in many instances shed light upon the far more complicated conditions obtaining in the brains of the higher mammals. The impulse to such comparison came in the first instance from morphology. On the side of physiology, it is the especial merit of J. STEINER to have shown, by his experiments on fishes and on the frog, supplemented by later work on reptiles and invertebrates, how extremely variable is the rôle assigned to the mesencephalon in the vertebrate series. Setting out from the spinal functions of Amphioxus, which, as we know, has no other central organ than the myel, STEINER has, further, attempted a general theory of the mesencephalic functions at large. But here, unfortunately, his foundation is uncertain, and the structure erected upon it still less secure. In the annelids, he says, the individual metameres and the corresponding terms in the series of ventral ganglia are all equivalent, so that any portion of the worm is, in its own right, just as capable of movement and, apparently, of sensation, as is the whole animal. Amphioxus is, now, to be regarded in the same way: its myel consists simply of a series of equivalent terms, not subordinated to any higher centre. Then, at the next stage, represented by the primitive fish, the shark, and at stages of progressive advance, represented by the other fishes, the myel is brought under the central superintendence of the mesencephalon, which henceforth remains, throughout the vertebrate series, the real directing centre: the prosencephalon is to be considered as merely supplementary. It is true that, in the mammals, the prosencephalon attains a marked preponderance; nevertheless, the mesencephalon and diencephalon contain the centres for the regulation of the whole system of bodily movements, and therefore still hold the part of the central organ proper. In this sense, STEINER defines a 'brain' as "the universal centre of movement, in connexion with the functions of at least one of the higher sensory nerves." The criterion of an 'universal centre of movement' consists, for him, in the occurrence of unilateral forced movements after injury to the one side of the organ. If, then, there is no part of the central organs at which these circus movements can be released, there cannot either be any unitary centre of direction within the nervous system; the entire central organ must consist of a number of equivalent metameres.[1] Now it is plain that the point of departure for all these theoretical considerations is furnished by the annelids. The bodily segments of these animals appear, when divided off, to represent independent vital units, every whit as capable of continued spontaneous movement as was the original, uninjured worm. The annelids, moreover, do not execute circus movements after removal of the dorsal ganglion of the one side. But the only inference that can be drawn from the latter fact is, surely, this: that the occurrence of forced movements is, in all probability, not an universal criterion of the presence of a directing centre from which lower centres are controlled. And further: we have no right to assume the complete functional independence and equivalence of all the terms in the series of ventral ganglia, unless the individual segments move just as independently while they are still connected with the total annelid body as they do after their separation. This, however, is not the case; in the uninjured animal all the metameres move in exact co-ordination with one another. We must, therefore, conclude that the whole chain of ganglia normally functions as an unitary system, of which, if we may judge from the anatomical relations, the dorsal ganglion is the directive centre. In just the same way the myel in Amphioxus is apparently controlled by its most anterior portion as in some sort the equivalent of the brain of the craniota (see p. 252 above). The word 'brain' is, in the first instance, an expression taken over by science from popular parlance, and on that account is, as ordinarily employed, extremely difficult of definition. If we are, nevertheless, to make the attempt, and are not to break with the general application of the term, we must say that the vertebrate brain is not a separate central organ, but rather the complex of all those central organs which share in the direction of the animal functions. In this sense, oblongata, mesencephalon and diencephalon, prosencephalon and cerebellum have equal claims to the name. If, on the other hand, we are to restrict the term 'brain' specifically to the central parts that are able in their own right to maintain the animal life—though perhaps on a reduced footing—after the removal of the rest, then the oblongata still has, at any rate, as good a claim as the mesencephalon and diencephalon. The point is that the brain, taken as a whole, is not *a* centre, but a complex of centres, and of centres so related to one another that, if one of

---

[1] STEINER, *op. cit.*, ii., 106; iii., 126; iv., 54 ff.

them is lost, a portion of its functions can, as a general rule, be taken over by another.

Experiments on completely decerebrised animals, especially the higher mammals, are of extreme importance, not only for the functions of the mesencephalic and diencephalic region, but also for the more general question of the functional representation of higher by lower centres. We therefore append here a somewhat detailed account of the phenomena observed by GOLTZ in the decerebrised dog that, of all operated on by him, longest survived the operation.[1] The animal was deprived of its left hemisphere in two experiments, performed on the 27th of June and the 13th of November, 1889; the entire right hemisphere was removed on the 17th of June, 1890. It was killed, with a view to *post mortem* examination, on the 31st of December, 1891. The general result of the autopsy was confirmatory; the cerebral hemispheres had been completely done away with, in part directly by the operations, in part indirectly by subsequent softening of the tissue. The animal had thus lived for more than eighteen months after the final operation. Immediately afterwards, it had been entirely motionless; but the capacity of spontaneous movement returned as early as the third day. The dog moved to and fro in the room, and was able to avoid obstacles laid in its way, without having first run against them. Placed on a smooth floor, it would slip up, but recover itself at once and of its own accord. If its toes were forced into an unnatural position, it corrected the displacement immediately as it began to walk, and stepped with the sole of the foot in the normal way. It lifted its leg, without falling in, from a hole that had been prepared for the purpose of the experiment. It once sustained an accidental injury to one hind paw, and thereafter, until the wound was healed, held up the injured leg in walking, precisely as a normal dog would do. The sense of touch was blunted; but the animal reacted to tactual stimuli of some intensity, though the localisation of the point stimulated remained, it is true, fairly uncertain. If, e.g., the left hind foot were seized, it would snap to the left, but generally in the air, without reaching the hand that held it. The auditory sensitivity was also greatly reduced; nevertheless, the animal could be aroused from sleep by intensive sound impressions. Gustatory stimuli were sensed. Meat dipped in milk and held before its mouth was seized and chewed up; meat dipped in a solution of quinine was taken, but spat out again, with wry movements of the mouth. The sense of smell was, of course, entirely abrogated: the olfactory nerves had been destroyed in the operations. At first, therefore, the dog took nourishment only when food was placed in its mouth. Later on, it became accustomed to seize and gulp down bits of meat, and to drink milk, as soon as its muzzle was brought in contact with them. It ate and drank of the solid and liquid food thus offered until its appetite was satisfied; it would then lie down and go to sleep. The functions of the sense of sight were shown—in addition to the avoidance of obstacles, mentioned above—in the reaction of the pupils to light stimuli. On the other hand, the animal was wholly insensitive to threatening gestures and movements, and to other animals presented for its notice. Consistently with this behaviour, it remained till its last day dull and apathetic. There was no question of any real 'cognition' and 'recognition' of the objects about it. The only expressions of feeling were snarling and biting when intensive stimulation was applied to the skin, and a tendency to restlessness under the influence of hunger. Nevertheless, the avoidance of

[1] GOLTZ, in PFLÜGER'S *Arch. f. d. ges. Physiol.*, li., 520 ff.

obstacles shows an adaptation of movement to the varying conditions of sense impressions; and the same fact is brought out still more clearly in the following experiment. Two long boards were put together to form a blind passage-way, about twice as long as the animal itself, and so narrow that it could not turn round. When the dog was introduced into this passage-way, it first walked to the farther end, and ran against the wall. For some time, it reared up vainly against this obstacle; but presently it began to back out, and finally, by this crablike movement, reached the open. Of all experiments on decerebrised animals, this is, without doubt, the experiment whose result seems to approach most nearly to what is termed an 'expression of intelligence.'. Nevertheless, it is plain that in this case, as in the others, the adaptation of the reacting movements to the sensory stimuli are still confined within limits where it is out of place to speak of any real 'reflection '—of a choice between different possibilities. The symptoms themselves, considered solely by themselves, might, naturally, be interpreted as voluntary actions. But it is another question whether the whole context in which the phenomena appeared permits of such an interpretation. And this question must, surely, be answered in the negative, for the same reason that we decline, e.g., to ascribe the avoidance of obstacles to a true 'cognition' of the objects,—the cognition in this instance being disproved by other symptoms. If, however, we rule out expressions of intelligence and voluntary actions, in the strict meaning of those terms, this attitude must not, of course, be construed as a denial that the actions of the decerebrised animal are, in part, *conscious* processes. On the contrary: it must be regarded as, at the least, extremely probable that they may be interpreted as conscious and, in this sense, not merely as purely mechanical reflexes. We cannot, however, enter upon this question with any fulness until we come to our psychological discussion of the idea of 'consciousness' (cf. Part V., Ch. xviii., below).

(b)—*Functions of the Mesencephalon and Diencephalon in Man*

In man, and indeed in all the other primates, who in this regard stand upon practically the same level as man, the preponderance of the prosencephalon, which becomes the more marked the higher we ascend in the vertebrate series, has reached a limit where the centres of mid brain and 'tween brain retain least of their original relative independence. This statement is justified both by the relations of the conduction paths and by the nature of the disturbances produced by pathological defects. We cannot, it is true,— and the reasons are obvious,—expect to find human cases that shall reproduce the conditions of total extirpation of the prosencephalon, with permanent retention of function in the middle brain regions. But in cases of restricted lesion of the quadrigemina and thalami, it would seem that a restitution of functions by way of vicarious representation in co-ordinated or superior parts may occur very extensively in the human brain. At the same time, the close connexion of the pregemina with the visual functions is evidenced by the derangement of ocular movements that accompanies injury to these parts; while disturbances of visual sensitivity in man appear, for the most part, only when the geniculum is involved. In individual cases—and the result accords with what we know of the course of the conduction paths—auditory disturbances have been observed after injury to the postgemina. Lesions of the thalami, as might, again, be expected from the anatomical facts and from the results of experiments on animals, are followed by anæsthesia or by motor disturbances or by both combined. Sometimes, it is true, affections of the thalami run their course without any sign of disturbance whatsoever :[1] a fact that testifies to the wide range of vicarious functioning possible, in this particular instance, within the human brain, and that constitutes a marked quantitative difference between man and the animals, in which the phenomena of abrogation are much more intensive. A second and still more striking difference is this : that the symptoms which in experiments on animals, from the fishes up to the mammals, are set up with the greatest uniformity by unilateral lesions of this area—the imperative circular movements—are represented in man, at the best, only by such reduced and vestigial forms as a permanent deflection of the eyes or an unilateral execution of mimetic movements.[2] The determining factors in this result are apparently two : on the one hand, the *voluntary* suppression of the symptoms, and, on the other, the greater scope of the automatic regulations and functional substitutions that, in the human brain, counteract the disturbances in question. Both factors indicate that, while the basal functions of this region of the human brain correspond to those discharged by the same region throughout the animal series, still its relative importance, as compared with the superior centres, has now become less. Compound reflex centres for the principal sense departments, sight, hearing and touch ; and comprehensive regulatory centres for the motor excitations issuing from the higher parts of the brain : these the mesencephalon and diencephalon have remained. But other regulatory mechanisms, and the independent processes of release within the prosencephalon, have increased in importance alongside of them : so that their assumption in man of such psychical function as has been observed to persist in the dog after removal of the prosencephalic parts can hardly be regarded as probable.

(c)—*Striatum and Lenticula*

Striatum and lenticula belong, morphologically, to the prosencephalon (pp. 128 f.). But little is known of their function. They appear, however, to be cortical areas, sunk into the substance of the hemisphere, and specifically correlated with the mesencephalic and diencephalic ganglia. This view is suggested by the extent of their fibre connexions, more especially with the thalami (Fig. 74, p. 179). It is borne out, further, by the phenomena observed in experiments on animals, and in cases of lesion in

---

[1] NOTHNAGEL, *Topische Diagnostik*, 204 ff. VON MONAKOW, *Gehirnpathologie*, 586 ff.
[2] WERNICKE, *Lehrbuch der Gehirnkrankheiten*, i., 370.

man, in which these structures are involved. The phenomena consist always of paralytic symptoms or, when excitatory influences are at work, of exaggeration of movement. Here again, however, and particularly in the case of man, the phenomena of abrogation are most pronounced when the lesion has been rapidly produced : slow growing tumours may, under certain circumstances, run their course without giving rise to any symptom whatever. NOTHNAGEL found, further, that mechanical or chemical stimulation of the striatum of the rabbit occasioned hurried running movements.[1] MAGENDIE observed the same result after complete removal of the striatum.[2] Anæsthesia, on the contrary, does not appear to be a consequence of injury to these structures.[3] For the rest, the intensive disturbances that ordinarily follow upon sudden lesions of the striatum are not beyond suspicion; they may be due to implication of the pyramidal paths ascending in the capsula to the cerebral cortex. Besides these relations to the mid brain and 'tween brain, the anatomical facts indicate a further connexion with the cerebellum. As a matter of fact, atrophy of the striatum, and especially of the lenticula, has been observed in cases of congenital failure of the cerebellum.[4]

§ 5. Functions of the Cerebellum

The functions of the cerebellum form one of the most obscure chapters in the physiology of the central organs. The obscurity is intelligible, when we remember the extensive connexions of the cerebellum with numerous other central parts,—with the oblongata, with the mesencephalon and diencephalon, and above all with the cerebral cortex. For, on the one hand, these connexions make it difficult to determine whether destruction of the other brain centres involves abrogation of the corresponding cerebellar functions. And, on the other, we are left equally in doubt whether the disturbances observed in cases of lesion or defect of the cerebellum are not due, in part at least, to the indirect implication of other parts of the brain with which it stands in connexion. To these is added the further difficulty, that the cerebellar derangements appear to be peculiarly easy of compensation by the enhancement or substitution of function in other central parts. We have, therefore, as many reasons to overestimate as we have to underestimate the importance of this organ; and our uncertainty is not a little increased by the ambiguity of symptoms, which characterises all the phenomena of central abrogation, but is especially marked in this particular case.

[1] NOTHNAGEL, in VIRCHOW'S *Archiv*, lvii., 209.
[2] MAGENDE, *Leçons sur les fonctions du système nerveux*, i., 280. Cf. also SCHIFF *Lehrbuch d. Physiol.*, i., 340.
[3] NOTHNAGEL,*Topische Diagnostik*, 262 ff. VON MONAKOW, *Gehirnpathologie*, 584.
[4] FLECHSIG, *Plan des menschl. Gehirns*, 41.

These symptoms themselves consist, for the most part, in *motor* disturbances. Complete extirpation of the cerebellum in animals renders all movements vacillating and uncertain, staggering or tremulous, though the influence of the will upon the individual muscle groups is not destroyed. Transsection of various parts of the cerebellum, as well as of the cerebellar peduncles,—whose radiations are, for that matter, involved in all deepgoing injuries to the organ,—is ordinarily followed by unilateral motor derangement. If the section passes through the most anterior portion of the vermis, the animals fall forwards; in spontaneous movements, the body is bent over anteriorly, always ready to fall and fall again. If it passes through the posterior portion of the vermis, the body is bent backwards, and there is a tendency to backward movements. If the one pileum is injured or removed, the animal falls towards the opposite side, owing to unilateral contraction of the corresponding muscles; violent movements of rotation about the long axis of the body are apt to follow. There occur also, at the moment of operation, convulsive movements of the eyes, usually succeeded by a permanent deflection. These abrogation symptoms agree, upon the whole, with the phenomena of stimulation observed with electrical excitation of various parts of the cerebellar cortex. Both alike are, without exception, same-sided, in contradistinction to the consequences of cerebral injury, which appear upon the opposite side of the body. The stimulation phenomena consist in spasmodic movements of the head, the vertebral column, and the eyes.[1]

As regards man, clinical experience is in accord with the results of the observations on animals. Motor disturbances are, again, the most constant symptom. They consist, chiefly, in an uncertain and vacillating gait, sometimes also in similar movements of the head and eyes. The arms appear to be less seriously involved; and it is but seldom that we observe, in man, those violent rotatory movements that, in the animals, accompany unilateral lesions of the pilea or the medipeduncles. For the rest, the motor disturbances in man are most intensive when the vermis is the seat of injury; while affections of the pileum of either side, especially if the change is merely local, may run their course without symptoms of any kind. Serious derangement occurs, seemingly, only with complete functional disability of the pilea, or in the rare cases of atrophy of the entire organ. Under such circumstances, however, the symptoms are not confined to motor dis-

---

[1] LUCIANI, *Il cerveletto, nuovi studi*, 1891, 49. The results of these experimental investigations, the most detailed made upon the cerebellum, serve in general to confirm the statements of NOTHNAGEL (VIRCHOW'S *Archiv*, lxviii., 33), FERRIER (*Functions of the Brain*, 174), and BECHTEREW (PFLÜGER's *Arch. f. d. ges. Physiol.*, xxxix., 362), as well as the older observations of SCHIFF (*Lehrbuch d. Physiol.*, i., 353). The only point upon which there is some divergence of opinion concerns the direction of the imperative movements set up by unilateral transsections. The differences are probably due to the fact that the cerebellar peduncles were cut at different places.

turbances; they become exceedingly complicated, and interpretation is correspondingly difficult.[1] Disturbances of cutaneous sensibility do not appear to result from affections that remain limited to the cerebellum, not even from total atrophy of the organ. On the other hand, a characteristic subjective symptom, more frequently connected with disease of the human cerebellum than with other central disorders, is the *dizziness* that accompanies the motor disturbances. It is therefore probable that the attacks of dizziness induced in the healthy subject by the passage of a strong galvanic current through the occiput are due, in part at least, to its influence upon the cerebellum.[3] And for the same reason we may suspect that this organ is involved in the dizziness produced by certain toxic agencies.[4] Now there are, in general, two conditions under which the phenomena of dizziness may be manifested: first, the functional derangement of certain *peripheral* sensory apparatus, whose impressions mediate the arousal of sensations that generate the idea of the static equilibrium of the body during rest and motion; and, secondly, such functional disorders of *central* areas as are in any way calculated to alter the normal relation subsisting between sense impressions and movements or ideas of movement. We shall presently become familiar with a sensory apparatus of the former kind in the ampullæ and canals of the labyrinth of the ear.[5] On the other hand, we appear to have in the cerebellum not the sole, but certainly the most frequent central seat of symptoms of dizziness. When we remember how near together are the labyrinth of the ear and this central organ, we can readily understand that the two forms of disturbance of equilibrium are difficult to discriminate. Besides, we have every reason to believe that they are functionally connected: the vestibular nerve, that supplies the vestibule and canals with sensory fibres, sends a large number of representatives to the cerebellum.[6] These relations to the vestibular division of the labyrinth are, perhaps, our best means of accounting for the influence of the cerebellum

---

[1] LUCIANI, *op. cit.* 32. LADAME, *Hirngeschwülste*, 93. WERNICKE, *Gehirnkrankheiten*, iii., 353. VON MONAKOW, *Gehirnpathologie*, 624.

[2] In a case in whch the cerebellum and pons were entirely lacking, voluntary movements were possible, but there was pronounced muscular weakness; the patient frequently fell, and her intelligence was extremely defective (LONGET, *Anatomie et physiologie du système nerveux*, i., 764). Observations by KIRCHHOFF, on certain cases of atrophy and sclerosis of the cerebellum, confirm this account upon all essential points (*Archiv f. Psychiatrie*, xii., 647 ff). In a case of HITZIG's, where, it is true, atrophy was only partial, the intelligence was affected, but there was no disturbance of movement. HITZIG himself supposes that the symptoms indicate a large measure of vicarious functioning, especially by parts of the cerebrum (*ibid.*, xv., 266 ff.).

[3] PURKINJE, in KUST's *Magazin d. Heilkunde*, xxiii., 1827, 297. HITZIG, *Das Gehirn*, 196 ff. *Der Schwindel*, 1898 (off-printed from NOTHNAGEL's *Pathologie*, ix.), 36 ff.

[4] FLOURENS, LUSSANA and RENZI also observed effusion of blood in the cerebellum as a result of intensive alcoholic poisoning; see RENZI, in SCHMIDT's *Jahrbuch*, cxxiv., 158.

[5] See Part III., Ch. xiii.

[6] BECHTEREW, *Die Leitungsbahnen im Gehirn und Rückenmark*, 361.

upon bodily movements. We know that all the other sense departments, and more especially those that mediate our spatial apprehension of sensory impressions, the senses of sight and touch, find abundant representation in it. And we find that where dizziness is set up by the action of definitely demonstrable subjective or objective causes, these may ordinarily be traced back to one general condition: disturbance of the normal correlation of sense impressions and bodily movements. Again, however, this disturbance may, in the individual case, be brought about, centrally and peripherally, in a great variety of ways. A man may be made dizzy by walking on the ice, if he is not accustomed to it. The uncertainty of vision that goes with amblyopia or strabismus, or that may be induced in a normal-sighted person by covering the one eye, is not infrequently attended by dizziness. The symptoms are still more evident in the walking movements of patients whose tactual sensations are dulled or destroyed by a degeneration of the dorsal columns of the myel. In such cases, the resistance of the ground is not sensed in the accustomed way: the patients lose their equilibrium; they stagger, and try to save themselves from a fall by balancing with the arms.[1] These phenomena show, at the same time, the indispensableness of the coordination of sense impression and movement for the correct execution not only of involuntary, but also of voluntary movements. In the latter, too, it is as a rule only the end to be attained that is clearly conscious; the means whereby this end is reached are entrusted to the automatic working of a motor mechanism, where movement interlocks with movement in the right order and to the right purpose. Each separate act in a compound voluntary action reveals, accordingly, a precise adaptation to the impressions that we receive from our own body and from external objects. But since the voluntary action is directed exclusively upon the end to be attained, the sense impressions that regulate the movements do not, ordinarily, take any part in the idea of movement. Even the sudden lapse of the regulatory impression is, in most instances, perceived only indirectly, by way of the consequent motor disturbance and the subjective phenomena dependent upon it.

Disturbances of movement due to central causes may now, in general, be brought about in four different ways. They may (1) be paralytic phenomena, i.e. they may be occasioned by a partial abrogation of voluntary movements. They may (2) appear as purely anæsthetic symptoms. They may (3) consist of disturbances of motor co-ordination. Or they may (4) result from disturbance of the normal relation obtaining between sensations and the movements depending upon them. The first of these possibilities is ruled out at once, since paralytic symptoms do not occur after removal

[1] VON LEYDEN and GOLDSCHEIDER, *Die Erkrankungen des Rückenmarks.* In NOTHNAGEL's *Handbuch d. Pathologie,* x., 149.

of the cerebellum or of separate parts of it; besides, dizziness is never observed in the train of purely motor disabilities. The second seems to promise better. Indeed, it has to a certain extent found acceptance; some authors have conjectured that the cerebellum is an organ of what is termed the 'muscular sense.'[1] But this view can hardly be reconciled with the fact that in cases of atrophy of the cerebellum in man, and after total extirpation of the organ in animals, the capacity of active movements of locomotion is still retained; the movements may be vacillating and uncertain, but they nevertheless allow us to posit a certain degree of sensation in the locomotor muscles. The abrogation of other sensations is equally out of the question. The third interpretation of the cerebellum, as centre of motor co-ordination, was first put forward by FLOURENS,[2] whose views have held their own, down to the most recent times, among physiologists and clinicians. But, first, this definition is too indeterminate to characterise the specific form of co-ordination mediated by the cerebellum. There is no single central motor area, from the myel upwards, that is not the seat of some sort of motor co-ordination. Secondly, the phenomena of dizziness also tell against FLOURENS' interpretation. They indicate that some kind of sensory disturbance is always involved along with the motor. We are thus forced to the conclusion that the fourth of the above hypotheses is the most probable: the hypothesis that inhibition of function in the cerebellum interferes with the action of those *sensory impressions* that exercise a direct regulatory influence upon the *motor innervation* proceeding from the cerebrum.

The acceptance of this hypothesis removes various difficulties. Thus, we can explain at once how it comes about that the disturbances produced by lesions of the cerebellum resemble the symptoms due to partial anæsthesia, and yet differ from them on the important point that abrogation of sensations never makes its appearance among the cerebellar phenomena. Where all conscious sensations persist, the only impressions that can be supposed to lapse are those that act upon movement directly and without previous translation into conscious sensations. Voluntary movements as such are as little affected as sensations; even after complete destruction of the cerebellum, the will retains its right of control over each individual muscle. This explains, again, how it is that the disturbances set up by injury to the cerebellum may gradually be compensated. Compensation takes place in this way, that the movements are regulated afresh by the conscious sensations that persist unimpaired. But a certain clumsiness and uncertainty never disappear. It is evident, as one watches, that the

---

[1] LUSSANA, *Journal de la physiol.*, v., 418; vi., 169. LUSSANA and LEMOIGNE, *Fisiologia dei centri nervosi*, 1871, ii., 219.
[2] FLOURENS, *Recherches expérimentales*, 2nd ed., 28.

movements must always proceed from a sort of reflection. The immediacy and certainty of movement shown by the uninjured animal are either lost or, if they may in some measure be regained, must be acquired slowly and gradually, as the result of a long continued course of renewed practice. Here too, therefore, the principle of the manifold representation of the bodily organs in the brain is seen in operation. The cerebellum appears to be intended for the *direct regulation of voluntary movements by sense impressions*. If this hypothesis be correct, it will, accordingly, be the central organ in which the bodily movements incited from the cerebrum are brought into harmony with the position of the animal body in space. This conception agrees sufficiently well with our anatomical knowledge of the course of the lines of conduction, incoming and outgoing. In the postpeduncles the cerebellum receives a representation of the general sensory path, reinforced, in all probability, by fibres from the optic nerve and the most anterior sensory cranial nerves which run in the valvula and the prepeduncles. Its connexion anteriorly is effected by the prepeduncles and medipeduncles, by which it is united partly to the anterior brain ganglia, partly to the most diverse regions of the cerebral cortex.[1] Finally, the extensive representations of the auditory nerve in the cerebellum (Fig. 77, p. 183) may be brought under the same point of view. For if the cerebellum deflects at all that sensory secondary path whose office it is to conduct impressions that influence voluntary movement directly, and not indirectly, by way of conscious sensations, then we shall certainly expect to find that this same path contains a representation of the eighth cranial nerve. The acusticus is precisely the sensory nerve that gives certain objective sense impressions a specific relation to movement; our movements adapt themselves involuntarily, in a corresponding rhythm, to rhythmical impressions of sound.

The question of the functions of the cerebellum cannot be answered, at the present time, with any degree of finality. The one point upon which physiologists are fairly unanimous is that this organ is set off in relative independence, anatomically and functionally, from the other parts of the central organ, and more especially from the cerebrum: so that no single function—in particular, therefore, neither sensation nor movement—is wholly abrogated even after its complete elimination, though profound derangements are produced in the co-ordinations of function. But this very fact of relative independence, which in man and the higher animals must be connected with a position of high functional importance,—a position attested, in any case, by the structure and volume

---

[1] In view of the close connexion of the olives with the conduction paths of the cerebellum (see pp. 170 ff.), it is readily intelligible that injury to these centres should produce motor disturbances akin to those set up by injury to the cerebellum itself. Such disturbances have, as a matter of fact, been observed by BECHTEREW (PFLÜGER's *Arch. f. d. ges. Physiol.*, xxx., 257). BECHTEREW found, further, that similar disturbances of equilibrium uniformly result from injury to the walls of the diacele (*ibid.*, xxxi., 479).

of the organ—renders the exact determination of the nature of the 'co-ordinations' or 'regulations' effected by the cerebellum a matter of extreme difficulty; and it is not altogether surprising that a good many of the physiologies are still satisfied to stop short at these indefinite terms,—terms that apply more or less to every central organ, and are therefore tolerably non-committal in the particular case. This position has been attacked, and rightly attacked, by LUCIANI. Aiming from the first at a definiteness of statement that should match the preceding indefiniteness, LUCIANI undertook to analyse the phenomena, so far as possible, along all their various lines, and thus to refer them to distinct groups of symptoms. He has thus been led to distinguish three principal symptoms of abrogation, which he regards as characteristic of cerebellar lesions: *asthenia, atony* and *astasia*. The movements lack their normal energy (asthenia); the tonus of the muscles is lowered (atony); and the movements are uncertain and incoherent (astasia).[1] It has been objected, with some justice, to this characterisation, that the symptoms which it discriminates are, in part at least, closely interconnected: atony and asthenia, e.g., always occur together.[2] But if the three terms are considered simply as collective expressions for certain partial states, they may be accepted as really denoting the essential features of the cerebellar symptoms. For the interpretation of the phenomena, however, the emphasis must fall, without any question, upon that member of the triad which is at once the most characteristic and also, unfortunately, the most complicated, upon 'astasia.' LUCIANI seems here, in some measure, to have missed the true perspective; he lays most weight upon the first two symptoms,—which, no doubt, admit of a simpler interpretation,—asthenia and atony. As a result of this mistake, he is inclined to regard the cerebellum as primarily an apparatus for the production of nervous force, an 'auxiliary' or 'intensificatory system' for the whole cerebrospinal organ, which is not the seat of any specific or peculiar functions, but reinforces the functional activity of the entire nervous system. In support of this view, he adduces the *trophic* disturbances that appear, in course of time, more especially after complete extirpation of the cerebellum, and that ordinarily take the form of muscular atrophy, cutaneous inflammations, decubitus, etc. Now these disturbances, as well as the striking lack of motor energy that perhaps stands in a certain relation to them, are unquestionably very important symptoms. But the possibility still remains that the 'atony' and 'astasia' of movement are interconnected phenomena, in which a part is played by the influence of sensory impressions. We saw, when we were discussing the myel, that the phenomena of tonus are straitly conditioned upon the continued effect of such impressions (p. 93). And trophic disturbances, of the kind observed after extirpation of the cerebellum, appear in all cases of permanent derangement of innervation; they result from the disability of sensory as well as of motor nerves; and they appear always to involve the co-operation of direct trophic influences, exerted by the nerve centres, and of indirect, which have their source in the abrogation of functions. LUCIANI lays special stress upon the fact, established by his observations, that dogs whose cerebellum has been destroyed are still able, when thrown into the water, to make the normal movements of swimming. But this experiment merely confirms, in a very complete way, the fact that all cutaneous impressions can be sensed, and all locomotor movements voluntarily

---

[1] LUCIANI, *Il cerveletto*, Germ. trans., 282.
[2] FERRIER, in *Brain*. xvii., 1894, 1 ff.

performed, without assistance from the cerebellum. Swimming is precisely the form of movement that may, under certain circumstances, bring into action a continuous voluntary regulation, compensating any inco-ordinations that have arisen involuntarily, for the reason that an intermission of movement means in its case the danger of drowning. The animal that constantly staggers as it attempts to walk or run is, in swimming, compelled at every movement to maintain itself above water by a maximal effort of will.

The view here taken of the cerebellar functions is in all essential points the same as that developed by the author in the first edition of this work.[1] It finds striking confirmation in the statements made by KAHLER and PICK, from the pathological standpoint, concerning the relation of other forms of 'ataxia,' as it is termed, to the cerebellar symptoms.[2] HITZIG, too, in his interpretation of cerebellar dizziness, seems to take up a very similar position.[3] In any attempt at explanation of this symptom, and, indeed, of the abrogation phenomena at large, especial attention must, in the author's opinion, be paid to the two facts brought out just now : that, in the case of voluntary impulses proceeding from the cerebrum, the individual terms in the series of purposive co-ordinations and regulations of the movements always succeed one another, under ordinary conditions, in independence of the will, i.e. automatically ; and that they must always, on the other hand, take their direction from the sensory impressions received by the organism.

The impressions conveyed to the central organs may, according to circumstances, be clearly or obscurely conscious,—may, in many instances, fail to come to consciousness at all. But, at any rate, it is not in consciousness that they are transformed into the motor impulses whose direction they determine. From this point of view we might, perhaps, characterise the cerebellum outright as an auxiliary organ which relieves the cerebrum of a large number of secondary functions : functions that were originally practised under the continuous control of the will, and that in consequence can always be partially resumed by the cerebrum itself. As for the first stage of practice, it may have occurred here, as in many other cases, either in the course of the individual lifetime or in the previous life history of the species, which has left its permanent traces, if anywhere, certainly in the organisation of the central parts. To ascribe to the cerebellum itself any share in conscious functions, or to endow it, as some have done, with a separate consciousness of the second order, a 'subconsciousness' is, as in the light of these arguments it seems to the author, entirely unwarranted. For the fact before us is that the cerebellum has developed into a centre of sensorimotor regulation, and that in the course of this development the individual co-ordinations of the separate acts of movement with the impressions of sense, all purposive and all subordinate to the ultimate end of the voluntary action, have gradually been withdrawn from consciousness. And there is, upon the whole, only one way in which this process can be envisaged : we must suppose that, under the influence of definitely directed cerebral innervations, there has developed a central mechanism, automatic in function, whose office it is to transmit the first, and only the first, discharging impulses to an auxiliary centre ; and that this auxiliary centre is endowed with self-regulating apparatus, again

---

[1] Edition of 1874, 220.
[2] KAHLER and PICK, *Beiträge zur Pathol. u. pathol. Anat. d. Centralnervensystems*, 1879, 58.
[3] HITZIG, *Der Schwindel*, 42 ff.

automatic in function, which adapt each several movement to the sense impressions coming in at the particular moment. These impressions may, of course, either come to consciousness by the way or remain unconscious: the former, if the conditions favour their special conduction to the sensory centre, the latter, if they are against it, or if the conduction is somewhere inhibited: for the self-regulations as such the matter is indifferent. On the other hand, it may very well happen, as a consequence of the direct conveyance of sensations to the cerebrum and of its response to them, that disturbances in the cerebellar mechanism of the sensorimotor self-regulations are presently compensated. Such compensation will, in particular, always be possible where the lesions are simply partial, so that a new course of practice may be entered upon and novel co-ordinations established. Where, on the contrary, the entire cerebellum is thrown out, a large draft upon the cerebral functions will suffice to hold the disturbances in check and so to mitigate the symptoms: but we can, it is true, expect nothing more.

We suppose, then, that these self-regulations of the voluntary movements are in some way mediated by the cerebellum. If, now, we are asked to give an account of them in detail, we must reply that the question is very difficult to answer, all the more since there is still much obscurity surrounding the directions and terminations of the conduction paths that meet within the organ. The anatomical relations suggest, and we may accept the suggestion as a provisional hypothesis, that the cerebellum, on the one hand, receives centripetal paths, derived from every sensitive portion of the body, and, on the other, sends out intracentral (as regards the organ itself, centrifugal) paths to every centromotor region of the cerebral cortex. We may imagine, accordingly, that the sensory components functioning in a movement, more especially sensations of touch and movement, are in the cerebellum united into a single resultant; and that this is then conducted onwards to the cerebral cortex, and makes connexion with the centromotor processes of discharge which are there in course. Thus, the regular sequence of walking movements is at every stage dependent upon the condition that the sensory impressions produced at each step by the movement itself are repeated in uniform succession. Suppose, now, that such a rhythmical sequence is summated to form a resultant which connects automatically with the voluntary impulses; and suppose that it remains unchanged so long as its components persist without change, while it varies at once when and as its components vary. We should then have, physiologically, a mechanism of self-regulation which at one and the same time reinforces and relieves the centromotor functions of the cerebral centres; and we should be able, psychologically, to explain by appeal to it the automatic, unconscious character of these self-regulations of our movements, which still leaves room for voluntary corrections and novel courses of practice.[1]

Over and above its influence upon the bodily movements,—of whose reality there can be no doubt, however various may be the interpretations put upon it,—the cerebellum has at times been accredited with functions of an entirely different order. Thus, the disturbances of intelligence observed in cases where the organ is lacking, combined perhaps with the anatomical fact that in the medipeduncles the cerebellum has extensive connexions with the prosencephalon, has persuaded several authors to attribute to it a share in what are called

---

[1] Cf. the discussion of the voluntary actions, Part IV., Ch. xvii.

the 'intellectual' functions. Apart, however, from these isolated observations, which may very probably be explained by concomitant affections of other parts of the brain, the hypothesis has no facts that are at all definite to support it. The view held by GALL and his pupils, that the cerebellum stands in relation to the sexual functions, is hardly held by any physiologist at the present day. The uncritical way in which GALL himself, and still more the phrenologists who followed him,—COMBE, for instance,—heaped together quotations from older authors, records of cases that had not been properly investigated, and observations in which the suspicion of self-delusion forces itself irresistibly upon the reader,—the whole forming a mass of evidential matter that should be impressive solely by its bulk,—would of itself forbid our devoting any attention to their writings, even if we did not find upon every page the mark of inveterate prepossession.[1] It should be mentioned, on the other side, that, now and again, observers who cannot be accused of any similar prejudice, men like R. WAGNER[2] and LUSSANA,[3] have regarded as possible this relation of the cerebellum to the sexual functions; though their standpoint, in making this admission, has generally been that the phrenological hypothesis cannot be certainly refuted. But this negative instance does not, of course, furnish any valid argument; and the general uncertainty of our knowledge of the organ necessarily implies that conjectures regarding its functions, of whatever nature they may be, cannot easily be met by apodeictic proof of the contrary. This does not mean, however, that they have become anything more than mere conjectures.[4] Moreover, the argument from the indemonstrability of the opposite can be rebutted, in the present case, by a sufficient number of positive instances, both experimental and pathological. LUCIANI was able entirely to extirpate the cerebellum in dogs without producing a disturbance of the sexual impulse; in many cases he observed an actual enhancement of the sexual phenomena.[5] The statistics of cerebellar tumours in man have, also, failed to yield the slightest confirmation of the phrenologists' view.[6] Finally, the symptomatology of cerebellar affections, so far as it is given objectively, on the ground of observations, affords no hint of sexual reference.[7]

§ 6. Functions of the Cerebral Hemispheres

(a)—*Phenomena of Abrogation after Partial Destruction of the Prosencephalon*

Our knowledge of the functions of mesencephalon and diencephalon is, it will be remembered, mainly derived from observations of the psychophysical activities left intact after removal of the prosencephalon (pp. 259 ff.). These same observations may, of course, be turned to account for a

---

[1] GALL, *Anatomie et physiologie du système nerveux*, iii., 1818, 85. COMBE, *On the functions of the cerebellum*, 1838.

[2] R. WAGNER, *Göttinger Nachrichten*, 1860, 32.

[3] LUSSANA, *Journal de la physiologie*, v., 140.

[4] On phrenology in general, see below, § 6.

[5] LUCIANI, *Il cerveletto*, Germ. trans., 198. Cf. also FERRIER, *Functions of the Brain*, 178.

[6] LADAME, *Hirngeschwülste*, 99.

[7] Cf., e.g., NOTHNAGEL, *Topische Diagnostik*, 78 ff. VON MONAKOW, *Gehirnpathologie*, 635 ff.

theory of the functions of the cerebral hemispheres themselves. Indeed, the results have, as a matter of fact, been applied more often to this than to the former purpose. It is clear, however, that the positive judgment of the persistence of certain activities is more definite and reliable than the negative judgment of their disappearance. Moreover, the prosencephalon is, obviously, far more seriously affected than are the lower lying brain centres by the indirect consequences of operation: whether these are the immediate disturbances produced by the diffusion of excitatory or inhibitory effects, or phenomena of a more gradual growth, changes wrought by compensation and substitution. In view of these facts, the symptoms of abrogation observed with defects of certain parts of the cerebral hemispheres cannot be accepted, without further examination, as the basis of inference regarding the functions of the parts in question. Physiological experiment and pathological observation show, both alike, that local lesions of the cerebrum are not necessarily followed by perceptible alteration of functions. If any extensive portion of the tissue is removed the animals appear heavy and stupid: but this change, too, disappears with time, very rapidly in the lower vertebrates, gradually in the higher, and if some small remnant of the cerebrum has been left uninjured may seemingly, as high up as the carnivores, give place to a complete restoration of functional capacity. A pigeon, from whose brain considerable masses of the cerebral lobes have been removed, is, after the lapse of days or weeks, indistinguishable from a normal animal. In rabbits, and still more in dogs, the mental dullness and general motor inertia are more evident than in birds. In man himself, textural changes of limited extent, if they are of gradual growth, sometimes run their course without external symptom. More extensive injuries, however, are, it is true, always accompanied in man by chronic disturbance of voluntary movement, of sense, or of the psychical functions.[1]

These abrogation phenomena and their compensations are of peculiar interest when the injuries from which they result are of definite character and considerable extent. Large portions of the brain substance may be lost, and the animal, notwithstanding, make a complete functional recovery. Thus GOLTZ found that dogs which he had deprived of the whole of one cerebral hemisphere conducted themselves, some months after the operation, in very much the same way as if they were normal animals.[2] There was a reduction of the cutaneous sensitivity on the opposite side; and when the animal was free to choose between the movements of its extremities, it preferred as a rule to use the muscles of the same side. The per-

---

[1] LADAME, *Hirngeschwülste*, 186 f. NOTHNAGEL, *Topische Diagnostik der Gehirn krankheiten*, 435 ff. VON MONAKOW, *Gehirnpathologie*, 376 ff.
[2] GOLTZ, in PFLÜGER'S *Arch. f. d. ges. Physiol.*, xlii., 1886, 484.

ceptions of sight and hearing had also become uncertain, though they were by no means destroyed.[1] GOLTZ afterwards made experiments, with like result, upon a monkey (Rhesus), which was almost entirely deprived of one hemisphere.[2] Where a considerable portion of both hemispheres is removed, the symptoms of disturbance are more acute, and at the same time take a definite direction. Thus, dogs deprived of both frontal lobes gave marked indications of motor derangement. The movements were awkward and clumsy, though the capacity of movement was not abrogated. There was no change of sensation. Extirpation of the two occipital lobes, on the other hand, produced disturbances of vision, which appeared, however, to consist less in an abrogation of sensitivity to light than in a serious impairment of the perceptual functions (cf. p. 196 above). In both cases, whether the frontal or the occipital lobes were removed, the intelligence of the animals also seemed to be somewhat diminished, though it was never wholly destroyed. As a general rule, emotive symptoms of like and dislike were still manifested; in this respect, therefore, there is a radical difference between these animals and the dog whose cerebrum was removed entire (cf. pp. 261, 268). At the same time, there were signs of emotive disturbance, which varied characteristically according as the frontal or occipital lobes were removed: in the former case, the animals appeared unusually irritable,—a fact that may, perhaps, be brought into connexion with the coincident symptoms of hyperæsthesia; in the latter, they became apathetic, probably in consequence of their partial anæsthesia; quarrelsome dogs were rendered, to all appearance, good-tempered, though it is true that they were also uninterested.[3]

The disturbances observed in man as the result of extensive cerebral deficiency appear, on the whole, to resemble these set up by operation in animals. This is true, more especially, of cases in which the one half of the cerebrum is wholly destroyed. Several instances are on record, in the literature of pathology, in which this condition was induced by external injury or by changes due to disease, and the patient nevertheless lived on for some period of time. Under such circumstances, the opposite side of the body was, of course, completely paralysed, owing to the decussation of the conduction paths. The intellectual functions, on the other hand, showed, so the report declares, no noticeable alteration. The only points signalised are incapacity for mental exertion, and an unusually rapid onset of mental fatigue.[4] Unfortunately, however, in no one of these cases, which all belong to the older medical literature, was the patient subjected to any

---

[1] LOEB, in PFLÜGERS' *Arch. f. d. ges. Physiol.*, xxxiv., 1884, 67.
[2] GOLTZ, *ibid.*, lvi., 1899, 411.
[3] GOLTZ, *ibid.*, xxxiv., 1884, 450; xlii., 1888, 439.
[4] LONGET, *Anatomie et physiologie du système nerveux*, Germ. trans. by HEIN, i., 539 ff.

accurate functional examination: so that we can draw from them simply the general conclusion that there occurs in man a partial compensation of the disturbances, similar to that observed in the corresponding experiments on animals. The abrogation symptoms that appear when the anterior or posterior portion of the cerebrum is wanting are also, it would seem, in agreement with the results of experiments on animals, both in psychical regard and with respect to the derangement of motor and sensory capacity. At the same time, the disturbances in this case are of a much more complicated kind, and their psychological analysis is accordingly too defective to allow of any certainty of inference. All the more prominent, on this account, is the position of certain territories of the cerebral cortex, which are connected with definite psychophysical activities of a compound order. These we shall discuss presently with some fullness: they are the only instances in which, in the present state of our knowledge, detailed functional analysis is possible.[1]

All these observations, which refer to the consequence of more or less extensive cerebral lesions, are, it is clear, of but comparatively slight importance for an appreciation of the functions whether of the hemispheres as a whole or of particular regions of the cerebrum. Their chief interest really lies in the evidence which they supply of the existence of very complete arrangements for the compensation of the disturbances. We have seen that in the lower vertebrates, and even in many of the mammals, such compensation is rendered possible, after removal of the entire prosencephalon, by the vicarious function of diencephalon and mesencephalon, which thus become autonomous centres of greatly increased activity. Within the cerebral hemispheres themselves, however, the possibility of substitution evidently goes much further. Under favourable conditions, more or less complete adjustment may be made, even in the human brain, to quite considerable defects. At the same time, we must accept the corollary that the definitive phenomena of abrogation, in cases of partial lesion of the cerebral hemispheres, may be turned to theoretical account only with the greatest reserve, and that our study of the separate functional departments of the cerebrum must be based rather upon the transitory than upon the chronic disturbances that follow in the train of cortical lesions. This point will appear more clearly when we undertake the special analysis of the functions of vision and speech.

(b)—*Phenomena of Abrogation after Total Loss of the Cerebral Hemispheres*

The phenomena of abrogation that result from the loss of certain parts of the cerebrum are, as we have seen, of doubtful significance; the in-

[1] Cf. the discussions of the centres of vision, speech and apperception, § 7, below.

fluences of compensation are incalculable. On the other hand, the symptoms that follow upon total loss of the prosencephalon have a definitive value, save only in the case of those animals in which this defect also can be concealed by the vicarious functioning of mesencephalon and diencephalon. Unfortunately, however, the effect of the operation is so extremely complex that here, again, the symptoms of chronic abrogation admit only of very general and, therefore, indefinite conclusions. In the first place, the psychophysical activities which continue after removal of the prosencephalon do not afford a safe basis for judgment, since it remains uncertain whether and how far they themselves owe their origin to some compensation of functions. But more than this : it is exceedingly difficult, indeed, in many cases it is impossible, to distinguish between complicated reflexes, that take place without any accompaniment of conscious sensations, and reactions that occur at the incentive of sensations and sense perceptions. Hence the investigator can never obtain more than a negative result. The functions that are permanently abrogated by removal of the prosencephalon are, in all probability, conditioned exclusively upon its integrity. But the activities that are temporarily deranged, and presently restored again, must remain of doubtful significance, since there is no means of determining the extent of possible compensations. Now we saw that birds, rabbits, and even dogs are not only capable, in the decerebrised state, of purposive reaction to tactual and visual stimuli, but also adapt their movements, like normal animals, to external impressions. They avoid obstacles, they recover their equilibrium by balancing, etc. ; nay more, they apparently execute spontaneous movements,—they run to and fro, seize and swallow the food that is offered them, and respond by expressions of pain to intensive sensory stimuli. That is to say, they appear to be in full possession of the sensory and motor functions. On the other hand, they give no signs of intelligence, and never express joy or any other of the complex emotions. Moreover, their spontaneous movements are more uniform and restricted than those of an uninjured animal (see above, p. 262). In a word, these final abrogation phenomena lead us to the general, and, we must also admit, indefinite conclusion that *the intelligence, the higher affective processes, and the compound voluntary actions* are conditioned upon the integrity of the cerebral hemispheres. We term this result indefinite, first, because the psychological terms that enter into the functional determination require a more exact psychological definition before any precise meaning can be attached to them, and secondly because it is clear, even without any such definition, that an absolute delimitation of the intelligence and the complex affective and volitional processes, as contrasted with the lower processes of the same kind that may possibly continue after the removal of the prosencephalon, is a matter of extreme difficulty. In any event, however, the distinction, so far as it is practicable at all, must also be left over for the detailed psychological analysis of the processes involved.[1]

(c)—Results from Comparative Anatomy and Anthropology

The general conclusion to be drawn from the abrogation phenomena, that the physiological function of the cerebral hemispheres stands in intimate relation to the intellectual activities and to the complex affective and volitional processes, is, upon the whole, confirmed by the results of comparative anatomy, evolutionary biology and anthropology. Comparative anatomy shows that the mass of the cerebral lobes, and more especially

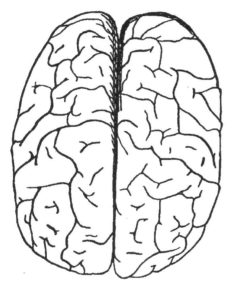 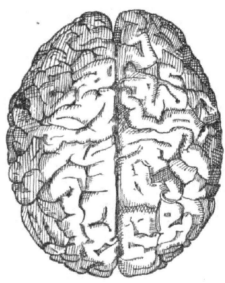

FIG. 100. Normal small brain, with fair fissural development.   FIG. 101. Brain of the mathematician, C. FR. GAUSS.

their superficial ridging by fissures and gyres, increase with increasing intelligence of the animal. This law is, however, limited by the condition that both factors, mass and superficial folding, depend primarily upon the size of the body. In the largest animals the hemispheres are absolutely, in the smallest, relatively larger, i.e., larger as compared with the weight of the whole body; and the ridging, as is natural from the relative decrease of surface with increasing volume of an organ, increases with the size of the brain: in all very large animals, therefore, the brain shows an abundance of fissures.[2] The physical organisation is another factor of great

---
[1] See below, Parts IV., V.
[2] LEURET and GRATIOLET, *Anatomie comparée du système nerveux*, ii., 290. OWEN, *Anatomy of Vertebrates*, iii.

importance. Of the terrestrial mammals, the insectivores have the least convoluted, the herbivores the most richly convoluted brain, and the carnivores stand midway; the marine mammals, although they are carnivorous, surpass the herbivores in the number of their brain gyres. It thus comes about that there are, after all, only two connexions in which the law quoted above has any claim to validity. It is valid if we take the widest possible comparative survey of the development of the brain in the vertebrate kingdom; and it is valid if we confine our comparison within the narrowest possible limits, and look at animals of related organisation and similar bodily size. Only in the latter case, again, can the result properly be termed striking. If we compare, e.g., the brains of different breeds of dogs, or the brains of man and of the man-like apes, there can be no doubt that the more intelligent breeds or species possess the larger and more highly convoluted hemispheres. By far the most significant of these differences is that between man and the other primates. The average brain weight of males of Teutonic descent between the ages of thirty and forty may be set at 1,424 grammes, and that of females of the same race and age at 1,273 grammes; the brain of a full-grown orang-utan amounted, e.g., only to 79·7 grammes. Still greater is the discrepancy if we consider, not the weight of the brain, but its superficial development, conditioned upon the number of gyres. Thus H. WAGNER gives for man a surface of 2,196 to 1,877, for an orang-utan a surface of 535.5 sq. cm.[1] Among the lower races of man the brain has also been found, as a rule, to be both smaller and less convoluted.[2] And numerous observations go to show that, within the same race and nationality, eminently gifted individuals possess large and richly convoluted hemispheres.[3] Figg. 100 and 101 illustrate this point in two especially striking cases. Fig. 100 is the dorsal view of the brain of a simple artisan of moderate, but not subnormal mental capacity; Fig. 101 is the corresponding view of the brain of the famous mathematician, C. Fr. GAUSS.[4]

---

[1] HUSCHKE, *Schädel, Hirn und Seele*, 60. H. WAGNER, *Massbestimmungen der Oberfläche des grossen Gehirns*, 1864, 33.
[2] TIEDEMANN, *Das Hirn des Negers mit dem des Europäers und Orang-Utangs verglichen*, 1837. BROCA, *Mémoires d'anthropologie*, 1871, 191.
[3] GALL and SPURZHEIM, *Anatomie et physiologie du système nerveux*, ii., 251.
[4] R. WAGNER, to whom we owe these reproductions, and those of certain other brains of eminent men (Dirichlet, C. Fr. Hermann, etc.), was himself somewhat hesitant about drawing this conclusion (*Göttinger gel. Anz.*, 1860, 65; *Vorstudien zu einer wissenschaftl. Morphologie und Physiologie des Gehirns*, 1860, 33). C. VOGT, however, justly remarks that it follows, without any question, from WAGNER's own figures, if we select from them the illustrations that really apply to individuals of acknowledged mental pre-eminence. See also BROCA, *Mémoires d'anthropologie*, 155. For the rest, it need not be pointed out that, here as elsewhere, the concurrent factors of race, height, age, sex, must be taken into consideration. A normal Hottentot brain in the skull of an European would, as GRATIOLET observed, spell idiocy.

(d)—The Hypotheses of Localisation and their Opponents. The Old and the New Phrenologies

These obvious differences in the superficial configuration of the cerebral hemispheres naturally suggest the hypothesis that the general connexion between brain development and mental endowment, which appears in them, is paralleled by *specific* relations between the relative development of various parts of the brain surface and definite directions of mental capacity. This hypothesis, which in itself is entirely justified, forms the point of departure of the system of 'phrenology' founded by FRANZ JOSEPH GALL. Unfortunately, however, the physiological and psychological premisses upon which GALL worked out his ideas are untenable, and the observations themselves and the conclusions drawn from them betray lack of accuracy and scientific caution. GALL regarded the mental functions as the business of a number of *internal senses*, to each of which, on the analogy of the external senses, he attributed a special organ. Nearly all of these internal sense organs he localised on the outer surface of the brain, assuming a parallelism of skull-form and brain-form which, as can easily be demonstrated, does not obtain, at any rate to the extent required. GALL distinguished twenty seven 'internal senses,' in naming which he makes use at need of the expressions sense, instinct, talent, and even memory: we find, e.g., sense of place, sense of language, sense of colour, instinct of propagation, instinct of self-defence, poetic talent, *esprit caustique, esprit métaphysique*, memory of things, memory of words, sense of facts, sense of comparison, etc. It is useless to repeat the statements of the phrenologists regarding these localisations. It may, however, be mentioned that in one case—and the fact shows that he possessed some gift of observation—GALL made a lucky hit: he localised his 'sense of language' in a region of the cerebral cortex approximately corresponding to the area whose lesions, as we shall see later on, have been proved in modern times to constitute the most frequent cause of the syndrome of 'aphasia.' Indeed, the discovery of the seat of aphasia is directly traceable to GALL's suggestion, as has been expressly acknowledged by BOUILLAUD, to whom it is due.[1] At the same time, we must not forget that even in this instance, where a pronouncement of GALL's has recceived a certain measure of confirmation from the facts, there is really an essential difference between what was actually discovered, viz., the anatomical seat of central derangements of speech, and the phrenological 'organ of language.' The two can, in truth, be identified only if we force a phrenological interpretation upon the phenomena of

---

[1] BOUILLAUD, *Recherches cliniques propres à demontrer que la perte de la parole corresponde à la lésion des lobules antérieures du cerveau et à confirmer l'opinion de M. GALL* etc. In *Arch. gén. de méd.*, viii., 1825.

aphasia, which in the light of actual analysis they will not bear. Cf. below, § 7b.

When physiology first took the field against the phrenological doctrine of localisation, it was itself but poorly armed for the combat. It was inclined to lay a disproportionate weight upon the indefinite or equivocal results of extirpation experiments on animals. It was easily influenced by false analogies, and did not hesitate to accept pyschological theories that at bottom were no less questionable than the 'internal senses' of the phrenologists. Thus FLOURENS, whose views long held undisputed sway in physiology, insisted strenuously upon the unity and indivisibility of the cerebral functions, and argued from it that their organ must be similarly indivisible. This opinion was largely determined by the analogy of other, unitarily functioning organs. Cerebellum, oblongata and myel were each endowed by FLOURENS with an independent and specific function, discharged by the organ as a whole. In the same way, the mass of the cerebral hemispheres stood for him upon a single physiological level, like the substance of a secreting gland, e.g. the kidney. He found confirmation of this view in the observations on the results of partial and total extirpation of the prosencephalon in animals that we have discussed above : for these experiments show, in general, that partial removal of the cerebral lobes simply weakens the mental functions, as a whole, and does not, as on the hypothesis of a localisation of functions might be expected, abrogate certain activities and leave the rest unimpaired ; while total extirpation of the cerebrum completely destroys all spontaneous expressions of the mental life, i.e., as FLOURENS phrased it, all 'intelligence and will.'[1]

This doctrine, of the specifically *psychical* function of the prosencephalon and of the indivisibility of that function, presently became untenable. It was overthrown partly by the pathological observations on the consequences of local lesion in man, partly by the growth of knowledge regarding the structure of the brain and the course of the conduction paths. Its place was taken by the *modern theories of localisation*, which to a certain extent attempt a *rapprochement* with the doctrine of phrenology. At the same time, they mark a twofold advance beyond GALL and his disciples. First, on the side of physiology, GALL's 'mental organs' are replaced by the idea of the separate 'centres,' correlated with peripheral spheres of function that are, upon the whole, definite and clearly distinguishable—the sense organs, the various muscular territories, etc. This change of view is evidently a reactive effect of the advance in knowledge of the anatomy of the conduction paths. Secondly, on the side of psychology, such monstrous terms as sense of facts, reverence, philoprogenitiveness, or—to take instances of another sort—sense of language, poetic talent, etc., are banished from

---

[1] FLOURENS, *Recherches expér. sur les fonctions du système nerveux*, 2nd ed. 1842.

the list of localisations, and the terms 'sensation and idea,' terms which, as the framers of the theories believed, represent the two fundamental forms of psychical process, and retained in their stead. 'Sensation' means, in this connexion, any conscious reaction evoked by external sensory stimuli, while 'idea' includes, in accordance with the nomenclature of the older psychology, all kinds of 'memory image.' From these general premisses, the doctrine of localisation or, as its close relations to the older phrenological theories justify us in calling it, 'modern phrenology' has developed in two directions. In both forms, it is based upon the assumption that the cerebral cortex is divided up into a number of sensory centres, in which the excitations brought in along the sensory conduction paths release the specific sensations. The centromotor regions are counted among these sensory centres, on the further assumption that a voluntary action may be adequately defined as the connexion of some reflex, arising either in lower centres or in the cortex itself, with a concomitant sensation of touch or movement. As we leave this common ground of general theory, however, opinions begin to diverge. The one form of the doctrine of localisation asserts that the centres of sensation and idea are strictly connected, so that every sensory centre covers both processes, and the entire cortical surface is therefore essentially composed simply of a number of adjacent sensory centres. The distinction of sensational and ideational functions within each centre is then conditioned solely upon the action of determinate—functionally, not morphologically discriminable—elements. It thus becomes necessary to posit the existence of two sorts of cortical cells: sensation cells and idea cells. The former are supposed to receive peripheral excitations by direct conduction; the latter take up excitations proceeding from the sensation cells, and thereby acquire the capacity of renewing these excitations,—a process that, for brevity's sake, has also been termed the 'deposition' of ideas in the specific memory cells. This form of localisation theory, which we may call the 'pure sense-centre theory,' was first worked out by MEYNERT on a morphological basis, and has since been employed by H. MUNK for the interpretation of his experiments on animals. It is widely current at the present day, both in physiology and in pathology,. The second form of the localisation doctrine differs from the first mainly by its assertion that the central areas which subserve the colligation of sensations, and therefore also the retention of ideas, the centres, in fact, which underlie the complex psychical functions at large, are spatially separate from the sensory centres, though connected with them by manifold systems of association fibres. It accordingly gives this second order of centres, whose office it is to colligate the various sense departments, the special name of 'association centres'; and we may therefore designate the second form of the localisation theory, briefly, as the 'theory of association centres.' According to this view, the essential activity of the cerebrum consists in the function of the association centres, while the sensory centres serve, on the whole, simply to take up the sense impressions, in the order in which they affect the peripheral organs, and to raise them to consciousness by their projection upon determinate cerebral surfaces. The expression 'association centre,' is used, in this connexion, both in a physiological and in a psychological sense: physiologically, it is the 'association fibres,' characteristic of these centres as such, that are connected only indirectly, viz., by way of the sensory centres with which they are correlated, with the periphery of the body; psychologically, these association centres are looked upon as the substrate of the associative processes upon which, as the psychology of association teaches, and as our theorists believe, all the higher psychical functions depend. This second form of the localisation doctrine is, unquestionably, superior to the first, in that it leaves a somewhat freer scope to hypotheses of the origin of the more complex psychical processes; the schematic antithesis of sensation cells and idea cells, which naturally leads to a corresponding and correspondingly untenable classification of the psychical processes themselves, is replaced by the broader antithesis of direct sensory excitations and associations. At the same time, however, the idea of association and of the association centre is left very indefinite. It is, in the last resort, bound down to the belief that cortical areas which stand in exclusive connexion with association fibre systems are the vehicle of the more complex psychical activities; so that, from the functional point of view, the expression 'psychical centres' would really be the more correct. But such a term shows very plainly that the second form of the localisation doctrine brings us perilously near, once more, to the doctrines of the older phrenology; and that, if it does not run altogether on the old lines, this is principally due to the praiseworthy caution of its representatives, who have so far refrained from correlating the different cortical areas of the association theory with complex psychical activities or endowments of a definite kind.

These modern hypotheses of localisation, like the old-time phrenology of GALL, have not been allowed to pass unchallenged from the side of physiological observation. GOLTZ and his pupils, in particular, have disputed the strict localisation of the psychical functions, on the ground of the defects observed after partial extirpations of the cortex. In opposition to the theory of sharply circumscribed sensory centres, these investigators insist upon the complex character of the disturbances following from local lesions, and upon the general reduction of the intellectual functions after partial removal of the cerebral lobes. They thus come back to a view which resembles that of FLOURENS: they emphasise the necessity of the *co-operation* of the different cortical regions in the psychical functions, though they have given up the hypothesis of the functional equivalence of all the parts of the cerebrum, as untenable in the present state of our anatomical and physiological knowledge.

If, now, we attempt an appreciation of these different theories, standing opposed to one another in the doctrine of the cerebral functions, we must, of course, try to do justice to all the departments of experience that our judgment involves: to anatomy and pathology, that is, not less than to physiology and psychology: and we must be the more careful, since the quarrels between the older and newer localisation theories and their opponents have evidently been due, in no small measure, to the all too common tendency to rely, exclusively and onesidedly, either upon the anatomical facts or upon the results of experiments with animals. In both events, we may add, psychology has usually been regarded as an unclaimed territory, with which either side might deal as seemed best to it. We will ourselves, therefore, begin by setting psychology in the foreground, though we shall, as was said just now, attempt an impartial treatment of the other sciences also. From the psychological point of view, then, the sense-centre theory must be pronounced untenable; neither of its constituent hypotheses can be accepted. In the first place, the 'sensory centres,' as is clear from the results of psychophysical analysis of the functions of perception and from pathological observations on man, are not simple repetitions of the peripheral sensory surfaces, but are in the strictest sense of the word 'centres,' that is, areas in which the different peripheral functions concerned in the activities of sense are centralised. Thus, the visual centres bring together the functions of visual sensation, of energy and synergy of movement in the visual organs, of the relations of these processes to the visual reflexes that run their course in lower centres, and so on. The sensory centres would not be centres at all, but superfluous duplications of the peripheral organs, if they possessed no other significance than that of repeating the excitations touched off at the periphery. In this regard, the view embodied in the sense-centre theory is the result partly of an inadequate and prejudiced reading of the anatomy of the conduction paths, partly of a wrong interpretation of the experiments on animals, which, as we know, are pre-eminently ambiguous upon the point at issue. In the second place, the theory opposes 'sense cells' to 'idea cells'; excitations are supposed to flow from the former to the latter, and there to be deposited in the form of memory images. It thus transforms a wholly inadmissible psychological distinction into an equally inadmissible physiological hypothesis. The idea that sensations and ideas are absolutely distinct conscious contents belongs to the older spiritualistic psychology, which taught that 'ideas,' as contradistinguished from the sensations evoked by physical stimuli, are purely mental processes, the prerogative of the mind itself. This spiritualistic distinction is, of course, a pure product of metaphysical speculation, and survives at the present time only in a psychology of reflexion that has turned its back once and for all upon the facts of psychical experience. No truly psychological observer will be found to assert to-day that ideas exist independently of sensations, or that the sensations which enter into our ideas differ in any other way than by their intensity, duration, and fragmentary character from the sensations aroused by external sensory stimuli.[1] This distinction, derived as we have said from the spiritualistic psychology, and then clothed about with the garb of materialism, stands in actual fact upon the same level, in psychology, as would, in anatomy, the dictum of some present day philosopher that the mind has its seat in the epiphysis.

As compared with the sense-centre theory, the theory of association centres has certain indisputable advantages. It has dissolved the unnatural alliance with the ideas of metaphysical psychology, and has attempted instead to enter into relations with the psychology of association, which agrees better with our modern conceptions. But, on the one hand, it still holds to the erroneous view that the 'sensory centres' are central repetitions of the peripheral sensory surfaces, which latter must be projected upon the brain cortex solely that they may be brought into touch with the consciousness which resides there; and, on the other, it confuses in a very dangerous way the purely anatomical idea of 'association fibres,' that connect different regions of the cerebral cortex with one another, and the psychological idea of association. We are forbidden to suppose that the association fibres are, so to say, the vehicles for the production of associations of ideas, by the simple fact that the commonest and most important associations are those obtaining between the sensation elements of one and the same sense department. Hence the paths that run between different sensory centres could, at most, be taken as the conjectural substrate only of what are called 'complications,' i.e. of associations between disparate ideational elements. But if the idea of 'association fibres,' understood in this restricted sense, would possess a fairly definite meaning, the same thing can hardly be said of the idea of an 'association centre.' Are we to imagine that the association fibres running between the various sensory centres are inadequate to mediate complications, and that the independent function of an organ that receives association fibres, and association fibres alone, is further necessary to their production? This is the obvious meaning to be put upon the term 'association centre'; but it is scarcely the meaning that really attaches to it. It seems rather that the theory is here influenced by reminiscence of the psychology of association, very much as the sense-centre theory, in its distinction between sensations and ideas, is dominated by the old spiritualistic view of mind. The psychology of association seeks, as we know, to derive concepts, judgments, complex intellectual and affective processes all and sundry,

---

[1] See Ch. vii. below.

from associations of ideas. And the theory of association centres is evidently inspired, in the last resort, by the idea that the various complex psychical products are originated in these centres,—always, of course, with the closest co-operation of the sensory centres with which they are connected by association fibres. Here, then, we have a justification for the expression 'psychical centres.' The further the distinction of such centres is carried, however, the more nearly do we approach to the 'internal senses' of the older phrenology. For the psychical functions ascribed to them must, naturally, become more special, and therefore more complicated, in proportion as they themselves increase in number.

This extreme subdivision of the psychical functions is opposed by the anti-localisation school of modern experimental physiologists. Its representatives are undoubtedly right in insisting upon the multiplicity of relations in which these functions stand, and in affirming, as a consequence, that we cannot speak of sensory centres, in the sense of a definitely circumscribed repetition of the peripheral sensory surfaces, or of psychical centres, in the sense of circumscribed seats of separate mental activities. Indeed, as the hypothesis of the functional equivalence of all parts of the prosencephalon has gradually fallen into disrepute,—an hypothesis, it will be remembered, which derives in the first instance from FLOURENS, and was revived in the early stages of reaction,—this principle of *functional interaction* has come to be our most valuable guide in the psychophysical analysis of the cerebral functions. The new anti-phrenological movement, like its predecessor, sets out from the results of experiments on animals. These abrogation experiments are, however, hardly qualified to lead up to any exact formulation of the principle: their outcome is indefinite and ambiguous, and they are seriously complicated by the effects of vicarious functioning, whose influence is in most cases greatly underestimated. What we rather need is, evidently, an *analysis of the individual central functions*, in the light of observations of pathological defects, carefully collected and compared. Hence instead of asking: What are the consequences of the lack of a given cortical area, and what functions are accordingly to be ascribed to it? we must now raise the question: What central changes do we find, when a given function (language, the act of vision, etc.) is deranged, and what is the nature of the parallelism between the functional and anatomical disturbances? The great advance that modern pathology, in particular, has made in this field may be attributed, without hesitation, to the fact that it has been forced, by the nature of its problems, to give up the first form of enquiry for the second. And the significance of the advance, for our knowledge of the central functions, lies in the further fact that the first form directs the attention onesidedly, from the very beginning, to a fixed and definite central area, while the second points at once to connexions with other areas and, in general, emphasises the principle of *functional analysis* as against the former centre of interest, the correlation of determinate functions with determinate parts of the brain. This change of standpoint means a breaking down of the barriers, not only between the different regions of the cerebral hemispheres, but even, to a certain extent, between the prosencephalon and the posterior brain divisions (more especially the diencephalon and mesencephalon) as well. For the complex functions prove, as a rule, to be functions in which all these departments of the brain are variously involved; so that it is about as sensible to localise a complex function in a restricted area of the cerebral cortex as it would be to throw the sole responsiblity for the movements of walking upon the knee joint, because they cannot be duly performed if that joint is ankylosed. In fine, the analysis of the complex functions themselves comes up as a further problem, whose solution will effectively supplement, at the same time that it transcends, the physiology of the central hemispheres. The solution, as things are, must, it is true, remain imperfect; there are but few functions, at the present time, that admit at all of this sort of analysis. Of those that do, the chief are the central act of vision, the functions of speech, and the processes of apperception.

The problem of the localisation of the psychical functions begins with the great anatomists of the sixteenth century. Among them, VESALIUS was especially instrumental in spreading the opinion that the *brain* is the seat of the mental activities. For a long time, however, the old doctrine of ARISTOTLE and GALEN, that made the heart the general centre of sensation, held its own alongside of the newer teaching. DESCARTES was the first to regard the brain as an organ subserving the interaction between mind and body. It is with DESCARTES, consequently, that a question arises which was destined thenceforth to play a great part in the discussions of physiologists and philosophers: the question of the *seat of the mind*. DESCARTES himself, in answering it, made the curious mistake of selecting the *epiphysis*, a structure which is probably a vestige of the old parietal eye of the vertebrates, and does not properly belong to the brain at all.[1] At the same time, increasing efforts were made, especially in the anatomy and physiology of the eighteenth century, to ascertain the significance of the various *parts* of the brain. Interpretations were based, as a rule, upon the results of anatomical dissection, though the psychological ideas prevailing at the moment were also of some influence. Thus, at a later time, the mental faculties of WOLFF's school, perception, memory, imagination, etc., were commonly chosen for localisation,—which was arbitrary and, of course, very differently worked out by different authors.[2] It is the service of HALLER, in particular, to have paved the way for a less artificial view, holding closely to the data of physiological observation. The reform is intimately connected with his doctrine of irritability, whose chief significance lay in the fact that it referred the capacities of sensation and movement to different kinds of tissue; the former to the nerves, the latter to the muscles and other contractile elements.[3]

[1] DESCARTES, *Les passions de l'âme*, I. See above, p. 124.
[2] See the list in HALLER, *Elementa physiologiæ*, iv., 1762, 397.
[3] See the historical critique of the doctrine of irritability in the author's *Lehre von der Muskelbewegung*, 1858, 155.

The source of these capacities HALLER finds in the brain. This organ is connected with the mind and the psychical functions only in so far as it is the sensorium commune, or the place where all activities of sense are exercised and whence all muscular movements take their origin. The sensorium extends over the whole substance of cerebrum and cerebellum.[1] It is therefore certain that every nerve receives its physiological properties from a definite central region; that, i.e., as is also attested by pathological observation, sight, hearing, taste, etc., have their seat somewhere in the brain. At the same time, the conditions of origin of the nerves seem to show that this seat is not sharply circumscribed, but as a general rule is spread over a considerable area of the brain.[2] To the commissural fibres HALLER assigns the function of mediating the vicarious function of sound for diseased parts. He deduces the inexcitability of the brain substance from the fact that the nerve fibres lose their sensitivity, in proportion as they split up within it into finer and finer branches.[3]

The position thus won was never lost by physiology. Nevertheless, the endeavours after a physiological localisation of the mental faculties were constantly renewed, the usual starting point, now as before, being furnished by anatomy. The views of the reactionaries were systematised by GALL, and in this form long continued to exert an influence upon the science. GALL, it should be remembered, did much real service in his investigations of the structure of the brain.[4] The phrenology[5] which he founded proceeds upon the assumption that the brain consists of internal organs, analogous to the external organs of sense. As the latter mediate our perception of the outer world, so do the former mediate what may be called a perception of the inner man. The individual capacities localised in the brain were, accordingly, also termed 'internal' senses. GALL distinguished twenty-seven; his pupil SPURZHEIM increased the number to thirty-five.[6] The mental faculties that are ordinarily recognised, such as understanding, reason, will, etc., have no place in the phrenological list. These fundamental forces of the mind are, in GALL's opinion, *not* localised, but are uniformly operative in the function of all the cerebral organs, and even in that of the external organs of sense. Every one of these organs is, therefore, as he puts it, an "individual intelligence."[7] His main argument for the analogy of the 'internal senses' with the external sense organs is derived from anatomical investigations; as every sensory nerve is a bundle of nerve fibres, so is the whole brain a collection of nerve bundles.[8] When, now, GALL and his followers came to put these theories into practice, they substituted 'skull' for 'brain': the form of the skull was to yield up information regarding the development of the individual organs. And this means, of course, that they intended, so far as possible, to localise the organs on the surface of the brain. Here, then, at the very outset, is evidence of a tendency to adapt observation

---

[1] *Elem. physiol.*, iv., 395.
[2] *Ibid.*, 397.
[3] "Hypothesin esse video et fateor," he cautiously adds. *Ibid.*, 399.
[4] GALL and SPURZHEIM, *Anatomie et physiologie du système nerveux*, i., 1810. Cf. also the same authors' *Recherches sur le système nerveux*, etc., 1809 (contains the memoir presented to the French Institute and the report of the Commissioners). GALL's two main services to brain anatomy are his introduction of the method of dissection from below upwards, and his demonstration of the universally fibrous character of the alba.
[5] GALL's system is set forth in detail in vols. ii.–iv. of the *Anatomie et physiologie*.
[6] COMBE, *System of Phrenology*, 1825 (Germ. trans. by HIRSCHFELD, 1833, 101 f.).
[7] *Anat. et physiol.*, iv., 341.
[8] *Ibid.*, i., 271; ii., 372.

to preconceived opinions: a tendency that crops up again in all the special investigations, and robs their 'results' of any sort of value. This apart, however, the monstrosity of the psychological and physiological ideas that underlie the teaching of phrenology marks a long step backward from the more enlightened position occupied by HALLER. The great Swiss already has an inkling of the true principle, that the peripheral organs of the body must in some way be represented and brought into mutual connexion in the central organs. The phrenologists make the brain an independent group of organs, for which they posit specific energies of the most complicated kind.

The fact remains that in *one* of his localisations, that of the 'sense of language,' GALL hit upon the right path. And in spite of all his errors, this fact has led certain authors in modern times, not only to seek a just recognition of his services to anatomy,—which are undeniable,—but also to attempt in some sort a rehabilitation of his phrenological doctrines.[1] It must, however, be remembered, on the other side, that even as regards the syndrome of aphasia the expression "organ of the sense of language" is inadmissible. We can imagine, if we are called upon to do so, that the conduction paths concerned in the function of speech run their course in these particular regions of the brain. We cannot possibly imagine, from what we know either of the brain or of the psychical processes, that a definitely circumscribed brain area is the seat of linguistic endowment, in the same sort of way that eye and ear are organs for the reception of light and sound stimuli, or the pyramidal paths lines of motor conduction. And even so, the faculty of speech is one of the comparatively simple 'internal' senses. How, then, are we to conceive of the mechanism by which the fear of God, philoprogenitiveness, the sense of facts, the impulse of self-preservation, and things like these are localised somewhere in the brain? Granted that GALL was, in his day and generation, one of the highest authorities on brain morphology: this honour is his, and is not to be taken from him. The phrenological system, nevertheless, is and remains a scientific aberration, the joint product—like its predecessor, the physiognomics of LAVATER—of charlatanism and unreasoning caprice. For this disease there is no remedy. Hence it is a questionable experiment to rehabilitate any other of the 'mental organs' that GALL pretends to have discovered, as P. J. MÖBIUS has undertaken to do in the interests of the 'organ of mathematical ability.'[2] Looked at as it stands, 'mathematical talent' comes perilously near the psychological monstrosity of GALL'S other localisations. But besides, the unusually marked development of the superior external orbital angle, which MÖBIUS has found confirmed in the case of three hundred mathematicians, admits of two different interpretations. In the first place, it may be—and this is, perhaps, the more probable hypothesis—a reactive effect of the mimetic tension of the muscles of the forehead, observable in profound thought, upon the bony skeleton of the face. Or again, it may be due to the fact that, in all highly developed brains alike, the frontal lobes are characterised by their mass and the number of their fissures, quite apart from the question whether or not the intellectual endowment of their owners takes the precise direction of a talent for mathematics. In other words: it must first be shown that the protuberance under discussion is not to be discovered in highly developed brains of poets, philosophers, philo-

---

[1] P. J. MÖBIUS, *Franz Joseph Gall*, in SCHMIDT's *Jahrbuch d. Medicin*, cclxii., 1899, 260.

[2] P. J. MÖBIUS, *Ueber die Anlage zur Mathematik: mit 51 Bildnissen*, 1900.

logians, etc., who at the same time were conspicuously lacking in mathematical ability. So far, this proof is not forthcoming. But suppose that it were given: what would follow? Certainly not, that there was a mathematical organ, in the sense of the phrenologists, but at best this: that we were in presence of a fact, which for the time being we could not explain, and which had about as much value for science as the law that most great men possess unusually large skulls.

The principal opponents of the phrenology of GALL and his followers, in the first half of the nineteenth century, were the French experimental physiologists, MAGENDIE and FLOURENS.[1] The views which these investigators developed of the significance of the central organs plainly represent a reaction against the phrenological doctrines. In MAGENDIE this spirit shows itself in the strict congruity of theory with observed facts.[2] FLOURENS had the more decisive influence upon the physiological ideas of the following period. His researches extended to the oblongata, quadrigemina, cerebellum and cerebrum. The first of these he determined as the centre for cardiac and respiratory movements: the quadrigemina as central organs for the sense of sight; the cerebellum as the centre of conduction of voluntary movements, and the cerebral lobes as the seat of intelligence and will.[3] He found, however, that different parts behaved differently, as regards the functions dependent on them. The central properties of the oblongata are confined within a small area, his *nœud vital*, destruction of which means instantaneous death. The higher central regions, on the other hand, discharge the functions assigned to them uniformly throughout their entire substance. This conclusion is an inference from the fact that the disturbances set up by partial removal of the cerebral lobes, cerebellum or quadrigemina, are gradually compensated as time goes on. It follows, therefore, that the smallest fragment of these organs can function for the whole. In his view of the cerebral hemispheres as the properly psychical centres, FLOURENS was evidently influenced, at the same time, by the traditions of the Cartesian philosophy. DESCARTES had emphasised the indivisibility of the psychical functions, more especially of the intelligence and will, and had on this very account demanded an unitary 'seat of mind.' As DESCARTES' choice of the epiphysis could not be sustained, in the face of more recent experience, FLOURENS substituted for it the total mass of the cerebral hemispheres. FLOURENS' doctrines thus came, in virtue of their spiritualistic prominence, into sharp conflict with the more materialistically coloured ideas of the phrenologists: a circumstance that was not without import for the issue of the struggle.

Their acceptance in scientific circles was, however, chiefly due to the fact that they gave a fairly accurate representation of the observational data in experiments on animals. It was not realised that the same psychological difficulties attach to them as to the phrenological theory of organs. Nevertheless, intelligence and will are also complex capacities. That they should have their seat in any the least fragment of the cerebral lobes is, after all, just as difficult of comprehension as that memory for languages, sense of place, etc., should

---

[1] A criticism of the teachings of phrenology from the standpoint of comparative anatomy is to be found in LEURET, *Anatomie comparée du système nerveux*, i.; a criticism based upon the writer's physiological experiments, in FLOURENS' *Examen de la phrenologie*, 1842.

[2] MAGENDIE, *Leçons sur les fonctions du système nerveux*, 1839.

[3] FLOURENS, *Recherches expér. sur les fonctions du système nerveux*, 2nd ed. 1842.

be somewhere localised. Moreover, it remains an open question what significance is to be ascribed to the separate parts distinguished by anatomical dissection of the cerebral hemispheres, if they are throughout as uniform in functional regard as, say, the liver.

So it came about, even before the dawn of the new era of localisation, that the anatomists, where they ventured at all upon speculation concerning the significance of the different parts of the brain, were apt to recur, urged doubtless by arguments derived from their own science, to the idea of localisation of particular mental capacities.[1] And as, in course of time, the connexion of anatomical, physiological and pathological observations became more intricate, the views introduced into physiology by FLOURENS gradually lost their hold upon men's minds. The determining factors in the change of opinion were two: first, the investigations into the elementary structure of the central organs, and, secondly, the physiological and pathological experiences regarding the localisation of certain sensory functions and motor effects. Epoch-making, in the latter connexion, was the renewal of interest by BROCA in the observations made long since by BOUILLAUD on the anatomical substrate of aphasia.[2] Still, a certain contradiction remained between these results and the consequences of partial removal of the hemispheres by FLOURENS' method. The permanent symptoms produced by the latter operation consisted, not in the abrogation of *particular* functions, but in the weakening of *all*: a fact verified in the most recent times by GOLTZ.[3] So, in the controversy carried on principally between H. MUNK and GOLTZ, we have repeated, in modern terms and within the limits of experimental physiology itself, the older issue between FLOURENS and the phrenologists. But the new phrenological view, as represented by the 'sense-centre theory' and the 'theory of psychical centres' discussed in the text, is indefinitely better fitted to make terms with science than was the old phrenology; and the newer antiphrenologists, in the same way, have given up their original and impossible assumption of the functional equivalence of the different parts of the brain, and lay increasing emphasis upon the principle of regional interaction in the various complex functions. This principle, now, taken together with the manifold phenomena of substitutive and auxiliary function, leads inevitably to the idea of a *relative localisation* of functions. We say 'relative' for two reasons: first, because it is never the complex functions themselves, but only their elements, that are localised; and, secondly, because these elementary functions may also suffer all sorts of shifts and changes as a result of the processes of vicarious function.

§ 7. Illustrations of the Psychophysical Analysis of Complex Cerebral Functions

(a)—*The Visual Centres*

Of all the sensory nerve conductions, it is those of the acusticus and opticus, shown schematiclly in Fig. 77 and 78 (pp. 183, 186), that, by the complicated course of their paths and the number of central areas which these

---

[1] Cf., e.g., BURDACH, *Vom Bau und Leben des Gehirns*, iii. ARNOLD, *Physiologie*, i., 836. HUSCHKE, *Schädel, Hirn und Seele*, 174.
[2] BROCA, *Sur la siège de la faculté du language*, 1861.
[3] Cf. especially his discussions in PFLÜGER's *Arch. f. d. ges. Physiol.*, xx., 1879, 10 ff.

paths unite, make the most insistent demand for physiological analysis. In the case of audition, however, we have not the data necessary for the functional interpretation of the various areas involved in the nervous conduction. The connexions with certain sensorimotor and regulatory centres, in particular,—centres like the pregemina, cerebellum, etc.,—can, in the present state of our knowledge, be referred only quite generally to the interactions between auditory impressions and rhythmical movements. The central mechanism of these movements themselves is still wrapped in so much obscurity that the general notion of interaction cannot be replaced by any more definite ideas. In the case of vision, the conditions are more favourable: not so much, perhaps, because the investigation of its anatomical substrate has been brought to greater completion, as because the physiological and psychological analysis of the functions as such has been carried further.

Anatomically and physiologically, the act of vision is, in the first instance, characterised by the fact—unparalleled, save in the one instance of olfactory sensations—that it is, from the very beginning, in some sort a *central* process. The retina, as we have seen, represents a brain area displaced to the periphery of the body. Hence it is by no means to be regarded as a simple receiving apparatus for external light stimuli, but rather as an organ of complicated structure, containing not only nerve terminations, but also manifold ganglionic formations that mediate connexion with other and higher nerve centres. The single elementary process that, in a certain sense, reaches its conclusion in this peripheral organ is, we must suppose, that transformation of the external light vibrations into some kind of photochemical process, the physical correlate of which we find in the sensations of light and colour. In all probability, the vehicles of this transformation are the specific sensory cells of the retina, the rods and cones (s, z Fig. 78).[1]

It is at this point that the process of vision proper begins. The photochemical changes have simply prepared the way for it, by impressing their peculiar qualitative *differentia* upon the excitations conveyed along the opticus paths. The process of vision itself is compounded from the manifold connexions into which these primary optical excitations enter, and by which they obtain their concrete contents. This latter always carries with it a number of secondary excitations, which are the principal factors in giving the particular optical stimulus its relations to other sensations, and thus mediating the *localisation* and *spatial arrangement* of light impressions. It is clear that the scheme of a simple and direct connexion between every point upon the retina and a corresponding point in the visual centre of the occipital cortex—a schema still to be found here and there in the physiologics—is not able to satisfy these conditions. How inadequate it is will be

[1] Cf. Part II., Ch. viii. below.

seen at once from a consideration of Fig. 78 (p. 186), although the Figure does no more than indicate the course of the simplest conduction paths, those that admit of relatively certain interpretation, and altogether omits such others as the pupillary reflex, which plays an important part in adaptation to brightness, and the branch conduction to the cerebellum, the function of which has not yet been definitely determined. The nearest approach to the original simple schema seems to be made by the direct optic radiation ss. But even this path is interrupted, as it passes through the thalamic region (AK), by nodal points, at which, in all probability, connexions are also made with other paths. Further: as we said above (pp. 188, 230 ff.), the decussation of the optic nerves occasions a partial transposition of the paths of the right and left sides: the rearrangement is adapted to the functions of binocular vision, but at the same time suggests a relation to the centrifugal motor innervations proceeding from the occipital cortex. This relation is also attested by the structure of the visual cortex (p. 219), and by the probable existence of centrifugal conductions issuing from it ($c'f'$ Fig. 78). Again, a second main conduction of the opticus paths, which, if we may judge from the position of the chiasma, is undoubtedly involved in the same plan of decussation that includes the principal path, leads to the mesencephalic region, where it enters, in the pregeminum (OV) into two connexions. The first of these is a reflex connexion to the nidi of the oculomotor nerves (rr). It is, probably, at once same-sided and crossed, according to the way in which the fibres are distributed in the chiasma, and the conditions laid down by the requirements of binocular (panoramic or stereoscopic) vision. The second is a sensory connexion; for the supposedly centrifugal terminations of the opticus in the retina (cf) also take their origin from the mesencephalic region. The excitations carried by this path may be brought in either along the centripetal path cp that ends in the same region of the brain, or along the higher centrifugal path $c'f'$ that reaches it from the visual centre. The functional arrangements warrant the conjecture that, in both cases, the paths will take a crossed course; for it is but natural to regard the centrifugal system $cf, c'f'$ as the substrate of the coexcitations, which can also be demonstrated psychologically as concomitant sensations, and which in all probability have a part to play in the functions of binocular vision. In view of the motor synergies which these functions engage, and of their dependence upon the sensory excitations of the visual centre, the central portion $c'f'$ of this centrifugal path will presumably make connexion, not only with its sensory continuation cf, but also with the motor path rr, so that the regulation of ocular movements by light impressions can be effected in two ways: the reflex, by direct release from cp, and the centromotor, by the excitations brought up from the visual cortex in $c'f'$.

Now we must, of course, assume, as a general rule, that every excitation of the peripheral organ of vision, whatever point it may strike, will discharge at one and the same time into all the different paths of conduction opening up before it, provided always that none of these paths have been rendered impassable by interruptions of conduction. In the entire complex of organs that thus work together in the particular act of vision, the retina on the one side and the visual centre of the occipital cortex on the other constitute the two principal centres. Their functions are in some sort antithetical. The retina, lying farthest out towards the periphery, plays the leading part in the origination of sensations; the visual cortex, lying farthest in towards the centre, plays this part in the final combination of the separate functional components of the act of vision.. The transformation of light vibrations into photochemical processes, which takes place in the elements of the retina, is at any rate indispensable for the first origination of light sensations: for observations made on the congenitally blind prove that the brain cannot mediate such sensations unless the retina has previously been in function. On the other hand, the visual functions, once originated, may persist after removal of the external sense organ; the victim of accidental blindness, despite the atrophy of his optic nerves, if he originally possessed any vivid sense of colour at all, sees coloured memory images and, more especially, can enjoy a wealth of colour in his dreams. We must accordingly suppose that the excitatory processes in the central apparatus, particularly in those of the occipital visual centre, come in course of time, through the influence which they exert upon the processes of external stimulation, themselves to resemble those processes. The change is an illustration of the great adaptability of the central nervous substance to the varying conditions of excitation, vouched for by many other facts. This capacity for adaptation is, indeed, evidenced by the central process of vision in two different ways: intensively, in the change just mentioned, and extensively, in the manifold functional substitutions that follow the loss of particular central parts. Apart from minor phenomena of this kind, which appear in cases of central lesion and are probably to be referred to the vicarious function of neighbouring parts of the same brain area, e.g. of particular divisions of the visual cortex, one for another, we have here to consider two principal substitutions, again of very different character, that occur between the two main departments of the optic conduction, the mesencephalic and prosencephalic regions. Both of these regions bring together sensory and motor conductions that belong to the same peripheral organs; so that, in the nature of the case, loss of either centre is compatible with the retention of certain essential visual functions, and a new course of practice may partially make good the defect. Observation, as we saw above, proves that these possibilities are realised. The visual centre in the mesencephalon is able, in particular, to discharge the most essential of the visual functions, independently of the visual centre in the occipital cortex (pp. 260 ff.). True, the defects that remain, even with the utmost extent of vicarious activity, demonstrate at the same time that under *normal* circumstances the act of vision is a complex function, conditioned upon the co-operation of all these centres, whose several functions are themselves of a complex nature.

In this analysis of the central functions of vision, we have still left out of account two principal factors, whose significance cannot at the present time be estimated in any sort of detail, though a rough guess may be made at their meaning. The first consists of the relations to the motor regulatory mechanisms situated in the cerebellum; the second of the connexions mediated by the association systems of the cerebral cortex both with other sensory centres and with yet more central brain regions, which are not directly correlated with definite sense departments, but themselves contain the junctions of various sensory and motor conduction paths. Now we cannot conceive of an optical excitation that does not, to some degree, release at any rate a certain proportion of these manifold excitations. Hence we might conclude without hesitation, merely from the morphological relations of the optic conduction and the physiological analysis of its processes, that the simplest act of vision is, physiologically, an occurrence of great complexity, even if we were not constrained to posit this complication of conditions by our psychological analysis of the visual processes.[1]

(b)—*The Speech Centres*

The name 'speech region' is ordinarily applied to a cortical area, lesions of which, whether they affect larger or smaller portions of its substance, are attended by *disturbances of the functions of speech*, without setting up at the same time other psychical disturbances, especially those of what is termed 'the intelligence,' of any noticeable kind. Where the intelligence is affected, there is always good reason to refer its impairment to more extensive changes involving other cortical areas. Psychical disturbances of this sort, due to diffuse cerebral disorder, may be accompanied by derangement of speech, or even by complete abrogation of the speech functions, without direct injury to the speech centre itself. In such cases, the disturbances of speech are evidently secondary symptoms. Hence the only phenomena that are important for the relations of speech to definite cortical areas are those observed when the seat of injury is strictly confined to the speech centre proper. This region, in contradistinction to the sensory centres, whose representation in the brain cortex is without exception bilateral, has the peculiarity that its development is exclusively *unilateral*. Since the majority of mankind are right-handed, it is situated, as a result of the decussation

---

[1] See below, Part III., Ch. xiv., on visual ideas.

of the conduction paths, upon the left hemisphere. The corresponding cortical area of the opposite side is not employed for any other function. Under normal circumstances it serves, we may suppose, though for the most part to a very limited extent, as an auxiliary to the principal speech centre. If, however, the function of the latter is abrogated, it enters under stress of the new conditions upon a special course of practice, and gradually takes the place of the lost organ. This appears, at any rate, to be the only way in which we can explain the restoration of function observed in cases where the speech centre of the left side has been destroyed over a wide extent of the cerebral surface.

According to pathological observations of the phenomena that result from its partial abrogation, the entire speech region divides into several

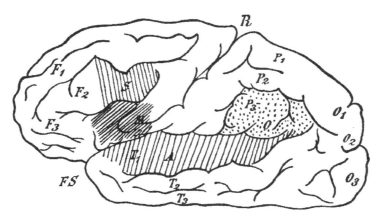

Fig. 102. Position of the speech centres in the cortex of the left cerebral hemisphere. M Motor, A acoustic, O optic speech centre. S Centre for writing movements. The remaining letters have the same meaning as in Fig. 65, p. 145.

sub-regions or 'speech centres,' as they are called, each of which would seem to preside over a definite phase of the total functions of speech. The first of these to be discovered, owing to the striking character of the symptoms produced by its injury, was the 'motor speech centre.' It occupies the posterior third of the subfrontal gyre (Broca's convolution : M Fig. 102). Destruction of this area and of its subcortical fibres gives rise to the phenomena of 'motor' or 'atactic aphasia,' which consists, according to the extent of the lesion, either in complete abrogation of the movements of speech, or simply in the abrogation or impairment of determinate articulations : the voluntary innervation of the muscles of speech is left intact. Of the remaining centres, we can distinguish most clearly the 'sensory' or 'acoustic speech centre,' by the characteristic form of the symptoms which accompany its lesions. It occupies the supertemporal gyre, more especially its posterior portion (about two-thirds of its whole extent: *A* Fig. 102); though this area cannot be sharply separated from the general auditory centre (WERNICKE's centre) which lies in the same neighbourhood. Destruction of the sensory speech centre gives rise to the phenomena of 'sensory' or 'amnestic aphasia'; words and phrases can, for the most part, be perfectly articulated, read or repeated from dictation; but the patient has lost the power of clothing his ideas in the corresponding phrases, and in extreme cases is able to hear but not to understand what is said to him, i.e., to associate a meaning contents to the sound of the words. This condition has been termed 'word deafness.' The disturbances again extend, according to the extent of the injury, either to the patient's whole vocabulary or only to certain of its constituents: the latter more especially in the minor degrees of 'amnesia,' which may range through all possible gradations to the condition of ordinary weakness of memory. Thus, sometimes it is merely certain classes of words, particularly proper names and names of objects, or in more severe cases all words whatsoever, with the exception of the particles and interjections most commonly employed, that are forgotten. It is therefore customary to distinguish total and partial amnesia. A special sub-form of partial amnesia is found, finally, in what is called 'paraphasia,' the symptoms of which, however, usually show a tendency to pass over into the syndrome of atactic aphasia. In its amnestic form paraphasia consists in the substitution of another, wrong word for the word required; in its atactic form, it consists in the substitution of certain sounds for others, so that the word is wrongly pronounced.

Somewhat less assured is the localisation of two further functions, functions that do not necessarily belong to speech in the stricter sense of the word, but that are intimately connected with it: the functions of *writing*, which, as a predominantly motor activity, connects with the articulation of sounds, and the functions of *reading*, which, as a more sensory process, connects in the first instance with the auditory perception of words. It has often been observed that abrogation of the movements of writing, with retention of the capacity of voluntary contraction of the muscles concerned, may be produced by lesion of a cortical area lying directly above the motor centre and belonging to the medifrontal gyre (*S* Fig. 102). This syndrome has been termed 'agraphia.' It seldom occurs, apparently, in pure form, but either accompanies motor aphasia or is connected with disturbances of the other voluntary movements of hand and fingers. A comparison with the position of the general motor centres (Fig. 88, p. 205) shows, also, that these and the centres for the special functions of speech and writing are either entirely coincident or, where that is not the case, directly apposed. As regards reading, we find that the relation of the *optic* to the acoustic speech centre corresponds to a certain extent with that of the writing centre to the centre for articulation. It appears, from numerous observations, that the optic speech centre belongs to a region of the subparietal and the second occipital gyres (the 'angular gyre': O Fig. 102) situated between the general centre for vision and the acoustic speech centre. Destruction of this region produces the peculiar syndrome of 'alexia' or 'word blindness': words can be spoken, and can also be heard, understood and remembered; but their written or printed symbols are not understood: they appear as meaningless pictures: although in other respects the visual functions remain unimpaired. All these disturbances, now, can not only occur in the most various combinations, with each component developed in a different degree, but may also be accompanied by further central disorders; so that it is but seldom that the syndromes of the typical forms of aphasia are seen pure, and unmixed with other phenomena. At the same time, the lesions of the different regions themselves produce somewhat divergent effects, according as the cortex proper or the subcortical parts are more seriously affected. Hence it is customary to distinguish cortical and subcortical disturbances. The latter are also termed intercortical or conductive disturbances, on the assumption that, while the cortical lesions involve the speech centres themselves, the subcortical injuries interrupt the connexions mediated between different centres by association fibres.[1]

These manifold gradations and combinations must here be followed out in some little detail, though only in so far as they furnish the necessary data for an appreciation of the psychophysical aspect of the phenomena, and afford an insight into the peculiar significance of that category of complex 'centres' to which the speech centres belong. An especial interest attaches, in this regard, to the connexions in which the typical cases of 'sensory' and 'motor' aphasia come under observation, and to the phenomena of mutual assistance and gradual recovery that follow in their train. The association paths anatomically demonstrable at all points between the centres marked out in Fig. 102 naturally suggest themselves as the substrate of these connexions. Since, however, nothing more can at present be learned from the anatomical maps than the general possibility of this synergy of the different centres, pathologists are accustomed, in order to explain the connexions in individual cases, to base their discussions upon a geometrical scheme, in which the centres themselves are represented by circles, and the paths of conduction to and between them by single lines of connexion joining the circles. A simple schema of this kind is shown, e.g., in Fig 103. It adopts, in all essential features, the arrangement suggested by LICHTHEIM.[2] The little circles M and S (A) denote the primary, motor

[1] WERNICKE, *Der aphasische Symptomencomplex*, 1874.
[2] LICHTHEIM, *Brain, a Journal of Neurology*, vii., 1885, 437. A still simpler plan, including merely the motor and sensory centres, was suggested by WERNICKE (*op. cit.*); it forms the basis of LICHTHEIM's schema, and is represented in Fig. 103 by the un-

and sensory-acoustic, speech centres; E and O are the secondary centres co-ordinated with them, E that of the movements of writing, O that of visual word-pictures. Besides these centres, however, all schematic representations of this sort are compelled to introduce a 'concept centre,' C, and lines of connexion running to it from the primary speech centres M and S (A), in order to indicate the relations with the ideational or conceptual contents of the words. It is obvious that this centre C, together with the name attached to it, is in reality only an indefinite expression for the manifold relations in which the various speech centres must stand with all the cortical areas that can claim a share in the origination of the ideational and affective contents of the constituents of speech. In what follows, we shall, for brevity's sake, include this contents under the single term 'meaning contents': an expression which, in the present instance, recommends itself by its very indefiniteness. It need, again, hardly be pointed out that such a meaning contents cannot possibly be conditioned upon any sharply circumscribed central area, but presupposes the combined activity of variously constituted groups of sensory centres and of many other of the regions that belong to the indeterminate category of 'association centres.' The circle C, therefore, can stand here simply as the indefinite symbol of these manifold relations. This presupposed, the schema first of all explains the occurrence of two general forms of speech derangement. *Abrogation of particular functions* will occur, whenever certain of the speech centres themselves, M, S (A), E, etc., are destroyed in whole or in part; *interruption of conduction* or, in psychological language, abrogation of the associations normally subsisting between the various phases of the speech function will occur, when the connexions between the centres are broken, e.g. at 3, 6, 10, etc. In the latter event, the phenomena will take on a different form according to the direction in which the processes are conducted or, in other words, the associations made. It is, however, generally assumed that the conductions may

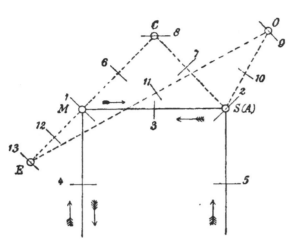

FIG 103. Schema of the speech centres and their connexions. After WERNICKE and LICHTHEIM.

broken lines. A plan resembling LICHTHEIM's, and factually accordant with it, but somewhat more complicated in outward appearance, had been drawn some years earlier by KUSSMAUL : *Die Störungen der Sprache,* 1877, 183.

take any direction as between the centres themselves, and that only the peripheral lines running to the two principal centres M and S convey their impulses towards a predetermined goal. The centre S receives its excitations centripetally from the direct auditory centres and, by way of these, from the peripheral organs of audition. The centre M gives out centrifugal impulses, first of all to the direct motor centres of the brain cortex, and then, from these again—probably with the co-operation of the co-ordinating and regulatory centres of diencephalon, mesencephalon and cerebellum—to the organs of articulation. So far, the directions of conduction are opposed. These articulatory movements are, however, accompanied by sensations, sensations of extreme importance for the uninterrupted flow of articulate speech; and we must accordingly posit, as their substrate, the existence of other, centripetal excitations, issuing from the motor organs. The conditions are indicated in Fig. 103 by the two arrows at 4.

From a plan of the speech centres and their connexions, such as is given by this Fig., we can read off without difficulty the different forms of speech derangement and their possible combinations. Thus, destruction of M will produce the syndrome of motor, destruction of S that of sensory aphasia; lesion of E will mean agraphia, lesion of O word-blindness. The schema also shows the more complex symptoms that may result from interruptions of conduction. Suppose, e.g., that connexion is broken at 3 between M and S. Words and phrases will still be heard; and, provided that the conduction from S to C is unimpaired, will be rightly understood. Further, if the conduction between C and M is intact, they may also, in contradistinction to the symptoms of cortical motor aphasia, be spontaneously uttered, with their right meaning upon them. On the other hand, *heard* words cannot be repeated, or can be repeated only with difficulty,—perhaps through the mediation of the idea centre, C,—because the requisite association path between M and S, the path which is supposed to run in the alba of the insula, is now out of function. Similar consequences follow from an interruption of conduction between M and E, S and O, O and E. A break at 12, e.g., would mean that the writing of words to dictation has become impossible, though printed or written words can still be copied from sight, provided that the conduction $O E$ remains uninjured; etc., etc.

Adequate, however, as this schema appears to be, for an understanding of the manifold forms of possible derangement, it nevertheless fails in two respects to do justice to the facts. In the first place, it represents certain disturbances as probable, even as necessary, which in reality do not occur at all, or, if they occur, do so only with very considerable limitations and modifications. In the second place, it leaves a large number of phenomena— more particularly the qualitative peculiarities of the disturbances, and the compensations due to interaction of the different functions—altogether unexplained.[1] On the former count, it may suffice here to mention the most striking example of incongruity between the anatomical plan and the actual functional conditions. According to the Fig., there may be interruptions of conduction between S and M that will prevent the translation of the heard into the spoken word, while the patient's apprehension of the meaning of words and power of spontaneous word formation remain unimpaired. But phenomena of this nature do not occur at all, in a pure form; the symptoms usually ascribed to the disturbance in question are paraphasic, and appear to be of more complex origin.[2] The incongruity thus made apparent between the schema and the facts is evidently due to an erroneous assumption which underlies the construction of the Fig.,—erroneous, because it disregards the actual psychological association of the speech functions: the assumption, namely, that the central areas C, whose activity is necessary for the origination of the meaning contents of a verbal idea, are connected in the same way both with the motor and with the sensory speech centres. Viewed in the light of the normal phenomena of speech associations, this assumption is wholly inadmissible. On the contrary, the possibility of a movement of articulation is so intricately associated with the acoustic word symbol, and the acoustic word symbol itself so frequently precedes articulation as a constituent of the total word complication, that the association may be much more probably referred to the indirect path $C\,S\,M$ than to the direct connexion $C\,M$. But if the indirect road is really followed, then the syndrome to be expected after interruption of conduction at 3 will, of course, be entirely different: spontaneous articulation and the translation of the heard into the spoken word must always suffer together. And if this conclusion, again, is not borne out in all cases, the result simply proves that in the preparation of the schema functional moments of such weight and importance have been left out of account that we may well doubt whether constructions of the kind can serve any useful purpose.

That these functional moments exert a real influence is shown with especial clearness in two groups of phenomena, whose whole character forbids the relegation of the aphasic symptoms, whatever they may be, to any rigid scheme of localisation. The first group consists in certain *qualitative* peculiarities, which attach to pathological amnesia in general precisely as they do to the normal lapse of verbal memory in advanced age. They find expression in the law that *those words disappear most readily from memory which are associated in consciousness with concrete sensible ideas.* The amnesic symptom that sets in most easily, and that is therefore the first to

---

[1] Cf. with this discussion the critical remarks in my *Völkerpsychologie*, i., 1, 1900, 495 ff.
[2] S. FREUD, *Zur Auffassung der Aphasien*, 1891. STÖRRING, *Vorlesungen über Psychopathologie*, 1900, 127 ff.

appear in old age, is, accordingly, forgetfulness of proper names. Next in order come the ideas of concrete objects: chair, house, table, etc. Somewhat more durable are the concrete verbs: go, stand, cut, strike, etc.; still more the abstract ideas, nominal and verbal: virtue, love, hate, have, be, become, etc. Finally, as most permanent of all, come interjectory words and the abstract particles: but, for, and, because, etc.[1] It is surely evident that no anatomical schema, however complicated its construction, can do justice to this sequence of phenomena. On the other hand, the order of impairment is explained at once by the associations in which verbal ideas are uniformly involved in consciousness. The more directly a verbal idea evokes a determinate object idea, the greater the converse possibility that the object idea itself represent the word in our thought. We are perfectly able to remember our acquaintances without at the same time reproducing their names. Concrete object ideas, like chair, house, table, may also come to consciousness immediately, without the words that denote them. But abstract ideas can be thought only by help of the corresponding words; and of these, again, the particles that are oftenest used naturally have the advantage. We are thus able, without difficulty, to explain the phenomena of progressive amnesia, in functional regard, from the psychological associations, on the one side, and the general effects of functional practice, on the other. Now these phenomena too have, of course, their physiological substrate. Only, the substrate cannot be conceived as in any way *stable*, given with fixed centres and their connexions, but must be thought of as *labile*, developing by function itself and continually changing as function changes.

We are led to this conclusion yet more directly by the second of our two groups of phenomena: the symptoms of auxiliary and vicarious function that regularly follow in the train of speech disturbances, and that point again to the universal validity of associations and their gradual establishment by practice. What is called amnestic aphasia still furnishes the most striking illustrations; it shows the phenomena of associative compensation in extraordinary variety. Thus, we not infrequently find that the word for an object is not directly at the patient's disposal, but that it is immediately remembered if other verbal ideas, that often occur in connexion with it, are intentionally reproduced. In one case, which has become classical, the patient, who suffered from an almost total amnesia induced by an injury to the head, was always able to discover the forgotten words *by writing them down*. Further, if he were required to name the attributes of an object, he failed to do so, both when the object itself was named and when the attributes in question were exhibited to him in other objects, but succeeded, after some improvement in his condition had set in, *if he saw the object before*

---

[1] KUSSMAUL, *Störungen der Sprache*, 163 f.

him.[1] Cases of this kind, which cannot be included in any rigid schema of localisation, are referred by certain authorities to a 'functional aphasia,' and thus distinguished from the typical forms of cortical and subcortical aphasia. In reality, however, instances of associative compensation are extremely common. We may unhesitatingly assume that if the phenomena are not recorded, and more especially if they are not recorded with minor degrees of derangement, this is merely because they have not been observed or not explicitly verified. All the aphasic disturbances are, indeed, at once functional and anatomical: and the functional disorder does not exclude structural defect as such, but only that rigid localisation which is presupposed in the schematisations of the centres and their connexions. The error that has crept in is the error of inversion. The anatomical conditions have been first laid down, and the functional symptoms that came under observation have then been assigned, as accurately as might be, to determinate cortical areas. But the first requirement evidently is that we analyse the functions themselves, and only then turn to consider how, in the light of this analysis, the anatomical conditions are to be envisaged.

If we take our stand upon this principle, we must necessarily begin by examining these psychological facts from which the associative relations may be ascertained that hold between the individual constituents of a verbal idea or between the different word ideas themselves. For the sake of brevity, these associative relations may be termed, in their entirety, the *psychological structure of verbal ideas*. We may, further, limit our enquiry to the constitution of consciousness that characterises the adult members of a civilised community, where the artificial development of the capacities of reading and writing has been superinduced by practice upon the natural function of speech. Proceeding on this basis to our task of a general appreciation of these activities, and of the disturbances which occur amongst them, we note, first of all, that every complete verbal idea is a *complicative association of three constituents*: the phonetic utterance, L; the script form, S; and the meaning contents, B. Each of these is, in turn, made up of two, more intimately compounded elements, Thus, the phonetic utterance, L, is composed of auditory idea (a) and articulatory sensation (m). The script form S is composed of visual idea (o) and movement sensations of writing (m'): these latter, we may suppose, corresponding originally to the pantomimic movements with which primitive man accompanies his talk, and then translated by civilisation later on into the specific form of writing

---

[1] GRASHEY'S case, *Archiv f. Psychiatrie*, xvi., 694 ff. This case, which is one of great interest, has been further investigated by R. SOMMER (*Zeits. f. Psych. u. Physiol. d. Sinnesorgane*, ii., 143) and G. WOLFF (*ibid.*, xv., 1 ff.). Cf. the detailed discussion in my *Völkerpsychologie*, i., 1, 1900, 502 ff., and in STÖRRING, *Vorlesungen über Psychopathologie*, 132 ff. A survey of the very extensive modern literature on aphasia and amnesia is given by O. VOGT, *Zeits. f. Hypnotismus*, vi., 1897, 215, 266 ff. Cf. also PICK, *Arch. f. Psychiatrie*, xxviii., 1 ff., and C. BASTIAN, *Aphasia and Other Speech Defects*, 1898.

movements. Lastly, the meaning contents B may be analysed, in general, into an ideational component (v), and a feeling (g) dependent both upon this and upon the whole configuration of consciousness, but more especially upon its relations to other contents, past and present. Not only B, however, but the other constituents of the verbal idea, L and S, as well, are associatively connected in the most various ways with further meaning contents and word ideas; so that a given combination $L\ S\ B$ never really occurs by itself alone, but always as a formation only relatively isolable from a more or less complicated tissue of associations. Now all the phenomena of speech, and all its disturbances also, indicate that these associations with other verbal and ideational contents vary within wide limits from case to case. But they indicate, further, that the different constituents of one and the same verbal idea may be associated in very different degrees of intimacy: this altogether apart from the fact that the vivacity and activity of these constituents must vary very considerably with the constitution of the individual consciousness, with the stage of practice attained, and with the specific conditions under which the ideas are formed. Thus, there are individuals who are but obscurely aware, in ordinary speech, of the elements o, or m, m', of the complex $L\ (a\ m)\ S\ (o\ m')\ B\ (v\ g)$; the auditory impression of the word dominates in consciousness. There are others, for whom m is especially prominent; and yet others, for whom even o is constantly noticeable. In reading, o naturally stands in the foreground of consciousness. It is, however, so closely associated with the terms $a\ m$ that these may always be perceived, more or less clearly, along with it. We find the most complete representation of all three constituents in the process of writing to dictation, where a directly arouses m, m' and o. In this instance, just because the word constituents proper force themselves all together upon consciousness, the meaning contents $v\ g$ may very easily be relegated to entire obscurity; it is a common experience that writing to dictation slips more readily than any other form of speech function, more readily even than repeating from dictation, into a meaningless routine. The degree of intimacy of the association between the meaning elements $v\ g$ is further conditioned, as we remarked above when discussing the phenomena of partial amnesia, upon the logical and grammatical value of the verbal ideas. It is owing to the influence of this factor that, in abstract word forms, the ideational constituent v entirely disappears behind the word elements proper, a and o, and only the affective element g remains. We shall treat later of this 'conceptual feeling'; here we have simply to note that it is firmly associated to the word constituents $L\ S$.[1]

Finally, there are two further phenomena, connected with this variation

[1] Cf. the fuller psychological discussion of the processes of association in Part V., Ch. xix. below.

in the intimacy of associative combinations, that require a special mention. They bring out, in a striking way, the quite extraordinary variety of tendency and disposition exhibited by the speech functions in the individual case. The first is this: that the closeness of any particular association, of the group here under discussion, depends not only upon the connected elements themselves, but also upon the *direction* of their connexion. It is but rarely that a speech association is of approximately equal strength on both sides. The principal instance of the kind is the connexion between the two components of the first term L of the complete verbal idea; here, under normal conditions, the auditory impression a is as powerful in arousing the tendency to articulatory movement m as the movement is to evoke the auditory idea. The same sort of reciprocal influence appears to be exerted, though on the whole with somewhat less of constancy, by the auditory word idea a and the feeling g which attaches to the meaning idea. A heard word first of all arouses a feeling of its meaning, before the meaning itself has come clearly to consciousness. This order of events obtains more especially in the case of unfamiliar or entirely unknown words; oftentimes, indeed, the whole process stops short with the arousal of the conceptual feeling. But we also observe, conversely, that in cases where the word that expresses a particular idea is for the moment beyond reach, in cases i.e. where we are " trying to think of " a word, a strong associative influence is exercised by the feeling accompanying the idea; so that it is clearly the association $g\ a$, and not (or, at any rate, only in a much slighter degree) the association $v\ a$, that is primarily responsible for the success of the act of recollection. In direct antithesis to these associations, in which the strength of the connexion is approximately the same for both sides, are those in which the one direction has a decisive advantage over the other. Here belongs, e.g., the association between o and m, where the direction $o\ m$ represents a much stronger associative tendency than the direction $m\ o$,—the script form arouses the movement of articulation, but this has very little power to call up the script form; or the association between m and m', where the movements of writing easily arouse the articulatory sensations of the organs of speech, but these require special conditions if they are to touch off the movements; and so on.

As a rule, then, the speech association runs more smoothly in the one direction than in the other. The second complicating condition is this. There is a continual fluctuation, not only in the strength of the connexions at large, but also and more particularly in the *preponderance of the one or the other direction* under the influence of practice. The effects of practice are seen most clearly in cases where some change has been produced in the normal intensity of the individual constituents of the idea, or where certain associations have lost their efficacy. In deaf-mutism, e.g., the elements *am* are entirely wanting. This loss is compensated by the development of the elements $o\,m'$ and of the two-way association between them: m', at the same time, appears in its original character as component of a mimetic movement. If the patient learns to speak, the connexion $o\,m$ develops as a two-way association of the most pronounced type, and completely replaces the normal connexion $a\,m$; and so on.

We may now attempt, in the light of the preceding paragraphs, to construct a plan of the whole number of associations that obtain between the elements of the complete word idea. Let the elements be denoted by the symbols, a, m, o, m', v, g; the associations between them by connecting lines; the direction of the associations by arrows; and their relative stability by the thickness of the lines. The ordinary course of the associations, within a complete word idea, will then be represented, in general terms, by the schema shown in Fig. 104. The effects of other word ideas, past or present, are indicated by the symbols v', g', and the interrupted lines proceeding from them.[1] This schema, it must be remembered, is not a

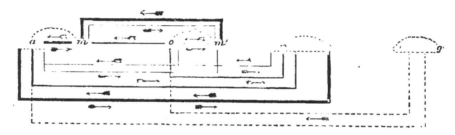

FIG. 104. Schema of the associations of a complete verbal idea.

stable structure; it varies from individual to individual, and from time to time. And the associations that enter into it are themselves variable processes, largely dependent, in particular, upon foregone associations and all sorts of other psychical conditions.

We began this discussion with a review of the 'speech centres.' From the point of view to which we have now attained by our functional analysis of verbal ideas, these centres, mapped out in Fig. 102 in accordance with pathological observations of the lesions underlying disturbances of speech, naturally acquire a very different significance from that assigned them in the plan of localisation and conduction laid down in Fig. 103. For it is clear that the constituents a, m, o, m' of a word idea can be brought into settled relation with definite brain areas only on condition that the associations between them may be regarded as relatively stable connexions. There

---

[1] This schema is taken from my *Völkerpsychologie*, i., 1, 1900, 519 ff. (section on the psychical structure of word ideas). The reader is referred to this passage for further explanation of the Figure.

are, however, two reasons why they may not be so regarded. In the first place, both the intimacy and the direction of the associations are throughout dependent upon individual practice. In the second place, the formation of at least one set of associations, those that include the terms o and m', cannot be explained save as the outcome of a development which is conditioned upon a certain level of civilisation, and which therefore began late in the history of the race. We might accordingly expect to find, as in fact we do, that these associations are subject to especially large individual variations. But variability in the conduction paths necessarily brings with it a certain degree of variability in the centres themselves: a conclusion which we need not hesitate to accept, since it is borne out, from another side, by the phenomena of restitution of function. In fine, then, the expression 'speech centre' cannot, under any circumstances, designate a central organ, in the sense in which this term is ordinarily employed,—an organ that presides, exclusively or even preponderantly, over a determinate group of functions. It can mean nothing more than an area which contains the most important nodal points of those conductions whose co-operation is indispensable for functions of this particular kind. In other words, the significance of the centres is rather that they comprise the *points of connexion* than that they include the *points of departure* of the elementary processes concerned in a certain complex activity. Such a conception harmonises very well with the idea suggested by the effects of practice and of restoration of function: the idea that it is not the centres but, in a certain sense, the *functions* that are the original things. The functions make their centres, and are constantly modifying them in accordance with the variable conditions of function itself. Hence the localisation of the functions is not stable, but labile; the boundaries of the functional areas are not fixed, but changing,—subject to the functional influences that modify the conditions of conduction, and with them the actual conduction paths. So it comes about that functional analysis of the very phenomena which first inspired the modern doctrine of strict localisations, the phenomena of derangement of speech, has at every stage thrown the intrinsic impossibility of this doctrine into clear relief. Such a result, however, is, after all, but the natural consequence of the extreme complexity of the speech functions, and of that many-sidedness and variability of the psychophysical conditions which they are peculiarly fitted to bring into open view. Understood in this way, it is also a result that must be generalised. What holds of the speech centres holds, in reality, of the 'sensory centres' as well, despite the fact that, even to-day, they are ordinarily interpreted as simple central projection surfaces. They, too, are 'association centres,' in the sense that they contain nodal points which serve to centralise the functions, but centralise them by bringing into connexion all the different partial functions, sensations, movements, reflexes, synergies of sensations

(c)—The Apperception Centre

There is an extensive region of the human brain that appears, so far as sensory and motor symptoms are concerned, to be comparatively indifferent whether to external stimulation or to internal change: the portion of the frontal lobes that lies anteriorly to the anterior margin of the motor zone (Fig. 88, p. 205). Pathological observations show that injuries to this region, sometimes involving the loss of considerable masses of the brain substance, have failed to produce any derangement whatsoever of the motor and sensory functions.[1] As a rule, however, the observers report, with equal definiteness, a permanent disturbance of the mental attributes and faculties In a famous American case, e.g., a pointed iron rod, one and a half inches in diameter, was driven through the head by the explosion of a blast, entering at the angle of the left lower jaw and emerging near the anterior extremity of the sagittal suture. The patient, who lived twelve and a half years after the accident, gave no indication of disturbance of sensation and voluntary movement, but suffered a complete change of character and activities. "He combines the animal passions of a man with the intellectual activities of a child," so writes the attending physician.[2] In other cases, decay of memory, inability to concentrate the attention, entire loss of will-power, etc., are quoted as characteristic symptoms.[3] These results agree with the observation that the pathological degenerations of brain tissue which accompany the decay of intelligence and will in cases of paralytic dementia usually have their seat in the frontal lobes,[4] and with the general law that intellectual development keeps even pace throughout the animal kingdom with the development of the prosencephalon.[5] It is also said that highly developed human brains are often characterised by an especially abundant formation of secondary gyres and fissures in the frontal lobes.[6] It can hardly be maintained, however, that in these cases there is any marked difference between the frontal and the other, e.g., the parietal and occipital regions.[7]

---

[1] Cf. the cases collected by CHARCOT and PITRES (*Revue mensuelle*, Nov., 1877), FERRIER (*Localisation of Cerebral Disease*, 1878), and DE BOYER (*Études cliniques*, 40, 54); also BIANCHI, in *Brain*, xviii., 1895, 497.

[2] The report is printed by FERRIER, *op. cit.*

[3] Cf. DE BOYER, 45, obs. iv.; 55, obs. xxvii. VON MONAKOW, *Gehirnpathologie*, 491 ff. The latter author reports a similar case from the Zurich clinic, and cites other analogous observations of JASTROWITZ.

[4] MEYNERT, *Vierteljahrsschrift f. Psychiatrie*, 1867, 166.

[5] FLATAU and JACOBSOHN, *Handbuch d. Anat. u. vergl. Anat. d. Centralnervensystems d. Säugethiere*, i., 536 ff. MARCHAND, *Die Morphologie des Stirnlappens*, in *Arbeiten des pathol. Instituts zu Marburg*, ii., 1893.

[6] H. WAGNER, *op. cit.*

[7] The reader may refer, for purposes of comparison, to the figures of the brains of GAUSS and of an individual of moderate intelligence, Figg. 100, 101, p. 285, above.

On the ground of these facts, it has been suggested by various investigators, among others by MEYNERT, HITZIG, FERRIER and FLECHSIG, that the frontal brain stands in intimate relation to the functions of the 'intelligence.' Now 'intelligence' is an exceedingly complex and indefinite term. If, as we have seen, the act of vision and the different functions concerned in speech are connected with 'centres' only in a very limited sense, it is, of course, impossible to conceive of a localisation of the intellectual functions, or to connect them with a specific 'organ of intelligence.' The utmost that we can say is that that this particular region of the cortex may contain certain nodal points of conductions, whose abrogation produces disturbances of an intrinsically elementary character, but manifesting themselves, in the complexity of functional co-operation, as impairment of the 'intelligence' and derangement of the compound feelings. On the anatomical side, the abundant connexions mediated by association fibres between the frontal brain and other brain regions, furnish a distinct support to the view that the frontal lobes contain nodal points of especial importance for the interrelation of the central functional areas. And the objection that lesions of the frontal brain have occasionally been observed to pass without permanent moral or intellectual injury is not decisive:[1] for local lesions in general are the more easily compensated, by vicarious function of other parts, the more numerous and varied are the connexions of the elements; and this condition is, on the whole, more adequately met by the cortical areas occupied by the 'association centres' than it is by the direct sensory and motor centres. Hence these negative results, in cases of local injury, are far outweighed by the fact, as stated by the brain pathologists, that "lesions of any extent at all are never observed to occur in this region without causing the most serious intellectual defects."[2]

Let us now attempt, so far as may be possible, to analyse the complex phenomena, grouped together under the indefinite rubric of 'intelligence,' into their elementary processes. These processes must be such as can be connected with a clear and simple psychological idea; and this must, in its turn, be capable of correlation with a correspondingly simple physiological idea. We find what we require in the elementary idea of the *apperception* of a mental contents, e.g. of a sensation. What apperception means in detail we shall show later on:[3] here we understand by it a psychological process in which, on the objective side, a certain contents becomes *clear* in consciousness and, on the subjective, certain *feelings* arise which, as referred to any given contents, we ordinarily term the state of 'attention.' Now the objective component of this complex process, the 'clarification'

---

[1] ZIEHEN, *Leitfaden der physiol. Psychologie*, 5te Aufl., 195; *Introduction to Physiological Psychology*, 1895, 231.
[2] VON MONAKOW, *Gehirnpathologie*, 492.
[3] Part IV., Ch. xvii.; Part V., Ch. xviii.

of a contents, is surely suggestive in the highest degree of determinate physiological concomitants. Just as, e.g., when a sensation grows stronger or weaker, there is a parallel increase or decrease of the physiological processes of excitation in particular nervous elements, so must we suppose that, when sensations or other conscious contents grow, as we have put it, clearer or more obscure, these changes are conditioned upon some sort of physiological substrate. And it is evident that this substrate may very well consist of certain simple processes, consistent with the general principles of nerve mechanics; whereas the idea of 'intelligence' is altogether so complicated that the search for any kind of definite or limited physical substrate would, in its case, be entirely hopeless.

It might, at first thought, be supposed that the elementary process of apperception which appears in its simplest form when a sensation becomes clearer, consists, on the physiological side, merely in an increase of the nervous excitation that runs parallel with the sensation; and that the physiological change, when the sensation becomes more obscure, is a corresponding decrease of the same concomitant excitation. But to say that a sensation 'grows clearer' or 'grows more obscure,' is, in reality, a very different thing from saying that it 'increases' or 'decreases in intensity.' To speak relatively, a weak sensation may be clearly, and an intensive sensation obscurely apperceived. And a little introspection suffices to show that a sensation, in growing stronger or weaker, alters its *own* intrinsic character; while, if it grows clearer or more obscure, the change is primarily a change in its relation to *other* conscious contents. A particular impression is always apprehended as 'clearer' in contrast to other impressions which, as compared with it, appear obscure. These facts suggest that the substrate of the simple apperception process may be sought in *inhibitory processes* which, by the very fact that they arrest other concomitant excitations, secure an advantage for the particular excitations not inhibited. If we postulate an inhibitory process of this kind, we are able to explain how it is that apperception as such does not consist in an intensification of the sensation contents. And if we assume, further, that the inhibitory influence, in this special case, is not exerted directly upon certain excitations in progress within the sensory centres, but rather upon the conduction of the excitations to the higher centres in which the sensory contents are combined to form complex resultants, we avoid doing violence to the obverse fact that the conscious contents obscured by inhibition do not on that account lose in intensity. The arousal of the inhibition, since on the psychological side it is ordinarily dependent upon particular conscious contents, past and present, must be physiologically conceived as analogous to that of the reflex inhibitions occurring in various forms in the lower nerve centres. There is, however, a difference. The inhibitory effects are liberated, here as elsewhere, by certain excitations that are conducted to the centre; but their liberation is at the same time influenced by that incalculable manifold of conditions which, for the most part, we can merely group together under the indefinite name of the current disposition of consciousness, as determined by past experience and the circumstances of the time.

We thus regard apperception as the one elementary process indispensable to any sort of 'manifestation of intelligence,' and, indeed, to the higher mental functions at large. The considerations put forward above with respect to its physiological substrate are, of course, hypothetical. We have far fewer data in this case even than we had for our discussions of the functions of the visual and speech centres, and we are accordingly thrown back upon conjecture and tentative hypothesis. These must be based, almost exclusively, upon the results of a psychological analysis of the functions. Except for the meagre analogy of reflex inhibition, physiology furnishes us with nothing more than the general principles of nerve mechanics. Nevertheless, it is worth while to attempt a schematic representation of our theory; we can at least show the general possibility of a physiological interpretation of the complex phenomena in question. Such a representation is given in Fig. 105. We assume that the central area of apperception AC stands in connexion with a twofold system of conduction paths: the one centripetal, ss', hh', that brings up sensory excitations from the primary sensory centres; and the other centrifugal, la, gf, etc., that carries, conversely, to subordinate centres the inhibitory impulses proceeding from AC. We then have, according as these impulses are transmitted to sensory or motor centres, either the apperception of sensations or the execution of voluntary movements. In the former case, it is other sensations, in the latter other motor impulses, aroused by internal or external stimuli, that are forced into the background. It is plain that the transmission here assumed presents a certain analogy to the reflex process, and particularly to the reflex inhibitions. At the same time, the way in which apperception depends upon the sensory excitations coming in at the moment marks a wide divergence from the schema of the reflex mechanism. In the reflex, we find the motor excitation or inhibition following of necessity from the action of the sensory stimuli; in apperception and voluntary movement, we can speak simply of a

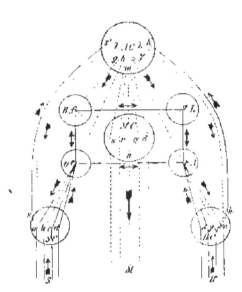

FIG. 105. Schema of the hypothetical connexions of the apperception centre. *SC* Visual centre. *HC* Auditory centre. *S* Central fibres of the opticus. *H* Central fibres of the acusticus. *A, O* Sensory, *L, B* motor intermediate centres. *MC* Direct motor centre. *M* Central motor fibres. *AC* Apperception centre. ss', hh' Centripetal paths to AC. la, gf, etc. Centrifugal connexions of AC.

regulative influence of the excitations in progress,—the implication being that a large number of intermediate terms, which our methods cannot reach, exert a determining influence upon the final result. The physiological character of these intermediaries is wholly unknown to us. We can only infer, from psychological experience, that definite dispositions take shape in every brain, as the consequence of generic and individual development, and determine the excitatory processes that run parallel with the act of apperception. If, then, we refer the apperceptive acts to a particular physiological substrate, we can do so only on the condition that we endow the central area in question with connexions to the other central parts, in virtue of which the excitations released in it are dependent upon these dispositions. Hence the centrifugal paths that issue from the apperception organ AC and serve to conduct the inhibitory excitations must, in general, take two directions: a centrifugal sensory and a centrifugal motor. In both directions they are connected, both directly and indirectly, by way of intermediate centres that represent nodal points of conduction for certain complex functions, with the direct sensory centres (SC, HC) and the motor centres (MC). The part of intermediary is played, within the centrifugal sensory path, by certain intermediate sensory centres (O and A); within the motor path, by analogous motor centres of complex character (B and L). The term 'centre' is here used, of course, only in the relative sense defined above, in the discussion of the visual and speech centres. We found, e.g., that the speech centres were not to be regarded as independent sources of the functions ordinarily ascribed to them, but simply as indispensable intermediaries in the mechanism of speech associations and apperceptions; and the same conclusion holds here. The physiological significance of these centres may be roughly illustrated in this way. We will suppose that various sensations, belonging to the domain of speech, have arisen in the sense centres proper, SC and HC. The corresponding excitations are at once combined, in the intermediate sensory centres O and A, into an unitary excitation process; whereupon the apperceptive inhibition can operate to render this, or the primary excitations in progress in the centres SC and HC, clearer or more obscure. The processes in O and A will thus have the significance of resultants, which correspond to the functional unification of the two associatively connected elements, phonetic utterance and script form. These resultants must not, we need hardly repeat, be regarded as traces, stamped indelibly upon certain cells, but rather as transitory processes of extremely complex character, embracing a large variety of elements,—processes akin to the stimulation processes in the peripheral sense organs, and to other processes in the central nerve substance, all of which leave a disposition to their renewal behind them. A like function must be assigned to the intermediate motor centres B and L, in which an act of apperception releases (by the paths $g f r s$, $\gamma \phi \rho \sigma$) a determinate motor excitation, corresponding to the sensory excitations brought up from SC and HC (by ss', hh'), or from O and A (by ek, $\epsilon\kappa$); or else an unmediated activity on the part of the two elements, phonetic utterance and script form, releases (by the paths ef, $\epsilon\phi$) the corresponding motor impulses, without interference from the apperception centre, i.e. by way of a direct reflex excitation. These impulses are then, in all cases, carried (by the paths $f r s$, $\phi \rho \sigma$) to the general motor centres MC, whence they are transmitted along the further nerve conduction to the muscles.

In the hypothetical schema of Fig. 105, the paths that lead towards AC and all paths of connexion between subordinate centres are represented by uninterrupted, the centrifugal paths that lead away from AC by interrupted lines, and the direction of conduction is further indicated by arrows. Besides the direct motor centres MC, and besides the auditory and visual centres SC, HC, chosen as the chief representatives of the sensory centres, the schema includes, as examples of more complex central areas, the four 'speech centres' mapped out in Fig. 102. Suppose, now, that a series of impressions is carried by the optic nerve S to the visual centre SC: we have, taking only the principal cases, the following possibilities. (1) The impressions are not conducted farther. Then the sensations remain in the state of mere perception or indistinct apprehension. (2) An individual impression a is apperceptively enhanced by inhibition of the impressions $b\ c\ d$: the inhibition is released by way of ss' and hh', and conducted to the centre SC by the path la. We then have perception of $b\ c\ d$ and apperception of a. (3) Besides the apperception of the impression a, there is a conduction by way of O to the centre A. Here a resultant is released, which produces in the auditory centre HC (by way of $e\ \epsilon\ \alpha$) the verbal idea a corresponding to the visual image a. At the same time, by means of inhibitions released in the centres A and SC along the paths $\kappa\epsilon$ and $\lambda\alpha$, the resulting word idea and the phonetic utterance are apperceived. (4) The processes described under (3) combine with (a) a conduction of the resultants from A by way of L to MC (along $\epsilon\phi$ and $\phi\rho\sigma$): involuntarily pronunciation of the word designating an apperceived idea ; (b) a conduction from AC by way of l to MC (along $\gamma\phi$ and $\phi\rho\sigma$): intentional pronunciation of the word in question ; (c) a conduction from HC by way of A to O, and from O again by way of SC to certain other elements, not shown in the Figure: involuntary association of the word idea to the script form. (5) If the original impression a is the script form of a word, we have the following possibilities : (a) direct apperception, again, by means of an inhibition la ; (b) conduction from SC to O, and apperceptive inhibitions along the paths la and ke : apperception of a word whose meaning is familiar ; (c) conduction from SC to O, and from O by way of A to HC, with the fourfold apperceptive inhibition la, ke, $\kappa\epsilon$ and $\lambda\alpha$: apperception of a visual and of the corresponding auditory word idea (the ordinary process in reading) ; and so on. For the rest, this Figure, too, necessarily leaves out of account all those moments that, in the nature of the case, cannot be given a place in any pure conduction schema : so, more particularly, the intimacy and direction of the associations, specially indicated in Fig. 104 for the functions of speech ; the influences of practice and of vicarious function, which are constantly at work to change the face of the phenomena ; and finally the influences, wholly rebellious, like the last, to any attempt at schematic representation, which are exerted, psychologically by the configuration of consciousness, physiologically by the general state of the nervous dispositions, upon the associations and apperceptions in progress at any given time.

§ 8. General Principles of the Central Functions

(a)—*The Principle of Connexion of Elements*

THE principle of the connexion of elements may be understood in an anatomical, a physiological, and a psychological sense. It may therefore be formulated in three different ways, each one of them individual, in contents and meaning, but each one again, in all probability, closely related to the others.

Anatomically regarded, the nervous system is an unitary complex of numerous elements; and every one of these morphological elements stands in more or less close connexion with others. This fact of interrelation is expressed in the very structure of the essential elements, the nerve cells. Not only are the connexions mediated, in general, by the cell processes, but the character of these processes, as dendrites and neurite, oftentimes indicates the direction in which the proximate connexions are made. It is the merit of the neurone theory to have shown how this principle of the connexion of elements is exhibited in the morphological relations of the central nervous system. And the merit would remain, even if the theory, in its present form, should ultimately prove untenable.

Physiologically, the principle of the connexion of elements implies that every physiological activity, which is open to our observation and analysis, is composed of a large number of elementary functions, the nature of which we may, under favourable circumstances, be able to infer, but which we can never completely isolate from the given complex activity. In particular, e.g., the physiological process underlying however simple a sensation or muscular contraction is a complex process, involving the activities of many elementary parts. This may be seen at once from its physiological analysis in a given case, whether the analysis be applied directly to the group of actual functions, or whether it be performed inferentially by a study of the connexions of the elements concerned in them. Our discussions of the act of vision and of the functions of speech bear witness, in both directions, to this physiological significance of the principle of elementary connexions.

Lastly, there is a psychological, as well as an anatomical and physiological, formulation of the principle. It means, psychologically, that the simplest psychical contents discoverable by analysis of the facts of consciousness always presuppose, as their physiological substrate, complex nerve processes, the result of the co-operation of many elementary parts. This complexity of the physical conditions of elementary psychical facts manifests itself in two ways: first, in psychological observation itself, in so far as the psychical elements, simple sensations or simple feelings, are always products of psychological abstraction, and never actually occur except in connexions (a simple colour sensation, e.g., is given as a coloured object in space, and so on): and secondly, in the physiological fact that no psychical process can be imagined, however simple it may be, which does not require for its origination a large number of functionally connected elementary parts. Thus, in the arousal of a sensation of light or tone we have not only the action of stimulus upon the peripheral structures, but also and invariably the processes of nervous conduction, the excitations of central elements in the mesencephalic region, and finally certain processes in the cortical centres. If the sensory excitation is of central origin, as is sometimes the case,—e.g. in memory images,—then, conversely, it is first co-ordinate centres and then peripheral regions that are involved in it. Hence every conscious contents, though it be as in these instances quite simple, conceived of in isolation from its connexions, and therefore, psychologically, insusceptible of further analysis, is always, physiologically considered, a complicated formation made up of various nerve processes spread over a large number of elementary parts.

(b)—*The Principle of Original Indifference of Functions*

The principle of the connexion of elements, in its anatomical and physiological signification, cannot but suggest the hypothesis that, wherever the physiological functions of the central elements have acquired a specific colouring,—recognisable psychologically, say, in the peculiar quality of a sensation, or physiologically in the release of a muscular contraction or the origination of a secretory or other chemical process,—this specific character of their activity is conditioned not upon the elements themselves, but upon their connexions. The connexions to which we must thus ascribe a determining influence upon the development of specific functions are, however, not so much the connexions of the nervous elements with one another, as rather their connexions, first, with the organs and tissue elements that directly subserve the functions themselves, and secondly, with the external stimuli by which the organs and elements are adequately excited. As regards sensation, in particular, which in virtue of its psychological significance is the most important of all specific functions, the determining factors cannot be found in the specific energy of any set of nerve fibres or nerve cells, but only in the physical action of the stimuli upon the sense organs and its immediate consequences, viz., certain changes in the sensory elements that serve to transmit the stimulation to the sensory nerves. It is a matter of indifference, for the present argument, whether these elements are themselves nervous in character, as they are in the olfactory mucous membrane and perhaps in the retina of the eye, or whether they simply represent epithelial appendages to the nervous system, as they do in the organs of touch and audition. But if, now, the specific activity of the nervous elements that belong to a particular sense department is the result of development, if it has been acquired under pressure of the external conditions of life, then the hypothesis of an *original indifference of function* follows of itself. And this principle, once formulated, immediately suggests the further hypothesis that the functional indifference will have persisted in all cases in which special conditions have not been at work to produce specific differences. There are, as a matter of fact, two phenomena which make it extremely probable that such functional indifference has persisted in a high degree among the central elements. The first is this: that a fairly long continuance of the function of the peripheral organs is required, if the sensations of the corresponding sense department are to appear in consciousness. Those who are born blind or deaf, and even those who have lost the sense of sight or hearing in early childhood, lack the sensation qualities of light and sound. And these sensation qualities are evidently wanting at a time when the atrophic degeneration of the central sensory elements, which results where the functions have been abrogated for a considerable period, cannot yet have set in.[1] The second phenomenon is this: that the functional disturbances occasioned by central lesions may be compensated without disappearance of the lesions themselves, i.e. under conditions that force us to assume a vicarious functioning on the part of other elements. But this clearly presupposes that, under stress of the conditions of life, the elements may take on novel functions of a special kind. In such cases, we are able to trace the rise of specific functions during the lifetime of the individual. We are, of course, bound to suppose that the conditions of the principal functional differentiations have been operative during the evolution of the race. Still, the facts just cited prove that we inherit nothing more definite than certain *dispositions*, which are given with the connexions of the nervous elements; and that the development of specific functions demands the actual discharge of these functions, and is therefore altogether dependent upon the direct action of the vital stimuli during the course of the individual life. This dependence of the elementary nervous processes upon external impressions must now be localised, primarily, in the nervous elements that come into closest contact with the sensory stimuli, i.e. in those situated at the periphery; it may be looked for far less probably in the more central regions, where, as we have said, substitution and exchange of functions play a leading part. Since, therefore, the immediate contents of consciousness always find expression in the elementary qualities originating in direct connexion with the peripheral functions, everything favours the view that the activities of the higher central elements consist solely in the effects which they produce by the combination and, under certain circumstances, by the inhibition of the excitations conveyed to them.

It follows, then, that the principle of the indifference of elementary functions admits, like its predecessor, of an anatomical, a physiological, and a psychological derivation. Anatomically, it is supported by the essential identity of structure that we find throughout the elements of the nervous system. The neurones differ both in form and in extent. But striking as these variations may sometimes be, the structural differences that they exhibit are, at most, such as indicate merely a difference in direction of conduction; and even these are apparently confined to the more highly dif-

[1] See p. 53, above; and cf. Part II., ch. viii., below.

ferentiated nerve cells (pp. 42 f.). Physiologically, the principle of indifference of function is attested by the uniform character of the forces that reside in the nervous elements. The two mutually supplementary forms of energy that we designated, from their mechanical effects, excitation and inhibition, or positive and negative molecular work (pp. 60, 80), appear throughout as the simple substrate of nervous function. It is true that, in working out the fundamental ideas of a physiological mechanics of the nervous system, we allowed ourselves to be guided, in the first instance, by the phenomena of muscle, i.e. of the mechanical structures appended to that system. At the same time, these peripheral phenomena came into consideration only in their symptomatic significance. We expressed the facts in a certain way, at the instance of external conditions. But, mode of expression apart, we have every reason to assume the essential identity of the nervous processes. Lastly, the principle derives its principal support, on the psychological side, from the fact that the specific differences in the sensory contents of consciousness, if they are of an elementary nature, may always be resolved into qualities of sensation and feeling that depend upon the functions of peripheral elements. In so far, therefore, as the central nervous system is concerned in the higher psychical processes, it must be occupied, not with the origination of new specific qualities, but solely with the indefinitely complex interrelation of these sensory elements of our mental life.

(c)—*The Principle of Practice and Adaptation*

'Practice,' in the ordinary acceptation of the term, consists in the perfecting of a function by its repeated performance. Hence the principle of practice, as applied to the functions of the nervous system, signifies that every central element, whether considered by itself or regarded as co-operating in some especial way, determined by the conditions of life, with other like elements, becomes better and better fitted to discharge or to share in the discharge of a particular function, the more frequently it has been called to its service by pressure of external conditions. We are already familiar with the elementary phenomenon of practice, in the increase of excitability by stimulation (p. 75). This elementary phenomenon is common to all elements of the nervous system : it may be demonstrated even in the isolated nerve, though it is observed at its best, and its aftereffects are more persistent, in the connected neurones and neurone chains. We thus have every reason to look upon it as responsible for the marked changes that are continually taking place, as the result of function, in the nervous apparatus and their appended organs: changes that, especially if we extend them beyond individual to generic development, represent the organs themselves as, in large measure, the products of their functions.

The obverse of the practice processes is seen, on the other hand, in the decrease and ultimate abrogation of functions which, as the result of functional inactivity, is at the same time connected with degeneration and waste of their morphological substrate (p. 53).

The effect of practice need not be limited to the quantitative enhancement of a given function. It may lead up to new combinations of elementary processes, by which the qualitative value of a complex function is altered, and the function itself, in accordance with the general character of practice, moulded into more complete correspondence with existing conditions. Under these circumstances, the process of practice is termed 'adaptation.' Adaptation, that is, can never be anything else than a result of elementary practice processes. At the same time, it is a more complex process, since it consists, by its very nature, in a number of concomitant practice courses, which culminate, definitely and purposively, in a single combined result. This complex character of adaptation makes it possible, further, that increase of practice in a given direction may coincide with decrease of practice in another, or that certain elements may be gaining in practice while other elements, alongside of them, are losing. Change in the conditions of life may thus render certain nerve paths more practicable, and others impassable. And the same shift of function that appears here, in the closure and improvement of conduction paths, may occur over whole regions of nerve cells. Hence the adaptations of chief significance for the nervous functions are those in which newly practised elements take the place of others, whose activity has been suspended under stress, internal or external, of adverse conditions. In view of their great importance for the central processes we may group the resulting phenomena under a special principle of vicarious function.

(d)—*The Principle of Vicarious Function*

Whenever it occurs, whether in the central nervous system or in other physiological departments, the phenomenon of vicarious function is simply a special case of practice and adaptation. In the present context, it may be termed a limiting case, in the sense that it extends to functions which the elements involved have never before been directly called upon to discharge, though they must, of course, have carried within them the latent possibility of their new offices. Habituation to the requirements of vicarious function may, as the preceding argument has shown, be brought about in two ways. On the one hand, elements and complexes of elements which, up to a certain time, performed only some *part* of a composite function, may afterwards, owing to the functional disability of the elements correlated with the remaining phases of the function, take upon them the duties of the whole. On the other hand, a certain group of elements may be compelled, by the incapacity of other elements with which they are in some way spatially co-ordinated, to play a part that is altogether strange to them. We may denominate the first of these cases a substitution by *extension of the area of function,* and the second a substitution by *acquisition of novel functions.* The first form is conditioned upon the original *functional* interdependence of departments of the nervous system that may be widely remote from one another; the second is conditioned, conversely, upon the *spatial* connexion of elements between which no original functional relation can be demonstrated. This spatial connexion may itself consist either in the immediate proximity of neurones lying upon the same side of the brain, or in the union of distant areas by association fibres. In the latter case, substitution occurs most often between the symmetrically situated cortical areas of the two cerebral hemispheres, and is mediated by the association systems that run from the one half of the brain to the other. This statement applies, e.g., in all probability, to the functional areas of the speech centres, whose development is usually unilateral (see above, p. 238).

The first of these two forms of substitution, that by extension of function, appears in general as a gradual *compensation* of the disturbances due to the partial impairment of a functional area of some magnitude, by way of enhancement of activity in other areas which, from the first, took their share in the same total function. These compensations may proceed from the higher centres, which, in favourable circumstances, almost entirely annul the disturbances produced by lesions in the lower; or may, contrariwise, be the work of the lower centres, which to a certain extent, though never completely, make good the loss sustained by the cessation of activity in the higher. Instances of compensation of the former kind, resulting from vicarious function on the part of superior centres, are not uncommon; we have them, e.g., in the gradual disappearance of the disturbances in cases of injury to the cerebellum, or of lesion of the diencephalic and mesencephalic region. An example of the second kind is the partial recovery of functions, normally conditioned upon the co-operation of certain cortical centres, by an enhanced compensating activity in the diencephalic and mesencephalic centres, such as may be observed more particularly in decerebrised animals (pp. 259 ff.). For both forms of substitution, the principle of connexion of elements is, besides that of practice and adaptation, of primary importance. None of these compensations would be possible, if the central function were not always divided into a number of partial functions, in each of which there is co-operation of all the factors necessary to the function as a whole; so that the higher central area contains the fundamental constituents required for the activity of the lower, and the lower in its turn those required for the function of the higher. Thus, to all appearances, we have repeated in the visual cortex, only on a higher plane and in more complicated form, the same relations of sensory and motor conditions that characterise the mesencephalic portion of the visual centres (cf. Fig. 78, p. 186). This is the reason that disturbances arising in the latter may be compensated from the visual cortex, and that, conversely, even cortical defects may, to a certain extent, be made good by the mesencephalic centres. At the same time, these compensations are, on the whole, the less likely to occur, in the case of *simple* functions, the nearer the lesions approach to the periphery; and are the less complete, in the case of *complex* functions, the higher the functional centre that is the seat of the disturbance. Interruption of the sensory nervous conductions in the myel and in the peripheral nerves is altogether beyond the reach of compensation by vicarious function. And, on the other hand, the disturbances of sense perception and of its associative connexions that are caused by destruction of cortical areas can never be more than imperfectly compensated by habituation of the lower centres.

The case stands very differently with those other forms of vicarious function which have their source in the spatial connexion, whether direct or mediated by association fibres, of the nervous elements. Here, the newly habituated parts apparently acquire wholly new functions. Under these circumstances, it is natural to suppose that the areas concerned are such as, before their assumption of the vicarious function, discharged no duties whatsoever. Indeed, there are many authors who take this assumption for granted,—connecting it, for the most part, with hypotheses regarding the complex functions of the elements themselves,—and who accordingly consider the cerebral cortex, in particular, as a functional department that contains within it a large number of reserve elements, intrinsically functionless, and provided simply as substitutes for elements that may have become defective. Now the fringe of teleological ideas that surrounds this notion of 'functional reserves' would alone make us hesitate to accept it. But, that apart, the hypothesis runs counter to the fact that functionless elements always evince a gradual degeneration and decay (Fig. 22, p. 53). Suppose, e.g., that the 'speech centres' of the right hemisphere were entirely functionless: it would then be impossible to understand why they do not become altogether atrophied in the course of a long individual life, still more in that of many generations. This difficulty disappears if, as the principle of the connexion of elements requires, we hold to the opinion that every complex function presupposes an intricate co-operation of central elements and their connecting conductions. But then we cannot fail to see that there is another hypothesis, indefinitely more probable than that which we have just been discussing: the hypothesis, namely, that, here too, the elements destined to vicarious duty have always had a certain, only a comparatively unimportant share in the normal function; and that the substitution consequently consists, again, simply in an enhancement of activities, along lines already familiar to the elements in their normal state. Looked at from this point of view, the appearance of aphasia after destruction of the speech centres of the left side would not imply that the speech functions had their exclusive seat in this left hemisphere, or, as has sometimes been suggested by those who support the hypothesis of word localisation, that only certain subordinate word forms, e.g. the interjections, are localised on the right. It is much more reasonable to suppose that the co-operation of neurone territories, where it is so extraordinarily complicated as it must be in a function of the complexity of speech, involves wide-spread areas in both halves of the brain; though, as a matter of fact, the areas of the left hemisphere are normally the more practised, and their destruction accordingly produces specially obvious defects. The larger practice of the motor organs on the right as compared with those on the left hand side of the body furnishes an admirable parallel to this functional habituation. Genetically, it is, in all probability, related to the unequal development of the speech centres; and factually, it repeats that inequality point by point. For the organs on the right hand side of the body are the more practised, but they are not the sole vehicles of function; and just because they are not, is substitution by new habituations possible.

(e)—*The Principle of Relative Localisation*

There can be no doubt that, in a certain sense, the central functions, like those of the peripheral organs, are spatially distinct. But there can also be no doubt that the central organ, as its names implies, represents in contradistinction to the peripheral organs a centralisation and thus, at the same time, an unification of functions; so that any absolute localisation of function, which should confine each separate activity within fixed limits, is *a priori* impossible, as it is also unsupported by the facts of observation. In the peripheral organs, where the demands of external function have produced diversity of structure, the principle of division of labour is strictly observed, and the localisation of function follows in the train of its observance. In the centres of the nervous system, the principle is broken through in two different ways. On the one hand, every central function divides, and divides the more definitely the higher its place in the ascending series of activities, into a number of subordinate and auxiliary functions, which of themselves embrace wide and, in part, widely remote areas of the central nervous system. On the other, the processes of practice, adaptation and vicarious function show that the spatial centralisation of a function is not fixed, but dependent upon its exercise, and upon the conditions under which this exercise is placed, so that any rigid spatial limitation is out of the question. The name of 'visual centre,' e.g., is by no means to be restricted to the region of the occipital brain known as the 'visual cortex.' The nodal points of the optic conduction in the lower nerve centres have good right to share in the title, seeing that they are not only constantly involved in the normal functions of vision, but are also able, to a certain extent, to do substitute duty for the functions of the higher region. Since, therefore, the principle of vicarious function, like the principle of practice and adaptation, implies a dependence upon external and internal conditions which allow the elementary functions a certain freedom of exchange, the localisation of the central functions at large cannot be looked upon as anything more than relative, i.e. dependent in this way upon the functional conditions of the time, and varying with their variation. The principle of localisation thus stands in the closest relation to the principles of the connexion of elements and of the original indifference of function. For without the connexion of elements that is required by every, even the simplest form of central activity, and without an original and, in the case of many central elements, a permanent functional indifference, there could be no shift of the limits of a function with change in its conditions. In fine, then, the principle of relative localisation gathers up and includes all the preceding principles, as its necessary presuppositions; while an absolute localisation of the central functions, such as is oftentimes assumed, comes into direct conflict with every one of them.

The five principles laid down in the text have gained ground but very slowly in the development of the theory of the central functions; and even at the present day they have failed, in many instances, to overcome the opposing views. Their progress was hindered, from the outset, by the authority of scientific tradition; in some measure, more particularly in the domain of anatomical and physiological research, it is so hindered still. Rightly to appreciate this resistance, we must remember that each one of them was obliged, before it could gain acceptance for itself, to oust a diametrically opposite opinion. These five dogmatic preconceptions had practical possession of the field; and the advance of modern nerve physiology has consisted in their gradual refutation, point for point, under compulsion by the facts.

(1) In opposition to the principle of the connexion of elements many physiologists, even now, prefer to posit an *autonomy of the elements*. Their assumption is, not that all contents of consciousness, even the simplest, presuppose complex functions in which numerous physiological elements take part, but contrariwise that these physiological elements, the nerve cells, can mediate extremely complex psychical functions. Thus, a single nerve cell may, according to circumstances, be the vehicle of a sensation or of a compound idea, a concept. The hypothesis is very seriously intended: its supporters have been at the pains to estimate the number of ideas that, on emergency, may be lodged in an individual consciousness, by counting the number of cells in the cerebral cortex.[1] Some-

---

[1] MEYNERT, *Vierteljahrsschrift f. Psychiatrie*, i., 1867, 80. H. MUNK, *Ueber die Functionen der Grosshirnrinde*, Einleitung, 9.

times, it is true, an attempt is made to mitigate its crudity by the remark that it is merely 'provisional' and 'tentative.' But even in this modified form it lacks all justification. For a provisional hypothesis is of use only so long as it groups the known facts together in a formula that can further the progress of investigation. If, on the other hand, the hypothesis points us to a road that undoubtedly leads in a direction diametrically opposed to the truth, then it has become nothing else than a pernicious prejudice.

(2) In opposition to the principle of indifference of function it is generally held, at the present time, that the *law of specific energy*, as it is termed, represents an especially valuable asset of modern nerve and sense physiology. Nevertheless, the history of the law shows a gradual regression. It slowly withdrew from the elements where advancing investigation had proved it to be untenable, to other elements whose functional attributes were less thoroughly worked out; and it has finally intrenched itself in those whose real differences of structure and function warrant the assumption of distinct modes of activity. First of all, a specific function was attributed to the nerve fibres. Then, as physiologists gradually became accustomed to consider the nerves as relatively indifferent conductors of the nervous processes, the nerve cells were selected as the vehicles of the specific functions. To-day, when the uniform character of these central elements also is impressing itself more and more strongly upon the investigator, we may confidently predict that the specific function will continue on its travels until it ultimately comes to rest in the peripheral sensory elements. Here it may, with a certain conditional propriety, be allowed to remain; whereas the central elements come into account only indirectly, in so far, i.e., as the influences of practice and adaptation play a part among them.[1]

The law of specific energy still holds its own in current scientific thought. More headway has been made against the dogmas that stand out in contrast and opposition to the principles of practice and adaptation and of vicarious function: the hypotheses (3) of the *originality* and (4) of the *immutability of functional attributes*. Neither possesses any present power in nerve physiology, save as it is properly a logical consequence of the strict interpretation of the law of specific energy. The numerous facts that bear witness to the influences of practice, adaptation and vicarious function will not be deprived of their rights. But this merely aggravates the division in modern physiological theory, and shows that it cannot maintain itself for any length of time. The same intrinsic unsoundness appears (5) in the hypothesis of an *absolute localisation*, which still persists in opposition to the principle of a merely relative localisation. It is the connexion of this hypothesis with those of specific energy and of the more or less complex character of the function of the nervous elements that constitutes the logical foundation of the phrenological edifice. And the constantly recurring tendency to a revival of phrenology in some modified form, adapted to the conceptions of current anatomy, physiology and psychology, is therefore an evidence not only of the extreme vitality of these dogmas, but also of their internal connexion. Indeed, if we grant the specific energy of the elementary functions, we have at the same time admitted their originality, their constancy, their complex character and their absolute localisation. Conversely, all these assumptions fall to the ground, as soon as we recognise the just claims of practice and adaptation. For then we must grant the possibility, within certain limits,

---

[1] For the limitations to be put upon the law of specific energy in its application to the peripheral sensory elements, cf. below Part III., ch. viii., § 4.

of vicarious function; and from this admission follow, in the last resort, a merely relative localisation of functions and, as regards the elements, an original indifference, which by the great majority of the central elements has in all probability been retained as a permanent possession. The five principles discussed above thus form an interdependent whole, no less than the five antagonistic dogmas of the older nerve physiology. That a view of the central functions which accords with the general status of our physiological and psychological knowledge should meet, even to-day, with serious opposition is, perhaps, sufficiently explained, first, by this very interpendence of the traditional doctrines, in which each assumption serves to support the rest; again, by the simple formulation of the older theories, as compared with the larger demands made by the new upon the physiological and psychological analysis of the phenomena; and, lastly, by the natural longevity of ingrained prejudice. To suppose that the specific contents of a sensation is given of itself with the existence of a central element; or that the act of vision is completed with the 'projection' of the retinal image upon a central sensory surface; or that 'memory for words,' 'intelligence,' and what not, that figure in popular psychology as simple and undivided concepts, are localised as simply in sharply circumscribed regions of the brain: to suppose all this is, naturally, very much easier than it is to work out the conclusions that follow from the five principles enunciated in the text. But apart from the objection that these various suppositions run counter to the facts, they are once and for all impossible, for the reason that they rest upon a wholly untenable psychology, upon erroneous physiological ideas, and, in the last instance, upon an antiquated conception of the structure of the nervous system. If, therefore, the anatomists are still to be found to-day among the most zealous champions of the phrenological view, they have really atoned for this fault in advance, by contributing the most valuable materials from which others may construct a tried and tested theory of the central functions.

Index

ABROGATION experiments, 191
— phenomena, motor and sensory, 242, 259, 264 f., 271 f., 280 f., 283 f.
Absolute localisation, principle of, 330 f.
Accommodation, centre for, 190, 301
Acid reaction of cinerea, 55
Acoustic nidi, 183
— speech centre, 303
Acusticus, origin and course of, 182 ff.
— Terminations of, in cochlea, 182
— Conductions of, 184 f.
— connexion of cochlearis and vestibularis, 185
Adaptation, principle of, 233 f.
— of visual centre to retinal impressions, 91
After brain, 107 f.
Aggregation, 62, 64
Aggregate state, 63
Agraphia, 208, 304
Alba, 39, 55, 111 f
Albicans, 119, 125, 127, 132
Alexia, 305
Alkaline reaction of alba, 55
Amblyopia, 211, 274
Amnesia, forms of, 304 ff.
— total and partial, 304
Amnestic aphasia, 304
Amoeba, 29, 33
Amoeboid movements, 33 f.
— — of dendrites, 43, 54
Amorphous sustentacular substance, 39
Amphioxus, nervous system of, 117, 260
Amygdala, 129 f.
Analysis, causal, of mental phenomena, 6 f.
— Methods of functional, 241 f.
— Illustrations of, 298 ff.
Anaesthesia, 160, 211, 274 f.
Anastomosis, 51
Angular gyre, 146
Animal and vegetable functions, 34
— impulses. *See* Impulse
— psychology, aim of, 5
— — Relation of, to ethnic, 5
— — Relation of, to generic or comparative, 6
Animals, experiments on, 191
Antiphrenological physiology, 293
Ape cleft, 146

Aphasia, 208, 287, 296, 298, 304 ff.
Apperception, 316
— centre, 315 ff.
Arbor, 121 f., 127, 141
Arsenic, 52
Ascending complication, principle of, 226 f.
Assimilation, 84 f.
Association centres, 217 f.
— Theory of, 290 ff.
— fibres, 213 ff.
— — function of, 214, 292
— — and projection fibres, 213 f.
Astasia, 277
Asthenia, 279
Atactic aphasia, 303
Ataxia, 278
Atony, 277
Atrophy, significance of, for investigation of conduction paths, 154 f.
— of a cerebral lobe, 176
— of an occipital lobe, 206
— of pregeminum and geniculum, 207
Atropin, 77
Attention, 316
Auditory centre, 197, 202, 206 ff.
— — Connection of, with speech, 310 f., 303
Aula, 113 f., 126, 131, 133
Automatic movements, 151
— — Centres for, 253 ff.
— — respiration and heart beat, 254 ff.
— imperative movements, 264, 270
Autonomy of elements, principle of, 329
Axis cylinder. *See* Neurite

BACTERIA, manifestations of life in, 30
Base of brain, 125, 132, 139, 143, 146
Bell's law, 156 f.
Bigemina, 107, 109 f., 123
— Function of, 258 ff.
Blindness. *See* Cortical, Mental, Word blindness
Blood cells, 30, 54
Bodily substrate of mental life, subject of Part I., 12, 27 ff.
— — Differentiation of, 33 ff.
— — General problems in investigation of, 105 f.

Body, 18
— Relation of, to mind, 20, 101 ff.
— — to spirit, 20
Brain, simplest form of, 36
— Development of, 106 ff., 112 ff.
  Development of outward form of, 137 ff.
— Law of growth of, 140, 147 ff.
— Law of fissuration of, 147
— Parts of, 106, 109, 118 ff.
— Conduction paths of, 167 ff.
— Functions of, 244 ff.
— Three vesicles of, 106 f.
— Five Divisions of, 107 ff.
— Ventricles of, 109 ff.
— surface, law of growth of, 140, 145 ff.
— ventricles. See Ventricles
— vesicles, 106 f., 113 f.
Broca's convolution, 301

CALCAR, 129, 132, 146
Callosal gyre, 114, 127, 135 f., 139, 142 f.
Callosum, 113, 127, 130, 134 ff.
— Tapetum of, 123, 135
— Rostrum and splenium of, 133
— Function of, 214
— Defect of, and atrophy of occipital lobe, 215
Canalisation, 100
Candicans. See Albicans
Capacity, nervous, 75
Capsular columns (fun. siliquae), 118
Caudatum, 129 f.
— Conduction in, 178 f.
— Function of, 270 f.
Caudex, 107
Causality, physical and psychical, 8 ff.
Cellifugal conduction in neurite, 42
Cellipetal conduction in dendrites, 42
Cells, organic, 30, 33
— Differentiation of, 33 ff. See Nerve cell
— Sensation, 289
Central colligation of remote functional areas, principle of, 229 ff.
— fissure, 144 f.
— organs, morphological development of, 104 ff.
— — Course of conduction paths in, 150 ff.
— — Physiological function of, 241 ff.
Centres, ideational, 289
— Nervous, first appearance of, 36 f.
— — Influence of, on processes of excitation, 85 ff., 243
— — Nutritive function of, 96
— — Cortical, 190 ff.
— — Centromotor and centrosensory, 191, 193 ff., 198 ff. 204 ff.

Centres, Nervous. Munk's direct sensory and mental, 203
— — Visual, 196 f, 200, 206
— — Auditory, 198, 200, 208, 211
— — Olfactory, 198, 209
— — Gustatory, 198, 209
— — for sensations of touch and movement, 198, 200, 209 f.
— — relation of centres for touch, movement and general sense to motor centres, 198, 200, 209, 211
— — for sensation and idea, 289
— — Functional development of, 212 f.
— — Functional interaction of, 293
— Psychical, 218, 290
— Sensation, 289
Centrifugal sensory paths, 151, 159, 182, 184, 186, 189
Cerebellar lateral column, 166, 174
— peduncles, 120 ff.
— — Conduction in, 172 ff.
— — Nidi of, 176
— — Function of, 272
Cerebellum, development of, 106 ff, 109, 110, 112, 121
— Position and parts of, 121 ff., 125, 127, 128
— Conformation of, 140 f.
— Conductions of, 167 ff. 172 ff.
— Structure of, 175
— Function of, 271 ff.
— Relation of, to acusticus, 273, 276
— — to sex functions, 280
— — to intelligence, 279 f.
Cerebrin, 54
Cerebrum, 107, 126 ff, 138 ff.
— Conductions in ganglia of, 178 f.
Cervical enlargement of myel, 117
Chiasma, 187 ff, 230 ff.
Child psychology, aim of, 5
— — Relation of, to ethnic, 5
— — Relation of, to individual, 5 ff.
Cholesterin, 55
Cholin, 55
Chorda tympani, 180 f.
Cilia, as motor organs, 34
— as tactual organs, 34
Ciliata, 29
Cinerea, 39
— Chemical constitution of, 55
— Three forms of, 112
— Nidi of, 112 118 f, 122, 126, 127
— Conduction in, 151 f, 160 ff.
— Irritability of, 160 f.
— Resistance in, 161
— Transference of excitation in, 161 ff.
Clarke's columns, 116
Classification of mental phenomena, 12 ff.

Claustrum, 129 f.
Coelenterates, 35, 37
Collaterals, 41
Commissural system of prosencephalon, 132 ff.
Commissures, dorsal, of myel, 116
— White and grey ventral, of myel, 116
— Medicommissure, 123, 125
— Postcommissure, 124, 127
— Precommissure, 114, 126, 132, 214
  See Callosum
Comparative psychology, also called generic, 6
— — Relation of, to animal and ethnic, 6'
Complex mental formations, 13, 15 f.
Conarium. See Epiphysis
Concept, conceptual feeling, 311.
Conduction, anatomical conditions of, 36, 48 ff.
— from motor nerve to muscle, 67 ff.
— Reflex, 85 ff. 151
— Transverse and longitudinal, 87
— Centripetal and centrifugal, 151
— Principal and auxiliary, 150 ff.
— Law of isolated, 151
— investigated by physiological method, 152 f.
— — by anatomical, 153 f.
— — by pathological, 154
— Waller's law of, 155
— in nerves and myel, 155 ff.
— in cinerea, 160 f.
— in oblongata, 167 ff.
— Branch, to cerebellum, 167, 169 ff.
— Direct, to cerebrum, 168 f, 173
— in pons and cerebellum, 172 ff.
— to and from the quadrigemina and thalami, 178 f.
— to striata, 179
— in nerves of taste, 180 f.
— — of smell, 181 f.
— in acusticus, 182 ff.
— in opticus, 185 ff.
— Terminations of, in cortex, 190 ff.
— of projection and association systems, 213 ff.
— Principles of central, 225 ff. See Intercentral paths
— Central, principles of, 225 ff.
— — Manifold representation, 225 f.
— — Ascending complication, 226 f.
— — Differentiation of directions, 227 ff.
— — Colligation of remote functional areas, 229 ff.
Connective tissue, sustentacular, 39
Connexion of elements, principle of, 320 ff.
Conscious contents as processes, 4
Consciousness, criteria and limits of, 27 ff.
— Primitive form of, 34
— Dissociation of, 54

Conservation of energy, 60 ff.
— Application of principle of, to mechanics of nerve, 65 ff.
Constrictions of primitive sheath, 45
Contact of dendrites and collaterals, 46 49, 51. See Neurone theory
Contractile vesicle, 34
Contractility, earliest evidence of mental function, 29 ff.
— an intrinsic character, 59
Contraction, muscular, as measure of nervous excitation, 58 f.
— after stimulation of motor nerve 67
— Isotonic, isometric and auxotonic curves, 68, 72
— increased by practice, 75
— and phenomena of fatigue, 77
— Superposition of, in tetanus, 76
— thermal and electrical consequences of, 80
— in reflex excitation, 85 ff.
— in enhanced reflex excitability, 88 ff.
— in investigation of conduction paths, 153
Convolution, of cerebrum, 138 ff, 145 ff.
— of cerebellum, 140 f, 147
— Two conditions of, 147 ff.
Corneal sheath, 45
Cornua of myel, 115 f.
— of paracele, 131
Corona, 130, 168
— Terminations of, in neighbourhood of central gyres, 168, 194, 212 (cf. 198, 200, 205, 210)
— Relation of, to association system, 214, 217
Cortex, cerebellar, 140 f, 175
— Cerebral, outward form of, 138 ff.
— — Conduction paths to, 190 ff.
— — Centromotor and centrosensory areas of, 191 ff.
— — Intercentral paths to. 191
— — Association system of, 213 ff.
— — Projection system of, 213 ff.
— — Structure of, 218 ff.
— — Relation of structure and function in, 220 ff.
— — Reflexes of, 252
— — Automatic excitations of, 256 ff.
— — Function of, 256 ff, 280 ff.
— — Substitutions in, 284
— — as seat of intelligence, 284
Cortical blindness, 201
— centres, methods for demonstration of, 190 ff.
— — Motor and sensory, in dog, 193 ff.
— — Motor and sensory, in monkey, 198 ff.

Cortical centres, motor and sensory, in man, 204 ff. 287 ff.
— — Visual, 298 ff.
— — Speech, 302 ff.
— — Apperception, 315 ff.
— deafness, 201
— epilepsy, 194
— stimulation, latent period of, 194
Coughing, reflex centres for, 245 ff.
Criteria of mind, 27 f.
Crura, 123, 125, 128
— Nidi of, 123
— Decussations in, 170, 174 f.
— Motor and mixed paths of, 177
— Functions of, 177
Crusta, 119, 123
— Conduction in, 176 f.
Cuneate funicles, 118 f.
— Conduction in, 166, 170
Cuneus, 143 f. 146
Curare, 47
Current of action, 80
— — Duration of, with momentary stimulation of nerve, 83
Custom, source of psychological knowledge, 5
Cylindrical columns (*eminentiae teretes*), 120

DECUSSATIONS, in myel, 159 ff.
— in oblongata, 168 f, 170, 172
— in pons and cerebellum, 173, 174 ff.
— of olfactorius, 182
— of acusticus, 184
— of opticus, 187 ff.
— of motor paths to cortex, 195, 205
— of sensory paths to cortex, 197
— in the transverse commissural system, 214
— Theory of, 230 ff.
Deafness. *See* Cortical, Mental, Word deafness
Degeneration of nerves, 52 f, 54 f, 168, 325
Deiters' cells, 44
Dendrites, 41
Dentatum, 118
— Conduction in, 173
Depressor nerves, 247
Derangement of central areas, 159, 160 f, 187, 191, 196, 201, 206 ff, 253 257, 264, 270 f, 273
Diacele, 109. *See* Ventricles
Diencephalon, structure of, 107, 124 ff.
— Function of, in lower vertebrates, 258 ff.
— in man, 269 ff.
Differentiation, of mental functions and their substrate, 33 ff.
— of animal and vegetable functions, 34
— of the three germinal layers, 34 f.
— of nerve cells, 36 f.
— of directions, principle of, 227 ff.

Dimensions of mental processes, 6
Disgregation, work of, 60
Dissimilation, 84 f.
Dissociation, work of, 60 f, 65
— of consciousness, 54
Dizziness, 273 ff.
Dorsal columns of myel, 116
— — of oblongata, 118
— — Conduction in, 166, 170
— — Continuations of, in cerebellum and pons, 173 f.
— Cornua of myel, 116
— — Terminations of conduction paths in, 163 ff.
— — Propagation of excitations in, 97 ff.
Dorsolongitudinal bundle, 169
Dualism, Cartesian, 32

ECTOCINEREA, 112, 127
Ectoderm, 35
Electrical changes of nerve in function, 58, 79 f.
— — Electric current as nerve stimulus, 58 ff.
Electrodes, differences in stimulation process at the two, 76, 79 f.
Electrolysis, 83, 95
Elements of mental life, sensations and feelings, 13
— — never given in isolation, 13
— — Subject of Part II., 13
Embryo, brain of, 106 ff.
Embryology of central organs, 106 ff.
Encephalin, 55
End-plate, 48
Energy, conservation of, 60 ff.
Entocinerea, 112, 123, 127
Entoderm, 35
Epencephalon, 107. *See* Cerebellum
Epicele, 110. *See* Ventricles
Epiphysis, 120, 123 f.
Equilibrium, disturbances of, from cerebellum, 272 ff.
— — from olive, 276
— — from walls of diacele, 276
— Organ of, 272 ff.
— Tendency towards, in nervous system, 82
Ethnic psychology, subject matter of, 5
— — Relation of, to experimental psychology, 5
— — Relation of, to generic or comparative, 6
Excitation, processes of, in stimulation of nerve, 70 ff, 93
— Theory of nervous, 80 ff.
— Reflex, 85 ff. 243 f.
— Resisted by central elements, 88
— by peripheral nerve mechanisms, 88
— Enhancement of reflex, 88 ff.

Excitation, chronic effects of, 93 f.
— Automatic, of myel and oblongata, 253 ff.
— of cortex, 256 ff.
Exhaustion and recuperation of nerve, 81
Experience, outer and inner, 1
Experiment, 3
— Physiological, 57 ff, 152, 241 f.
Experimental psychology, how far identical with physiological, 3
— — cannot investigate relations of physical and psychical, 3
— — Limitations of, 5
— — Relation of, to ethnic, 5
— — Relation of, to individual, 5 f. 8
— — Aim of, 7
— — Connexion of, with psychophysical materialism, 9 ff.
— — Relation of, to hypnotism and suggestion, 11
Extirpation, 154, 242

FACIALIS, 119, 171, 180 f.
Fascia dentata, 136
Fasciola, 136
Fatigue, 77 f, 85
Feelings, definitio of, 13
— Complex, 13
— correlated with sensations, as mental elements, 15
— Intellectual, 16, 311
— as mental faculty, 18, 21
— in apperception, 316
— in hypnotic state, 11
Fibre tracts of myel, 116
— — of oblongata, 118 ff.
— — of cerebellum, 121 f.
— — of mesencephalon, 123
— — of diencephalon, 126, 128
— — of prosencephalon, 128 ff.
— — of tenia, 128
— — of corona, 129 f.
— — of fornix and commissural system, 132 ff.
Fibres. See Nerve fibres
Fibrillar structure of nerve cells, 41, 51 f.
— — of intercellular substance, 51
Fibrils of dendrites, 40 f.
— of muscular and cutaneous nerves, 41
— of the peripheral nerve endings, 47
— unaffected by stains, 41. See Primitive fibrils
Fimbria, 137
Fissuration of cerebrum, law of, 147 ff.
Fissures of cerebrum, 139 ff.
— — Longitudinal and transverse, 141 f.
— — of the primate brain, 143 ff.
— — Embryology of, 145 ff.
— — Significance of, 285 f.

Flexures of central nervous system, 112
Flocculus, 141
Foramen of Monro. See Aula, Porta
Fore brain, 107 f, 112 ff.
Fornix, 114, 132 ff.
Fossa rhomboidalis, 110, 119, 176
— Nidi of, 118 f, 184
Frontal gyres, 125, 144 f.
— — Function of, 198, 205, 210 302 ff, 315 ff.
— lobes, 139
— — Function of, 207, 209, 315 ff.
— — Connexion of, with temporal, 215
— — Gyres of, 125, 144 f.
— — Relation of, to centre of general sense, 200
— — Relation of, to motor speech centre, 303
Function, physiological, of central parts, 241 ff.
— — Sensory and motor, of nerves, 36, 42, 48 ff.
— — Development of mental, 26 ff.
Functional analysis, 241 ff, 298 ff.
— aphasia, 310

GANGLIA, of invertebrates, 36 f.
— Peripheral, 99
— Brain, 170, 174 ff, 178 ff.
— Cerebral, 178 ff.
— Spinal, 88, 115, 182 f.
Ganglion, spiral, 183
Gelatinosa, 116
Gemüthsbewegungen, 15 f.
Generic psychology, also termed comparative, 6
— — Relation of, to animal and ethnic, 6
Geniculum, 120, 126
— Conduction in, 188
— Atrophy of, 207
Giant pyramidal cells, 220
Glomeruli olfactorii, 181
Glossopharyngeus, 180
Golgi's cells, 44
Goll's columns (fun. graciles), 119 f.
Ground reticulum, 39, 51, 116
Gustatory centre, 198, 209
Gyres, 140
— General cause of, 140
— Callosal and olfactory, 139, 141
— Longitudinal and transverse, 142 ff.
— the individual, 143 ff.
Gyrus fornicatus, as olfactory centre, 209

HEART BEAT, centres for, 171, 245 ff, 254 ff.
— — Government of, 247
— — Automatism of, 255 f.
— — Connexion of, with respiration, 247

Heart beat, connexion of, with vascular innervation, 255
Heat of combustion, of constituents of nerve substance, 55
Hemianaesthesia, 160, 211, 264
Hemianopsia, 187, 201, 232
Hemiplegia, 211
Hemispheres. See Cerebrum, Cortex
— Function of, 280 ff.
— of cerebellum. See Pilea
Hind brain, 107 f.
Hippocampal gyre, 135 ff.
Hippocampus, 129, 132, 135 ff.
— Function of, 198
Histological basis of neurone theory, 50 ff.
— Method for investigation of conduction paths, 153 f.
Homocerebrin, 55
Hydra, 35
Hylozoism, attitude of, 27
— Confuses latent with actual life, 31 f.
Hyperaesthesia, 282
Hyperkinesia, 89 f, 194, 256, 258
Hypnotism, experiments during, 11
Hypophysis, 124 ff.

IDEA, definition of, 13
— confusion of with sensation, 13 f.
— sense idea, 15
— does not exist apart from feeling and volition, 20
— Localisation of, 289, 291
Immutability of functional attributes, principle of, 330
Impulse, nutritive and sexual, relation of, to voluntary action, 28 f.
— Conduction of voluntary, 169
Indeterminate magnitudes, mental processes as, 7
Indifference of functions, principle of, 322 ff.
Individual psychology, 5 f.
Inexhaustibility, relative, of nerve substance, 78, 81 f.
Infundibulum, 109, 119, 125, 130
Inhibition, processes of, in nerve stimulation, 70 ff, 90, 93
— best tested by weak stimuli, 72
— Transitory, at end of twitch, 73
— Duration of, dependent on nature of stimulus, 74
— diminished, in exhausted nerve, 75
— developed at anode by constant current, 79
— — at cathode by break of current, 79 f.
— and negative molecular work, 81 f.
— of excitation by central elements, 88, 161, 242, 281

Inhibition, by interference of stimuli 91 ff, 243
— Centres for, 91, 317
— Chronic effects of, 93 f, 244
— Influence of poisons on, 92
— Theory of, 98 f.
— in apperception, 317
Innervation, centres of vascular, 244 ff.
— pressor and depressor fibres, 247
— Relation of, to heart beat, 247
— Automatic excitation, 245
— Mechanics of, 57 ff.
— Theory of central, 94 ff.
Insula, 139
— Conductions of, 216
Intensity, a dimension of mental processes, 6
Intercalatum, 123
— Conduction in, 177
Intercellular substance, 55, 114
Intercentral paths, from cerebellum, 177, 279
— — of association system, 213 ff.
Interference of stimuli, 91 ff.
Intergyral fibres, 215
Intermediary nerve cells, 44
Introspection, requires aid of experiment, 4 ff.
— Importance of, 7
— Results of naïve, 17
Irritability, doctrine of, 58, 294

LANGUAGE, source of psychological knowledge, 5
— embodies system of concepts, 17
Laqueus. See Lemniscus
Latent period, 68
— — Tests during, 73
— — Change of, by test stimuli, 73
— — Explanation of, 81, 97
— — of reflex twitch, 86 ff.
Lateral columns, of myel, 116
— — of oblongata, 118 ff.
— — in mesencephalon, 123
— — Conductions of, 168 f, 174, 177
— cornua of myel, 115 f.
— stria, 135 f.
Lecithin, 54 f.
Lemniscus, 123
— Conduction in, 170, 177
Lenticula, 129 f, 133
— Conduction to, 173, 178
— Function of, 270 f.
Life, adequate definition of, 3
— Lowest manifestations of, how explicable, 29
— Latent, not a function of matter, 32
— Beginnings of, identical with beginnings of mind, 31
Lingualis, 180

Localisation, 190 ff.
— Methods of investigating, 190 ff.
— of will, 212
— Older and newer hypotheses of, 287 ff.
— of sensations and ideas, 289 ff.
— Goltz' objections to, 290 f.
— History of, 294 ff.
— of visual centres, 298 ff.
— of speech centres, 302 ff.
— of apperception centre, 315 ff.
— principle of relative, 328 ff.
Lumbar enlargement of myel, 117

MACULA LUTEA, 187
Manifold representation, principle of, 225 f.
Marginal arch, 113 f.
Matter, 18
— Concept of, ground of objective phenomena, 32
Mechanical materialism, 9
Mechanics of nerve substance, 57 ff.
— Problem of, 59
— Law of conservation of energy, in its relation to nerve substance, 65 ff.
— Theory of nerve excitation, 80 ff.
— Theory of central innervation, 94 ff.
Medipeduncles, 120, 122
— Conduction in, 173 ff, 276
Medusae, 35
Memory, lapse of verbal, in old age, 308
Mental blindness, 201
— deafness, 201
— development, subject of Part VI., 16
— — Origin of, becomes a question of origin of life, 31
— faculty, 18 f., 295 f.
— — Uselessness of concept of, 19
— — Influence of, at present day, 19 f.
— — Higher, 21
— — Lower, 21
— — Threefold division of Plato, 21 f.
— — of Aristotle, 22
— — scheme of Wolff, 22
— — of Kant, 23
— function, organic evolution of, 27 ff.
— — Criteria of, 27 f, 32
— — Beginnings of, 29 ff.
— — Range of, 33
— — Differentiation of, 33 ff.
— processes, subject matter of psychology, 1
— — Connexion of, with vital, 1, 31 f.
— — subject matter of physiological psychology, 2, 11

Mental processes included in definition o life, 3
— — Elementary, 13
— — Interconnexion of, subject matter of Part V., 16
— — Relation of, to nervous processes, 101 ff.
Mesencephalon (bigemina or quadrigemina), development of, 107
— Structure of, 123 f.
— Reflexes of, 244 ff.
— Functions of, in lower vertebrates, 258 ff.
— — in man, 269 f.
Mesocele, 109 f. See Sylvian aqueduct, Ventricles
Mesoderm, 35
Metabolism, 65, 84 f, 95 f.
Metacele, 110. See Fossa rhomboidalis, Ventricles
Metencephalon, 107. See Oblongata
Methods, of physiology, how adapted to psychology, 3
— Experimental, necessary to introspection, 4 ff.
— Limits of experimental, 5
— Aim of experimental 7
— Value of experimental, 7 f.
— of mechanics of innervation, 57 ff.
— of investigation of conduction paths, 152 ff.
— of functional analysis, 241 f.
Mid-brain, 107 f.
Mind, definition of, 17 f.
— Relation of, to spirit, 18 ff.
— — to body, 20
— Beginnings of, 27 f.
— of plants, 32
— Seat of, 124, 177, 218, 294 f.
Molecular work, 63
— — Relation of, to work of disgregation and to mechanical work, 60 ff.
— — External and internal, 62
— — Positive and negative, 67
— — Change of, by stimulation, 81
— — and recovery and exhaustion of nerve, 81
— — Curves for relation of positive and negative, 75, 82
— — Tendency of, to equilibrium, 82
— — under stimulation by constant current, 83
— — and electrolysis, 83
— — and assimilation and dissimilation, 84 f.
— — in theory of central innervation, 94 ff.
— — and nutritive influence of central substance, 96
— — in the two cell regions, 96 f.
— — and enhancement of reflex excitability, 98

Molecular work, explains inhibitory phenomena, 98 f.
— — explains practice, 100 f.
— — Relation of, to mental qualities, 102 f.
Molluscs, 37
Monera, 31, 34
Monkey, brain of, 131, 132, 143 f, 198 ff.
Morphology of nervous system, significance of, for psychology, 104 ff.
Motor aphasia, 303
— centres of cortex, 193 ff, 198 ff, 204 ff.
— — of cortex, relation of, to sensory centres, 198, 200, 209, 211
— speech centre, 303
Movement, centres for, 191, 193 ff.
— — in dog, 196 ff.
— — in monkey, 204 ff.
— — in man, 242 ff, 245, 254, 256, 264, 269 ff, 304 ff.
— Mechanism of, in protozoa, 33 f.
— sensation, centre for, 198
Movements, concomitant, 161
— Conduction paths of, 161 f.
— Instances of, 196, 248 f.
— Unconscious, 28
— Conscious, criteria of, 28 ff.
— of plants, 30
— Amoeboid, 33 f.
— Co-ordination of, 162, 246 ff.
— Disturbances of, 264 ff, 269 ff, 272 ff, 276 f.
— after stimulation of cortical sensory areas, 211
— symmetrical, in stimulation experiments, 194
— Regulation of, by sensation, 264 273 f.
— Circus, 264, 270
— Clockhand, 264

Muscle, nerve endings in, 48
— seat of fatigue, 78
— sense, 275
Myel, development of, 37, 106
— Structure of, in higher vertebrates, 114 ff, 163 ff.
— Columns of, 116
— Continuation of, in oblongata, 118
— Conduction in, 155 ff, 159 ff.
— Origin of nerves in, 156
— Distribution of nerves in, 156 f, 163 ff.
— Deccussation in, 159 f.
— Principal and secondary paths of, 161 ff, 163 ff.
— Branch conductions of, 163
— Connexion of, with higher centres, 166
— Reflexes of, 242 ff.
— Automatic excitations of, 253 ff.

Myelinic sheath, 39, 44 f.
— — Degeneration of, 53, 154
— — Chemical constitution of, 55
— — Sequence of formation of, 155, 212 f.
Myelocele, 106, 110, 115 f.
Myth, source of psychological knowledge, 5

NEOPLATONISM, 23
Nerve cell, 39
— — Nucleus of, 40
— — Processes of, 40 f.
— — Fibrillar structure of, 41, 51
— — Granular deposits in, 41, 52 f.
— — Types of, 42, 43 f, 220 f.
— — Molecular processes in, 95 ff.
— — Regions of, 96
— — of cortex, 218 ff.
— — of olfactory organ, 180 f.
— — of gustatory organ, 180 f.
— — Homogeneous turgescence of, 53
— — Function of, 53, 85 ff.
— — Uniformity of, in cortex, 224
— — Indifferent function of, 322, 330
— centres, general survey of, 104 ff.
— — Development of, 106 ff.
— — Structure of, 114 ff.
— — Course of conduction in, 150 ff.
— — Morphological elements of, 39 ff, 175, 218 ff.
— — Function of, 242 ff.
— fibres, 39
— — Structure of, 44 ff.
— — Peripheral endings of, 47 f. See Nerve terminations
— — Connexion of, with cells, 48 ff, 163 ff, 181
— — Degeneration of, 53
— — Trophic influence of nerve cells upon, 53, 96
— — Processes of stimulation in, 67 ff.
— — Indifference of function of, 322 ff, 330
— plexus, 156
— rings of coelenterates, 37
— roots, myelic, 115 f.
— terminations, peripheral, 47 f, 180 ff.
— — in the cerebral cortex, 190 ff, 298 ff.
— — in the cerebral ganglia, 175 f.
— tissue, ectodermal, 35
— — Chemical constitution of, 54 ff.
Nerves, cranial, origin of, 170 ff.
— Inhibitory, 247
— Mixed, 156
— Motor, in neurone chain, 50

Nerves, Motor, of myel, 115 f, 155 ff, 159 f, 163 ff.
— — of oblongata, 119 f, 168 ff.
— — of oculomotor system, 171, 184, 189 f, 203
— — of pons and cerebellum, 173 ff.
— — of mesencephalon and diencephalon, 178 f.
— — in reflex connexion with acusticus, 182 ff.
— — of corona, 194
— Oculomotor, 171, 184, 189 f, 203
— Sensory, in neurone chain, 50
— — of myel, 115 ff, 155 ff, 164 ff.
— — of oblongata, 119 f, 125, 168 ff.
— — Principal path of, to cerebrum, 172
— — of pons and cerebellum, 173 ff.
— — of mesencephalon and diencephalon, 177 f.
— — Conduction paths of the higher, 179 ff.
— — Centrifugal, 182, 184 f, 189 f.
— — and motor, 155 ff.
— — and motor, are indifferent conductors, 157
— — and motor, of taste and smell, conduction in, 179 ff.
— — and motor, acoustic, conduction in, 182 ff.
— — and motor, optic, conduction in, 185 ff.
Nervous system, structure of, 39 f.
— — Nerve cells, 40 ff, 94 ff.
— — Nerve fibres, 44 ff, 67 ff.
— — Peripheral nerve terminations, 47 f, 88
— — Neurone theory, 48 ff, 158
— — Chemical constituents of, 54 ff.
— — and principle of conservation of work, 65 ff.
— — Seat of practice, 75, 100
— — Theory of nervous excitation, 80 ff.
— — Relation of, to mind, 101 ff.
— — *See* special headings
Neural tube, 37 f, 106 ff, 114, 117
Neurite, 40 f, 44 f.
— Structure of, 45
— Terminations of, in nerve cell or between other tissue elements, 47
— Degeneration of, 53
— Chemical constitution of, 55
Neurodynamic interaction, 96
Neuroglia, 39, 54
Neurokeratin, 54
Neuromuscular cells, 35
Neurone theory, 48 ff, 150, 326
— — connexion of neurones, 49
— — motor and sensory neurone chains, 50

Neurone theory, peripheral connexions, 50, 182
— — History of theory, 51 ff.
Nidal cinerea, 112
Nissl's corpuscles, 41
Noeud vital, 297
Nuclein, 56
Nucleus of nerve cell, 40
Nutritive function of ganglion cells, 53, 96

OBLONGATA, development of, 107 ff, 112
— Structure of, 118 ff.
— Conduction in, 167 ff.
— origin of cranial nerves, and nidi of cinerea, 170 ff.
— Reflex functions of, 244 ff.
— Automatic excitations in, 254 ff.
Occipital lobes, 139
— — Conduction to, 196 f, 200, 206, 211
— — and the visual centres, 298 ff.
Olfactorius, origin and course of, 181 f.
— connexion with peripheral cells 181
— Conductions in, 182
— Decussation of, 182, 214
Olfactory bulbs. *See* Rhinencephalon
— centre, 197, 207, 208 f.
— mucous membrane, nerve endings in, 47, 181
Olives of oblongata, 118 f.
— — and conduction paths, 172
— — Olivary path of dorsal columns, 174
— — Function of, 276
— — Superior, *See* Trapezium
Operculum, 139, 145
Opticus, conductions of, 185 ff.
— Peripheral terminations of, 186
— Decussation of, in lower vertebrates, 187
— its significance, 230 ff.
— Decussation of, in man, 187 ff.
— its significance, 235 ff.
Originality of functional attributes, principle of, 330

PALLIUM, 107, 122, 127
Paracele, *See* Ventricles
Paralysis, motor, from transsection of ventral nerve roots, 155 f.
— of the myelic columns, 161
— from lesion of pyramids, 168
— from extirpation of centromotor areas, 195, 200, 205
— in apoplexy, 160
Paraphasia, 304
Parietal lobe, 139
— — Function of, 195, 198, 209
Perception, outer, 1
— Inner. *See* Introspection
— Derangements of, 196, 198, 282
— Centres for, 201

Pericellular reticulum, 43
Perineurium, 39
Photochemical process in retina, 299
Phrenology of Gall, 105, 287 f.
— — Newer, 288 ff.
— — Criticism of newer, 290 ff.
— — History of doctrines, 295 ff.
Physiological psychology, problem of, 1 ff. 8 f, 11, 14
— — as title of this work, 2
— — Explanation of term, 2
— — Force of adjective, 2
— — Relation of, to experimental, 3
— — adapts methods of physiology, 3
— — investigates relations between physical and mental process, 3
— — Relation of, to psychophysics, 3
— — reforms psychological investigation, 4
— — System of, 11 ff.
— — Relation of, to physiology and psychology, 15
Physiology, 1
— Relation of, to psychology, 2, 10
— processes based on general properties of matter, 31
— See Physiological psychology
Pigment spot, of infusoria, 34
Pilea, 122, 272
Pineal body. See Epiphysis
Pons, 119, 122
— Conduction paths of, 168, 172 ff.
— Function of, 175 f.
Porta, 126 f, 133
Postcentral gyre, 145
Postcribrum, 119, 125
Postpeduncles, 120, 173
Practice, elementary phenomenon of, 76
— Direct, 76
— Property of nerve substance, 78, 100
— Indirect, 78
— Specialised in principles of localisation and vicarious function, 101
— Principle of, 324 f.
Precentral gyre, 145
Precribrum, 119, 125, 131
Precuneus, 127, 144, 146
— Conductions of, 173
Prepeduncles, 120, 173 ff, 176
Prepsychological concepts, 16 ff.
Pressor nerves, 247
Primate brain, Sylvian fissure in, 138
— — Olfactory gyres in, 142
— — Difference of, from other mammalian brains, 144 f.

Primitive fibrils, 46, 53
— groove, 106
— sheath, of Schwann, 39, 45, 54
— streak, 37
Problems of psychology, 1
— of physiology, 1
— of psychophysics, 3 f.
— of physiological psychology, 4
— of psychogenesis, 5
— of ethnic psychology, 5
— of beginning of mental life, 29 ff.
— of physiological mechanics of nerve substance, 59 f.
— of a mechanics of innervation, 57 ff.
Projection system of cortex, 213
Protagon, 54
Protoplasm, 29 ff, 55
Protoplasmic processes, 41 f.
Protozoa, 29 ff, 33 ff.
Processes of nerve cell, 40 f. See Conscious contents, Mental processes
Prosencephalon, structure of, 126 ff.
— brain cavities and surrounding parts, 126 ff.
— Fornix and commissural system, 132 ff.
— Outward conformation of, 137 ff.
— Results of partial destruction of, 280 ff.
— of total destruction of, 283 ff.
— Comparative anatomy and anthropology of, 285 ff.
Psychogenesis, problems of, 5
Psychology, subject matter of, 1
— Relation of, to physiology, 2
— adapts methods of physiology, 3
— Observation in, 4
— Physiological, 1 ff, 8 f, 11 ff, 14, 15
— Generic, 6
— Individual, 5 f.
— Comparative, 6
— Ethnic, 5 f.
— Experimental, 3, 5, 7 ff.
— Animal, 5 f.
— Child, 5 ff.
— Rational, 7 f.
— Pure empirical, 8
— Scientific, 17
Psychophysical materialism, 9 ff.
Psychophysics, defined by Fechner, 3
— Relation of, to physiology and psychology, 4
Pulse, relation of, to breathing, 247
Pulvinar, 119, 126
Pupillary reaction, centre for, 190
Purkinje's cells, 44, 175
Pyramidal cells, 43 f, 221
— path, 168 f.
— — Decussation, 169, 174
— — Lateral column, 166, 174

Index

Pyramidal ventral column, 166, 174
    Function of pyramidal tract, 168 f.
Pyramids, 118

QUADRIGEMINA, development of, 107, 111
— Structure and position of, 123 f.
— Conductions of, 173, 178 f., 183, 186, 188 ff.
— Degeneration of, after destruction of occipital lobe, 206 f.
— Functions of, 269 f.

RATIONAL PSYCHOLOGY, 7 f.
Reason, before Kant, 24
— in Kant, 24 ff.
— Herbart's criticism, 25 f.
Reflex, 85 ff, 250 ff.
— and the muscular contraction following direct stimulation of motor nerve, 86 ff.
— time, 87
— Directions of conduction, 87
— Influence of cinerea on, 88, 242 f.
— tetanus, 88 f.
— poisons, 89 ff.
— Inhibition of, 91 ff, 243
— Spinal, 242 ff.
— Metencephalic and mesencephalic, 244 ff, 261, 269 f.
— Self-regulation of, 247 ff.
— Specific stimuli for, 249
— Diffusion of, 162, 244, 249 f.
— Purposiveness of, 250 f.
— Range of, 252 f.
— Cortical, 252 f.
— and automatic excitation, 253
— centres, dependent on other central areas, 242
— — Interaction of, 245 ff.
— — Quadrigemina and thalami, complex, 262
— — of audition, 184, 270
— — of vision, 184, 190, 264, 270
— — of touch, 270
— — of heart beat, respiration, etc., 245 ff.
— convulsions, 250
— excitability, 86 ff.
— — Enhancement of, 88 ff, 242 f.
— — with repetition of stimulus 88 f.
— — by chemical means, 89 f.
— — by removal of superior centres, 242
— — Theory of, 98
— inhibition, 91 ff, 243
— — Theory of, 98 f.
— paths of acusticus, 184
— of opticus, 190
— tonus, 94, 244
Relative localisation, principle of, 298, 328 f, 330 f.

Respiration, motor paths of the respiratory muscles, 171
— Respiratory centres, 171, 244 ff, 254
— Relation of, to pulse 247
— Self-regulation of, 254 f.
Restes, 119
— Conduction in, 173
Rhinencephalon, 125, 130, 139, 142
— and olfactorius, 181 f.
Rhizopods, 31, 34, 43
Right-handedness, 238 f.
Rods and cones, 48, 186, 299
Rostrum, 133
Rubrum, 124, 130
— Conductions of, 173, 176, 178

SARCOLEMMA, 48
Seat of mind, 124, 177, 218, 296 f.
Sensation, definition of, 13
— Confusion of, with idea, 13
— correlated with feeling as mental element, 15
— as mental faculty, 21
— as psychical quality, 32
— of touch, in lowest organisms, 33 f.
— of light, in infusoria, 34
— Concomitant, 161 f.
— — Conduction paths of, 161 f.
— — in painful excitations, 162
— — Regions of, 162
— Conjugate, 162
Senses, internal, of phrenology, 288, 295
Sensory aphasia, 304
— centres of cortex, 196 ff, 198 ff, 206, 206 ff.
— — Theory of, 289, 290 ff.
— speech centre, 303
Septum, 127, 133
Sexual impulse, 28
— and cerebellum, 280
Sinus rhomboidalis, 117
Skin, nerve endings in, 47
Slender columns (*fun. graciles*), 118, 120
— — Conduction in, 166, 170
Smell, organ of, 181 f.
Sneezing, reflex centres for, 245 ff.
Specialisation of function, in compound organisms, 34
Specific energy, of cortical areas, 224
— — of the central functions, 322 ff,
— — Law of, 330
Speech, derangements of, 303 ff.
— — atactic aphasia, 303
— — amnestic aphasia, 304
— — paraphasia, 304
— — word deafness, 304
— — word blindness, 305
— centres, 208, 302 ff.
— — Motor and sensory, 303
— — Optic and acoustic, 303 ff.
Spindle-shaped cells, 220

Spirit, definition of, 18
— Relation of, to mind, 18 ff.
— — to body, 20
Spiritualism, Cartesian, 27
Splenium, 133
Staining, histological, 153
Stellate cells, 221
Stimulation, processes of, in nerve fibre, 67 f, 79 f, 158
— Excitatory and inhibitory processes in, 70 ff, 79 f.
— After-effects of, 75 ff.
— experiments, 242, 259
Stimulus, definition of, 58
— Internal and external, 58
— Interference of stimuli, 91 ff.
— Transformation of, 299
Striata, 128 f.
— Conductions of, 173, 178 f.
— Function of, 270 f.
Sulci, dorsal and ventral, of myel, 115 f.
Swallowing, reflex centres for, 245 ff.
Sylvian aqueduct, 110, 176
— fissure, 113, 138, 143 ff, 146
— fossa, 112 f., 138
Sympathetic system, 247
System of transverse association fibres, 214
— of longitudinal, 215
— of intergyral fibres, 215

Taste beakers, 181
— cells, 48
— nerves, 179 ff.
— Terminations of, in peripheral cells, 181
Tegmentum, 119, 123
— Conduction in, 170, 173, 175
Temporal lobes, 139
— — Terminations of conduction paths in, 198, 200, 208 f.
Tenia, 128 f.
— tecta or lateral stria, 135 f.
Terma, 113, 127, 132
Tetanus, 76
Tigroid bodies, 41
Time, a dimension of mental processes, 6
Tongue, nerve endings in, 48
Tonsil, 125, 141
Tonus, 93 f, 244
— Loss of, from cerebellar lesion, 277
Touch, centres for, 198, 200, 209, 211
Transsection of nerves, 154 f, 159, 161
Trapezium, 172, 183 f.
Trigeminus, 181
Tuber cinereum, 125
Tuberculum acusticum, 183
Turgescence, homogeneous, 53
'Tween brain, 107 f.

Uncus, 143
— Function of, 198

Vagus, 247
Valvula, 120 f.
— Conduction in, 173
Velocity of stimulus process in nerve, 69
— of anodal inhibition, 79 f.
— of current of action, 80
Velum medullare ant. See Valvula
Ventral columns of myel, 115 f, 166
— — of oblongata. See Pyramids
— cornua of myel, 115 f.
— — of myel, conductions of, 164 f.
— — of myel, propagation of ex citations in, 99
Ventricles, development of, 109 ff.
— Structure and position of, 119 f. 123 ff, 126 ff, 131, 134 f.
Vermis, 121 f, 127, 141
— Conduction of, 173, 175
Vertigo, 273 ff.
Vestibularis, 185
Vicarious function, and neurone theory 51
— — and branch paths of conduction, 150, 161
— — Compensation by, 153, 193, 216, 260, 261 ff, 269, 271, 281 ff
— — in lesions of visual centres, 301
— — of speech centres, 303
— — Principle of, 325 ff, cf. 225 f, 275
Vision, organ of, 34, 185 ff.
Visual centres, 196, 200, 206 ff.
— — Complex character of, 208
— — Function of, 298 ff.
— — Optic speech centre, 304 f.
Vital processes, interdependence of physical and psychical, 1, 3, 31 f.
— — in definition of life, 3
— — show adaptation to ends, 29
Vitalism, 58
Voluntary action, external, criterion of mental life, 28
— — Relation of, to animal impulses, 28
— — not demonstrable in contractile movements, 30
— — Duration of, 89
Vomiting, centre for, 245

Waller's law, 155
Wernicke's centre, 304
Will as idea of movement, 212
— Localisation of, 212
Winking reflex, 249
Work, 60
— Three forms of, 60
— Conservation of, 60 ff, 65 ff.
— Mechanical, definition of, 61
— Molecular, internal and external, 62

Work, molecular, positive and negative, 67, 81 ff, 91, 94 ff.
— performed in nerve substance, 55 f.
Word blindness, 208, 305, 307
— deafness, 208, 304, 307

YOLK, 34 f., 54

ZONAL fibre system, 120
— — Conduction of, 172

Index of Names

APATHY, 52
Aristotle, 20, 22, 294
Arnold, 40, 52, 129, 157, 298

BAGINSKY, 203
Bastian, 244, 310
Battestini, 55
Baumann, 56
Baxt, 89
Beaunis, 89
Bechterew, 29, 166, 179, 185, 188, 190, 264, 272, 273, 276
Beevor, 199, 200
Bell, 156, 157
Bernstein, 80, 83, 84
Bert, 240
Bethe, 32, 40, 41, 52, 53
Bianchi, 315
Bidder, 115
Biedermann, 85, 91
Binswanger, 250
Bischoff, 107, 146
Bötticher, 91
Bojanus, 110
Bouillaud, 287, 298
Bowditch, 77
de Boyer, 205, 315
Braune, 240
Bresler, 187, 223
Broca, 240, 286, 298, 303
Brondgeest, 93
Bubnoff, 92, 194
Bütschli, 31, 52
Burdach, 298

CARUS, 121
Charcot, 154, 168, 211, 315
Chittenden, 54
Christiani, 204, 259, 260, 261
Clausius, 64
Combe, 280, 295
von Cyon, 92, 93

DARWIN, 30
Déjerine, 213, 217
Deiters, 41, 42, 44, 51, 164
Descartes, 32, 294, 297
Diakonow, 55
Donaldson, 207
Duval, 43, 54

ECKER, 146, 148, 240

Edinger, 153, 168, 169, 171, 178, 179, 180, 213, 214, 215, 217
Ehrlich, 153
Engelmann, 30, 46, 100, 248
Ewald, 44, 46, 248
Exner, 100, 205, 209

FAMINZYN, 29
Fechner, 3, 6, 7, 32, 33
Ferrier, 193, 194, 198, 204, 206, 210, 265, 272, 277, 280, 315, 316
Fetzer, 154
Fichte, 9
Fick, 68, 80
Flatau, 147, 315
Flechsig, 154, 166, 168, 206, 207, 209, 212, 213, 216, 217, 224, 238, 271, 316
Fleming, 52
Flourens, 259, 260, 266, 273, 275, 288, 290, 293, 297, 298
Forel, 154
Franck, 194
Freud, 308
Freusberg, 253
von Frey, 72
Freytag, 54
Friedmann, 53
Fritsch, 193, 194
Fürstner, 207

GALEN, 294
Gall, 280, 286, 287, 288, 290, 295, 296, 297
Gauss, 286, 315
Gegenbaur, 109, 118, 128
Gerlach, 51
Gillet, 187
Goldscheider, 274
Golgi, 41, 43, 44, 51, 153, 224
Goll, 174
Goltz, 91, 193, 196, 201, 204, 239, 248, 253, 259, 260, 266, 268, 281, 282, 290, 298
Grashey, 310
Gratiolet, 144, 240, 285, 286
Griffith, 89
Gscheidlen, 55
Gudden, 53, 154, 187

HALLER, 58, 294, 295, 296
Hartley, 9
Hegel, 8
Heidenhain, 69, 92, 93, 194, 254

Hein, 259, 282
Held, 41, 52, 183, 185
Helmholtz, 68, 72, 76, 89
Henschen, 188, 189
Herbart, 6, 7, 25, 26, 177
Hering, 94, 162, 243
Hertwig, 35, 38
Herzen, 91
His, 38, 41, 51, 112
Hitzig, 193, 194, 195, 198, 217, 273, 278, 316
Horsley, 89, 199, 200
Huschke, 286, 298
Huxley, 132

JACOBSOHN, 147, 315
Jastrowitz, 315

KAHLER, 208, 278
Kaiser, 59
Kant, 6, 9, 23, 24, 25
Kessel, 54
Kirchhoff, 273
Kleinenberg, 35
Kölliker, 43, 44, 46, 51, 112, 224
Kowalewsky, 162
Kraepelin, 257
von Kries, 72, 76, 89
Kronecker, 72, 88, 89
Kühne, 44, 45, 46, 48, 54
Kupffer, 115
Kussmaul, 256, 306, 309

LADAME, 273, 280, 281
Lange, 8
Langendorff, 91
Lavater, 296
Lemoigne, 275
von Lenhossek, 41, 49, 51, 52
Leuret, 285, 297
von Leyden, 274
Lichtheim, 305, 306
Liebreich, 54
Loeb, 204, 282
Longet, 259, 273, 282
Lubavin, 56
Luchsinger, 256
Luciani, 193, 194, 195, 196, 197, 204, 207, 208, 209, 210, 272, 273, 277, 280
Ludwig, 160, 161
Lussana, 273, 275, 280
Luys, 154

MAGENDIE, 271, 297
Marchand, 315
Marinesco, 53
Masius, 253
Meyer, J. B., 25
Meyer, L., 149
Meynert, 154, 155, 211, 213, 224, 225, 239, 289, 315, 316, 329
Miescher, 56

Mihalkovics, 108
Minot, 35
Möbius, 296
Mönckeberg, 52, 53
Moleschott, 55, 160, 256
von Monakow, 154, 186, 187, 189, 190, 205, 206, 207, 208, 209, 211, 217, 232, 270, 271, 273, 280, 281, 315, 316
Mosso, 257
Mott, 160, 244
Müller, J., 23, 109, 157
— W., 55
Münsterberg, 9
Munk, 200, 201, 202, 203, 204, 210, 211, 223, 289, 329

NANSEN, 51
Neumeister, 55
Nissl, 41, 42, 52, 53
Nothnagel, 204, 205, 206, 207, 209, 211, 250, 265, 270, 271, 272, 270, 274, 280, 281

OBERSTEINER, 153
Ogle, 239, 240
Owen, 132, 285

PANSCH, 146
Parcus, 55
Paschutin, 91
Pfeffer, 30
Pfluger, 69, 80, 163
Pick, 208, 278, 310
Piersol, 39, 46, 48
Pitres, 194, 315
Plato, 20, 21, 22
Purkinje, 44, 175, 273

QUERTON, 54

RABL-RÜCKHARD, 43, 54
Ramon y Cajal, 42, 43, 50, 51, 52, 99, 165, 169, 171, 181, 187, 189, 190, 217, 219, 221, 222, 223, 224, 228, 230, 231, 232, 233, 238
Ranvier, 45
Reichert, 130
Reinhard, 207
Remak, 45
Renzi, 273
Retzius, 36, 51
Rolando, 145
Rollett, 59
Romanes, 29
Rosenthal, 91
Rüdinger, 149

ST. CLAIRE DEVILLE, 64
Schäfer, 89, 199, 200, 203
Schelling, 8, 85
Schenck, 59
Schiff, 160, 211, 259, 264, 271, 272

Schitscherback, 198
Schmidt, 113
Schrader, 260
Schultze, 30, 46, 52
Schwann, 39, 45
Seppilli, 195, 196, 204, 207, 208, 209
Setschenow, 91
Sherrington, 94, 162, 243, 244
Siemerling 213, 217
Sömmering, 177
Sommer, 310
Soukhanoff, 54
Spencer, 10
Spurzheim, 286, 295
Stanley Hall, 72, 89
Steiner, 259, 260, 264, 266, 267
Stieda, 110, 111
Stilling, 154, 176
Stirling, 88
Störring, 308, 310
Stransky, 162
Strecker, 55
Stricker, 46, 48, 52, 154, 213, 224
Szymonowicz, 48

TENNER, 256
Thudichum, 54
Tiedemann, 132, 286
Tiegel, 69

Tigerstedt, 59
Translator, Notes by, 16, 16 f, 18, 21, 34 f, 35, 38, 39, 44, 46, 48, 100, 127
Türck, 154, 211

VAN DEEN, 160
Verworn, 29, 30, 49
Vesalius, 294
Vialet, 187, 188
Vogt, C., 154, 286
— O., 11, 213, 217, 310
Vulpian, 259

WAGNER, H., 286, 315
— R., 280, 286
Waldeyer, 49, 52
Waller, 155
Wasmann, 32
Weigert, 153
von Wendt, 53
Wernicke, 171, 208, 257, 270, 273, 304, 305, 306
Wolff, C., 7, 21, 22, 24, 25, 294
— G., 257, 310
Woroschiloff, 160, 161
Wundt, 3, 6, 7, 8, 10, 12, 35, 76, 77, 80, 212, 254

ZELLER, 6
Ziehen, 9, 257, 316

Errata

P. 193, last line: *for* central *read* crucial
P. 195, 11, 16, 17: *for* frontal *read* parietal
P. 162, n. 2: *for* LOWALEWSKY *read* KOWALEWSKY

CPSIA information can be obtained at www.ICGtesting.com
Printed in the USA
LVOW022217091112
306408LV00003B/407/P